# RESPONSES TO DISASTERS AND CLIMATE CHANGE

## Understanding Vulnerability and Fostering Resilience

# RESPONSES TO DISASTERS AND CLIMATE CHANGE

## Understanding Vulnerability and Fostering Resilience

edited by

**Michèle Companion**
**Miriam S. Chaiken**

CRC Press
Taylor & Francis Group
Boca Raton London New York

CRC Press is an imprint of the
Taylor & Francis Group, an **informa** business

CRC Press
Taylor & Francis Group
6000 Broken Sound Parkway NW, Suite 300
Boca Raton, FL 33487-2742

First issued in paperback 2021



ISBN 13: 978-1-03-224229-3 (pbk)
ISBN 13: 978-1-4987-6096-6 (hbk)

DOI: 10.1201/9781315315928



Publisher's Note
The publisher has gone to great lengths to ensure the quality of this reprint but points out that some imperfections in the original copies may be apparent.

**Library of Congress Cataloging-in-Publication Data**

Names: Companion, Michèle, editor. | Chaiken, Miriam S., editor.
Title: Responses to disasters and climate change: understanding vulnerability and fostering resilience / edited by Michèle Companion and Miriam S. Chaiken.
Description: New York, NY : CRC Press is an imprint of the Taylor & Francis Group, an Informa Business, [2017] | Includes bibliographical references and index.
Identifiers: LCCN 2016028208| ISBN 9781498760966 (hbk) | ISBN 9781315315928 (ebk)
Subjects: LCSH: Disasters--Social aspects--Case studies. | Disaster relief--Social aspects--Case studies. | Natural disasters--Social aspects--Case studies. | Climatic changes--Social aspects--Case studies.
Classification: LCC HV553 .R394 2017 | DDC 363.34--dc23
LC record available at https://lccn.loc.gov/2016028208

**Visit the Taylor & Francis Web site at**
**http://www.taylorandfrancis.com**

**and the CRC Press Web site at**
**http://www.crcpress.com**

*This book is dedicated to our amazing colleagues and the professionals who are working to improve community resilience, reduce risks, and give voice to often marginalized populations to ensure that their cultures and livelihoods are protected and respected. We are proud to showcase a small sample of their work in this volume.*

# Contents

# List of Figures

# List of Tables

# Editors

**Michèle Companion** is a Professor of sociology at the University of Colorado–Colorado Springs. She received her PhD (2003) from the University of Arizona. Her work has focused on Native American reservation nutritional dynamics, including impacts of low-income diets on overall health and on reservation food security issues. She has also been documenting tribal participation in the food sovereignty movement to reclaim cultural aspects of traditional foods. More recently, she has been focusing on food security and long-term health implications of food access for urban Indian populations by examining cultural barriers to healthy eating among low-income urban Indian populations.

Dr. Companion works as a food and livelihood security consultant to international humanitarian aid organizations. She has worked extensively across Africa in countries including Malawi, Mozambique, Angola, South Africa, Ethiopia, Egypt, and Somalia with organizations that include Save the Children–US, US Agency for International Development, Counterpart International, FEWSNET, International Relief and Development, and Global Food and Nutrition, Inc. Her current work focuses on the expansion of food security indicators to increase local sensitivity to food crisis triggers, especially in local markets, and on population displacement, migration, and resettlement. She edited the volume *Disaster's Impact on Livelihood and Cultural Survival: Losses, Opportunities, and Mitigation* (2015, CRC Press) and coedited *Street Food: Culture, Economy, Health, and Governance* with Ryzia de Cassia Vieira Cardoso and Stefano Marras (2014, Earthscan from Routledge).

**Miriam S. Chaiken** currently holds the position of Dean of the William Conroy Honors College at New Mexico State University and Distinguished Professor of anthropology. She is a cultural anthropologist with decades of experience in international economic development, having conducted field research on issues of population resettlement and migration, food security and hunger, livelihoods and agricultural production, and maternal and child health. Most of this work was done in collaboration with humanitarian nongovernmental organizations such as the United Nations Children's Emergency Fund and Save the Children. Her earliest long-term field work was on Palawan Island in the Philippines, followed by extensive work in Kenya, Ethiopia, and Mozambique.

Dr. Chaiken's recent publications include "Understanding Famine and Severe Food Emergencies" published in *Research Methods for Anthropological Studies of Food and Nutrition* (2017, eds. John Brett and Janet Chrzan, Berghahn Press). In a different vein, she published an account of the trials and tribulations of anthropological field research entitled "No Heads, No Feet, No Monkeys, No Dogs: The Evolution of Personal Food Taboos" in *Nutritional Anthropology: Biocultural Perspectives on Food and Nutrition* (2013).

# Contributors

**Sara E. Alexander** is an applied social anthropologist at Baylor University, whose research interests focus on economic development strategies with emphasis on livelihood security and vulnerability, food and nutritional security, indigenous populations and natural resource management, risk perceptions regarding climate change, and resilience to natural disasters and climate-derived shocks. She recently completed a two-year field study funded by the National Oceanic and Atmospheric Administration in several coastal communities in the Meso-American Barrier Reef System to determine resilience of vulnerable households to climate-related events. The project continues to work to facilitate new coalitions within and outside communities to identify linkages that can be enhanced to increase resilience at household and community levels. She is also currently investigating how West Texas wheat farmers are adjusting to changing climate patterns.

**Sudha Arlikatti** is an Associate Professor with the Integrated Emergency Management and Business Continuity Management Program, Rabdan Academy, Abu Dhabi, United Arab Emirates. Dr. Arlikatti has over a decade of experience working as an architectural and planning consultant in Oman and India. Her research focuses on risk communication, protective action decision making, postdisaster sheltering and housing recovery, organizational and community resiliency to disasters, and sustainable land use planning. Her teaching at both the undergraduate and graduate levels focuses on emergency management, disaster response and recovery, international disaster management, special populations in disasters, introduction to planning and environmental planning and hazards management, among others.

**Cathy Banwell** is an Associate Professor with the National Centre for Epidemiology and Population Health at The Australian National University. She brings social science theories and research methods, derived from her background in anthropology, to the development of explanations for public health problems. She has extensive experience working with multidisciplinary teams with expertise in epidemiology, statistics, sociology, psychology, and geography. She has specialized in conducting research on risky consumption (drugs, alcohol, and food) in Australian and Thai community settings.

**Roberto E. Barrios** is an Associate Professor of anthropology at Southern Illinois University Carbondale. During the last 16 years, Dr. Barrios has conducted ethnographic research on disaster recovery in post-Hurricane Mitch Honduras, post-Katrina New Orleans, Southern Illinois in the aftermath of the 2011 Mississippi River Floods, and Chiapas, Mexico, following the Juan de Grijalva Landslide. His work focuses on the implicit cultural assumptions on the part of expert planners and nongovernmental organization programs concerning the nature of personhood, community, and social well-being and the ways members of disaster-affected populations negotiate, interpret, and contest these assumptions.

**Shiloh-Kay Bennett** is a senior at Mandan High School in Mandan, North Dakota. In her sophomore year of high school, she was invited to attend the first Future Physicians Conference in Washington, DC. Soon after, she was nominated for the Science Award at her local high school. She spent five summers working with the National Aeronautics and Space Administration's Tribal Colleges and Universities Project/Experiential Learning Opportunity Program out of Haskell Indian Nations University in Lawrence, Kansas. She spoke at Rising Voices 3 in Boulder, Colorado and is a leader in the Rising Voices Youth Climate Initiative. When Shiloh graduates from high school, she plans to major in political science and ethics at the university level.

**Barrett P. Brenton** is a Professor of anthropology and Director of the Center for Global Development and Graduate Program in Global Development and Social Justice at St. John's University in Queens, New York. As a specialist on the nutritional anthropology of sustainable food systems, Dr. Brenton's cross-cultural applied fieldwork experience across five continents has ranged from studies of dietary biodiversity, food insecurity, and health in Indigenous Native American and Ecuadorian Amazon communities, to research on food aid and food sovereignty in Zambia, to community-based urban food systems and health disparities research in New York City.

**Catherine Bwerinofa** holds a master of science degree in Development Studies from the Women's University in Africa. She is a practicing social scientist with a specific focus on gender, girls and women's empowerment, and the environment. Catherine is an emerging African scholar with a passion for research and enjoys environmental photography in her free time.

**Matthew Carroll** is a Senior Research Fellow in the Monash School of Rural Health. He has managed major state and national epidemiological studies and has extensive connections with research, policy, and practice, having overseen the national Australian Research Council/National Health and Medical Research Council Research Network in Ageing Well. He has a wide-ranging research program focused on healthy ageing, in terms of resilience post disasters, lifelong learning, heat-health risks, and social isolation. He is currently one of the chief investigators on the large-scale Hazelwood Health Study examining the effects of the Hazelwood mine fire.

**Mary Ann Castle** is a social anthropologist. For 35 years, she has conducted applied research and evaluation with marginalized and disadvantaged populations throughout the United States and internationally (e.g., India, Kenya, South Africa, Turkey, and Zambia). Her substantive work has been on health and social welfare issues, including environmental determinants of health and illness. Her work is holistic, participatory, and committed to social change and creating a more equitable world. Dr. Castle is a Senior Associate at Planning Alternatives for Change, a consulting firm with a strong focus on sustainable development and a Senior Consultant Evaluator at Cora Group, Inc.

**Miriam S. Chaiken** is a cultural anthropologist with extensive experience working with humanitarian nongovernmental organizations to improve food security, standards of living, maternal and child health, and gender equity. She has worked in Southeast Asia and east and southern Africa. She currently holds the positions of Distinguished Professor of anthropology and Dean of the William Conroy Honors College at New Mexico State University.

**Karletta Chief** is an Associate Professor in soil, water, and environmental sciences at the University of Arizona (UA). Her research focuses on unsaturated flow in arid environments and climate change impacts on indigenous communities. She received BS and MS degrees in civil and environmental engineering from Stanford in 1998 and 2000 and her PhD in hydrology at UA in 2007. In 2011, she completed her postdoctorate at Desert Research Institute in Nevada. Dr. Chief was named the 2011 American Indian Science and Engineering "Most Promising Scientist or Scholar," received the 2013 Stanford University Distinguished Alumni Scholar Award, and was named the one of the "2015 Native American 40 under 40."

**Manase Kudzai Chiweshe** is a Senior Lecturer in the Centre for Development Studies at the Chinhoyi University of Technology in Zimbabwe. He is a widely published author whose work revolves around the sociology of everyday life in African spaces with special focus on promoting African ways of knowing. He has published in journals such as *Critical African Studies*, *African Identities*, *Agenda*, *Agrarian South*, and *Journal of Asian and African Studies*, among others. His research work concentrates on agrarian studies, rural sociology, and sustainable livelihoods.

**Morgan Chow** is a Faculty Research Assistant in the AquaFish Innovation Lab at Oregon State University (OSU) who recently completed her MS in marine resource management at OSU. Morgan's interest in natural resources began at the University of California–Davis where she received a BS in environmental science. After working on global water issues for The Nature Conservancy and the World Resource Institute in Washington, DC, Morgan became a Coastal Resource Management Extension Worker for the US Peace Corps/Philippines. She worked with small-scale fishers, women's fishing cooperatives, and youth groups. The devastating typhoon that swept through the Philippines one year later sparked her interest in gender dimensions in disaster management.

**Logan Cochrane** is a Vanier Scholar and doctoral candidate in interdisciplinary studies at the University of British Columbia (Okanagan). He completed an MA in sustainable development and a BA in anthropology. For the last ten years, he has worked overseas in Afghanistan, Benin, Burundi, the Democratic Republic of Congo, Ethiopia, Saudi Arabia, Tanzania, and Uganda. Logan has served as a director for two nongovernmental organizations and worked as a consultant with clients that have included Management Sciences for Health, The Liaison Office, the United Nations Children's Fund, and the Joint United Nations Programme on HIV and AIDS. His doctoral research analyzes the dynamics of food security in rural southern Ethiopia.

**Michèle Companion** is a Professor of sociology at the University of Colorado–Colorado Springs. She is a food and livelihood security specialist, working in countries across Africa with international nongovernmental organizations. This work focuses on the expansion of market-based food security indicators to increase local sensitivity to food crisis triggers and on population displacement, migration, and resettlement. She also researches Native American nutritional dynamics, including impacts of low income diets on overall health and food security and tribal participation in the food sovereignty movement. She has recently been looking at cultural barriers to healthy eating among low-income urban Indian populations.

**Lori A. Cramer** is an Associate Professor of sociology in the School of Public Policy at Oregon State University. Dr. Cramer has over 25 years of experience in rural community research. Most of her teaching and research centers on how rural communities are affected by, and adapt to, social and ecological change. Her current work includes research on community resilience to hazards, in particular offshore earthquakes and subsequent tsunamis off the Oregon coast. Specific interests include public perceptions of risk, social vulnerability, and decision making.

**Shona V.Z. de Jong** is with the Department of Earth Sciences, Laurentian University, Ontario, Canada. Her interests are corporate and social responsibility, sustainable economic development, earth sciences, and public health and safety. She has worked in various roles in government, academia, nongovernmental organizations, and industry in Canada, New Zealand, Zimbabwe, and the United States. Currently, she is developing the Geohazards Program at the Ontario Geological Survey, Canada, and serving on the Board of the Canadian Risk and Hazard Network and the Canadian Geoscience Education Network. Recently, Shona received awards from the United Way and the Hollyhock Social Venture Institute.

**Carla May Dhillon** is a PhD candidate in environmental social sciences at the University of Michigan School of Natural Resources & Environment and a licensed civil engineer. Her doctoral research focuses on climate change, environmental inequality, and the study of boundaries. Carla has also researched uses of citizen science to pursue environmental justice in urban Southern California. She has over 10 years of professional experience in engineering, green/ecological building, and appropriate technologies. Carla's current work investigates collaborations in climate change science networks and inequalities in climate adaptation.

**Michelle Duffy** is a Senior Lecturer in sociology at Federation University Australia, Gippsland campus. Her research explores how interactions between people and place contribute to notions of community and identity and, hence, the concepts and processes of belonging or alienation. This includes exploring the role that culture plays in shaping our lives at different spatial levels and local processes operating within and between individuals, communities, and societies. She is Director of the Centre of Research for Resilient Communities, which undertakes interdisciplinary community-engaged research in regions such as the Latrobe Valley and, more broadly, in Gippsland and is currently the Community Wellbeing Stream leader on the large-scale Hazelwood Health Study examining the effects of the Hazelwood mine fire.

**Hillary Egna,** Director of the Feed the Future AquaFish Innovation Lab at Oregon State University, leads multi-institutional, multidisciplinary, international projects and has collaborated with researchers from 40 countries. With a master's in fisheries science and a PhD in geography, she has mentored 50 students and created two graduate student fellowships to encourage international dimensions of aquatic resources management. Dr. Egna has authored 60 publications in aquaculture and international development, including impact assessment and gender mainstreaming in aquaculture. She received the Women in Leadership Award from the Northwest Chapter of the United Nations Development Fund for Women, an Asian Fisheries Society Merit Award, and the World Aquaculture Society Honorary Life Award.

**A.J. Faas** is an Assistant Professor of anthropology at San Jose State University. His research focuses on practices of exchange and social organization in contexts of crisis, including disasters, displacement and resettlement, development, and violent conflict. A.J.'s research has been funded by the National Science Foundation and the Public Entity Risk Institute's Dissertation Fellowship in Hazards, Risk, and Disasters. His work has been featured in a number of peer-reviewed journals. A.J. coedited (with Roberto Barrios) a special issue of the journal *Human Organization* on the applied anthropology of risk and disaster. He is a founding member of the Risk and Disaster Topical Interest Group at the Society for Applied Anthropology and served as its chairperson (2014–2015). A.J. has also served as a consultant for nonprofits, universities, and community-based initiatives.

**Preety Gadhoke** is an Assistant Professor in the Master of Public Health Program, Department of Pharmacy Administration and Public Health, College of Pharmacy and Health Sciences, at St. John's University in Queens, New York. Dr. Gadhoke engages in interdisciplinary, collaborative community-based research to inform culturally tailored programs and policies for chronic disease prevention. Her research lies at the intersections of health disparities, resiliency, and food and nutrition. Her current work focuses upon tailoring visual anthropological methods to address resiliency and coping among homeless women and children living in transition in New York City, social ecological approaches to chronic disease prevention in Native American households, and family health and wellness through the application of livelihood models and visual anthropology in indigenous Ecuadorian Amazon Shuar communities.

**Yishak Gecho** is an Assistant Professor and the postgraduate program coordinator in the Department of Rural Development and Agricultural Extension at Wolaita Sodo University, Ethiopia. Dr. Gecho completed his doctorate at Haramaya University (Ethiopia) on livelihood strategies and food security in rural southern Ethiopia.

**Bob Gough** is a US attorney and cultural ecologist of Irish, English, French, and Lenape descent, with 40 years of experience in tribal natural and cultural resource issues. As founding secretary of the Intertribal Council on Utility Policy (COUP), Gough has advocated for indigenous rights and resource relations with interest in building sustainable energy-based reservation economies. Gough and COUP President Patrick Spears were the recipients of the Inaugural World Clean Energy Award–Special Award for Courage from Facktor Four, Basel, Switzerland (2007). They also cochaired the Native Peoples/Native Homelands workshops (1998 and 2009). Gough contracted with the National Renewable Energy Laboratory's Wind Powering Native America program (2000–2009), receiving the Department of Energy Wind Energy Program Outstanding Technology Acceptance Award (2004). He was lead author for the "National Climate Assessment's Indigenous Peoples, Lands and Resources" chapter (2014), cofounded the Rising Voices gatherings at University Corporation for Atmospheric Research/National Center for Atmospheric Research, and is a member of Pacific Risk Management 'Ohana (PRiMO) Indigenous Knowledge and Environment Hui (working group).

**Deanna Grant-Smith** is a Lecturer in the School of Management, Queensland University of Technology, in Brisbane, Australia. Deanna researches stakeholder engagement practices in a range of sustainability contexts and is interested in the role emotions play in shaping policy decisions for "wicked" or unspeakable problems and the implications on professional practice. Before joining academia, she worked in the public sector planning, delivering, and evaluating participatory processes and intergovernmental transport and safety programs. Deanna has published on a range of social justice, management, and planning issues, including the provision of transport and other lifeline services, particularly for disadvantaged communities.

**Kathryn Henderson** is Associate Professor of sociology and women's and gender studies at Texas A&M University. Her research employs visual methods investigating the visual culture of design engineers, standardization in straw bale building, and mind maps and visual memory of Katrina survivors. She has taken graduate and undergraduate students to post-Katrina New Orleans and post-wildfire Texas towns to assist survivors in recovery efforts through volunteer work and teach students to conduct participant observation and in-depth interviews. Her current research employs action research, ethnography, and participant-directed photography in examining wildfire survivors' changing networks of people, animals, and things along with gender assumptions.

**Chad Huddleston** is a cultural anthropologist and an Instructor in the Department of Anthropology at Southern Illinois University Edwardsville. His research interests focus primarily on the interactions between people and their landscapes. For the past six years, he has focused on how people adapt to changing social and physical landscapes due to disaster or "adverse events," such as social collapse or a zombie apocalypse. This has led him to spending time with and learning from those who are preparing to do just that.

**Katherine J. Johnson** is a PhD candidate at the University of Maryland working on the Deal Island Marsh and Community Project. Her research focuses on vulnerability and resilience as understood and experienced by a diverse stakeholder network representing a rural coastal system impacted by climate change. She is interested in vulnerability and resilience on the local level and in collaboratively using individual and community knowledge to leverage adaptive planning outcomes. She prioritizes interdisciplinary and collaborative work to create outcomes suitable to wide range of needs and interests across the social-ecological system.

**David Kim** is Senior Pastor at The Garden Christian Fellowship in Chatsworth, California. He earned his doctorate at Fuller Theological Seminary and his bachelor's degree at the University of California, Berkeley. His dissertation examined the role and impact of personal discipleship programs in Asian American ministries. For the past 20 years, he has been actively engaged in community empowerment and global outreach and has established several churches. He has been involved in forging long-term partnerships between local leaders and organizations in the developing world and faith-based organizations in the United States. He is interested in the role of religion in promoting resilience and well-being in people's lives.

**Sharon Kim** is an Associate Professor in sociology at the California State University Fullerton. Her widely published research focuses on the intersection of race, religion, and immigration. She examines the development and growth of hybrid third spaces of worship among second generation Korean Americans. She is the author of *A Faith of Our Own: Second Generation Spirituality within Korean American Churches* (2010, Rutgers University Press). Currently, she serves as a consultant at University of Southern California's Center for Religion and Civic Culture on a project that examines religious innovation and competition.

**Linda Kruger** is a social scientist with the US Forest Service in Juneau, Alaska, studying the effects of climate change on Alaska Natives and rural communities, community adaptation, sustainability, and resilience. She is the Alaska Native and American Indian Special Emphasis Program Manager and Tribal Liaison for the Pacific Northwest Research Station. She works with tribal elders and youth to document traditional harvest and use of forest products, exploring experiences and observations of climate change. She coedited *Place-Based Conservation: Perspectives from the Social Sciences* with Daniel Williams and William Stewart (2013, Springer Publishing).

**James LaGro, Jr.** is a Professor of urban and regional planning at the University of Wisconsin-Madison. His graduate education (Cornell University) is in landscape architecture and natural resource policy and planning. He has over 30 years of combined professional experience in academia, government, and the private sector. His research, teaching, and outreach focus on the structure and function of the built environment across multiple spatial scales. The third edition of his textbook (*Site Analysis: Informing Context-Sensitive and Sustainable Site Planning and Design*) was published in 2013 by John Wiley & Sons.

**Heather Lazrus** is an environmental anthropologist and a project scientist at the National Center for Atmospheric Research in Boulder, Colorado. She earned a PhD in anthropology from the University of Washington in 2009. Using the theories and methods in the anthropological toolkit, Dr. Lazrus investigates the cultural mechanisms through which all weather and climate risks are perceived, experienced, and addressed. She focuses on the interface between extreme weather and climate change; her research contributes to improving the utility of weather forecasts and warnings, reducing social vulnerability to atmospheric and related hazards, and understanding community and cultural adaptations to climate change.

**Erlidia F. Llamas-Clark** is a medical specialist in obstetrics and gynecology. She is a Clinical Associate Professor of the University of the Philippines–Philippine General Hospital. She earned her PhD at the Australian National University, National Centre of Epidemiology and Population Health and has worked in the Philippines, Kiribati, Australia, and Fiji as a consultant clinician, public health practitioner, academic, health administrator, and program coordinator. She engages in multidisciplinary research interests and advocacies and applies combined quantitative and qualitative research methods involving women, children, and reproductive health, climate change-health impacts, food and nutrition security, gender, and disaster risk reduction.

**Julie Maldonado** is the Director of Research for the Livelihoods Knowledge Exchange Network, is a Lecturer in the University California–Santa Barbara's Environmental Studies Department, and consults for the Institute for Tribal Environmental Professionals to facilitate the development of tribal climate adaptation plans. Julie obtained a PhD in anthropology from American University in 2014, focusing on sociocultural effects of environmental change for tribes in coastal Louisiana. Julie worked for the US National Climate Assessment, was a lead author on NCA3's Indigenous Peoples, Land, and Resources chapter, and was the lead editor and organizer for the special issue of *Climatic Change* and book, *Climate Change and Indigenous Peoples in the United States: Impacts, Experiences and Actions* (Springer 2014).

**Victor Marchezini** has a PhD in sociology from Federal University of São Carlos, São Carlos, Brazil (2013), and earned a master's in human rights, global risk management, and disaster prevention policies from Henry Dunant Foundation, Chile (2012). He has spent the past 11 years focusing on social dimensions of disasters. He is the author of *Campos de desabrigados: a continuidade do desastre* (*Homeless Camps: The Disaster after the Disaster*) (2014, RiMa Publishers) and coeditor of *Sociologia dos Desastres: Construção, interfaces e perspectivas no Brasil* (*Sociology of Disasters: Development, Interface and Perspectives in Brazil*) (2009, RiMa Publishers). Currently, he is a researcher at the National Early Warning and Monitoring Centre of Natural Disasters (CEMADEN).

**Seven Mattes** is a PhD candidate specializing in the anthropology of Japan, human–animal studies, and disaster at Michigan State University. She is also pursuing a certificate in community engagement. Her doctoral research uses multispecies ethnography to understand the shifting animal welfare landscape in Japan following the 2011 Tohoku earthquake. Locally, she engages in numerous academic and advocacy projects exploring and aiding the multifaceted relationships people have with the animals in their lives, from the pigs they eat to the cats they love.

**Edward Morgan** is a postdoctoral research fellow based at the Urban Research Program at Griffith University. He is working with the Cooperative Research Centre for Water Sensitive Cities and the Griffith Climate Change Response Program. His current research is looking at catchment-scale landscape planning for water-sensitive city regions in an age of climate change. It uses an urban metabolism framework to integrate water management and land-use planning to improve urban water governance and help cities build resilience and adapt to climate change. His PhD research analyzed the use of science in water governance to understand how governance, politics, and values affect the interactions between science and policy. His research interests are the interactions between knowledge and society, particularly how science can be used to support sustainability, resilience, and environmental justice.

**Jeff Morisette** is the Director of the Department of the Interior's North Central Climate Science Center, which is working to provide the best available climate science to natural and cultural resource managers in the region. His existing research includes large-scale species habitat mapping and work on land surface phenology estimates from satellite data.

**Brian A. Needelman** is an Associate Professor of soil science at the University of Maryland in the Department of Environmental Science and Technology. He teaches and performs research in the fields of soil science, coastal wetlands, and coastal resiliency. His coastal wetland research focuses on management and restoration practices to increase tidal marsh sustainability including studies on prescribed burns, accretion, carbon sequestration, methane emissions, and the restoration of ditch-drained marshes. His coastal resiliency research focuses on the integration of natural and social science approaches to better understand and increase the resilience of coastal socioecological systems.

**Josephine Nummi** is pursuing her PhD in sociology at Texas A&M University. She received her BA in global studies from Hamline University. Her research interests include antiracist movements online, gender and gender assumptions in everyday life, and international immigration issues. She has presented on internalized dominance and white privilege at the National Conference on Race and Ethnicity in Higher Education. To explore how offline racism is criticized online, she is currently analyzing Twitter data surrounding the killing of Michael Brown, an unarmed black teenager, by Darren Wilson, a white police officer in Ferguson, Missouri, on August 9, 2014.

**Natalie Osborne** is a Lecturer in the School of Environment, Griffith University, Gold Coast, Australia. Natalie researches community-based activism and transition planning, resilience and adaptation, social and environmental justice, mine closure, community development, collective trauma, and the socio-spatial construction of identities, communities, and experiences. Her work is geared toward a better understanding of how social, environmental, political, and economic shifts can trigger transformative change for a more just, resilient, and sustainable future. Natalie has published work on climate change adaptation, intersectional feminist theory, mining, neoliberalism and Indigenous Peoples, and emotional geographies.

**Michael Paolisso** is a Professor of anthropology at the University of Maryland, College Park. He has conducted short- and long-term fieldwork in the areas of environment and development in Venezuela, Honduras, Ecuador, Kenya, and Nepal. For the past 15 years, he has focused his research on the human dimensions of a range of environmental issues confronting the Chesapeake Bay, including management of natural resources, particularly fisheries and agricultural lands, water pollution, restoration, social justice, socioecological resilience, and climate change.

**Stefan Petrovic** was a senior (2015–2016) at Lawrence High School in Lawrence, Kansas, at this writing. Stefan has worked under the guidance of, and in partnership with, Dr. Daniel Wildcat of Haskell Indian Nations University, the Indigenous Peoples' Climate Change Working Group, and the Rising Voices: Collaborative Solutions for Climate Science program to emphasize the importance of youth research and climate activism. Stefan cofounded the Rising Voices Youth Climate Initiative and is currently serving on the Environmental Protection Agency's National Environmental Justice Advisory Council Youth Climate Justice Workgroup. Stefan is currently attending Harvard University.

**Andrew Prelog** is an Assistant Professor of sociology at the University of Northern Colorado. His research interests include environmental sociology, social deviance, the sociology of law, and social policy. His research focuses on risk, risk perceptions, and the empirical relationship between disasters and crime.

**Jason D. Rivera** is an Assistant Professor at State University of New York–Buffalo within the Department of Political Science (Public Administration Division). He earned his PhD in public affairs from Rutgers, The State University of New Jersey. His research focuses on social vulnerability to and recovery from natural and manmade disasters with an emphasis on racial/ethnic minority and low-income experiences in addition to representational bureaucracy and bureaucratic discretion. He is the coeditor, along with DeMond S. Miller, of several volumes, including *Comparative Emergency Management: Examining Global and Regional Responses to Disasters* (2011, CRC Press).

**Norma Tan** is Principal of Cora Group, a consulting consortium established in 1988 to help organizations meet new workplace challenges through learning systems that promote the capacity for change and innovation. Trained as an educational psychologist, her research has focused on cognitive and perceptual processes in learning. She currently advises leaders and provides technical assistance to support organizational learning and capacity building through coaching, systems design, assessment, and evaluation. In prior years, she conducted evaluation studies as a research director in the Metro Center for Urban Education of New York University and in Baruch College of the City University of New York.

**Rachel Trajber** has a PhD in anthropology from Purdue University (United States), revalidated at Federal University of São Carlos, Brazil (1988). She was the coordinator of environmental education at the Ministry of Education in Brazil (2004–2011) and a member of the Steering Committee, United Nations Decade on Education for Sustainable Development/United Nations Educational, Scientific, and Cultural Organization and the Treaty on Environmental Education for Sustainable Societies and Global Responsibility. Currently, she is the Education Project Coordinator at the National Early Warning and Monitoring Centre of Natural Disasters (CEMADEN) in Brazil.

**Kyle Powys Whyte** is an Associate Professor of philosophy and community sustainability and holds the Timnick Chair in the Humanities in the Department of Philosophy at Michigan State University. He is a faculty member of the Environmental Philosophy & Ethics graduate concentration and serves as a faculty affiliate of the American Indian Studies and Environmental Science & Policy programs. His primary research addresses moral and political issues concerning climate policy and Indigenous peoples and the ethics of cooperative relationships between Indigenous peoples and climate science organizations. He is an enrolled member of the Citizen Potawatomi Nation.

**Sue Whyte** is a Research Assistant with the Centre of Research for Resilient Communities at Federation University, Australia, Gippsland campus. Her research interests include the role of place on people's sense of identity and well-being and on community well-being and resilience. She explores alternative methods that enable different stories to be told of how people understand and can be in their place(s) and how this can change both individual and community well-being.

**Pamela Wood** is an Associate Professor in the School of Nursing at the Eastern Institute of Technology in New Zealand. Her background is in nursing and history, and her research focuses on the history of nursing practices, particularly in contributing to primary health care and regional health services in collaboration with communities. These nursing initiatives have strengthened community resilience in the past. She was formerly the Associate Dean of Research in the Faculty of Health and codirector of the Centre of Research for Resilient Communities (CoRRC) at Federation University Australia. CoRRC undertakes interdisciplinary community-engaged research in regions such as the Latrobe Valley and, more broadly, in the Gippsland region of Victoria, Australia.

**Hao-Che Wu** is an Assistant Professor of political science at Oklahoma State University. He teaches courses in the Fire and Emergency Management Administration Program, with an expertise in disaster response and methods. His research areas focus on disaster information use, household disaster response, perceptions of environmental threats, and GIS applications. Within disaster information, his research has focused on the mental model of information search, social media use, and disaster information content.

**Clayton Wukich** is an Assistant Professor of political science at Sam Houston State University. His research interests include intergovernmental relations and collaborative governance, particularly within the policy domain of disaster and emergency management. His research focuses on how public sector and nonprofit organizations use information and communication technology to increase public participation and interagency coordination.

**Susan Yell** is a Senior Lecturer in media at Federation University Australia, Gippsland Campus. She has published in the fields of communication and media studies, linguistics, and semiotics. Her work examines the relationship between social practices and discourse and the role of communication technologies in enabling (or hindering) social connection. Her recent research focuses on media coverage of natural disasters and the formation of emotional communities during and after disasters. She is a member of the Community Well-being stream within the large-scale Hazelwood Health study, examining the effects of the Hazelwood mine fire, and of the Centre of Research for Resilient Communities based at Federation University.

**Qiaoyun Zhang** is a PhD candidate in anthropology at Tulane University, New Orleans. Her master's research examined how New Orleans' food and restaurant heritage has become an essential part of the city's recovery after Hurricane Katrina in 2005. Ms. Zhang's NSF-funded dissertation research explores how Chinese ethnic minority Qiang culture is restored and promoted through the state-led projects after the 2008 Sichuan Earthquake. Her study focuses on the interplay of the vulnerability and resilience of the affected communities, state-ethnic relationships, and the transformed identity and ways of life of local people.

# Introduction

*Michèle Companion and Miriam S. Chaiken*

## THE NEED FOR UNDERSTANDING FACETS OF VULNERABILITY IN A CHANGING CLIMATE

As the global climate shifts, communities are faced with a myriad of mitigation and adaptive challenges. Evidence suggests that the physical environment around us is changing. While politicians debate, scientific research indicates that global climate change has altered sea levels and water temperatures, thereby increasing the frequency and intensity of hurricanes and named storms (Cai et al. 2015; Knutson et al. 2010; Wong and Teixeira 2016). More intense storms are associated with increased ferocity of wind, storm surges, and heavier rates of precipitation. These, in turn, increase the likelihood of flooding, rates of subsidence and salt water incursions, and land and mudslides, contributing to higher overall property damage and morbidity and mortality rates in affected zones. They also result in technological and commercial interruptions due to damaged power, communication, and transportation systems, generating economic impacts beyond the cost of repairs and rebuilding.

Not only has climate change altered the severity of disaster events, it has also shifted their geographical impacts. Altered rainfall patterns and increasing droughts (Bergaoui et al. 2015; Wang, Lin, Gillies, and Hakala 2016) increase wildfires, pest infestations, and food insecurity (Dale et al. 2001), threatening biodiversity (Seim et al. 2016), biomass (Olmo, Lopez-Iglesias, and Villar 2014), and agricultural output (Woli, Jones, Ingram, and Hoogenboom 2014). This has tremendous implications for staple crops and the larger global food chain (Daryanto, Wang, and Jacinthe 2015; Li, Angeles, Radanielson, Marcaida, and Manalo 2015).

Disasters come in many forms; they can be sudden and devastating or emerge slowly and remain chronic problems. Human interventions, such as river diversion, construction of dams, generation of pollutants and carbon emissions, logging, mining, and oil and gas extraction techniques, alter existing risk factors and generate new ones. Technological failures, such as oil spills and contamination from nuclear fallout, exemplify the changes that require populations and governments to rethink distributions of risk and how they should best respond to these challenges. Growing awareness of these risks and vulnerabilities fosters political dissent, exposes capacity/response shortcomings, and challenges power structures. In the extreme, this has led to civil unrest and destabilization of governments.

Social inequalities are further exposed as changes in the physical world alter access to resources, such as water, arable land, and food. Livelihood opportunity structures related to fishing, various forms of harvesting and traditional gathering practices, pastoralism, and farming shift in favor of large-scale corporate enterprises with vast economic resources and political power. This threatens the survival of traditional people and their cultures (e.g., Bamforth 2015; Gill and Ritchie 2015; Laska et al. 2015; Maldonado et al. 2015) and has a disproportionate impact on women (e.g., Enarson 2012) and groups that are not well integrated into existing power structures (e.g., Alfirsaus 2014; Potter 2007).

Disasters and challenges posed by climate change highlight the political, cultural, economic, social, and physical vulnerability of social groups, communities, families, and individuals. As Schipper and Pelling (2006, 19) remind us,

> The impacts of Hurricanes Katrina and Rita on world oil prices show how uncertainty is not restricted to local or agricultural economies. It feeds into cycles of resource degradation and poverty, affecting both human well-being and the environment. In such cycles, climate change and natural hazards play significant roles, just as the state of development influences their ramifications for society and the environment.

Research in the fields of risk and hazard management, humanitarian response, food security programming, agricultural development, gender-equity programming, epidemiology, sociology, and anthropology has sought to understand the factors that create vulnerability. Through an exploration of these factors, researchers and practitioners have been identifying strategies to enhance resilience at all levels.

## SITUATING DISASTER RESEARCH IN A CASE STUDY FORMAT

This volume brings together case studies from communities around the globe to illustrate the dyadic concepts of resilience and vulnerability. Specifically, the volume examines programs and community-based responses that have helped reduce risks brought on by political instability, climate change, natural disasters, chronic food insecurity, inequality, and other problems that cause human suffering. Our goal is to both foster a richer understanding of the variations in risk and susceptibility to negative impacts and to derive lessons that can be employed on a broader scale to mitigate such risk. Documenting the best practices and programming strategies for building resilience and reducing vulnerability is a major focus of the book.

The chapters in our volume employ a human ecology focus; they contribute to the study of the relationship between humans and the natural, built, and social environment. Collectively, they examine how risk factors and vulnerability to the negative consequences of events are compounded by demographic factors, such as the age and sex distribution of the local population, their physical capabilities, and how populations are dispersed and clustered. They illustrate how economic and social factors, such as endemic and chronic poverty and gender-based inequality, heighten these factors. This is important, because disasters are complex phenomena; their impacts are simultaneously economic, political, geographical, physical, political, social, and cultural.

Consequently, understanding resilience at the level of the individual, household, community, and social group is essential, as the effects of disasters affect all of these tiers of social organization simultaneously. Resilience is shaped by politics and social constructions as much as by geography and ecology, as race, ethnicity, religion, gender, disability, class, and social cohesion all influence the degree of impact of disaster and climate change. These characteristics have also been correlated with the likelihood of receiving aid to effectively rebuild, as well as the speed and thoroughness of the recovery and response following a shock. However, they are understudied dimensions that can contribute to resilience in the face of catastrophic events. This volume directly addresses these dimensions.

## SECTION I: METHODOLOGY, POLICY, AND EARLY WARNING SYSTEMS

The first section of the book is devoted to the evaluation of dimensions of resilience and vulnerability to improve disaster risk reduction and enhance recovery, with a focus on presenting "best practice" models. The first chapters highlight the need for deeper collaboration with and input from local stakeholder communities. These chapters reveal the barriers often created between "experts" and the local communities, where academic knowledge and pedigree or governmental status become elevated over lived experience and traditional observations. Cultural sensitivity necessitates incorporation of a broader array of voices, such as marginalized and indigenous people, in the discussion. This ensures the building of effective and collaborative communication structures and provides opportunities for creative programming and thinking outside the "expert" box.

These studies demonstrate that listening to, respecting, and incorporating local experiential knowledge into formalized programming initiatives produce a more comprehensive set of responses that are also sensitive to local conditions. This increases ownership of local programming efforts and can improve relationships with government departments or agencies and nongovernmental organizations (NGOs). It can speed up activation of response resources through earlier identification of a crisis situation, thereby mitigating impacts. It can also improve chances of survival for acute events, such as flooding, by improving community preparedness and ability to respond.

Johnson, Needelman, and Paolisso (Chapter 1) expose the contested dynamics of stakeholders in their work with the Deal Island Marsh and Community Project. They highlight the importance of using a collaborative science approach to improve communication and knowledge exchange between the community and "outsider" program stakeholders. They focus on removing barriers between groups that had become entrenched in an "us" versus "them" dynamic. Employment of collaborative learning models helped to develop a more robust and inclusive partnership that provided the flexibility to meet the needs of the community, built a broader socioecological response system, and improved opportunities to enhance effectiveness in programming at a variety of levels.

Collaborative learning strategies are critical for underserved or often ignored communities, as demonstrated in Chapter 2. Maldonado et al. point to the high level of threats faced by indigenous communities as a result of climate change and ecological dispossession. They stress the importance of boundary organizations in facilitating communication and collaboration between often oppositional world views. Facilitated processes contribute to community empowerment, greater cultural sensitivity among programming authorities, and broader, more sustainable partnerships.

Barriers to resilience and the need to build more bridges to reduce vulnerability are global issues. In Chapter 3, Marchezini and Trajber provide an example of an education program in Brazil that empowers local citizens and youth to contribute to a broader social protection network. As with the discussion in Chapter 2, Marchezini and Trajber find that youth are underutilized as citizen scientists and local responders. They present an integrated educational program that trains youth to work with their communities and forges links between multiple levels of government representatives and the citizenry.

The impact of local and traditional knowledge on response to disaster scenarios varies but represents a crucial and understudied facet of disaster research. Wu et al. (Chapter 4) provide a comparison of flood responses in a community in the United States and one in India. Given previous exposure to floods in recent history, the United States community was more reliant on their observations of risk indicators, combined with sociotechnical systems. Despite the lack of flash flood warning systems or governmental education programs, residents of Uttarakhand used their knowledge of their local environment to improve their chances of survival.

Chaiken (Chapter 5) follows up the first four chapters with a discussion that integrates indigenous knowledge systems and expertise in disaster and humanitarian responses to create partnerships to generate innovative solutions. This approach respects and fosters local human agency while building on traditional knowledge, resulting in solutions such as community-based early warning systems. She notes that Save the Children programs reestablished social safety-net functionalities that had been destroyed by long-term conflict in rural Mozambique, and she purports that promoting partnerships to address local issues improves community buy-in and ensures cultural sensitivity in humanitarian response. This chapter contributes to the "best practices" focus by concluding with a detailed checklist of community-based early warning indicators that can be modified and added to through collaboration with local partners.

### Policy, Evaluation, and "Best Practices" Models

The remaining five chapters in Section I focus on evaluating existing policies. These chapters take a "lessons learned/best practice" approach, using case studies to frame policy evaluations and to generate recommendations to build stronger responses and preventative measures at a variety of levels. These recommendations can enhance the pace of recovery and reduce personal, household, and community experiences of trauma by improving communication structures, mitigating risk prior to the occurrence of an event, accounting for cultural factors such as the inclusion of animal companions in response, and protecting culturally unique social groups from exploitation.

For example, Rivera (Chapter 6) finds fault with formal recovery mechanisms provided by the United States' Federal Emergency Management Agency. He notes that messages about how to apply for disaster relief in the aftermath of Super Storm Sandy often missed their intended targets. Instead, social capital (the ability to maximize and actualize the use of formal and informal social networks for resource access and accumulation) was a critical component in accessing the appropriate information needed to apply for recovery assistance. He proposes that stronger social capital networks need to be built at the community level to improve disaster preparation and response and need to be fostered continually over time. Castle et al. (Chapter 7) build on this theme by examining an NGO's capacity-building program. They find that social networks, in the form of peer-to-peer learning platforms, facilitated knowledge exchange, skill building, and leadership development.

In Chapters 8 through 10, we see the problems that occur when governments fail to prioritize local knowledge, engage in culturally sensitive dialogue, and create partnerships with the local community to address its needs. de Jong (Chapter 8) is deeply critical of the Canadian government's failure to adequately consult with First Nation peoples with regard to oil spill response and the creation of regulatory frameworks for hydrocarbon transport activities. Making a similar argument to Maldonado et al. (Chapter 2), she notes that ignoring the experiential, technical, and science-based knowledge of First Nations places traditional coastal communities at even greater peril from a catastrophic spill. Zhang and Barrios (Chapter 9) focus on the way culture is reimagined and constructed by the power elite to the disadvantage of Chinese ethnic minority groups in the aftermath of the Wenchuan earthquake. Like de Jong, they find that these reconstruction programs serve to reinforce the legitimacy and the authority of the State rather than to aid in the cultural survival of a unique group and heritage. Thus, risk planning and disaster response are used to reinforce existing power disparities.

Government and policy failures can serve to retraumatize or add additional layers of suffering to survivors in the aftermath of disasters. Mattes (Chapter 10) tackles this in her discussion of the impact of the 2011 earthquake, tsunami, and consequent nuclear power plant catastrophe in Japan. She notes that hundreds of thousands of companion and working animals were abandoned to their fates as a result of policies that failed to provide space for them in shelters or to account for them as part of emergency evacuation protocols. Not only were these animals exposed to suffering and death, but their companions were also faced with the additional heartache resulting from guilt, loneliness, and relational loss. She advocates for improved disaster policy that takes into account the human–animal bond and its relationship with emotional, physical, economic, and livelihood recovery issues.

## SECTION II: IMPACTS ON RESILIENCE AND VULNERABILITY

The second section of the book takes a more focused look at social dynamics that can contribute to both vulnerability and resilience. Social, political, religious, and economic inequalities structure levels of vulnerability and predict the likelihood of food insecurity. Food security is a major predictor of resilience and recovery, so it is explored in depth (Chapters 11 through 13). It is intimately linked with livelihood systems, which integrate strategies and coping mechanisms for physical and economic survival (e.g., agriculture, pastoralism, fishing, petty trading, wage labor, or a combination). These systems are shaped by local contexts, such as agro-ecological zones and climate, social, economic, and political environments, and by access to assets including human, social, natural, physical, and financial capital.

Chapters 11 through 14 explore the links among livelihood systems, food security, and community resilience. Llamas-Clark and Banwell (Chapter 11) find that preflooding investments in child nutrition in the Philippines proved inadequate in the aftermath of Tropical Storm Ketsana and Typhoon Parma. Much of this could be attributed to government and program integration failures that increased social and economic disadvantages. They argue that programming that includes sustainable livelihood assistance, social welfare support, and gender-sensitive disaster risk reduction strategies could drastically alter the impacts of future disasters on food insecurity.

Similar policy failures increase the vulnerability of displaced urban families in New York. As Gadhoke and Brenton (Chapter 12) note, single mothers face extreme barriers to providing food for their families and transitioning out of homelessness. These are further compounded by the lack of coordination across agencies that are tasked with addressing these issues and the social invisibility constructed around the issue of homelessness in American society.

Cochrane and Gecho (Chapter 13) and Companion (Chapter 14) focus on adaptive livelihood strategies employed in the face of enormous challenges, including lack of capacity to deal with or interest in their conditions on the part of the State. Small-holder, rural farmers in southern Ethiopia lack political, social, or economic capital to compel large-scale responses from their government, which also has limited resources. This leaves them to find survival strategies on their own. These farmers have been facing more erratic rainfall patterns and extended periods of drought, exacerbating vulnerability to food insecurity. However, they identify individual and community strategies to capitalize on opportunities, such as education and diversification of crops. The key to impact mitigation, they find, is agency, flexibility, and adaptation.

These findings are echoed in Companion's chapter (14), in which she focuses on impelled migrants, who comprise a new class of environmental refugee. Due to lack of political, social, or economic clout, Malawian people have been forced from their traditional lands by ecotourism and development needs. Her work investigates livelihood shifts and identity formation around what had been considered secondary or "hobby" skills, such as making jewelry, carving masks and figurines, and generating other forms of material goods. She finds that the production of material goods represents an adaptation to changing local conditions that empowers individuals to take greater control over their identity formation and continuity and carve out new competitive economic niches.

Companion finds this to be especially important for women, who have fewer options for education, land holding, and occupations in many areas around the globe. Gender dimensions impact the ability of both men and women to plan, actively mitigate, respond to, and rebuild from disasters. Gender both shapes and is shaped by levels of poverty and social, political, and economic marginalization. Chapters 15 through 17 highlight the need for in depth discussions of gender dynamics in planning and programming. Chow, Cramer, and Egna's (Chapter 15) policy analysis of gender integration into disaster management in fishing and aquaculture communities in the Philippines after new legislation and two major storms finds shortcomings. These need to be addressed, they argue, to foster more resilient communities.

Gender dynamics can both empower and constrain responders, survivors, and programming initiatives, impacting overall community and individual response and recovery. Nummi and Henderson (Chapter 16) and Bwerinofa and Chiweshe (Chapter 17) explore how gender dynamics shape the way fires and floods are experienced differently by those most immediately impacted by them. They both find that gender-balanced approaches benefit both men and women.

## SECTION III: COMMUNITY-BASED FACTORS THAT IMPACT RESILIENCY AND VULNERABILITY

In the last section, this volume explores multiple facets of communities and how these dynamics shape and are shaped by disaster events. Scholars examine how dimensions such as faith and the composition of collective memory alter vulnerability and resilience, thereby impacting mitigation planning, emergency response, and rebuilding. Disaster events place tremendous strain on existing community-based groups, organizational structures, and public policies. The identification of communication and structural breakdowns and the new organizational forms that emerge as a result have broad public policy and community planning implications. Emergent groups can engage in responsive mobilization, as they are unconstrained by preexisting power structures (Gardner 2015). This facilitates collective action. Community mechanisms for resilience and mobilization and organization building are explored in depth in this section.

Alexander (Chapter 18) examines strategies employed by poor communities in coastal Belize that are dependent on reef-based tourism. Climate change is increasing their vulnerability to storms and large-scale destruction of their homes and livelihood resources. She finds that collective, cooperative responses provide the greatest benefits across communities affected by disaster. This responsiveness enhances communication avenues for the spread of adaptive strategies, resource sharing, and trust-building. It also provides better communication and collaboration with government agencies who oversee tourism development and tourist safety.

Duffy et al. (Chapter 19) also highlight the tremendous capacity for community-level self-help and agency. In the aftermath of the coal mine fire, individuals felt disconnected from each other, ignored by state and local officials, and subject to the power disparities between them and the energy interests culpable for the disaster. Through the use of social media and the formation of new groups, the community was able to generate a strong collective voice and response that compelled government action on their behalf. Their action resulted in an independent inquiry into the fire and a long-term, government-sponsored study into the health impacts of exposure to contaminants.

Emergent collectives or organizations are also the focus of Kim and Kim's chapter (20). Their study of Best Family Rwanda examines how organizational formation and its religious foundation empower and equip surviving orphans of the Rwandan genocide with hope and economic and social coping skills. They stress the learning opportunities that Western disaster responders can glean from such organizations if they are willing to engage in true partnerships and respectfully engage with in-country partners. They note that power dynamics or assumptions about the role of religion in society can create barriers to developing resilience and rebuilding programs. Their case study demonstrates that religious belief can be a powerful mobilizer for action that should not be trivialized or marginalized in disaster response tool kits.

Social movement groups and collective action organizations often form in response to government failures, as well as community need. This is clear in the case studies of "guerrilla governance" of Osborne et al. (Chapter 21). These emergent organizations provide community, structure, and mechanisms for response to both government action, inaction, and perceived inappropriate action in disaster response. Huddleston (Chapter 22) continues this theme, noting that prepping is an emerging and growing social movement to improve resilience at the micro level in communities. Preppers recognize the shortcomings in government response agencies and are actively trying to situate themselves as responders instead of victims. Organizations of preppers are spreading across the United States and Canada to reduce personal and community vulnerability and improve disaster resilience, forming nascent social and logistical safety nets.

Faas (Chapter 23) rounds out this discussion by reminding us that communities are the sites where collective narratives are negotiated and memories constructed. How this process unfolds is driven by relationships within the communities, as structured by all dimensions of inequality, and among communities, institutions, and the environments in which disaster scenarios occur. Understanding the construction of collective memory is critical, as it informs practices that follow dealing with mitigating impacts in the future and facilitating recovery and resilience.

## CORE ELEMENTS OF THE VOLUME

Twenty-three essays are included in this volume, investigating 17 countries around the world. Different dimensions of community, household, individual, or social group vulnerability to disaster and strategies are investigated in each essay, to better understand and improve resilience. This volume represents a broad forum to discuss the impacts of disasters on communities. All of the studies emphasize the importance of integrated responses for community-based recovery and preparation mitigation. Issues such as gender and poverty affect how governments channel policy at vulnerable populations and contribute to the complexity and efficacy of community-based responses. Multiple forms of disasters (e.g., climate change, hurricanes/typhoons, earthquakes, fires, and floods) are explored to provide a comprehensive discussion of the topic. Resulting conditions, such as population displacement, malnutrition and food insecurity, emotional trauma, distrust of political systems, and livelihood loss are also examined.

The collected works emphasize the need for community-driven *applied methodology*. This encourages community participation in and ownership of programs. It recognizes the value of traditional and experiential knowledge in constructing solutions to local issues. This process includes incorporating cultural sensitivity by not marginalizing voices of the less powerful or cultural practices, including religious beliefs. It emphasizes the continued identification and discussion of "Best Practices" before, during, and after disasters and the constant search for new assessment models or tools for disaster risk reduction, including early warning systems.

To successfully identify vulnerability and build resistance at all levels, the impact of political dynamics, history of contestation between groups, social inequalities, levels of trust between communities and governments, and a host of other issues must be accounted for in all phases of planning and policy enactment. Our goal with this volume is to provide a comprehensive, holistic examination of the ways in which vulnerabilities to risk and disasters can be enhanced or minimized. By emphasizing a global focus, the inclusion of indigenous perspectives, and presenting alternative and emergent collective action structures, this collection of works exposes essential elements that need to be incorporated into successful disaster mitigation and community resilience-building initiatives.

## REFERENCES

Alfirsaus, L.K. 2014. Disaster and discrimination: The ethnic Chinese minority in Padang in the aftermath of the September 2009 earthquake. *Journal of Social Issues in Southeast Asia* 29(1): 159–183.

Bamforth, T. 2015. The social impact of Typhoon Bopha on indigenous communities, livelihoods, and conflict in Mindanao. In *Disaster's impact on livelihood and cultural survival: Losses, opportunities, and mitigation*, ed. M. Companion, 199–210. Boca Raton, FL: CRC Press, Taylor & Francis Group.

Bergaoui, K., D. Mithcell, R. Zaaboul, R. McDonnell, F. Otto, and M. Allen. 2015. The contribution of human-induced climate change to the drought of 2014 in the southern Levant Region. *Bulletin of the American Meteorological Association: Supplement Explaining Extreme Weather Events*, December: S66-S70. DOI: 10.1175/BAMS-D-15-00129.1

Cai, W., G. Wang, A. Santoso, M.J. McPhaden, L. Wu, F.-F. Jin, A. Timmermann, M. Collins, G. Vecchi, M. Lengaigne, M.H. England, D. Dommenget, K. Takahashi, and E. Guilyardi. 2015. Increased frequency of extreme La Nina events under greenhouse warming. *Nature Climate Change* 5: 132–137.

Dale, V.H., L.A. Joyce, S. McNulty, R.P. Neilson, M.P. Ayres, M.D. Flannigan, P.J. Hanson, L.C. Irland, A.E. Lugo, C.J. Peterson, D. Simberloff, F.J. Swanson, B.J. Stocks, and B.M. Wotton. 2001. Climate change and forest disturbances: Climate change can affect forests by altering the frequency, intensity, duration, and timing of fire, drought, introduced species, insect and pathogen outbreaks, hurricanes, windstorms, ice storms, or landslides. *BioScience* 51(9): 723–734.

Daryanto, S., L. Wang, and P.-A. Jacinthe. 2015. Global synthesis of drought effects on food legume production. *PLoS ONE* 10(6): 1–16. DOI: 10.1371/journal.pone.0127401.

Enarson, E. 2012. *Women confronting natural disaster: From vulnerability to resilience*. Boulder, CO: Lynne Rienner Publishers.

Gardner, R.O. 2015. The emergency community: A grassroots model for post-disaster redevelopment. In *Disaster's impact on livelihood and cultural survival: Losses, opportunities, and mitigation*, ed. M. Companion, 257–268. Boca Raton, FL: CRC Press, Taylor & Francis Group.

Gill, D.A. and L.A. Ritchie. 2015. Sociocultural survival in the face of looming disaster: The Gitga'at First Nation's opposition to the Enbridge Northern Gateway Pipeline Project. In *Disaster's impact on livelihood and cultural survival: Losses, opportunities, and mitigation*, ed. M. Companion, 211–224. Boca Raton, FL: CRC Press, Taylor & Francis Group.

Knutson, T.R., J.L. McBride, J. Chan, K. Emanuel, G. Holland, C. Landsea, I. Held, J.P. Kossin, A.K. Srivastava, and M. Sugi. 2010. Tropical cyclones and climate change. *Nature Geoscience* 3: 157–163.

Laska, S., K. Peterson, C.L. Rodrigue, T. Cosse', R. Philippe, O. Burchett, and R.L. Krajeski. 2015. "Layering" of natural and human caused disasters in the context of sea level rise: Coastal Louisiana communities at the edge. In *Disaster's impact on livelihood and cultural survival: Losses, opportunities, and mitigation*, ed. M. Companion, 225–238. Boca Raton, FL: CRC Press, Taylor & Francis Group.

Li, T., O. Angeles, A. Radanielson, M. Marcaida, and E. Manalo. 2015. Drought stress impacts of climate change on rainfed rice in South Asia. *Climate Change* 133(4): 709–720.

Maldonado, J.K., A.P. Naquin, T. Dardar, S. Parfait-Dardar, and K. Bagwell. 2015. Above the rising tide: Coastal Louisiana's tribes apply local strategies and knowledge to adapt to rapid environmental change. In *Disaster's impact on livelihood and cultural survival: Losses, opportunities, and mitigation*, ed. M. Companion, 239–255. Boca Raton, FL: CRC Press, Taylor & Francis Group.

Olmo, M., B. Lopez-Iglesias, and R. Villar. 2014. Drought changes the structure and elemental composition of very fine roots in seedlings of ten woody tree species: Implications for a drier climate. *Plant & Soil* 384(1/2): 113–129.

Potter, H. 2007. *Racing the storm: Racial implications and lessons learned from Hurricane Katrina*. Lanham, MD: Lexington Books.

Schipper, L. and M. Pelling. 2006. Disaster risk, climate change and international development: Scope for, and challenges to, integration. *Disasters* 30(1): 19–38.

Seim, A., G. Omurova, E. Azisov, K. Musuraliev, K. Aliev, T. Tulyaganov, L. Nikolyai, E. Botman, G. Helle, I.D. Liñan, S. Jivcov, and H.W. Linderholm. 2016. Climate change increases drought stress of juniper trees in the mountains of Central Asia. *PLoS ONE* 11(4): e0153888. DOI: 10.1371/journal.pone.0153888.

Wang, S.-Y.S., Y.-H. Lin, R.R. Gillies, and K. Hakala. 2016. Indications for protracted groundwater depletion after drought over the Central Valley of California. *Journal of Hydrometeorology* 17(3): 947–955.

Woli, P., J.W. Jones, K.T. Ingram, and G. Hoogenboom. 2014. Predicting crop yields with the Agricultural Reference Index for Drought. *Journal of Agronomy and Crop Science* 200(3): 163–171.

Wong, S. and J. Teixeira. 2016. Extreme convection and tropical climate variability: Scaling of cold brightness temperatures to sea surface temperature. *Journal of Climate* 29(10): 3893–3905. DOI: http://dx.doi.org/10.1175/JCLI-D-15-0214.1.

# *Section I*

## *Methodology, Policy, and Early Warning Systems*

# *Methodological Strategies and Early Warning Systems*

Chapters in this section highlight the need for deeper collaboration with and input from local stakeholder communities. These chapters reveal the barrier often created between "experts" and the local communities, where academic knowledge and pedigree or governmental status become elevated over lived experience and traditional observations. Cultural sensitivity necessitates incorporation of a broader array of voices, such as marginalized and indigenous people, into all planning, mitigation, and response discussion. This ensures the building of effective and collaborative communication structures and provides opportunities for creative programming and thinking outside the "expert" box.

# 1 Vulnerability and Resilience to Climate Change in a Rural Coastal Community

*Katherine J. Johnson, Brian A. Needelman, and Michael Paolisso*

## CONTENTS



**Abstract**

The Deal Island Marsh and Community Project is an ongoing collaborative effort among scientists, environmental managers, and local community members to improve resilience and reduce vulnerability to climate change impacts in a coastal socioecological system. Using the toolkit of collaborative learning, which relies upon adult and experiential education, conflict resolution, and systems thinking (Feurt 2008), we are building a stakeholder network to engage participants. Alongside experiential and collaborative activities, formal research and data collection produces knowledge from across the socioecological system that can be used to inform environmental management strategies, further research interests, and share with local community members. Knowledge and social ties built through our network are integral to complex and lively understandings of vulnerability and resilience and determining their leverage points. This chapter discusses four strategies that help us understand ecological and community vulnerability and potential resiliencies while maintaining a systems perspective. These tools and methods can provide best practices and inform work elsewhere.

## INTRODUCTION

Producing resilience to climate change impacts among communities is important, but multiple challenges impede these efforts. In academic and practitioner arenas, differences in disciplinary commitments and theoretical approaches can hamper collaboration. For instance, integrating social and natural science research and data can be problematic. Ideological divides can also undermine progress. This is particularly true when cultural norms lead people to distrust key findings of climate science. Perhaps most critical is a lack of long-lasting partnerships bridging institutional and organizational boundaries to address community and ecological vulnerability. These challenges are overcome by linking vulnerability and resilience to climate adaptation planning using strategies for systems thinking and collaboration.

The Deal Island Marsh and Community Project (DI Project) is an effort to build resilience to climate change in a rural coastal community. A collaborative stakeholder network and research are key project outputs. In particular, findings relate to vulnerabilities and resiliencies for the socio-ecological system and inform adaptation planning. Resilience is often positioned as a positive and relational attribute of a system: "the ability to cope with shocks and keep functioning in much the same kind of way" (Walker and Salt 2012, p. 3). Vulnerability, correspondingly, is a negative system attribute: "[the] degree to which a system is likely to experience harm owing to exposure and sensitivity to a specified hazard or stress and its adaptive capacity to respond to that stress" (Chapin et al. 2009, p. 241). Vulnerability and resilience are best considered together to understand complex relationships related both to impacts and efforts to recover from disturbance events.

The impact of environmental and physical change on communities is a product of social and relational features influencing vulnerability and resilience for an area. For example, residents of low-lying areas may not agree that sea-level rise is a significant threat because they have more immediate and pressing concerns. Consensus in definitions of vulnerability and resilience cannot be assumed. The DI Project is a model for connecting climate change research and a community of stakeholders to develop solutions to problems in unique ways.

## DEAL ISLAND PENINSULA VULNERABILITY TO CLIMATE CHANGE

The Chesapeake Bay is the United States' largest estuary and a site of contentious resource regulation and increasingly strict environmental management for conservation and pollution reduction (Chesapeake Bay Program 2014; Ernst 2010). The Deal Island "peninsula" is 18 square miles of landscape and islands dominated by marsh, tidal waterways, and forests, interspersed with agricultural and residential land use along the Maryland shorelines of the Bay (Figure 1.1). One main road traverses marsh, creek, and open water to connect several small and unincorporated hamlets across flat coastal plain with an average elevation of only 3 feet. Long-time community members distrust

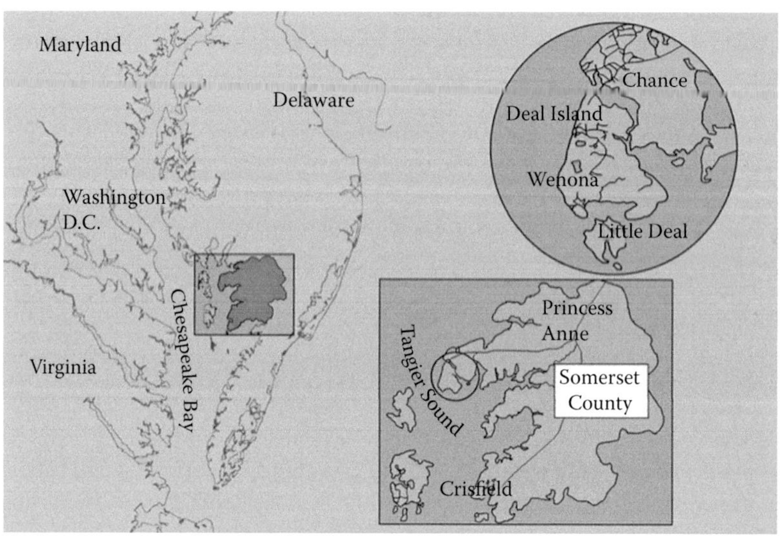


**FIGURE 1.1** Deal Island Peninsula, Somerset County, Maryland, is adjacent to the Tangier Sound of the Chesapeake Bay. (Courtesy of iStock.com/crossroadscreative and Maryland Sea Grant.)

outsiders and government involvement. This has escalated with management of fisheries and marshlands; many feel the government unfairly burdens them with regulation. As climate change adaptation proceeds, the community position should be acknowledged. They can be both marginalized and, at the same time, central to contestations over environmental management (Paolisso 2005).

Bay livelihoods have changed with increased development and the decline of water-based economies. Many rural communities have disappeared due to out-migration, economic decline, or encroachment of Chesapeake waters (Cronin 2005; Erwin, Brinker, Watts, Constanzo, and Morton 2010; Leatherman, Chalfont, Pendleton, McCandless, and Funderburk 1995). Some, like those in the Deal Island peninsula area, have maintained vibrant communities despite population decline and an aging population. Today, about 1000 people are dispersed between historical inland communities and private waterfront homes developed by vacationers and retirees (American Fact Finder 2013). Two small convenience stores (one selling gas) are available for food and amenities, but many more existed in the area's heyday of seafood harvesting and processing industries, regular steamboat commerce, and United Methodist Church revivals and camp meetings (Rhodes 2007; Roberts 1905; Wallace 1978).

Watermen (commercial fishermen) still catch crabs, oysters, and fish year-round. Hard working and independent, watermen provide a cultural and economic backbone for the community despite their dwindling numbers. Heritage is an ongoing and lived experience for peninsula residents, linking past to present on a daily basis (Paolisso 2002 and 2003; Power and Paolisso 2007). When you ask someone what is special about the area, they talk about faith, family, quietness, and the community's commitment to a slower pace of life. During semistructured interviews conducted with 25 DI Project stakeholders in spring 2014, many local community members indicated that they identify so strongly with the area that they couldn't imagine living anywhere else.

### Expected Environmental Change

The region's relative sea level has increased 30 centimeters over the last century (Titus and Strange 2008). It is predicted to rise another 110 centimeters within the next century (Boesch et al. 2013), increasing flooding, storm surge, wave height, and tidal flows (Spanger-Siegfried, Fitzpatrick, and Dahl 2014). Geologically induced land subsidence has been measured at 5 millimeters per year in the Chesapeake region (Eggleston and Pope 2013), while the peninsula's rates of erosion are significantly greater than Maryland's average (Maryland Department of Natural Resources [MDDNR] 2008). Anticipated impacts also include temperature fluctuations, changes in rainfall, increased storm frequency and severity, and salinity intrusion, all with profound effects on landscape and hydrology (Najjar et al. 2010).

Brackish marshes are a prominent feature of the area's landscape and provide habitat for important species (Scott 1991). The marshes are managed by MDDNR to promote fish spawning, wildfowl hunting, and mosquito reduction. Along the Atlantic seaboard, coastal marshes are declining rapidly due to sea-level rise and other environmental stressors with dramatic consequences for coastal ecosystems and local communities (Needelman 2012). Land subsidence and anthropogenic disturbance, particularly extensive ditching in the early 20th century, have compromised the natural ability of marsh to accrete. As sea levels rise, marsh erosion and submergence will impede storm surge mitigation and other socioecological services. Local communities seek cost-efficient restoration and conservation approaches to increase resilience in marshes and communities in the face of these impacts.

## THE DEAL ISLAND MARSH AND COMMUNITY PROJECT

The DI Project (www.dealislandmarshandcommunityproject.org) was originally funded by the National Oceanic and Atmospheric Administration's (NOAA's) National Estuarine Research Reserve Science Collaborative Program (Fall 2012–Summer 2015) and has received additional support from the University of Maryland's College of Behavioral and Social Sciences and College of Agriculture and Natural Resource, MDDNR Chesapeake and Coastal Service, and the US Geological Survey Water Resources Research Program. The project is managed by Drs. Needelman and Paolisso, in partnership with representatives from MDDNR. Significant involvement by local organizations and churches has helped to extend project leadership into the local community. Paolisso has been working as an environmental anthropologist in the area for over 15 years; he was integral to engaging local community members.

The DI Project is an ongoing collaborative effort among social and natural scientists, environmental managers, and local community members. The project improves resilience and reduces vulnerability to climate change impacts across the socioecological system using several objectives to restore and conserve marshes and local communities. This includes establishing collaboration among stakeholders, developing and testing a broadly transferable process of engagement, and producing a better understanding of socioecological services by marsh systems and decision-making processes within the stakeholder community using integrated anthropological, economic, and ecological applied science.

Four key strategies have enabled success toward objectives and promoted development of a more nuanced understanding of ecological and community vulnerabilities and resiliencies. These include the conceptualization of vulnerability and resilience as part of a socioecological system, the implementation of collaborative learning to deepen insight, trust, and sharing among project participants, and the creation of a network of stakeholders to diversify views and skills available to address issues. Finally, there is the use of collaborative science, which brings an interdisciplinary perspective.

## A Socioecological Systems Framework

Resilience researchers (Adger 2000; Folke 2006) highlight the importance of socioecological systems frameworks. Using "systems thinking" emphasizes holistic and complex perspectives, giving equal footing to environmental and social concerns. The DI Project's framework is similar to the "situated resilience approach" described by Cote and Nightingale (2012), prioritizing institutional and functional configurations in the socioecological system and also "processes and relations" supporting the system (p. 480). This framework allows exploration of system features, dynamics and feedbacks between those features, supporting institutions and arrangements, and the relationships and perspectives of network stakeholders that contribute to climate change resilience.

As Nelson, Adger, and Brown (2007) argue, defining resilience in a systems context increases understanding of vulnerability and adaptation in three ways. First, more sociocultural factors are included. These reveal tensions in environmental and social relations and identify vulnerabilities that can be historically or politically constructed. This includes a focus on vulnerability as systemically embedded in socioecological systems due to inequitable distributions of resources, wealth, and security (Oliver-Smith 2013, p. 279). Second, the system-oriented approach creates a broader research agenda. Individual and group knowledge, values, and practices can be investigated and contextualized in relation to climate change vulnerabilities and adaptations (Adger et al. 2009; Oliver-Smith 2013; Orlove 2009). This increases the potential for the development and implementation of adaptation strategies. It can also contribute to more successful adaptation planning, since information is more robust. Finally, this perspective allows individuals and communities to define goals for the socioecological system and work together to achieve them. This broadens the potential for environmental governance through planning and adaptation, while also providing space for agency (Nelson, Adger, and Brown 2007, p. 412).

The socioecological framework simultaneously serves as a useful conceptual planning tool, a reminder of commitment to resilience for the entire peninsula area, and a site for action and negotiation. It enables expanded scope, requires diversification and incorporation of multiple research perspectives, and necessitates engagement with stakeholders across the system. This framework is essential to the development of our understanding vulnerability and resilience and the creation of strategies to cope and adapt with climate change.

## Collaborative Learning

Collaborative Learning is an experiential learning and conflict-resolution approach used in cases of contentious environmental issues generative of cultural and economic conflict (Daniels and Walker 2001; Feurt 2008). It can help craft adaptive processes using appropriate science and technology and emphasizes strategies that are both implementable and have low transactions costs (Daniels and Walker 2001, p. 3). Daniels and Walker (2001, p. 10) argue that collaborative processes have potential to achieve balance between technical competence and inclusive deliberation, noting: "Collaboration involves interdependent parties identifying issues of mutual interest, pooling their energy and resources, addressing their differences, charting a course for the future, and allocating implementation responsibility among the group."

The DI Project promoted collaborative learning through group outreach activities, particularly community conversations and workshops. Four evening community conversations were held in Fall 2014 and early 2015, with attendance ranging from 24 to 28 individuals. DI Project stakeholders, including academic researchers, environmental managers, and local community members, presented valuable sociocultural and environmental information to each other and community residents. Topics included Federal Emergency Management Agency policies and flood insurance, scientific assessment of marsh vulnerability and restoration options, shoreline erosion and opportunities for building living shorelines, and religion, faith, and climate change.

Six day-long workshops were also held for DI Project stakeholders between April 2013 and April 2015, with attendance ranging from 20 to 38 individuals. Workshops were designed to ensure that interactive data collection and collaboration activities occurred alongside general project updates and presentations of research findings. Data were gathered on beliefs and values regarding climate change, understanding of the local environment and the human position within it, and vulnerabilities and resiliencies in the Deal Island Peninsula socioecological system. Scientific presentations covered a variety of topics, such as geologic and shoreline change of the area through time, socioecological services valuation, mosquito population dynamics, and experimental testing and data collection concerning marsh hydrology and health. In addition, informal conversation was encouraged with breaks, a long lunch, and frequent small-group activities. The workshops proved to be the core activity of the stakeholder network and allowed diverse stakeholders to come together to share knowledge and information in meaningful ways.

Collaborative learning activities have been effective at establishing rapport within the project's network. While stakeholders do not always agree on the problems and solutions, they have learned and benefited from each other's views, particularly in relation to environmental and social vulnerabilities and resiliencies. In a survey following the last workshop, 30 out of 31 project stakeholders said that they "strongly agree" or "agree" that "I have been able to share my knowledge and expertise" through project activities. All 31 project stakeholders "strongly agree" or "agree" that "I have learned from other's knowledge and expertise." The ongoing collaborative learning commitment has served to establish rapport, build new connections among the diverse subgroups of the stakeholder network, and contribute to shared knowledge and understanding of diverse system components, threats/vulnerabilities, and sources of resilience.

## Network of Stakeholders

Social network analysis (SNA) is an increasingly popular technique used to quantify social relations among individuals by mapping individual's relationships to one another within a group (cf. Prell 2012). Examples include friendships, working relationships, comembership in organizations, groups based on geographic vicinity, or groups defined by a topical area of interest. To gather this information, researchers often ask participants to respond to a series of questions about other individuals to whom they may or may not be associated within a network. An alternative strategy is for individuals to respond to a survey that seeks information on the duration and strength of relationships between every individual in the network. Mapping these relationships enables researchers to discover how social relations form patterns or structures.

SNA can be used to understand how the flow of information, social capital, natural resources, or influence and power travel throughout a network (Prell 2012). How networks are connected influences the rate and direction of flow, impact, and outcomes of sharing (or nonsharing) within a group. Key points of analysis relate to strength of ties, sparseness and density of the network, isolates and subgrouping, similar thinking according to group, actor centrality in the network, and how these features affect the flow of information. Such data have been successfully studied in a range of natural resource management contexts (Bodin and Prell 2011; Crona and Hubacek 2010).

In our case, we first had to create a viable social network representing the full socioecological system. Social relations on the peninsula coalesce around familial relations, church and civic organization membership, and ties built through work relationships, e.g., one's trusted boat mechanic or a regular crewmember during the crabbing season. Since there is no local government and few ties with county and local representatives and managers, the community is quite independent. Local community members are often uninformed and not consulted on management decisions for the substantial marshlands in their vicinity. It was evident that additional work was needed to bridge local and nonlocal stakeholders. Therefore, in creating our network, we emphasized the inclusion of those involved with regional and state level governance and environmental management.

More than 50 project stakeholders were invited to participate by the NOAA Science Collaborative Grant team, based on academic qualifications, areas of expertise in governmental or nongovernmental management, and leadership standing within the local communities. This new and unique network includes 40% representation from the local community and 20% representation each from university researchers, state agency environmental and policy managers (including outreach specialists and coastal planners), and representatives of environmental and heritage nonprofit organizations. The network is experientially, professionally, and geographically diverse, enabling discussions across the system. By confronting concerns together, the stakeholder network increases the resilience of the area. In the future, we anticipate implementing an SNA to measure network structure and effectiveness.

## Collaborative Science Approach

Since the beginning of the DI Project, social and natural science research activities have helped to engage the stakeholder network through a commitment to collaborative science. A significant portion of project support went to academic research in the fields of ecology, anthropology, and economics. Social-science data collection focused on local and system-level understandings of climate change, vulnerability, resilience, heritage, and valuation of socioecological services (understandings of vulnerabilities and resiliencies will be covered in the following section).

The DI Project's ecological research focused on marshes and particularly on hydrological restoration of ditch-drained marshes. Marshes were ditched in the 1930s as a means to mitigate mosquitoes and facilitate salt hay harvesting. Plugging of ditch-drained marshes was identified by a subset of stakeholders prior to the project's initialization as a potential restoration and adaptation strategy. Studying marsh systems before and after restoration was necessary to understand whether this would restore natural hydrology and improve habitat quality and marsh resilience, or increase vulnerability to sea-level rise. Data gathered relate to hydrology, mosquitoes, fish, plants, soils, and elevation change, with a focus on vulnerable components of the ecological system that may become more resilient through restoration activities. In each of these research components, additional emphasis was placed on developing interactive and collaborative exercises to share knowledge within the network. As a result, information exchange proceeded via a combination of traditional research and nontraditional stakeholder interaction. Collaborative research projects (CRPs) are a key example of our collaborative science activities.

CRPs were developed through initial project stakeholder discussions at workshops. Three CRP groups of 10 to 15 stakeholders coalesced on topics related to flooding and shoreline erosion, marsh restoration, and community heritage. With an open research agenda, small groups conducted facilitated activities, leading to the codevelopment of key research questions, paying attention to relevant features of vulnerability and resilience. For example, the marsh restoration CRP has conducted data collection on historical environmental change in the area and organized a field trip to share on-the-ground knowledge about the marsh among local community members and MDDNR representatives. CRP research findings complement ongoing scientific research and provide a platform for social learning, particularly concerning stakeholder knowledge and values. Local knowledge was given equal consideration to scientific knowledge in these groups, aiding in the development of a shared and deeper understanding of complex socioecological problems and interactions and additional needs for future investigation.

These collaborative science research activities serve three purposes within the broader project. First, it allows for the creation of knowledge about the socioecological system and the sharing of this knowledge with project stakeholders and other community members through collaborative learning activities. Second, stakeholders learn how research is conducted by scientists and about how that research can be influenced through their involvement. Finally, it enables the heightened involvement of researchers, who often have limited time available to participate in outreach activities. These activities provided opportunities for shared learning between researchers from the three scientific disciplines and between scientists and nonscientists within the stakeholder network.

## RESULTS: A MORE NUANCED UNDERSTANDING OF VULNERABILITY AND RESILIENCE

> The experience of having considered these challenges together and having developed potential solutions and contingencies together, to me, means that the true essence of that community will live on regardless of its position in the landscape.
>
> **DI Project Stakeholder**

Through the four strategies described earlier, we have increased detail and complexity in understandings of vulnerabilities and resiliencies across the stakeholder network. A summary discussion of results is given here, starting with vulnerabilities and then tying these to socioecological system resiliencies.

Vulnerabilities identified include expected items, such as sea-level rise, shoreline erosion, flooding, land subsidence, low-lying buildings, isolation, and increased storm ferocity. Less expected features include distant management and governance, weak economics, changing demographics, and denial of vulnerability. Through discourse at community conversations, workshops, and in interviews, it is clear that perceptions of vulnerabilities are not universally held or defined. For example, the idea among some participants that locals "deny their own vulnerability" was uncovered through semistructured interviews. This was then highlighted for discussion at subsequent stakeholder workshops. Local community members feel that environmental managers and government officials from outside the community hold this perspective, seeing them as liabilities rather than people maintaining livelihoods in their historic homeland.

Focusing on vulnerability is not sufficient to understand complex positioning in relation to climate change. Detailed analysis of resiliencies is also needed. Those identified include protected shorelines, protection provided by marshlands, the ability to handle low flooding, and social networks enabling families to seek shelter elsewhere during major storms. Additional resiliencies include adaptability to change, an ethic of cooperation, self-reliance, and strong attachment to place. These capture cultural and historical features of the Deal Island Peninsula area. Since colonial times, people have been assiduous, building the community and livelihoods that have sustained them for generations. Adaptability is inherent to their way of life, as they experience and expect unpredictability in the world around them. Discussion of this topic at workshops revealed that underlying features of resilience might be hidden from environmental managers and government officials, who do not perceive locals in an active process of adaptation. Local community members, in turn, see managers as advocating detailed climate change planning in the face of uncertainty. They argue this is illogical, since one can never know the future, only have faith and fortitude in their ability to cope. Environmental managers respond that they are not promoting a single solution. Instead, they are interested in looking at a suite of options alongside communities. This example indicates that facilitating continued conversation is imperative to minimize contestation and support cooperation in future decision making.

Project stakeholders have made it clear they do not want investments in restoration and adaptation made until the group better understands the benefits and limitations of these strategies. Therefore, our next project is to develop a detailed coastal resilience assessment of the area to inform the development of potential strategies. Our partners at MDDNR are initiating a geospatial study that will provide quantitative data on a parcel-by-parcel basis. And we are bringing in new partners to model the effects of sea-level rise and climate impacts. These activities will produce maps and visualizations of environmental change projected into the future. These efforts, combined with continued collaboration, stakeholder feedback, and ground verification of data, should result in a comprehensive assessment and stakeholder-driven prioritization process.

## LESSONS LEARNED AND CONCLUSIONS

We encourage others in natural resource management and climate change adaptation fields to apply four strategies: framing at the socioecological system scale, early focus on collaborative learning, reliance on a robust stakeholder network, and integrating science into the collaborative process. Framing at the socioecological system scale enables consideration of social and natural environmental interests simultaneously and promotes a "what's best for everyone" attitude. Focus on collaborative learning at the outset builds a solid base from which a learning community can effectively transition to a decision-making community. Developing a robust stakeholder network can take significant time and energy, but reliance on a network enables social ties to become flexible and evolve. Integrating science increases ease communication of scientific, technical, and experiential knowledge and supports partnership in knowledge creation.

These lessons emphasize collaboration and sharing across multiple scales. The DI Project has marshaled resources and linked skills to build camaraderie and openness to alternative views and opinions. Newly established social relations are more capable of handling complex and diverse information, such as additional focus on vulnerability and resilience. The collective knowledge gleaned on these topics would not have been possible without utilizing the previously mentioned strategies. Project work identified sociocultural and ecological vulnerabilities and resilience features that take into account community viewpoints and therefore reinforce the understanding of and commitment to addressing these needs in ways that make sense to the entire stakeholder network. The resulting organizational structure meets local needs and builds socioecological system resilience but also has the potential to inform work in other areas.

Overall, project stakeholders have a sense of success in tackling this complex issue together and are excited to contribute with their knowledge and expertise. Planned future work will build on existing information and incorporate new perspectives. Additional research includes SNA, cultural consensus analysis, participatory modeling, continued heritage work, and a coastal resiliency assessment. Despite some clear conceptual divides within the group, the network acknowledges change is happening and is interested in continuing to work together. As a local Deal Islander said, "It ain't right, but it's perfect."

## REFERENCES

Adger, N.W. 2000. Social and ecological resilience: Are they related? *Progress in Human Geography* 24(3): 347–364.

Adger, N.W., S. Dessai, M. Goulden, M. Hulme, I. Lorenzoni, D.R. Nelson, L.O. Naess, J. Wolf, and A. Wreford. 2009. Are there social limits to adaptation to climate change? *Climate Change* 93(3): 335–354.

American Fact Finder. 2013. US Census Data from 2010 for the Deal Island Area. http://factfinder2.census.gov, accessed January 15, 2013.

Bodin, Ö. and C. Prell. 2011. *Social network analysis and natural resource management.* Cambridge: Cambridge University Press.

Boesch, D.F., L.P. Atkinson, W.C. Boicourt, J.D. Boon, D.R. Cahoon, R.A. Dalrymple, T. Ezer, B.P. Horton, Z.P. Johnson, R.E. Kopp, M. Li, R.H. Moss, A. Parris, and C.K. Sommerfield. 2013. *Updating Maryland's sea-level rise projections: Special report to the Scientific and Technical Working Group to the Maryland Climate Change Commission.* Cambridge, MD: University of Maryland Center for Environmental Science. http://www.umces.edu/sites/default/files/pdfs/SeaLevelRiseProjections.pdf, accessed January 15, 2013.

Chapin III, F.S., S.R. Carpenter, G.P. Kofinas, C. Folke, N. Abel, W.C. Clark, P. Olsson, D.M.S. Smith, B. Walker, O.R. Young, F. Berkes, R. Biggs, J.M. Grove, R.L. Naylor, E. Pinkerton, W. Steffen, and F.J. Swanson. 2009. Ecosystem stewardship: Sustainability strategies for a rapidly changing planet. *Trends in Ecology and Evolution* 25(4): 241–249. doi: 10.1016/j.tree.2009.10.008, accessed July 9, 2014.

Chesapeake Bay Program. 2014. Chesapeake Bay Watershed agreement. http://www.chesapeakebay.net/documents/FINAL_Ches_Bay_Watershed_Agreement.withsignatures-HIres.pdf, accessed August 20, 2014.

Cote, M. and A.J. Nightingale. 2012. Resilience thinking meets social theory: Situating social change in socio-ecological systems (SES) research. *Progress in Human Geography* 36(4): 475–489.

Crona, B. and K. Hubacek. 2010. The right connections: How do social networks lubricate the machinery of natural resource governance? *Ecology and Society* 15(4): 18. http://www.ecologyandsociety.org/vol15/iss4/art18/, accessed May 13, 2015.

Cronin, W.B. 2005. *Disappearing islands of the Chesapeake.* Baltimore, MD: The Johns Hopkins University Press.

Daniels, S.E. and G.B. Walker. 2001. *Working through environmental conflict: The collaborative learning approach.* Westport, CT: Praeger.

Eggleston, J. and J. Pope. 2013. Land subsidence and relative sea-level rise in the southern Chesapeake Bay region. Washington, DC: United States Department of the Interior, United States Geological Survey Circular no. 1392. http://pubs.usgs.gov/circ/1392/pdf/circ1392.pdf, accessed August 20, 2014.

Ernst, H.R. 2010. *Fight for the Bay: Why a dark green environmental awakening is needed to save the Chesapeake Bay.* Plymouth, UK: Rowman and Littlefield Publishers, Inc.

Erwin, R.M., D.F. Brinker, B.D. Watts, G.R. Constanzo, and D.D. Morton. 2010. Islands at bay: Rising seas, eroding islands, and waterbird habitat loss in Chesapeake Bay (USA). *Journal of Coastal Conservation* 15(1): 51–60.

Feurt, C. 2008. *Collaborative learning guide for ecosystem management.* Wells, ME: Wells National Estuarine Research Reserve. http://www.wellsreserve.org/sup/downloads/collaborative_learning_guide.pdf, accessed January 23, 2013.

Folke, C. 2006. Resilience: The emergence of a perspective for social-ecological systems analyses. *Global Environmental Change* 16(3): 253–267.

Leatherman, S.P., R. Chalfont, E.C. Pendleton, T.L. McCandless, and S. Funderburk. 1995. *Vanishing lands: Sea level, society and Chesapeake Bay.* Washington, DC: United States Department of the Interior, Fish and Wildlife Service. http://www.fws.gov/slamm/VanishingLandsSeaLevelSocietyandChesapeakeBay2.pdf, accessed March 20, 2015.

Maryland Department of Natural Resources Coastal Zone Management Program. 2008. *Somerset County, Maryland: Rising sea level guidance.* Annapolis, MD: Maryland Department of Natural Resources. http://www.dnr.state.md.us/irc/docs/00014600.pdf, accessed September 17, 2012.

Najjar, R., C. Pyke, M. Adams, D. Breitburg, C. Hershner, M. Kemp, R. Howarth, M.R. Mulholland, M. Paolisso, D. Secor, K. Sellner, D. Wardrop, and R. Wood. 2010. Potential climate-change impacts on the Chesapeake Bay. *Estuarine, Coastal and Shelf Science* 86(1): 1–20.

Needelman, B.A. 2012. Climate change and coastal habitats. In *Restore-adapt-mitigate: responding to climate change through coastal habitat restoration*, eds. B.A. Needelman, J. Benoit, S. Bosak, and C. Lyons, 14–22. Arlington, VA: Restore America's Estuaries. http://americaswetland.com/photos/article/rae%20climate%20chg%20report%204-19-2012.pdf, accessed December 6, 2015.

Nelson, D.R., W.N. Adger, and K. Brown. 2007. Adaptation to environmental change: Contributions of a resilience framework. *Annual Review of Environment and Resources* 32: 395–419.

Oliver-Smith, A. 2013. Disaster risk reduction and climate change adaptation: The view from applied anthropology. *Human Organization* 72(4): 275–282.

Orlove, B. 2009. The past, the present, and some possible futures of adaptation. In *Adapting to climate change: Thresholds, values, governance*, eds. W.N. Adger, I. Lorenzoni, and K. O'Brien, 131–163. Cambridge: Cambridge University Press.

Paolisso, M. 2005. *Chesapeake environmentalism: Rethinking culture to strengthen restoration and resource management.* College Park, MD: Maryland Sea Grant College, University of Maryland.

_____. 2003. Weather, blue crabs and Chesapeake Bay watermen: Implications for harvest strategies and fishery management policies. In *Weather, climate and culture,* eds. S. Strauss and B. Orlove, 61–82. New York: Berg Publishers.

_____. 2002. Blue crabs and controversy on the Chesapeake Bay: A cultural model for understanding watermen's reasoning about blue crab management. *Human Organization* 61(3): 226–239.

Prell, C. 2012. *Social network analysis: History, theory, and methodology.* Thousand Oaks, CA: Sage Publications.

Power, L. and M. Paolisso. 2007. Linking estuarine research to local community heritage & environmental values: Lessons from the Chesapeake Bay. *Practicing Anthropology* 29(1): 29–34.

Rhodes, J. 2007. *Somerset County, a brief history.* Mount Pleasant, S.C.: The History Press.

Roberts, W. 1905. *The crab industry of Maryland.* Washington, DC: Government Printing Office. http://babel.hathitrust.org/cgi/pt?id=hvd.hwgm3l;view=1up;seq=11, accessed April 15, 2015.

Scott, J. 1991. *Between ocean and bay: A natural history of Delmarva.* Centreville, MD: Tidewater Publishers.

Spanger-Siegfried, E., M.F. Fitzpatrick, and K. Dahl. 2014. *Encroaching tides: How sea-level rise and tidal flooding threaten U.S. East and Gulf Coast communities over the next 30 years.* Cambridge, MA: Union of Concerned Scientists.

Titus, J.G. and E.M. Strange. 2008. *Background documents supporting climate change science program synthesis and assessment product 4.1. coastal elevations and sensitivity to sea-level rise.* Washington, DC: United States Environmental Protection Agency, Office of Air and Radiation.

Walker, B. and D. Salt. 2012. *Resilience practice: Building capacity to absorb disturbance and maintain function.* Washington, DC: Island Press.

Wallace, A. 1978 [1861]. *The parson of the islands: The life and times of the Reverend Joshua Thomas.* Centreville, MD: Tidewater Publishers.

# 2 The Story of Rising Voices

## *Facilitating Collaboration between Indigenous and Western Ways of Knowing*

*Julie Maldonado, Heather Lazrus, Shiloh-Kay Bennett, Karletta Chief, Carla May Dhillon, Bob Gough, Linda Kruger, Jeff Morisette, Stefan Petrovic, and Kyle Powys Whyte*

### CONTENTS



We include, we understand, we act.

**Rising Voices Youth Climate Initiative Guiding Ethos**

**Abstract**

Indigenous community self-determination, cultures, and ways of life are at high risk from climate change impacts and ecological dispossession. Partnerships between experts with backgrounds in Indigenous and western knowledge may be productive and effective ways to reduce vulnerability and foster resilience. This chapter examines collaborations among scientific and Native American, Alaska Native, and Pacific Island communities to support climate solutions. We draw examples from the "Rising Voices: Collaborative Science with Indigenous Knowledge for Climate Solutions" program (Rising Voices) to examine how boundary organizations function cross-culturally to increase communities' adaptive capacity through knowledge exchange, as well as building the decision-making capacity needed to exercise sovereignty and make adaptive decisions in a changing climate.

### BACKGROUND

Indigenous peoples' cultural beliefs and practices have guided their adaptation to environmental change for millennia (Tsosie 2007). However, Indigenous community self-determination, cultures, and ways of life are at high risk from climate change impacts and ecological dispossession.

Indigenous communities maintaining subsistence livelihoods, practices, and traditions are dependent on an intact environment, which climate change is rapidly disrupting (Bennett et al. 2014). Many also live within fixed jurisdictional boundaries, such as reservations in the United States, or on small tracts of land, such as islands, that circumscribe their capacities to adapt to ecological change (Whyte 2014).

Indigenous peoples' traditional knowledges* and adaptive strategies are becoming more vulnerable due to combined effects of changing climatic conditions, increasing social and ecological stressors, such as resource extraction on and around tribal lands, and limited economic resources. Traditional knowledges are defined as Indigenous communities' ways of knowing that both guide and result from their community members' close relationships with and responsibilities toward the landscapes, waterscapes, plants, and animals that are vital to the flourishing of Indigenous cultures (Climate and Traditional Knowledges Workgroup [CTKW] 2014). These provide a crucial foundation for community-based adaptation measures to climate-related transformations (Barros et al. 2014; Bennett et al. 2014; CTKW 2014; Lazrus 2012; Maldonado et al. 2016).

Until recently, the voices of Indigenous peoples have been largely excluded from the local, national, and international discussions on climate change governance. Their exclusion is a continuation of colonial power that continues to silence Indigenous concerns, agency, and collective practices through numerous political obstructions (Whyte 2013a). For example, in the United States, colonial-driven processes, such as the 1830 Indian Removal Act, forced Indigenous communities into fixed boundaries in fragile new territories (Reo and Parker 2013). This systemic marginalization continues through processes of federal land management, which stems from the colonial concept of land ownership, that inhibit Indigenous communities in the United States from enacting traditional adaptation strategies (Redsteer, Kelley, Francis, and Block 2010; Redsteer, Krupnik, and Maldonado in press). The 567 federally recognized tribes in the United States have to compete for climate adaptation funding from the federal government, and the many state-recognized and nonrecognized Indigenous communities do not qualify to participate (Whyte 2013a). In addition, government-led adaptation decisions generally do not take into consideration the cultural practices and traditions on which Indigenous adaptation strategies are based (Middleton 2015).

Traditional knowledges relevant to climate change and adaptation strategies are largely shared through oral tradition. They are often discounted as nonscientific because they are not academically peer reviewed, published in academic journals, and/or expressed quantitatively. The ways that Indigenous peoples understand, communicate, and know about climate change do not necessarily fit into categories dictated by western science (Maldonado et al. 2016; Williams and Hardison 2013). Thus, at the root of many decisions to implement adaptation "lie differentials in power: power to tell the story of the future and then to enact it" (Westman 2013, p. 112).

This chapter focuses on the successes and challenges of one effort to transform the issues just described through convening Indigenous communities, scientists, and government agency representatives together to discuss climate change adaptation. The idea for Rising Voices developed from a conversation between a social scientist (Lazrus) at the National Center for Atmospheric Research (NCAR) in Boulder, Colorado, and an Indigenous cultural ecologist (Gough), who was a visiting scientist at NCAR in 2011. NCAR is internationally renowned as a research and development center devoted to service, research, and education in the atmospheric and related sciences, including facilitating cultural diversity in the field.

Rising Voices was initiated at NCAR to increase engagement among Indigenous communities in the United States and Indigenous and non-Indigenous scientists by asking the question, "What are the elements of successful co-production of science and policy in the fields of extreme weather and climate change?" (Lazrus and Gough 2013). The goal is to address the challenges of understanding and responding to a changing and variable climate, extreme weather events, and research and

* "Knowledges" is used in the plural form, following the Guidelines for Considering Traditional Knowledges in Climate Change Initiatives (CTKW 2014).

policy needs. The program has evolved into a movement of engaged Indigenous and non-Indigenous individuals, including leaders, environmental experts, students, and scientific professionals from across the United States, including Alaska and the Pacific Islands. Rising Voices functions as a boundary organization among these diverse individuals by building relationships based on mutual trust and respect. Partners include NCAR, Colorado State University, Global Breadfruit Heritage Council, Indigenous Peoples' Climate Change Working Group, Intertribal Council on Utility Policy, Livelihoods Knowledge Exchange Network, National Disaster Preparedness Training Center, National Oceanic and Atmospheric Administration, Pacific Risk Management 'Ohana, and US Department of Interior's Climate Science Centers.

Participation in Rising Voices occurs through annual workshops and an active listserv that is used to share updates and coordinate follow-up projects. To date, NCAR has hosted three Rising Voices workshops, which aim to provide a space for participating individuals to convene and exchange scientific results, challenges, and solutions for long-term capacity building and increased resilience. The meetings transform how communication occurs within western scientific institutions. The workshops begin and end with traditional ceremonial protocol. The agenda include topical breakout groups, presentations by students, early career Indigenous scientists, and others sharing relevant activities, discussion panels, informal evening gatherings, and time for unstructured conversation over food. In bringing together people from diverse backgrounds, the aim is to shift from a conventional western-style meeting format to a more engaged conversation that includes traditional protocol while respecting the cultural diversity of the participants.

Across three Rising Voices workshops (2013–2015), the number of attendees increased from 45 to 119 people. Striving for an intimate, collective conversation, the first Rising Voices workshop (2013) issued invitations primarily through the Indigenous Peoples' Climate Change Working Group and the people involved with tribal input into the Third United States National Climate Assessment. It has evolved organically through initial participants reaching out to their greater networks. By the third workshop, there were more representatives from remote communities, such as Shishmaref, Alaska, and Mescalero Apache, as well as increased involvement of youth, tribal leaders, scholars from diverse disciplines, government agencies, and engaged citizens from nearly every US region. For the remainder of the chapter, we consider examples from this event-inspired movement. We examine how ethical and cultural protocols can be used to establish effective and appropriate collaborations that bring together diverse Indigenous and non-Indigenous voices of individuals from different generations, cultures, professions, levels of authority, and walks of life.

## BOUNDARY ORGANIZATIONS

Rising Voices is an example of what many Indigenous peoples have been doing for some time: creating networks with new partners to gain influence in areas in which they previously had little involvement (Grossman 2005). As such, it functions as a boundary organization for the participating individuals and the communities they serve. Rising Voices seeks to transcend boundaries that often separate science and science policy from society (Guston 2001) and which exclude members of society from influencing and benefiting from scientific research. Rising Voices seeks to lower the barriers for boundary-crossing in ways that create usable and actionable science for Indigenous peoples (Meadow et al. 2015). Lowering barriers is especially important in situations where collaborators may have little experience working together, high levels of distrust, and wield disproportionate degrees of power. Indigenous peoples have complex histories of exploitation at the hands of bureaucrats and scientists, leading to justified concern about how their knowledges are valued, credited, and respected in research relations (Mahoney 2011; Middleton 2015).

As a boundary organization, Rising Voices seeks to be a credible, salient, and legitimate collective across epistemological, research/practice, and generational communities (Cash et al. 2002; Meadow et al. 2015). Boundary organizations work by establishing accountability in multiple arenas, using ideas and objects that are meaningful in various contexts, facilitating participation from diverse groups, actively demonstrating the permeability of boundaries, translating across boundaries, and coordinating complementary expertise (Cash et al. 2002). The primary Rising Voices activities, mainly collaboration building, annual gatherings, website maintenance (http://risingvoices.ucar.edu/), a Facebook page, e-mail/listserv communication, and position papers, provide opportunities for establishing participation from both western and Indigenous sciences and traditions.

One important facet of Rising Voices engages professionals who "have a foot in both worlds" (Ward 2015). In some ways, these are "boundary individuals." Their contributions and engagement help bridge a selectively permeable boundary of diverse ways of knowing. That is, how they choose to engage and their contributions to the workshops create their own pathways between knowledge and action. Multiple "worlds" are also brought together by stressing mutual respect and growing a shared vision to address compelling human needs and resource concerns.

The complex challenges of climate change call for a kind of multiplicity in understanding around a central issue. For example, western scientists and Indigenous people have different ways of telling the history of changing drought conditions in particular regions and use different techniques, from storytelling to sampling methods, to understand baseline drought conditions. While drought presents questions about the water cycle to a hydrologist, it raises concerns about maintenance of water-based ceremonies essential for spiritual livelihoods on the Navajo Reservation (Redsteer 2012). At Rising Voices, concepts such as drought risk are explored through multiple forms of expression. Strong effort is made to avoid one form of knowledge or history dominating discussions. Through a culture of mutual respect and a focus on important issues, participants are driven to accountability across boundaries.

## AGENCY–TRIBAL ENGAGEMENT

The Rising Voices movement is growing in tandem with increased engagement and collaborations between Indigenous communities and federal agencies. For example, the United States Department of Agriculture's (USDA) Forest Service Research and Development (USFS-RD) branch has initiated a program to identify tribal climate change research and information needs, building a portfolio of integrated research with Indigenous communities. The USFS-RD's Tribal Engagement Roadmap outlines six objectives to enhance working relationships with tribes and build on a commitment to government-to-government relationship and trust responsibilities (USDA-USFS 2015).

The Roadmap's first objective is to build new partnerships while enhancing existing ones. For example, and in line with this stated objective, the US Forest Service's Pacific Northwest Research Station initiated the Pacific Northwest Tribal Climate Change Network (PNWTCCN) cohosted and facilitated through the Tribal Climate Change Project at the University of Oregon. The PNWTCCN strengthens communication among tribes, agencies, and other entities on policies, programs, grants, training opportunities, and other issues. They are publishing a synthesis of climate change impacts and experiences of Indigenous peoples. This includes identifying knowledge gaps and needs for future research in this area that is tribally led or conducted with direct tribal engagement and consent (CTKW 2014; see also http://tribalclimate.uoregon.edu/).

Some of the contributors became involved through relationships formed at Rising Voices workshops. Presenting the synthesis at the workshops and receiving feedback on the content and process enhanced the work; it also provided an opportunity for outreach into the broader community to whom the work is geared. Participation in Rising Voices workshops and other activities provides an ideal venue for continued efforts to meet the Roadmap's first objective.

The following four objectives, which guide USFS-RD's work, cover institutionalizing trust responsibilities and tribal engagement. They include increasing and advancing Indigenous values, knowledge, and perspectives within the agency; coordinating and networking with other agency branches to increase program efficacy; and using collaboration and participatory approaches to work with tribes and tribal organizations. These represent another point of intersection with Rising Voices. These have been implemented through activities such as the Region 10 Alaska Tribal

Leader's Committee's monthly conference calls and annual face-to-face meetings and joint cultural awareness training. Recognizing the importance of engaging young people, Rising Voices youth interns working with USFS have partnered with mentors in six Native communities in Southeast Alaska to explore local observations and experiences of a changing environment.

Finally, the Roadmap's sixth objective is to develop and deploy research and technologies to support tribal decision making on natural resource issues. Scientists with both the Pacific Northwest and the Pacific Southwest Research Stations work closely with the Institute for Tribal Environmental Professionals and tribes across Alaska and the western states to design and present webinars and training on climate change and adaptation strategies. These have included several Rising Voices participants. Similar collaborations and partnerships have emerged in other USFS regions as well.

## ETHICAL AND CULTURAL PROTOCOLS FOR COLLABORATIONS

A primary goal of Rising Voices activities is to increase cultural diversity in science by promoting meaningful and ethical collaborations between Indigenous and non-Indigenous partners. These require transparent dialogue, with Indigenous communities leading the formulation and designing of the goal and purpose of the partnership and projects, as exemplified with USFS partnerships presented previously. Approaches must be appropriate for each specific community, as native communities are different from one another; there are also many practices and knowledges within communities. Thus, Indigenous local partners need to be included from the beginning in guiding the research process (Whyte 2013b).

Respect and regard for Indigenous traditional knowledges, practices, and beliefs are critical in applying appropriate methodologies and approaches. Collection of physical, human, and biological samples is extremely sensitive and requires consideration of cultural beliefs and practices. This is significant, given the long history of misconduct by the US government and scientists in expropriating the remains of Indigenous peoples (Bieder 1990). This exploitation ultimately led to the Native American Graves Protection and Repatriation Act and the National Museum of the American Indian Act (Smithsonian 2016).

The first question in collaborations is whether the research will benefit the community and its needs. Non-Indigenous collaborators must actively learn about the culture, history, and governance of the community with whom they plan to work, including traditional and colonial governments; recognize the diversity of Indigenous communities and nations; and identify and understand culturally sensitive topics. A community partnership can take years to develop trusting and respectful relationships. Achieving this requires understanding the cultural protocols and process for engaging with a tribe, obtaining support for a particular objective from each unique tribe, and learning the various processes of approval at different levels of government. For example, some tribes have their own internal review board that requires a formal application to work with human subjects. Identifying and observing these protocols are essential for demonstrating respect for tribal sovereignty and self-governance and for the community.

At Rising Voices gatherings, research is discussed as part of Indigenous governance and self-determination. A distinct goal is for all participants to see themselves collectively as part of developing stories of adaptation to climate change, instead of seeing Indigenous peoples as primarily sources of data that can help to advance careers (CTKW 2015; Whyte 2013b). Indigenous research methodology, with a strong focus on the importance of overcoming barriers imposed by colonization and advancing governance and self-determination, can help facilitate this process (Smith 2007).

Two rules of engagement are emphasized at Rising Voices, which are cornerstones of Indigenous research methodology. First, "cause no harm." This refers to identifying and avoiding risks that could lead to the loss or misappropriation of traditional knowledge. The second is free, prior, and informed consent (Williams and Hardison 2013). "Free" means that Indigenous communities have complete control over decisions to be involved in a partnership. "Prior" refers to the involvement of Indigenous peoples from the very beginning of the collaboration, specifically in the conceptual design. "Informed" means that all relevant information must be made available and provided in language understandable to Indigenous people. "Consent" means that Indigenous peoples have a right to decline engaging at any time. Though this is only a snapshot, adhering to these rules can help progress toward research that matters to Indigenous lives and resists colonial power (CTKW 2015).

## CULTURAL AND GENERATIONAL DIVERSITY

Cultural diversity at Rising Voices gatherings is evident not only among the participants but also in how the workshop is run. Opening and closing ceremonies are important components of the meeting, which honor people's time and contributions. They also show respect and gratitude to the ancestors of Indigenous peoples local to the workshop location. Intergenerational diversity is fostered by actively engaging youth participants in panel and breakout discussions, as well as allowing space for their reflections on the workshop agenda.

At Rising Voices 3, youth participants included high school students from Kansas, North Dakota, Colorado, and Hawai'i. They were active in all workshop activities, shared their reflections, and initiated the Rising Voices Youth Climate Initiative. It is vital to emphasize the lived experiences of youth in conjunction with quantitative scientific data to create responsible and effective policy. The goal is to energize those who are often left out of the conversation but are the ones who will bear the brunt of changes in the Earth's climate.

Youth today seem to straddle the line between lassitude and an innate impulse to be part of the solution to climate change (Partridge 2008). The Youth Initiative aims to harness this "activist itch" and mold it in a lifelong commitment to environmental sustainability and a deeper understanding of diverse knowledge systems. The Youth Initiative calls for the inclusion of all Indigenous and non-Indigenous youth who share a common goal: taking action to mitigate global climate change.

## EVALUATION

As Rising Voices evolved in response to Indigenous communities' needs, an evaluation of its achievements and challenges became of interest to the funders, organizers, and participants. Indigenous peoples have dynamic methods for evaluating how programs, networks, and events can foster relationship building, which incorporate both time-tested knowledge and insights from recent experiences. One key tenet of Indigenous evaluation is that participants must be involved in, not just subjects of, the evaluation process. This is important for boundary organizations at the intersection of Indigenous and scientific knowledge systems and for successful collaborations (Dockry, Hall, Van Lopik, and Caldwell 2015; LaFrance and Nichols 2010).

Rising Voices participants developed an evaluation process that suits both the particular kind of event and its goals and outcomes. The Sustainable Development Institute at the College of Menominee Nation (an Indigenous organization) and several Indigenous and non-Indigenous researchers and scientists worked with participants in advance of Rising Voices 3 to find out what kinds of relationships (e.g., family-like) and relationship-building activities participants desired in order to achieve the aim of ethical and meaningful collaborations.

The evaluation team created a questionnaire based on this feedback, focusing on how collaborative relationships are developed, which activities provided the greatest support, and whether the workshop fostered stronger appreciation for cultural knowledge and protocols in Indigenous–scientific partnerships. The evaluation included questions about collaborations and climate-related work over the past year. The online questionnaire, sent out shortly after the workshop, had a 68% response rate.

Table 2.1 shows results for how well various types of relationships were supported. For example, approximately 78% responded that relationships that develop collaborative scientific–Indigenous partnerships were supported "extremely well" or "a lot," with 19% responding that such relationships

**TABLE 2.1**
**Evaluation Results from Rising Voices 3**

| Evaluation Question: *Rising Voices 3 supported...* | Response in Percentage | | | | | |
|---|---|---|---|---|---|---|
| | Extremely Well | A Lot | In a Satisfactory Way | A Little | Not at All | Unable to Comment |
| Relationships that develop collaborative scientific–Indigenous partnerships for adaptation in response to climate variability and change ($n$ = 75) | 49 | 29 | 16 | 3 | 0 | 3 |
| Cultivation of professsional relationships ($n$ = 76) | 43.5 | 43.5 | 9 | 2.5 | 0 | 1 |
| Cultivation of family-like relations ($n$ = 75) | 32 | 18.5 | 16 | 21 | 4 | 5 |
| Cultivation of mentorship relationships ($n$ = 76) | 26 | 18.5 | 29 | 9 | 4 | 13 |

were supported "in a satisfactory way" or "a little." The three activities that most supported these partnerships were interactive breakout sessions, break times between sessions, and lunches with open seating. Approximately 80% of respondents said they would pursue future collaborations due to the re/connections they made.

The evaluation asked to what degree attendees gained a stronger appreciation of the cultural knowledge and protocols for Indigenous–scientific partnerships in four key subject areas: relocation, water, phenology, and health and livelihood hazards. Table 2.2 indicates that 54% to 60% of respondents improved their understanding of cultural protocols "extremely well" or "a lot," with minor variations based on the climate adaptation focus topic. A more detailed summary of the evaluation process is being compiled for attendees, funders, and organizers to share areas of success and further improvements as a boundary organization.

As Rising Voices continues to develop, participants, organizers, and funders want to understand what relationships are forming at events and whether those relationships evolve into future partnerships and achieve other outcomes. The evaluation team will analyze the network connections and resurvey participants at future gatherings to learn more about how relationships are evolving.

**TABLE 2.2**
**Cultural Protocol Results for Rising Voices 3**

| Evaluation Question: *To what degree do you have a stronger appreciation of the cultural knowledge and protocols required for Indigenous–scientific partnerships on the key subject areas of Rising Voices 3?* | Response in Percentage | | | | | |
|---|---|---|---|---|---|---|
| | Extremely Stronger | A Lot | In a Satifactory Way | A Little | Not at All | Unable to Comment |
| Relocation ($n$ = 73) | 24.5 | 35.5 | 20.5 | 8 | 2.5 | 8 |
| Water ($n$ = 72) | 26.5 | 34.5 | 22 | 7 | 0 | 9 |
| Phenology ($n$ = 70) | 24.5 | 30 | 28.5 | 10 | 0 | 7 |
| Health and livelihood hazards ($n$ = 72) | 30.5 | 26.5 | 22 | 8.5 | 1.5 | 1 |

## OUTCOMES AND CHALLENGES

Rising Voices, in its function as a boundary organization, has facilitated adaptation partnerships between Indigenous communities, scientists, academics, researchers, students, and government agencies. This includes a focus on student and early-career involvement in climate science and adaptation planning and ideas for evaluating these partnerships. For example, Indigenous participants with the US Federal Emergency Management Agency's National Disaster and Preparedness Training Center (NDPTC) in Hawai'i provided training to community members in Kivalina, Alaska. Tribal college students have pursued certification as NDPTC trainers and have been connected to agencies through a project examining phenology on tribal lands at the US Department of Interior's North-Central Climate Science Center. Numerous research proposals and projects have been sparked at Rising Voices meetings, carrying forward ideas and recommendations generated in breakout groups. The workshops have also facilitated bringing the needs of some coastal tribes to Congress and audiences across the United States. These tribes are without options for in situ adaptation and have decided to relocate to maintain community and cultural integrity and sovereignty.

Participants have jointly written reports, which have become part of the US National Climate Assessment's network of partner organizations' toolkit. These include the Letter to the US Presidential Task Force on Climate Preparedness and Resilience in 2014 and the Letter of Recommendations to the United Nations Framework Convention on Climate Change 21st Conference of Parties in 2015. Thus, Rising Voices is much more than an annual gathering; it is an ongoing network involved in collaborative activities.

The process of working to bring together diverse knowledges, governance structures, and institutional systems has exposed some of the very challenges that Rising Voices aims to address: limited funding available for sustained Indigenous–scientific interaction; misaligned institutional, administrative, and community or subsistence timelines; and difficulty of broadening the reach of the program beyond the US context. For example, the strong social cohesion among Rising Voices participants is both a challenge and a strength. While this helps foster long-term relationships of trust, it also means that members of certain social networks are more likely to learn about and seek to attend the workshops.

To address these challenges, organizers continue to seek sustained funding to expand venue size and networking opportunities. Organizers have adjusted planning around and timing of the workshops and are seeking to introduce Rising Voices to new networks to expand outreach. The active listserv, in particular, is a venue for people who have not yet attended to interact with previous workshop participants. This stimulates interest in workshop participation and extends information flow to broader networks.

## "WE'RE ALL IN THE SAME CANOE": RECOMMENDATIONS FLOWING FROM RISING VOICES

The Rising Voices Youth Climate Initiative mission statement reminds us that we are "guided by a simple premise that the future of our species and the future of the Earth are one and inseparable: We rise or fall together." In this spirit, participants put forth several recommendations based on workshop discussions. We offer several overarching recommendations here with a tangible sense of the hope for a mutually viable, ethical, and culturally enriched future. At the first Rising Voices workshop, participants invoked the metaphor that "we are all in the same canoe" to help frame an understanding that we are all searching for ways to reduce climate risks. This recognizes that problem-focused collaboration must bring people together from multiple perspectives and places. As such, creating effective boundary organizations builds the accountability, trust, understanding, collaboration, and participation that is necessary to focus on large-scale problems. Essential to this is an explicit respect for diverse ways of knowing and doing, which leads to rich insight and meaningful collaboration.

At the second and third Rising Voices gatherings, the recommendations that came out of the discussions included convening a federal-level climate migration task force with Indigenous representation to address population displacement, creating a formalized structure for Indigenous participation in and leadership of the US National Climate Assessment, and establishing an institutional framework to ensure support for tribes in defining and utilizing their water rights. This includes financial and scientific support to address climate change impacts on water. Finally, they recommended supporting and enhancing educational curricula, especially in tribal and Indigenous schools, to address climate change, variability, adaptation, and mitigation in all levels of academic education.

These recommendations arise from and continue to inform participants' regular work tasks and advocacy opportunities. Thus, the discussions held among participants and their colleagues are able to move forward and be actualized through everyday activities, as well as exceptional events. While finalizing this chapter, several Rising Voices participants have been involved in President Obama's visit to Alaska. He became only the second president to visit a glacier and the first to visit north of the Arctic Circle. The spirit of Rising Voices was behind their entreaties to take seriously the rapid rates of change experienced by Arctic communities. On his visit, President Obama recognized that "[c]limate change is no longer some far-off problem; it is happening here, it is happening now" (The White House 2015a). To address it, "we've got to do more. We've got to move faster" (The White House 2015b). We believe the fastest way to make effective, appropriate, and lasting change is through collaborations built on mutual trust and respect that unite our voices together and draw from diverse ways of knowing and knowledge systems.

## ACKNOWLEDGMENTS

Rising Voices annual workshops are made possible through the support of and partnership with the NCAR, Colorado State University, Global Breadfruit Heritage Council, Indigenous Peoples' Climate Change Working Group, Intertribal Council on Utility Policy, Livelihoods Knowledge Exchange Network, National Disaster Preparedness Training Center, National Oceanic and Atmospheric Administration, Pacific Risk Management 'Ohana, and US Department of Interior's Climate Science Centers. Any use of trade, product, or firm names is for descriptive purposes only and does not imply endorsement by the US Government or related authors.

## REFERENCES

Barros, V.R., C.B. Field, D.J. Dokken, M.D. Mastrandrea, K.J. Mach, T.E. Bilir, M. Chatterjee, K.L. Ebi, Y.O. Estrada, R.C. Genova, B. Girma, E.S. Kissel, A.N. Levy, S. MacCracken, P.R. Mastrandrea, and L.L. White. 2014. *Fifth assessment report: Impacts, adaptation, and vulnerability, Working Group II contribution to the fifth assessment report of the Intergovernmental Panel on Climate Change*. New York: Cambridge University Press, Intergovernmental Panel on Climate Change. http://ipcc-wg2.gov/AR5/report/final-drafts/, accessed August 28, 2015.

Bennett, T.M.B., N.G. Maynard, P. Cochran, R. Gough, K. Lynn, J. Maldonado, G. Voggesser, S. Wotkyns, and K. Cozzetto. 2014. Indigenous peoples, lands, and resources. In *Climate change impacts in the United States: The third national climate assessment*, ed. J.M. Melillo, T.C. Richmond, and G.W. Yohe, 297–317. Washington, DC: US National Climate Assessment, US Global Change Research Program.

Bieder, R.E. 1990. *A brief historical survey of the expropriation of American Indian remains*. Boulder, CO: Native American Rights Fund. http://www.narf.org/nill/documents/NARF_bieder_remains.pdf, accessed January 27, 2016.

Cash, D., W.C. Clark, F. Alcock, N.M. Dickson, N. Eckley, and J. Jäger. 2002. *Salience, credibility, legitimacy and boundaries: Linking research, assessment and decision-making*. Harvard, MA: John F. Kennedy School of Government Working Papers Series RWP02-046, Harvard University. http://poseidon01.ssrn.com/delivery.php?ID=674066092020083066126001005094021101006046007020059

034127067093113124120031041121125052059044123066076120019029006035042008049090002105087105123119077005121033030078125099022086028068088075018125010075026093027121085029025088123077071018103101&EXT=pdf, accessed August 17, 2015.

Climate and Traditional Knowledges Workgroup. 2015. The ethics of traditional knowledge exchange in climate change initiatives. *Earthzine* July 31, 2015. http://earthzine.org/2015/07/31/the-ethics-of-traditional-knowledge-exchange-in-climate-change-initiatives/comment-page-1/, accessed January 22, 2016.

_____. 2014. Guidelines for considering traditional knowledges in climate change initiatives. https://climatetkw.wordpress.com, accessed August 15, 2015.

Dockry, M., J.K. Hall, W. Van Lopik, and C.M. Caldwell. 2015. Sustainable development education, practice, and research: An indigenous model of sustainable development at the College of Menominee Nation, Keshena, WI. *Sustainability Science* 11(1): 1–12, doi: 10.1007/s11625-015-0304-x.

Grossman, Z. 2005. Unlikely alliances: Treaty conflicts and environmental cooperation between Native American and rural white communities. *American Indian Culture and Research Journal* 29(4): 21–43.

Guston, D.H. 2001. Boundary organizations in environmental policy and science: An introduction. *Science, Technology, & Human Values* 26(4): 399–408.

LaFrance, J. and R. Nichols. 2010. Reframing evaluation: Defining an indigenous evaluation framework. *The Canadian Journal of Program Evaluation* 23(2): 13–31.

Lazrus, H. 2012. Sea change: Climate change and island communities. *Annual Review of Anthropology* 41: 285–301.

Lazrus, H. and R. Gough. 2013. "We're all in the same canoe": The rising voices of indigenous peoples in weather and climate science and policy. Boulder, CO: National Center for Atmospheric Research, Rising Voices I Workshop Report, July 1–3.

Mahoney, M. 2011. This land is your land, this land is my land: An historical narrative of an intergenerational controversy over public use management of the San Francisco Peaks. MS Thesis. Tempe, AZ: Arizona State University.

Maldonado, J.K., T.M.B. Bennett, K. Chief, P. Cochran, K. Cozzetto, B. Gough, M.H. Redsteer, N. Maynard, K. Lynn, and G. Voggesser. 2016. Engagement with Indigenous peoples and honoring traditional knowledge systems. *Climatic Change* 135: 111–126.

Meadow, A.M., D.B. Ferguson, Z. Guido, A. Horangic, G. Owen, and T. Wall. 2015. Moving toward the deliberate coproduction of climate science knowledge. *Weather, Climate, and Society* 7: 179–191.

Middleton, B.R. 2015. Jahát Jatítotòdom: Toward an indigenous political ecology. In *The international handbook of political ecology*, ed. R.L. Bryant, 561–576. United Kingdom: Edward Elgar Publishing.

Partridge, E. 2008. From ambivalence to activism: Young people's environmental views and actions. *Youth Studies Australia* 27(2): 18–25.

Redsteer, M.H. 2012. Disaster risk assessment case study: Recent drought on the Navajo Nation. Presented at Climate Adaptation Futures International Conference, Tucson, AZ.

Redsteer, M.H., K.B. Kelley, H. Francis, and D. Block. 2010. Disaster risk assessment case study: Recent drought on the Navajo Nation, southwestern United States. In *Annexes and papers for the 2011 global assessment report on disaster risk reduction*, United Nations, http://www.preventionweb.net/english/hyogo/gar/2011/en/what/drought.html, accessed February 11, 2016.

Redsteer, M.H., I. Krupnik, and J.K. Maldonado. In press. Native American communities and climate change. In *Handbook of North American Indians*, ed., I. Krupnik. Washington, DC: Smithsonian Institution Scholarly Press.

Reo, N.J. and A.K. Parker. 2013. Re-thinking colonialism to prepare for the impacts of rapid environmental change. *Climatic Change* 120(3): 671–682.

Smith, L.T. 2007. On tricky ground. In *The landscape of qualitative research*, eds. N.K. Denzin and Lincoln, 113–144. Thousand Oaks, CA: Sage Publications.

Smithsonian. 2016. Is the Smithsonian institution subject to NAGPRA? Washington, DC: Department of Anthropology, Repatriation Office. http://anthropology.si.edu/repatriation/faq/#general04, accessed February 20, 2016.

Tsosie, R. 2007. Indigenous people and environmental justice: The impact of climate change. *University of Colorado Law Review* 78: 1625–1677.

United States Department of Agriculture–United States Forest Service. 2015. Forest Service research and development: Tribal engagement roadmap. http://www.fs.fed.us/research/docs/tribal-engagement/consultation/roadmap.pdf, accessed September 26, 2015.

Ward, D. 2015. Doing something about the weather. *Winds of Change* 30(2): 40–45. http://www.nxtbook.com/nxtbooks/pohlyco/woc_2015spring/#/44, accessed September 2, 2015.

Westman, C.N. 2013. Social impact assessment and the anthropology of the future in Canada's tar sands. *Human Organization* 72(2): 111–120.

The White House Office of the Press Secretary. 2015a. Remarks by the President at the GLACIER Conference—Anchorage, AK. https://www.whitehouse.gov/the-press-office/2015/09/01/remarks-president-glacier-conference-anchorage-ak, accessed September 10, 2015.

_____. 2015b. Remarks by the President at Kotzebue High School, Kotzebue, AK. https://www.whitehouse.gov/the-press-office/2015/09/03/remarks-president-kotzebue-high-school-kotzebue-ak, accessed September 10, 2015.

Whyte, K.P. 2014. A concern about shifting interactions between indigenous and non-indigenous parties in U.S. climate adaptation contexts. *Interdisciplinary Environmental Review* 15(2–3): 114–133.

_____. 2013a. Justice forward: Tribes, adaptation and responsibility. *Climatic Change* 120(3): 517–530.

_____. 2013b. On the role of traditional ecological knowledge as a collaborative concept: A philosophical study. *Ecological Processes* 2(1): 1–12.

Williams, T. and P. Hardison. 2013. Culture, law, risk and governance: Contexts of traditional knowledge in climate change adaptation. *Climatic Change* 120(3): 531–544.

# 3 Youth-Based Learning in Disaster Risk Reduction Education

## *Barriers and Bridges to Promote Resilience*

*Victor Marchezini and Rachel Trajber*

**CONTENTS**



**Abstract**

Governments are developing early warning systems (EWSs) to protect citizens from hazards. However, distrust of authorities hampers disaster prevention. Some literature criticizes EWS as a linear model with a top–down approach whose technological aspects receive more attention than human contributions do. We examine barriers and bridges to promote resilience and vulnerability reduction through an educational project on disaster risk reduction (DRR) and EWSs in São Luiz do Paraitinga, Brazil. We study a DRR learning module at a high school and analyze social representations that emerge from this experience. Student participants developed hands-on research, integrating interdisciplinary science methodologies. They established a Committee for Disasters Prevention and the Protection of Life (*Com-VidAção*) to promote a social protection network. Through this project, we identify some variations in vulnerability and windows of opportunity to enhance resilience.

## INTRODUCTION

The Global Survey of Early Warning Systems (EWS) (United Nations International Strategy for Disaster Reduction [UNISDR] 2006) highlighted notable advances in the capacity of agencies to forecast natural hazards and reinforced the importance of governments' role in establishing EWS to reduce human and economic losses in disasters. The report made five main recommendations. One of them highlights the task of building national people-centered EWSs, with calls for a national multiparty roundtable on early warning, a national plan based on a survey of capabilities, a warning dissemination strategy, community-based approaches, public education, and mock exercises. In spite of these recommendations, the prevalent national policies still depend upon command-and-control and top–down frameworks, which prioritize scientific knowledge and government intervention to the detriment of local actions (Gaillard and Mercer 2012).

Public education about EWS remains one of the main difficulties in building national people-centered paradigms. The challenge for educators is to integrate knowledge, innovation, and education to build a culture of safety and resilience (UNISDR 2005). Young people are an important audience in EWS and disaster risk reduction (DRR) because they represent 50%–60% of those affected by disasters (United Nations Children's Fund 2012). At the end of the twentieth century, an estimated 66.5 million children were impacted annually (Penrose and Takaki 2006). Examples of events with mass casualties of children include the 1988 Armenian Spitak Earthquake (17,000+ students died in schools), the 2001 Bhuj Earthquake in India (971 students and 31 teachers perished) (Tuladhar, Yatabe, Dahal, and Bhandary 2014), the 2004 Indian Ocean tsunami (60,000+ children), and the 2005 Pakistan earthquake (19,000+ children died, most of them in collapses of school buildings) (Earthquake Engineering Research Institute 2006). In 2006, an elementary school in the Philippines was buried in a landslide, killing 245 children and teachers. In 2008, more than 10,000 children were killed during the Sichuwan Earthquake in China (Tuladhar, Yatabe, Dahal, and Bhandary 2014). In the 2011 Brazilian disaster, 698 persons were classified as missed people; 34% of them (128) were young people (Valencio 2012).

While young people are at risk for injury or death, they may also develop various behavioral, psychological, and emotional issues in the aftermath of disaster (Peek 2008). Policymakers, researchers, and practitioners typically don't recognize these different forms of physical and emotional vulnerability. Youths' needs and experiences are neglected because they do not set the research agenda, do not carry out research, and are not in policy making or relevant professional positions to push these issues forward (Anderson 2005). One of the challenges for youth-centered DRR programming is that the prevailing adult perception views the role of young people as vulnerable recipient-participants not as proactive protagonists (Cumiskey, Hoang, Suzuki, Pettigrew, and Herrgard 2015; Mitchell, Tanner, and Haynes 2009).

In this chapter, we examine barriers and bridges to promote resilience and vulnerability reduction in Brazil. We focus on São Luiz do Paraitinga, a city that experienced a great flood in January 2010, which covered nearly 80% of its urban area. One of the lessons learned is that policymakers have to include sociocultural dimensions in EWS, adjusting them for multiple audiences and contexts. A heterogeneous blend of knowledge and practice reveals a more trusted authority—the community. Effective participation and diversity, which incorporate local knowledge and generates a sense of belonging and action, are key to fostering the culture of disaster prevention and resilience. Empowering principles, such as the "youth educates youth" and "one generation learns from another," are also recommended.

## CHALLENGES OF PEOPLE-CENTERED EWS

Some literature criticizes the traditional view of EWS as a linear model with a top–down approach (Garcia and Fearnley 2012; Thomalla and Larsen 2010). In the top–down approach, technological aspects receive more attention than human aspects do. The technical equipment detects a hazard event and delivers warnings to the people at risk. This is the last step of EWS, also known as the "last mile" approach. This approach posits that only technical equipment (e.g., radar and rain gauges) and experts have data, information, and knowledge about hazards and risks. Vulnerable communities affected by hazards are not viewed as endowed with information, knowledge, or applicable wisdom. Thus, they are warning receivers in EWS, the last ones to be involved.

In opposition to this is the "first mile" approach, which assumes that local people should be involved as the central component of the design and operation of EWS (Kelman and Glantz 2014).

The effectiveness of EWS demands a strong focus on the people exposed to risk, incorporating all of the relevant factors in that risk, whether arising from natural hazards or social vulnerabilities (Basher 2006). It also depends on being more inclusive. To do this, different forms of knowledge must be recognized, allowing for the integration of both scientific and local. Action must occur along different scales, from top–down and from the bottom–up, involving multiple stakeholders in dialogue and collaboration at all points in the process (Gaillard and Mercer 2012). In other words, EWS must become people-centered, horizontal, decentralized, participatory, and knowledge-based public policies.

Three preconditions are essential when designing a people-centered EWS (Villagrán de León 2012). First, a strong governance model that considers the value of conducting activities in the context of DRR is needed, rather than one that only recognizes the need to respond after an event has occurred. The second condition is empowering communities to participate in the design, implementation, and routine operation. The third is based on the assumption that the system can be operational only if it involves the active participation of a variety of individuals and institutions in the four subsystems of EWS. These are risk knowledge of the relevant hazards and vulnerabilities, monitoring of the hazards and issuing warnings, dissemination and communication of understandable warnings and prior preparedness information, and response capability, which implies the knowledge, plans, and capacities for timely and appropriate communication by authorities and those at risk.

EWS can also be used to promote resilience (Thomalla and Larsen 2010) and vulnerability reduction (Kelman and Glantz 2014). To do this, it must take into account the demographic, gender, cultural, and livelihood characteristics of the target audiences (UNISDR 2005). To address the concerns of multiple audiences, system planners need to consider the different forms and degrees of vulnerabilities and capacities of people. To effectively achieve this, they need to confer with gender experts, people with disabilities, representatives of all religious, ethnic, caste, and cultural groups, those representing different age groups, and others.

Mainstream approaches and theoretical debates in disaster management tend to ignore the role of young people as communicators of risk and as facilitators of DRR (Cumiskey, Hoang, Suzuki, Pettigrew, and Herrgard 2015; Mitchell, Tanner, and Haynes 2009). Most DRR research and literature produced by organizations and governments traditionally consider that youth are passive victims with very little role to play in preventing risks and responding to disasters (Fernandez and Shaw 2014; Mitchell, Haynes, Hall, Choong, and Oven 2008). Although there is research on young people's vulnerability to disasters, less has been published regarding capacities and contributions of youth in DRR activities (Peek 2008). Youth should be recognized as capable of advocacy and action. They should have the right to participate in their own protection. In order to appreciate the roles they can play in EWS, it is important to understand barriers and bridges to their active involvement.

São Luiz do Paraitinga provides a good living lab for such research. Located in the northeastern region of São Paulo state, Brazil, the town has experienced extensive floods in 1863, 1967, 1971, and 1996. In January 2010, the Paraitinga River reached 12 meters above its normal level, submerging several neighborhoods, including the historical center. This severely damaged two churches, two schools, and left half of the population homeless (5000 persons). São Luiz was chosen by convenience, since we investigated the disaster recovery process from January 2010 to June 2013 (Marchezini 2015). Moreover, the local public high school agreed to be the pilot for the Cemaden Education Project.*

## RESEARCH METHODS

The analysis is based on literature reviews, documentary research, and field work. Field work, rooted in action research methodology (see Yamori 2009), combines observation and qualitative

* Cemaden—National Center for Monitoring and Early Warning of Natural Disasters created the project "Cemaden Education in 2014," which is in a pilot stage. See the website for more details: http://educacao.cemaden.gov.br.

data collection. It was conducted from October 2014 to August 2015, during the nine workshops organized at the Monsenhor Ignacio Gioia High School. The authors designed the workshops' methodology, invited experts to conduct presentations, and were participant-observers at the research site in the school. Every workshop lasted three hours and included 15 voluntary students (10 girls and 5 boys, ages 15 to 17). Students were enrolled in three different grades (3 in the first, 6 in the second, and 6 in the third). Ten students were from urban areas, and 5 lived in rural areas.

Workshops promoted student participation in research activities designed by experts. We observed how they interacted in these activities, which integrate traditional wisdom and interdisciplinary scientific methodologies, to build their own knowledge. Using oral history and tradition, participatory monitoring, and mapping, high school students identified memories about disasters and perceptions about climate changes and risks in their map sectors. Based on anthropology of risk and disasters (e.g., Garcia and Fearnley 2012), we analyze the building of DRR knowledge and social representations of youth, highlighting some barriers and bridges to their involvement in EWS.

## FINDINGS

### Top–Down Barrier

One of the main barriers to increased youth and school participation in DRR and EWS activities is related to the awareness of different actors about its importance. Fernandez and Shaw (2014, p. 284) state that "the discussion on youth participation in DRR has been largely limited to pragmatic research and publications made by NGOs and researchers who are working independently." They note that the involvement of young people is not a feature in the broader DRR discourse, including the Hyogo Framework for Action (UNISDR 2005) and UNISDR Global Assessment Reports (2011). Their absence is also found in many developed and developing countries.

Convery, Carroll, and Balogh (2014) note that, although the city of Hull, England, faces a high risk of flooding, the schools were not prepared for them in the summer of 2007. They find that a top–down institutional approach, with a command-and-control structure, underestimated the risks to schools and disregarded their involvement in EWS. They state (p. 150), "The head teachers and staff reported surprise at the amount of rain and the speed of the flooding in their schools...Head teachers were concerned about the health and the safety of the students."

In Kenya, 30 schools in Nyando District were damaged by the December 2006 floods. To foster disaster prevention strategies, Ochola, Eitel, and Olago (2010) recommended community-level workshops addressing vulnerability reduction in schools. In Brazil, floods and landslides affected more than 1800 schools in 311 municipalities from January to March 2004 (National Secretariat of Civil Defense 2004). The top–down institutional approach with a command-and-control structure of militarized civil defense hampered the development of public policies for DRR activities. For instance, in São Luiz do Paraitinga, the old school building was destroyed during the 2010 flood, and the new one was reconstructed in a flood-prone area. Due to a disaster reconstruction policy that does not involve participatory risk management, the school's community keeps being exposed to flood risk. Only one local civil defense agent monitors the hazards and holds data and information about risk mapping.

### Distrust of Authorities: An Obstacle for Change

Trust is a crucial element for disaster prevention at several levels. It is widely agreed that distrust between local communities and government or scientists lies in the absence of space for dialogue across the hierarchy of scales (Gaillard and Mercer 2012; Pennesi 2013; Yamori 2009). If there is no trust of the public on the part of organizations, there will be no room for approaches relying on citizen-generated data. This leaves data gaps and many people and countries behind (Teschenhausen 2015).

**FIGURE 3.1** Workshop for planning the future—wish tree, rocks on the way, and bridge of actions. (Courtesy of Victor Marchezini, 2015.)

In Brazil, families who lost their homes in disasters remain in public shelters for long periods. There is also a long delay in the restructuring of damaged public schools and health centers (Marchezini 2014). When informed about disaster risks, people tend to remain in their homes and not evacuate because they believe authorities will abandon them. Iwama (2014) examines the risk perception among dwellers of the coastal region of São Paulo and finds that they tend to refuse the warnings to evacuate risk-prone areas. There are some practical reasons for their resistance to evacuation. Many do not have the ability to leave, due to a lack of financial means. Those of strong faith leave their destiny in God's hands. They also have emotional bonds with their house and the neighborhood.

The authors observe a gap between what is expected from citizens in order to protect life and concrete official actions, due to a top–down institutional approach. This generates a lack of trust in authorities. During a workshop designed to create a Committee for Disasters Prevention and the Protection of Life (*Com-VidAção*) at the school, a participatory methodology (*Oficina de Futuro* or "Workshop for the Future") was organized with students, teachers, and civil defense agents. Participants were divided into four groups. Each group envisioned a collective dream (*wish tree*) for a disasters safe community, identified the main barriers (*rocks on the way*) for making their dream real, and planned (*bridge of actions*) ways to overcome barriers (Figure 3.1). All four groups stated their distrust of authorities and identified corruption as the main obstacle for reaching their objectives. Embezzlement is the main structural problem associated with corruption. However, they didn't perceive the civil defense agents that were participating in the workshop as belonging to that group of government agents that were involved in corruption. These claims were consistent across groups in the two workshops about *Com-VidAção.*

## Disaster Risk Education as a Bridge

Despite the fact that schools are considered some of the most revered and trusted institutions in local communities, worldwide practices show fragility in the face of shocks. Selby and Kagawa (2012, p. 9), reporting on mapping of global DRR integration into education curricula, find that, with only "a few exceptions, an assessment of student DRR learning is thin on the ground." Sometimes, DRR education is impeded by the lack of relevant teaching materials (Izadkhah and Hosseini 2005). It is also impacted by the lack of training of teachers to enable them to use available DRR curriculum materials effectively and to adapt and develop them for non-formal education (Fernandez and Shaw 2014).

In the age of the Internet, large amounts of data and information are available. However, availability does not guarantee that knowledge and wisdom will be generated. For example, weather data are widely disseminated in the media, but some types of information can be abstract to everyday lives. For example, what does it mean for a community or household if 60 millimeters of rain fall in one hour? It is difficult to analyze and contextualize the amount and intensity of rainfall, as well as correlate weather data with the potential risks of landslides and floods. As Morin (1999) notes, learning to live is the object of education. Learning needs to transform information into knowledge, knowledge into wisdom (and science), and that wisdom needs to be incorporated into everyday life.

Participatory methodologies of teaching–learning can provide bridges to make data and information useful, opening windows of opportunity to knowledge production and enhancement of adaptation strategies. These educational methods are not always seen as essential by DRR practitioners and researchers. For example, through analyzing the effects of different educational interventions on schoolchildren's knowledge of earthquake protective behavior in Israel, Soffer, Goldberg, Avisar-Shohat, Cohen, and Bar-Dayan (2010, p. 212) find that "the theoretical knowledge…may be interesting, but not essential to the goal of preventing injury and saving lives." Focusing on hazards adjustments is not sufficient to face the challenge of DRR and climate change adaptation.

In Nepal in 2008, the Ministry of Home Affairs promulgated the National Strategy for Disaster Risk Management. This recognized schools as important centers for propagating DRR knowledge. Tuladhar, Yatabe, Dahal, and Bhandary (2014) analyzed some of the initiatives that were developed in schools. They find that implementation, especially at the individual level, is one of the major challenges. The authors note (p. 205), "pedagogy always has a key role in knowledge transmission and learning competences," so students should be encouraged to gain basic disaster-related knowledge through the curriculum and extracurricular activities. This may lead them to a better understanding of their vulnerability through data and information sharing, allowing for the generation and transmission of broader knowledge, thus reducing their overall vulnerability. Community members should participate in school activities to broaden student access to knowledge and learned experience, and the students should be involved in disaster awareness and adaptation actions of the community members. These meaningful intergenerational activities are recommended by Cumiskey, Hoang, Suzuki, Pettigrew, and Herrgard (2015) as a strategy to build a network of knowledge and develop short- and long-term strategies for a resilient society.

The Cemaden Education Project aims to contribute to the development of curriculum skills and competencies, as each school becomes a local knowledge producer rather than a reproducer of information. All the activities are interdisciplinary, intended to develop scientific thinking. This leads high school students through new paths of discovery and dialogue with people from their region that are familiar with their surroundings, as well as external technicians, academics, and researchers. The so-called "transdisciplinarity" includes the diversity of traditional and original people's culture and wisdom, knowledge, and techniques, which has accumulated in each community. Inspired by the concept of "circles of learning and culture," Cemaden Education Project proposes that high schools create a *Com-VidAção*. Alongside the introduction to scientific studies, the *Com-VidAção* is a horizontal, informal organization where "everyone has voice, everyone reads and writes the world; as a workspace, for research, show practices and experiences that enable the collective construction of knowledge" (Freire 1999, p. 111).

## WINDOWS OF OPPORTUNITIES: YOUTH, CITIZEN SCIENCE, AND CROWDSOURCING

The development of people-centered EWS demands a new and integrated approach of educational methods. Citizen science can offer a great opportunity to youth to be proactive and empowered. Using oral history techniques, the students interviewed persons affected by the 2010 flood (two women and two men), who had been invited to participate at the workshop about Oral History and Disasters. An oral history expert at a regional university presented some basic concepts and methodological procedures to the students. They then divided into four groups, chose one person to interview, and formulated questions based on each person's profile. For example, one group interviewed Mrs. Fide, an elderly woman. Their questions included the following: when you were a child, did many floods occur; at that time, were the floods larger, smaller, or similar; when you were younger, did disaster prevention exist; and, how did people cope with floods before the 2010 disaster? During Mrs. Fide's narration, new questions emerged about the level of the Paraitinga River during the floods, how people exchanged information, and what coping strategies were then adopted. The students audio-taped more than 15 questions and answers and transcribed the tapes.

The next step was a communication activity: the production of a wall newspaper. This was composed of the highlights from the interviews and pictures collected on the Paraitinga disaster. This exercise is designed to give voice to and empower participants. Consequently, the workshop created an opportunity for intergenerational learning and for turning youngsters into risks communicators. Sharing oral histories with other schools from different Brazilian regions and cities may provide bridges for knowledge integration and foster resilience, especially in the context of EWSs.

Another window of opportunity was the study of the watershed through various complementary renderings, including Google maps, field trips, and 3D models. Participatory social cartography, a tool mostly utilized by nongovernmental organizations (NGOs) (Gaillard and Mercer 2012) was also employed. For this, we elicited some basic concepts, such as what they consider risk, hazard, and vulnerability, as well as the types of risks they identify in their town. The purpose was to turn students into actors who can promote similar workshops with their community and then share results with other schools.

The students were divided into three groups and given a Google Earth satellite photograph of the town's urban area. Each group plotted elements, such as well-known landmarks (rivers, schools, churches, roads). They then identified the places most likely to have vulnerable groups (schools, asylums, hospitals), areas considered as risky, and what type of hazards can occur there (floods, landslides). They also plotted what they considered to be safe areas. The civil defense agent pointed out that some areas identified as safe for floods by students were actually susceptible to landslides. Students correctly identified more flood-prone areas. Using local knowledge, many of them mentioned that the third step of the main church was the historical high water mark reached by the Paraitinga River, only exceeded by the 2010 flood. Finally, they identified flood protective measures, such as planting and maintaining riparian forests, using and monitoring rain gauges, lifting their belongings above historic flood levels, and monitoring river levels.

Students added the legend and used symbols, numbers, and colors to show different aspects of the map. They classified risk intensity of areas by assigning likelihood of risk. The four levels were represented by colors, based on the ones used in the situation room at Cemaden—high risk (red), medium risk (orange), low risk (yellow), and normal (green).

Following this, we engaged in the Protection Map Game, designed by the Cemaden Education Project. This was inspired by the Disaster Imagination Game, a Japanese method for disaster prevention, in which participants brainstorm and design local disaster planning. The students were given a mission: each team should formulate a plan to rescue one vulnerable group from a risky area and lead them to a safe place. Within 10 minutes, they had to choose a type of hazard (flood or landslide), identify one vulnerable group (children in schools, elderly in asylums), find a shelter, draw two escape routes to safe areas, and define needs and strategies to accomplish their mission.

The teams presented results to those present, and the local civil defense representative gave feedback. Students knew that the rafting team had rescued children in schools and elderly in asylums during the 2010 flood. They retrieved this local sociocultural information, demonstrating the value of retaining memories and past experiences in order to build up resilience. When asked about the mapping process at the final debate, a student said, "Before the participatory mapping, we never stopped to think about risk zones and escape routes." One commented, "When we look through the map, we see that the flood-prone area is much larger than we imagined." Another observed, "The map helps to understand the scale of the disaster, since you look at the entire city, not just your home." This participatory strategy decision game was an excellent tool for all levels, including the civil defense officers and teachers who participated at the workshop.

Another workshop focused on hydro-meteorological monitoring. Scientists asked students if they knew what a rain gauge was and what the weather data (in millimeters) meant for ground saturation and water levels. Since the students did not know that precipitation could be measured, they had to learn some basic concepts about weather, monitoring, and data collection. They used plastic bottles to make rain gauges, planned where to install them in the school's neighborhood, and georeferenced their positions with a *Global Positioning System*. Finally, they learned how to share data using the Cemaden mobile app.

Citizen Science, applied through crowdsourcing techniques, engaged students in all the activities of the project, from monitoring rainfall and river levels to interacting with the community to learn about memories and oral tradition. These activities "provide the perfect teachable moment for a lesson on disaster risk science, while developing an archive of data that could serve both community needs and science" (International Federation of the Red Cross and Red Crescent Societies 2012, p. 45).

## EDUCATION AND LOCAL ACTIONS TOWARD RESILIENCE: SOME LESSONS LEARNED

Gathering and sharing experiences and knowledge about the youth involvement in DRR and EWS activities are important bridges to encourage people to learn about disasters, vulnerability, and hazards, as well as to provide tools for policymakers and stakeholders. Key lessons were learned throughout the process and may be widely replicated. First, starting activities at the high school level is appropriate. This provided a myriad of opportunities due to the wider scope of student interests, more freedom to utilize different scientific research methods, and the ability to access and use information and communication technologies. Young adults have greater emotional maturity than younger children do, allowing them to deal with risks. This, combined with more physical capabilities, allows them to act to help children, the elderly, and people with disabilities in case of need. Moreover, they can establish links with local authorities concerning action for preventive interventions, which is empowered by *Com-VidAção*.

Second, creative and innovative platforms that promote access to information are vital to help students develop their skills. "Young people are ready to be part of the open data revolution by collecting, verifying, communicating, and using open data in a fast and responsible manner" (Cumiskey et al. 2015, p. 157). These platforms also foster new forms for the organization of school's time, spaces, and internal relations for knowledge production (not just reproduction) of basic scientific research. Although activities are led by students, teachers' guidance is fundamental for in-depth conceptual learning and curriculum embedding. In this way, education can include the study of uncertainties that have emerged in the physical, biological, social, and historical sciences (Morin 1999), as well as in the fields of climate change education and DRR education. Citizen science and crowdsourcing can provide windows of opportunities to do this.

Many challenges remain, however. These include the limited impact of DRR in education policies and programs, the need to assess the effectiveness of the existing programs, a need for continuity in capacity-building, and a need for schools-based DRR policies to scale up and reach the totality of schools located at disasters vulnerable areas. Despite these challenges, one should take into account the findings of case studies about DRR in school curricula from 30 countries. Another issue, particularly in this area of Brazil, is scaling up from the pilot project to reach all vulnerable municipalities monitored by Cemaden (about 957). According to Selby and Kagawa (2012, p. 23), "pilot initiatives are instigated and driven forward by a ministry or department of government other than the ministry responsible for education; the pilot outputs and outcomes may receive only passive or reluctant support when planning for movement to scale." For a successful protective network to be built for the benefit of Brazilian communities, the Ministry of Education in DRR and EWS must work together with the youth to engage in sustainable and meaningful vulnerability reduction.

## REFERENCES

Anderson, W. 2005. Bringing children into focus on the social science disaster research agenda. *International Journal of Mass Emergencies and Disasters* 23(3): 159–175.

Basher, R. 2006. Global early warning systems for natural hazards: Systematic and people-centered. *Philosophical Transactions A* 364(1845): 2167–2182.

Convery, I., B. Carroll, and R. Balogh. Flooding and schools: Experiences in Hull in 2007. 2014. *Disasters* 39(1): 146–165.

Cumiskey, L., T. Hoang, S. Suzuki, C. Pettigrew, and M.M. Herrgard. 2015. Youth participation at the third UN World Conference on Disaster Risk Reduction. *International Journal of Disaster Risk Science* 6(2): 150–163.

Earthquake Engineering Research Institute. 2006. Learning from earthquakes—The Kashmir Earthquake of October 8, 2005: Impacts in Pakistan. https://www.eeri.org/lfe/pdf/kashmir_eeri_2nd_report.pdf, accessed June 3, 2015.

Fernandez, G. and R. Shaw. 2014. Youth participation in disaster risk reduction through science clubs in the Philippines. *Disasters* 39(2): 279–294.

Freire, P. 1999. *Educação como prática da liberdade* [*Education as a freedom practice*]. Rio de Janeiro: Paz e Terra.

Gaillard, J.C. and J. Mercer. 2012. From knowledge to action: Bridging gaps in disaster risk reduction. *Progress in Human Geography* 37(1): 93–114.

Garcia, C. and C.J. Fearnley. 2012. Evaluating critical links in early warning systems for natural hazards. *Environmental Hazards* 11(2): 123–137.

International Federation of the Red Cross and Red Crescent Societies. 2012. *Community early warning systems: Guiding principles*. Geneva, Switzerland: IFRC.

Iwama, A.Y. 2014. Riscos e vulnerabilidades às mudanças climáticas e ambientais: Análise multiescalar na zona costeira de São Paulo—Brasil [Risk and vulnerability to climate and environmental changes: Multiscale analysis in the coastal zone of São Paulo—Brazil]. PhD dissertation, Campinas State University.

Izadkhah, Y. and M. Hosseini. 2005. Towards resilient communities in developing countries through education of children for disaster preparedness. *International Journal of Emergency Management* 2(3): 138–148.

Kelman, I. and M.H. Glantz. 2014. Early warning systems defined. In *Reducing disaster: Early warning systems for climate change*, eds. Z. Zommers and A. Singh, 89–108. London: Springer.

Marchezini, V. 2015. The biopolitics of disaster: Power, discourses and practices. *Human Organization* 74(4): 362–371.

Marchezini, V. 2014. La producción silenciada de los "desastres naturales" en catástrofes sociales [The silenced production of "natural disasters" in social catastrophes]. *Revista Mexicana de Sociología* 76(2): 253–285.

Mitchell, T., K. Haynes, N. Hall, W. Choong, and K. Oven. 2008. The roles of children and youth in communicating disaster risk. *Children, Youth and Environments* 18(1): 254–279.

Mitchell, T., T. Tanner, and K. Haynes. 2009. *Children as agents of change for disaster risk reduction: Lessons from El Salvador and the Philippines*. Brighton, UK: Institute of Development Studies, Working Paper No. 1. http://www.plan-uk.org/resources/documents/37225/, accessed May 5, 2014.

Morin, E. 1999. *Seven complex lessons in education for the future*. Paris, France: UNESCO. http://unesdoc.unesco.org/images/0011/001177/117740eo.pdf, accessed June 1, 2013.

National Secretariat of Civil Defense. 2004. *Relatório sala de situação—enchentes 2004* [Crisis situation report]. Brasília: SEDEC.

Ochola, S.O., B. Eitel, and D.O. Olago. 2010. Vulnerability of schools to floods in Nyando River catchment, Kenya. *Disasters* 34(3): 732–754.

Peek, L. 2008. Children and disasters: Understanding vulnerability, developing capacities, and promoting resilience—An introduction. *Children, Youth and Environments* 18(1): 1–29.

Pennesi, K. 2013. Predictions as lies in Ceará, Brazil: The intersection of two cultural models. *Anthropological Quarterly* 86(3): 759–789.

Penrose, A. and M. Takaki. 2006. Children's rights in emergencies and disasters. *The Lancet* 367: 698–699.

Selby, D. and F. Kagawa. 2012. *Disaster risk reduction in school curricula: Case studies from thirty countries*. Paris, France: UNESCO and UNICEF. http://www.unicef.org/education/files/DRRinCurricula-Mapping30countriesFINAL.pdf, accessed March 12, 2014.

Soffer, Y., A. Goldberg, G. Avisar-Shohat, R. Cohen, and Y. Bar-Dayan. 2010. The effect of different educational interventions on schoolchildren's knowledge of earthquake protective behaviour in Israel. *Disasters* 34(1): 205–213.

Teschenhausen, A.R.R.V. 2015. In the crowd we trust: Role and challenges of crowdsourcing and citizen science in the context of the data revolution—A transdisciplinary approach. Masters Thesis, Universities of Leipsich and Vienna.

Thomalla, F. and R.K. Larsen. 2010. Resilience in the context of tsunami early warning systems and community disaster preparedness in the Indian Ocean region. *Environmental Hazards* 9(3): 249–265.

Tuladhar, G., R. Yatabe, R.K. Dahal, and N.P. Bhandary. 2014. Knowledge of disaster risk reduction among school students in Nepal. *Geomatics, Natural Hazards and Risk* 5(3): 190–207.

United Nations Children's Fund. 2012. *UNICEF and disaster risk reduction.* http://www.unicef.org/malaysia/UNICEF_and_Disaster_Risk_Reduction.pdf, accessed June 6, 2014.

United Nations International Strategy for Disaster Reduction. 2011. *Global assessment report on disaster risk reduction: Revealing risk, redefining development.* Geneva, Switzerland: UNISDR.

_____. 2006. *Global survey of early warning systems: An assessment of capacities, gaps and opportunities towards building a comprehensive global early warning system for all natural hazards.* Geneva, Switzerland: UNISDR.

_____. 2005. *Hyogo Framework for Action 2005–2015: building the resilience of nations and communities to disasters.* Geneva, Switzerland: UNISDR. http://www.refworld.org/docid/42b98a704.html, accessed July 2, 2015.

Valencio, N.F.L.S. 2012. *Para além do "dia do desastre": O caso Brasileiro* [Beyond the "day of the disaster": The Brazilian case]. Curitiba, Brazil: Editora Appris.

Villagrán de León, J.C. 2012. Early warning principles and practices. In *Handbook of hazards and disaster risk reduction and management*, eds. B. Wisner, J.C. Gaillard, and I. Kelman, 481–492. Abingdon, Oxfordshire: Routledge.

Yamori, K. 2009. Action research on disaster reduction education: Building a "community of practice" through a gaming approach. *Journal of Natural Disaster Science* 30(2): 83–96.

# 4 Household Response to Flash Flooding in the United States and India

## *A Comparative Study of the 2013 Colorado and Uttarakhand Disasters*

*Hao-Che Wu, Sudha Arlikatti, Andrew Prelog, and Clayton Wukich*

**CONTENTS**



**Abstract**

Flash floods are dangerous weather-related disasters. There are no recent studies focused on immediate household response to floods that examine two countries, using comparable approaches, to acquire those data. This chapter fills this gap by presenting an empirical analysis of two disaster events: the June 2013 flash flood in the Himalayan State of Uttarakhand, North India, and the September 2013 flood in Colorado, United States. This study examines immediate flood response data from the perspective of local residents, including their flood emergency information source, perceived flood risk, and response. The results show that there are behavioral and emotional response differences between the Indian sample and Colorado sample.

## INTRODUCTION

Flood hazards claim approximately 20,000 lives worldwide annually and adversely affect millions of others (Kellens, Terpstra, and De Maeyer 2013). Flash floods are especially dangerous because individuals often lack knowledge about exposure to risk and immediate danger (Knocke and Kolivras 2007). It is critical to understand issues related to risk perception and different sources of warning information, such as changes observed in the environment. These include seeing the flash flood or noting rising water levels in lakes and rivers. Environmental cues portent imminent threat; these influence decisions taken to protect oneself.

In the United States, public understanding of flash flood risks remains varied (Bell and Tobin 2007). Previous research suggests that, when compared to slower moving threats such as hurricanes (Wu, Lindell, and Prater 2012, 2014), people have less time to identify risks, seek out information, and act. Official warning systems, created to quickly disseminate alerts and information, contribute considerably to individual responses (Morss, Wilhelmi, Downton, and Gruntfest 2005).

There is general agreement that effective risk communication strategies increase community and individual protective actions (Terpstra and Lindell 2013; Terpstra, Lindell, and Gutteling 2009; Wu, Lindell, and Prater 2015). However, research on flash flood warnings in developing countries is limited (Kellens, Terpstra, and De Maeyer 2013), as is related literature on community members' behavioral responses to these threats. Where official warning systems are rare, understanding the community's social organization, including traditional knowledge, prior experiences, and integration into improvised peer warning networks, can advance our understanding of immediate reactions to flash floods and, ultimately, community resilience.

It is imperative to examine immediate responses to flash floods in different geographical, political, social, and cultural settings. Arlikatti and Prater (n.d.) emphasize this because policymakers are increasingly looking beyond national borders for ideas to address challenges at home. Advances in communications technology have also made it possible for governments, citizens, and nongovernmental organizations to engage in cross-national learning and real-time information exchanges, thereby benefiting the global community (Comfort, Boin, and Demchak 2010).

Kellens, Terpstra, and De Maeyer (2013, p. 46) find that, although there has been significant growth, there is more to be done. They suggest that "future research should strive for more theoretical support and more 'methodological openness'...Profound empirical testing of previous theories may lead to new insights and model improvements assuming that the selection and measurement of constructs is 'open' and well-grounded." This research answers their call for action by using the Protective Action Decision Model (PADM) as a guiding framework to test the effects of flood risk communication and perception on people's behavior following the 2013 flash floods in Colorado, United States, and Uttarakhand, India.

## THEORETICAL FRAMEWORK AND RESEARCH QUESTIONS

Perry, Lindell, and Greene (1981) tested a multistage path model of evacuation decision making that incorporated measures of the respondents' social context, environmental cues, warning characteristics (sources, channels, and messages), risk perceptions, and behavioral response. Lindell and Perry (1992, 2004, 2012) revised and extended this model, now known as the PADM. PADM integrates information derived from social and environmental cues with messages that social sources transmit through communication channels to those at risk. Social cues are signals we receive verbally (face-to-face or via television, radio, or phones) or nonverbally (watching others evacuate) from family, friends, or people around us who are part of our social network. Environmental cues are nonverbal signals that our natural environment gives us, such as rising water levels.

PADM identifies three core drivers that cause an emotional reaction in humans and influence decisions about how to respond or protective actions to take. These apply to both imminent and long-term threats. These drivers are (1) the severity of the threat and the perceived destruction from it; (2) the ability or inability to take actions to protect oneself and ones family; (3) the knowledge, responsibility, and trustworthiness of stakeholders in the community, including the local, state, and federal government, media, and peers, to protect them from the threat.

The outcome of the protective action decision-making process, together with situational facilitators and impediments, produces a behavioral response. This model has guided studies of evacuations from Hurricane Ike (Huang, Lindell, Prater, Wu, and Siebeneck 2012) and the 2009 Samoa earthquake and tsunami (Lindell et al. 2015), as well as the immediate behavioral response to the earthquakes in Christchurch, New Zealand and Hitachi, Japan (Lindell et al. 2016). However, none of these have examined the differences in the sources of disaster information, risk perception, protective action decision making, and emotional responses between developing and developed countries.

International initiatives, such as the United Nations Office for Disaster Risk Reduction Hyogo Framework for Action 2005–2015 (2015b) and the recent Sendai Framework for Disaster Risk Reduction 2015–2030 (2015a), have inspired developing and developed countries to invest heavily in a variety of warning systems and garner national and local support for disaster preparedness and response. However, emergency management research that study the efficacy of these efforts have mostly been done in English-speaking or developed countries (Arlikatti and Prater n.d.; Lindell, Prater, and Perry 2007). Therefore, there is a need to conduct similar research by collecting comparable variables in both developing and developed counties. This would allow emergency personnel to better use this information to communicate with residents of different social contexts internationally.

To address this, we are comparing the flash flood response experiences in Colorado, United States, and Uttarakhand, India. Guided by PADM, this chapter aims to answer three research questions (RQ). First (RQ1), we seek to determine how primary sources of flash flood risk information inform protective action decision making and how these differ by respondents' demographic characteristics (e.g., education level, age, gender, marital status, household size, and number of children). Second (RQ2), are there significant correlations between individuals' flood risk perception, flood behavioral response, and emotional response variables for both countries? Finally (RQ3), to what extent do US and Indian respondents differ in terms of risk perceptions and emotional responses?

We identify key issues in effective flash flood warning systems; physical, social, and emotional factors that affect risk perception; and associated civilian responses that protect lives and property. The chapter notes the unique needs, strengths, and weaknesses of current policies and practices in the United States and India. We conclude by offering policy recommendations and identifying the remaining research gaps that deserve future attention.

## BACKGROUND AND METHODOLOGY

### Hazard Settings

Colorado is situated in the center of the North American Rocky Mountains and is home to over 5 million people. Due to the varied terrain (mountains, foothills, and plains), many reside in areas susceptible to flooding. Over the course of two days in September 2013, over 20 inches of rain fell in the mountains and eastern foothills. This fed into local rivers and streams in what would later be characterized as a 500-year flood event. The flooding resulted in eight deaths and an estimated $2 billion in damages (Henson 2013).

Uttarakhand, in northern India, includes parts of the Himalayan mountains and is home to approximately 10 million people (Government of India, Census of India 2011). The summer months of 2013 were abnormally warm, causing glacial melting and increased runoff. This inundated dammed lakes and caused rivers to swell. This was compounded by the onset of the monsoon season, which brought incessantly heavy rains for over 60 hours (50 mm–500 mm) from June 14 to 17 (Global Shelter Cluster 2013; Singh 2013). This resulted in a devastating flash flood and numerous landslides, causing widespread damage in 13 of the 14 districts (Indian Red Cross Society 2013).

By July 16, 2013, the state government confirmed 1000 deaths and over 5700 individuals were missing and "presumed dead" (Solanki 2013).

## Site and Sample Selection

Eleven counties in Colorado needed individual and public assistance following the flood (Federal Emergency Management Agency 2014). Five counties (Adams, Arapahoe, Boulder, Larimer, and Weld) were selected for this study because of the severity of flood impact (Colorado Climate Center 2014). All experienced major flash flood damage and had areas with mandatory evacuation orders. Stratified random samples of households from evacuated and 500-year flood risk areas in these counties were used to generate a statistically relevant set of households within each county and also provide variation in terms of mountain and foothill communities. The household addresses were provided by Infogroup, a private company. Following Dillman, Smyth, and Christian's (2000) survey methodology, each household was sent an initial questionnaire. Two subsequent reminders were sent to nonresponders.

Two separate waves of questionnaires were implemented. The first was sent approximately seven months after the floods to residents of Adams and Boulder County. The second wave was sent to additionally sampled households (in Arapahoe, Larimer, and Weld Counties) 14 months after the floods. A total of 1811 questionnaires were mailed, with 401 households participating, for a response rate of 22.1%. Although low, this rate is common in survey research with disaster survivors (Lindell, Kang, and Prater 2011).

In India, flash flood survivors from Uttarkashi district were selected. This district is located in the extreme northwest of Uttarakhand state, bordering Tibet and Himachal Pradesh. It encompasses an area of 8016 km$^2$, with a population of 40 per km$^2$. The district is located between the Bhagirathi and Asi Ganga rivers. It has 673 villages, of which 300 were severely affected by the flash floods and accompanying landslides (Uttarkashi District Administration 2014).

Flood survivors were identified and interviewed face-to-face in the local language (Hindi) between October 16 and November 1, 2013, by a five-member research team of graduate students from the University of Delhi, led by one of the authors. Interviews took place either at the homes of the respondents, in the central market by the side of the highway, or at government and/or nonprofit-sponsored makeshift tent shelters scattered across the villages. As the study was conducted four months after the event and there was no access to many of the remote locations due to infrastructure damage and ongoing recovery and rebuilding activities, a convenience sampling strategy was used to identify respondents (Singleton and Straits 2010). In all, 316 respondents from 17 villages were surveyed using a snowball sampling procedure. Potential participants were first identified by village leaders or local liaisons; these participants then suggested other potential contacts. Secondary information was also collected from government reports, blogs, and news media reports.

## Respondent Demographics

Colorado respondents range in age from 18 to 93, with a mean of 55.56 years. Approximately 47.10% of the respondents are male. Approximately 62.1% of the respondents identify as married, with 34% identifying as single, divorced, or widowed. The average household size is 2.49 people, with 0.53 children under the age of 18. The modal education level was "college degree." According to the 2010–2014 US Census data (United States Census Bureau 2016), the percentage of people with bachelor's degrees in Boulder, Larimer, Arapahoe, Weld and Adams Counties are 58%, 44%, 35%, 26%, and 21%, respectively. Our survey data indicated comparable education levels for each county.

In India, respondents' ages range from 18 to 85 years, with a mean of 43.06. Approximately 58.50% of the respondents are male. Roughly 75% of the respondents identify as married, and 35% as single, divorced, or widowed. Respondent households include an average of 6.42 people, with approximately 2.04 children under the age of 18. The modal education level of survey respondents is "less than 9th grade."

## Measures

Similar survey instruments were used in both countries, but each was adapted for the specific sociocultural contexts of the research sites. The questions aim to measure respondents' emotional responses, perceived potential for personal and community property loss, flood behavioral response, and how they received flood information. For emotional responses, nine measures were selected from the University of Wales, Institute of Science and Technology's Mood Adjective Checklist. The variables (optimistic, depressed, annoyed, nervous, fearful, relaxed, energetic, alert, and passive) measure respondents' hedonic (pleasant), tense, and energetic tone (Lindell et al. 2016). The hedonic arousal scale (optimistic, depressed, and annoyed) measures feelings of pleasantness–unpleasantness during the flood (Matthews, Jones, and Chamberlain 1990). The tense arousal scale (nervous, fearful, and relaxed) and energetic arousal scale (energetic, alert, and passive) measure respondents' anxiousness and activeness (Thayer 1978). For example, energetic means respondents actively evacuated; passive means respondents were not very responsive to the situation. Survey respondents were asked to report the extent to which they felt the above emotions during the flood. These variables were measured from "not at all = 1" to "a very great extent = 3."

"Perceptions of personal and familial risk" measures include questions on how likely respondents thought the flood might have resulted in the following: "severely damage or destroy your home," "injure or kill you or your family," "destroy or severely damage many homes in your community/town," and "injure or kill many people in your community." These variables were also measured from 1 to 3. Flood behavioral response measures include six variables (all coded 1 = yes, 0 = no): (1) continued what I was doing before the flood; (2) stopped what I was doing but stayed where I was; (3) stopped what I was doing and went to a higher ground; (4) tried to protect other people nearby; (5) tried to protect property nearby from the water by lifting it; and (6) immediately left the building I was in.

Respondents identified their primary sources of information about the floods, the content of that information, and subsequent protective actions taken as a result (e.g., sheltering in place or evacuation). They were also asked about secondary information sources and whether they sought out confirmation about potential risks. Finally, respondents were asked about their previous experiences with disasters. The survey concludes with standard sociodemographic questions, including sex, number of children below 18, total household size including children, income, and education level (some high school, high school graduate, some college/vocation school, college graduate, graduate school). Respondent ages are collapsed into 4 groups (under 18, 19–30, 31–64, and 65 and older). Marital status is identified as either married or unmarried (including single, divorced, or widowed).

The survey questions were adopted from previous PADM risk perception studies on earthquakes, hurricanes, and tsunami (Huang, Lindell, Prater, Wu, and Siebeneck 2012; Lindell et al. 2015, 2016; Wu, Lindell, and Prater 2012). Since these questions have not been tested during a flood emergency, the survey instruments were adjusted to fit the new context. The questions were also modified to meet the social structure in India. For example, "community" was reworded as "village" in the India survey.

## Data Analysis

Quantitative data analysis is presented in the subsequent section. Cross-tabulation analyses test the difference among demographic groups using chi-square. Correlation analyses measure the degree of association among the flood risk perception and behavioral and emotional response variables using Pearson's *R* (see Appendix for full correlations in Table A4.1). Analysis of variance (ANOVA) examines the differences among risk perception and emotional response variables and country groups. The SPSS 22 Statistic Analysis Package was used for the computations.

## RESULTS

With respect to RQ1, the extent to which primary sources of flood risk informed protective action decision making differs by demographic characteristics. The cross-tabulation analyses (see Table 4.1) show that education level of the respondents is significant ($\chi^2 = 54.92$, $p < .01$) for the Colorado sample. Of the 143 respondents who were aware that the torrential rains could cause a flood, 44.10% had graduate degrees, 38.50% had a bachelor's degree, 11.90% had some postsecondary education, and 5.60% graduated high school. Results indicate that Colorado respondents' primary flood information sources were different, based on education level. The Indian sample did not show statistically significant differences based on demographic characteristics and their primary sources of flood information.

Respondents also reported their primary information sources about the emergency. The descriptive statistics show that 40% of the Colorado respondents generated their initial understanding of the situation through personal observations, 18% relied on radio and/or television, and 12% relied on their friends/relatives. Only 2% of the Colorado respondents relied on websites. The Indian sample suggests that 46% received their primary flood risk information from their friends/relatives, 42% from personal observations, and only 7% from the police, who serve as disaster management authorities in these communities.

To examine RQ2, are there significant correlations between individuals' flood risk perception and flood behavioral and emotional response variables for both countries, a correlation analysis was conducted (see Appendix for table of results). Colorado respondents who believed the flood would severely damage/destroy their home were more likely to protect their property ($r = .19$, $p < .01$), leave the building ($r = .11$, $p < .05$), and feel depressed ($r = .40$, $p < .01$), annoyed ($r = .30$, $p < .01$), nervous ($r = .48$, $p < .01$), fearful ($r = .50$, $p < .01$), energetic ($r = .12$, $p < .05$), and alert ($r = .28$, $p < .01$). Respondents who believed the flood would result in injury/kill someone in their family were more

**TABLE 4.1**
**Primary Emergency Information Source by Education Level for Colorado Sample**

| | Education Level | | | | | |
|---|---|---|---|---|---|---|
| **Source of Information** | **Some High School (%)** | **High School Graduate/ GED (%)** | **Some College/ Vocational School (%)** | **College Graduate (%)** | **Graduate School (%)** | **Total (*N*)** |
| Torrential rains could cause a flood | 0 | 5.6 | 11.9 | 38.5 | 44.1 | 143 |
| Noticed unusual changes | 0 | 0 | 0 | 100.0 | 0 | 2 |
| Saw people evacuate | 0 | 0 | 0 | 100.0 | 0 | 1 |
| I saw the flood coming | 0 | 26.7 | 33.3 | 20.0 | 20.0 | 15 |
| Warned by siren | 0 | 0 | 3.4 | 37.9 | 58.6 | 29 |
| Others warned me face to face | 3.8 | 7.7 | 15.4 | 34.6 | 38.5 | 26 |
| Someone called or texted to warn me | 8.8 | 11.8 | 20.6 | 29.4 | 29.4 | 34 |
| I received the warning from a particular source | 1.2 | 6.0 | 19 | 33.3 | 40.5 | 84 |
| Other | 3.2 | 6.5 | 29 | 30.6 | 30.6 | 62 |

*Note:* $\chi^2 = 54.92$, $p < .01$

likely to protect their property ($r = .16, p < .01$) and feel depressed ($r = .22, p < .01$), annoyed ($r = .17, p < .01$), nervous ($r = .33, p < .01$), fearful ($r = .42, p < .01$), and alert ($r = .16, p < .01$). Respondents who believed the flood would severely damage/destroy homes in their community were more likely to stay where they were ($r = .20, p < .01$), protect others ($r = .12, p < .05$), and feel depressed ($r = .34, p < .01$), annoyed ($r = .20, p < .01$), nervous ($r = .42, p < .01$), fearful ($r = .38, p < .01$), and alert ($r = .34, p < .01$). In addition, people who believed the flood would result in injury/killing someone in their community were more likely to feel depressed ($r = .30, p < .01$), annoyed ($r = .17, p < .01$), nervous ($r = .38, p < .01$), fearful ($r = .33, p < .01$), and alert ($r = .25, p < .01$).

Results for the Indian sample differed. Respondents who believed the flood would severely damage/destroy their homes reported being more likely to feel depressed ($r = .21, p < .01$), nervous ($r = .22, p < .01$), and fearful ($r = .21, p < .01$). However, the flood risk perception for home damage was not significantly correlated with any of the flood response variables. Respondents who believed the flood would result in injury/kill someone in their family were more likely to leave the building and feel depressed ($r = .17, p < .01$), nervous ($r = .17, p < .01$), fearful ($r = .19, p < .01$), and passive ($r = .11, p < .05$). Further, respondents who believed the flood would severely damage/destroy homes in their village were less likely to continue what they were doing ($r = -.19, p < .01$), stay where they were ($r = -.16, p < .01$), and were more likely to feel depressed ($r = .20, p < .01$), annoyed ($r = .13, p < .05$), nervous ($r = .21, p < .01$), fearful ($r = .18, p < .01$), and alert ($r = .13, p < .05$). Not surprisingly, those who believed the flood would result in injury/kill someone in their community were also less likely to continue what they were doing ($r = -.24, p < .01$) and stay where they were ($r = -.11, p < .01$). They felt depressed ($r = .21, p < .01$), nervous ($r = .19, p < .01$), fearful ($r = .23, p < .01$) and alert ($r = .14, p < .01$).

These results indicate that the risk perception variables are positively correlated with the negative hedonic arousal measures (depressed and annoyed), higher tense arousal measures (nervous and fearful), and higher energetic arousal measures (energetic and alert) in both Colorado and Uttarakhand. However, the data were not able to identify significant correlations between home risk perception variables and protective action variables in Uttarakhand. It only shows correlations between village damage perception variables and protective action variables.

RQ3 examines the differences, if any, between US and Indian respondents with regard to risk perception and emotional responses. ANOVA compares the two sets of respondents. Table 4.2 shows

**TABLE 4.2**
**Emotional Response and Flood Risk Perception between India and Colorado**

| | | Colorado | | India | | |
|---|---|---|---|---|---|---|
| **Variable** | | **Mean** | **N** | **Mean** | **N** | **ANOVA Results** |
| Emotional response | Optimistic | 2.55 | 383 | 3.06 | 316 | $F_{1,697} = 21.42, p < .01$ |
| | Depressed | 2.18 | 385 | 4.47 | 316 | $F_{1,697} = 605.80, p < .01$ |
| | Annoyed | 2.35 | 383 | 2.70 | 316 | $F_{1,697} = 8.26, p < .01$ |
| | Nervous | 3.19 | 386 | 4.63 | 316 | $F_{1,697} = 230.21, p < .01$ |
| | Fearful | 2.73 | 392 | 4.61 | 316 | $F_{1,697} = 395.28, p < .01$ |
| | Relaxed | 2.05 | 383 | 1.91 | 316 | $F_{1,697} = 1.92$, *ns* |
| | Energetic | 2.88 | 387 | 3.46 | 316 | $F_{1,697} = 26.78, p < .01$ |
| | Alert | 4.06 | 389 | 3.72 | 316 | $F_{1,697} = 11.68, p < .01$ |
| | Passive | 1.81 | 385 | 2.64 | 316 | $F_{1,697} = 59.96, p < .01$ |
| Risk perception | Damage at home | 2.15 | 396 | 3.92 | 316 | $F_{1,710} = 254.44, p < .01$ |
| | Injury at home | 1.35 | 391 | 3.18 | 316 | $F_{1,705} = 307.51, p < .01$ |
| | Damage in community/village | 3.35 | 394 | 4.12 | 316 | $F_{1,708} = 52.02, p < .01$ |
| | Injury in community/village | 2.57 | 395 | 4.20 | 316 | $F_{1,709} = 249.36, p < .01$ |

that there are significant differences on the emotional response variables between the two samples, except for feeling relaxed. Indian respondents felt more depressed ($F_{1, 697} = 605.80$, $p < .01$), annoyed ($F_{1, 697} = 8.26$, $p < .01$), nervous ($F_{1, 697} = 230.21$, $p < .01$), fearful ($F_{1, 697} = 395.28$, $p < .01$), and passive ($F_{1, 697} = 59.96$, $p < .01$) and less alert ($F_{1, 697} = 11.68$, $p < .01$). Colorado respondents reported feeling alert much more often than Indian respondents ($F_{1, 697} = 11.68$, $p < .01$). This may be due to a lack of flash flood awareness and education programs, official warning systems, lack of savings and insurance for rebuilding following disasters, poor infrastructure and difficulties in accessing aid in these remote Himalayan villages.

Indian respondents are simultaneously more optimistic ($F_{1, 697} = 21.42$, $p < .01$) and energetic ($F_{1, 697} = 26.78$, $p < .01$). According to Rautela (2015), they have traditionally depended on social norms and religiosity to devise ways of maximizing resources and mitigating against natural hazards even when the Indian government is slow in responding. The analyses of risk perception variables indicate that Indian respondents are more likely to believe the flood will result in some type of damage at their homes ($F_{1, 710} = 254.44$, $p < .01$) and communities ($F_{1, 708} = 52.02$, $p < .01$). Similarly, they also tend to believe there could be some injuries within their households ($F_{1, 705} = 307.51$, $p < .01$) and their community ($F_{1, 709} = 249.36$, $p < .01$).

## DISCUSSION

This chapter highlights the differences in experiences by flash flood survivors in communities in the United States and rural mountain communities in India. Contrary to previous research findings (Lindell, Kang, and Prater 2011; Wu, Lindell, and Prater 2012), there were no clear demographic distinctions for risk perception in Colorado; the Uttarakhand data suggest such differences. Possible explanatory factors could include the intensity of the floods and the damage wrought in Uttarakhand, where 80.04% of respondents had homes that were severely damaged. Data show that the Colorado flood was perceived to be less intense compared to the one in Uttarakhand. There were also flash flood warnings disseminated through social media and emergency management personnel in the United States, but not in India.

Similar to the findings of Lindell et al. (2016), this study confirms that physical damage and injury to household members are correlated with variables such as "depressed," "nervous," and "fearful" during disasters. This study finds that people with higher risk perceptions are more likely to take protective actions in both countries, with few variations. For example, in the case of Uttarakhand, only the perception of having village houses damaged or family members injured/killed increased respondents' sense of urgency to leave the building/area.

Finally, regarding RQ3, respondents in Uttarakhand reported lower levels of alertness during the flood. This stands in contrast to Colorado respondents. This finding may be a product of the more robust risk communication infrastructure in the United States and the fact that respondents in Uttarakhand did not have the same level of access to information.

## CONCLUSION

The results of these three RQs identify some risk information use differences in these two countries. Colorado residents' response to flash flooding is statistically significantly correlated with flood risk perception variables, possibly indicative of a better warning communication system and self-reliance. Congruent with previous research (Arlikatti and Prater n.d.), these results suggest that public evacuation strategies in developing countries are notably different from those in developed countries and need to be closely examined to inform better warning communication and disaster management policies

With respect to primary flood information sources, we observe that Colorado survey respondents relied predominantly on their own observations. Given the region's history of flooding, we would assume that individuals have some experience with the recognition of risk. Risk detection is augmented by various sociotechnical systems, as well as informal social networks (see Comfort, Boin, and Demchak 2010; Lindell and Perry 2012). To a lesser extent, respondents indicated that they relied on similar means (e.g., radio and television and friends and relatives).

Findings demonstrate that, although an overwhelming majority (98.23%) of Uttarakhand respondents had never experienced a flash flood in the past 10 years, their social perceptions motivated them to take adequate protective actions that saved the lives of their families and themselves. Despite a lack of a well-established flash flood warning system, or educational campaigns and assistance from the government and the mass-media, these villagers' traditional knowledge about their environment helped the survey respondents survive. Rautela (2015) notes that the indigenous people of Uttarakhand, Himalayas, have an advanced understanding of resource management and hazards. Relevant techniques include water harvesting, an understanding of recharge and discharge and flooding, landslide mitigation through terrace farming, seasonal migration, selection of land for habitation and vernacular architectural construction techniques and are sustainable.

Encouraging traditional mitigation practices, adopting owner-driven housing reconstruction, using local masons or residents, and training them on how to use stronger building materials are essential to make the built environment safer (i.e., amalgamating the old and new). Scientists and policy makers should not advocate climate change adaptation or mitigation without tying it to livelihood development and religious and cultural beliefs. How this can be done warrants further exploration.

A limitation of this study, however, is that the Colorado sample included a disproportionate percentage of older respondents and more formally educated respondents. These individuals may have been quite experienced with flash flooding and more sophisticated warning systems. Therefore, they might not be representative of the entire communities we examined. Future research could focus on younger and more diverse populations and how they detect and recognize flash flooding risk, or, perhaps, fail to do so. Relatedly, social media platforms may play a more pronounced role in this process than we identify in our study and, therefore, deserve future attention.

## REFERENCES

Arlikatti, S. and C.S. Prater. n.d. Emergency preparedness and immediate response to disasters: An international perspective. In *Planning for disaster resilience,* eds. S. Van Zandt and W.G. Peacock. New York: Routledge Publishing.

Bell, H.M. and G.A. Tobin. 2007. Efficient and effective? The 100-year flood in the communication and perception of flood risk. *Environmental Hazards* 7(4): 302–311.

Colorado Climate Center. 2014. Colorado flood 2013. http://coflood2013.colostate.edu, accessed March 8, 2016.

Comfort, L.K., A. Boin, and C.C. Demchak. 2010. Resilience revisited: An action agenda for managing extreme events. In *Designing resilience: Preparing for extreme events*, eds. L.K. Comfort, A. Boin, and C.C. Demchak, 272–284. Pittsburgh, PA: University of Pittsburgh Press.

Dillman, D.A., J.D. Smyth, and L.M. Christian. 2000. *Mail and Internet surveys.* New York: John Wiley & Sons.

Federal Emergency Management Agency. 2014. Colorado severe storms, flooding, landslides, and mudslides. http://www.fema.gov/disaster/4145, accessed March 10, 2016.

Global Shelter Cluster. 2013. Uttarakhand floods: Joint shelter assessment 22 August 2013. https://www.sheltercluster.org/sites/default/files/docs/Uttarakhand%20Joint%20Shelter%20Assessment%20Report.pdf, accessed November 8, 2015.

Government of India, Census of India. 2011. Provisional population totals: Uttarakhand: Census 2011. http://www.censusindia.gov.in/2011-prov-results/prov_data_products_utt.html, accessed November 10, 2015.

Henson, B. 2013. Inside the Colorado deluge. *AtmosNews*, September 3. National Center for Atmospheric Research. http://www2.ucar.edu/atmosnews/perspective/10250/inside-colorado-deluge, accessed November 12, 2015.

Huang, S.-K., M.K. Lindell, C.W. Prater, H.-C. Wu, and L. Siebeneck. 2012. Household evacuation decision making in response to Hurricane Ike. *Natural Hazards Review* 13(4): 283–296.

Indian Red Cross Society. 2013. Uttarakhand flash floods—A report. http://reliefweb.int/report/india/uttarakhand-flash-floods%E2%80%93-report, accessed November 12, 2015.

Kellens, W., T. Terpstra, and P. DeMaeyer. 2013. Perception and communication of flood risks: A systematic review of empirical research. *Risk Analysis* 33(1): 24–49.

Knocke, T.E. and K.N. Kolivras. 2007. Flash flood awareness in Southwest Virginia. *Risk Analysis* 27(1): 155–169.

Lindell, M.K., J.E. Kang, and C.S. Prater. 2011. The logistics of household hurricane evacuation. *Natural Hazards* 58(3): 1093–1109.

Lindell, M.K. and R.W. Perry. 2012. The Protective Action Decision Model: Theoretical modifications and additional evidence. *Risk Analysis* 32(4): 616–632.

_____. 2004. *Communicating environmental risk in multiethnic communities*. Thousand Oaks, CA: Sage.

_____. 1992. *Behavioral foundations of community emergency planning*. Washington, DC: Hemisphere Press.

Lindell, M.K., C.S. Prater, C.E. Gregg, E.J. Apatu, S.-K. Huang, and H.-C. Wu. 2015. Households' immediate response to the 2009 American Samoa earthquake and tsunami. *International Journal of Disaster Risk Reduction* 12: 328–340.

Lindell, M.K., C. Prater, and R.W. Perry. 2007. *Introduction to emergency management*. New York: John Wiley & Sons.

Lindell, M.K., C.S. Prater, H.-C. Wu, S.-K. Huang, D. Johnston, J. Becker, and H. Shiroshita. 2016. Immediate behavioral responses to earthquakes in Christchurch, New Zealand and Hitachi, Japan. *Disasters* 40(1): 85–111.

Matthews, G., D.M. Jones, and A.G. Chamberlain. 1990. Refining the measurement of mood: The UWIST Mood Adjective Checklist. *British Journal of Psychology* 81(1): 17–42.

Morss, R.E., O.V. Wilhelmi, M.W. Downton, and E. Gruntfest. 2005. Flood risk, uncertainty, and scientific information for decision making: Lessons from an interdisciplinary project. *Bulletin of the American Meteorological Society* 86(11): 1593–1601.

Perry, R.W., M.K. Lindell, and M.R. Greene. 1981. *Evacuation planning in emergency management*. Lexington, MA: Heath Lexington Books.

Rautela, P. 2015. Traditional practices of the people of Uttarakhand Himalaya in India and relevance of these in disaster risk reduction in present times. *International Journal of Disaster Risk Reduction* 13: 281–290.

Singh, J. 2013. What really happened in Uttarakhand. *Down to Earth*, July 3. http://www.downtoearth.org.in/news/what-really-happened-in-uttarakhand-41550, accessed November 12, 2015.

Singleton, R.A. and B.C. Straits. 2010. *Approaches to social research*. New York: Oxford University Press.

Solanki, A. 2013. India raises flood death toll reaches 5700 as all missing persons now presumed dead. *CBS News*, July 16. http://www.cbsnews.com/news/india-raises-flood-death-toll-reaches-5700-as-all-missing-persons-now-presumed-dead/, accessed November 11, 2015.

Terpstra, T. and M.K. Lindell. 2013. Citizens' perceptions of flood hazard adjustments: An application of the Protective Action Decision Model. *Environment and Behavior* 45(8): 993–1018.

Terpstra, T., M.K. Lindell, and J.M. Gutteling. 2009. Does communicating (flood) risk affect (flood) risk perceptions? Results of a quasi experimental study. *Risk Analysis* 29(8). 1141–1155.

Thayer, R.E. 1978. Factor analytic and reliability studies on the activation–deactivation adjective checklist. *Psychological Reports* 42(3): 747–756.

United Nations Office for Disaster Risk Reduction. 2015a. Sendai framework for disaster risk reduction. http://www.unisdr.org/we/coordinate/sendai-framework, accessed March 23, 2016.

United Nations Office for Disaster Risk Reduction. 2015b. Hyogo framework for action (HFA). https://www.unisdr.org/we/coordinate/hfa, accessed March 23, 2016.

United States Census Bureau. 2016. United States quick facts. http://www.census.gov/quickfacts/table/PST045215/00, accessed March 10, 2016.

Uttarkashi District Administration. 2014. Social sector plan Uttarkashi: Status report 2014. http://uttarkashi.nic.in/files/Disaster/Uttarkashi_Social_Sector_Status_Report_till_March 2014.pdf, accessed March 23, 2016.

Wu, H.-C., M.K. Lindell, and C.S. Prater. 2015. Strike probability judgments and protective action recommendations in a dynamic hurricane tracking task. *Natural Hazards* 79(1): 355–380.

_____. 2014. Effects of track and threat information on judgments of hurricane strike probability. *Risk Analysis* 34(6): 1025–1039.

_____. 2012. Logistics of hurricane evacuation in Hurricanes Katrina and Rita. *Transportation Research Part F: Traffic Psychology and Behavior* 15(4): 445–461.

# APPENDIX

## TABLE A4.1
## Correlations between Demographic, Risk Perception, and Emotional Variables

| Variables[a] | | | 1 | 2 | 3 | 4 | 5 | 6 | 7 | 8 | 9 | 10 | 11 | 12 | 13 | 14 | 15 | 16 | 17 | 18 | 19 |
|---|---|---|---|---|---|---|---|---|---|---|---|---|---|---|---|---|---|---|---|---|---|
| Flood Risk | 1 | HmPercep | – | **.48[c]** | **.48[c]** | **.43[c]** | **–.08** | **–.02** | **–.02** | **.05** | **–.01** | **.04** | **.01** | **.21[c]** | **.06** | **.22[c]** | **.21[c]** | **–.04** | **–.07** | **.05** | **–.10** |
| Perception | 2 | HmInjPercep | .48[c] | – | **.35[c]** | **.32[c]** | **–.07** | **–.03** | **.08** | **.08** | **–.03** | **.12[b]** | **–.10** | **.17[c]** | **–.13[b]** | **.17[c]** | **.19[c]** | **–.24[c]** | **.10** | **.08** | **.11[b]** |
| | 3 | ComPercep | .48[c] | .30[c] | – | **.67[c]** | **–.19[c]** | **–.16[c]** | **–.02** | **.03** | **.03** | **.10** | **.08** | **.20[c]** | **.13[b]** | **.21[c]** | **.18[c]** | **.02** | **.07** | **.14[b]** | **–.01** |
| | 4 | ComInjPercep | .27[c] | .33[c] | .67[c] | – | **–.24[c]** | **–.11[c]** | **.05** | **.01** | **.11** | **.10** | **.07** | **.21[c]** | **.08** | **.19[c]** | **.22[c]** | **.00** | **.05** | **.15[c]** | **–.09** |
| Flood | 5 | ContinWrk | –.32[c] | –.21[c] | –.38[c] | –.20[c] | – | **–.09** | **–.09** | **–.08** | **–.06** | **–.20[c]** | **–.16[c]** | **–.18[c]** | **–.13[b]** | **–.16[c]** | **–.12[b]** | **–.07** | **–.10** | **–.07** | **–.03** |
| Behavioral | 6 | StopStay | .08 | .02 | .20[c] | .09 | –.43[c] | – | **–.10** | **–.12[b]** | **–.09** | **–.31[c]** | **.01** | **–.04** | **–.02** | **.04** | **.00** | **.00** | **–.30[c]** | **–.28[c]** | **.09** |
| Response | 7 | StopClimb | .08 | .09 | .03 | .06 | –.18[c] | –.13[c] | – | **–.12[b]** | **–.09** | **–.32[c]** | **–.07** | **.14[b]** | **–.12[b]** | **.04** | **.03** | **.10** | **.19[c]** | **.14[b]** | **–.06** |
| | 8 | ProtectOth | .10 | .07 | .12[b] | –.02 | –.13[c] | –.09 | –.04 | – | **–.08** | **–.27[c]** | **.12[b]** | **.01** | **–.04** | **–.03** | **–.09** | **.07** | **.14[b]** | **.14[b]** | **.09** |
| | 9 | ProtectProp | .19[c] | .17[c] | .08 | .09 | –.19[c] | –.14[c] | –.06 | –.04 | – | **–.22[c]** | **.15[c]** | **.02** | **.10** | **.01** | **.02** | **–.05** | **.06** | **.07** | .07 |
| | 10 | LeftBldg | .11[b] | .03 | .09 | .03 | –.13[c] | –.10[b] | –.04 | –.03 | –.04 | – | **–.11[b]** | **.07** | **.05** | **.10** | **.17[c]** | **–.19[c]** | .06 | .04 | .05 |
| Flood | 11 | EmOptimistic | –.22[c] | –.07 | –.11[b] | –.10[b] | .12[b] | –.03 | –.02 | .04 | –.08 | –.01 | – | **.11** | **.27[c]** | **.00** | **–.01** | **.34[c]** | **.32[c]** | **.28[c]** | **.05** |
| Emotional | 12 | EmDepressed | .40[c] | .22[c] | .33[c] | .30[c] | –.25[c] | .05 | .02 | .02 | .14[c] | .10[b] | –.22[c] | – | **.26[c]** | **.55[c]** | **.50[c]** | **–.05** | **.17[c]** | **.23[c]** | **–.01** |
| Response | 13 | EmAnnoyed | .30[c] | .17[c] | .20[c] | .18[c] | –.12[b] | –.06 | –.01 | –.05 | .17[c] | .03 | –.06 | .48[c] | – | **.21[c]** | **.22[c]** | **.08** | **.05** | **.13[b]** | **.29[c]** |
| | 14 | EmNervous | .48[c] | .33[c] | .42[c] | .38[c] | –.33[c] | .19[c] | .11[b] | .01 | .10 | .16[c] | –.23[c] | .50[c] | .31[c] | – | **.88[c]** | **–.15[c]** | **.09** | **.06** | **.05** |
| | 15 | EmFearful | .50[c] | .42[c] | .38[c] | .32[c] | –.32[c] | .16[c] | .10[b] | .04 | .10[b] | .11[b] | –.21[c] | .51[c] | .28[c] | .78[c] | – | **–.21[c]** | **.05** | **.06** | **.03** |
| | 16 | EmRelazed | –.28[c] | –.10[c] | –.24[c] | –.20[c] | .22[c] | –.07 | –.05 | –.04 | –.09 | .02 | .38[c] | –.32[c] | –.12[b] | –.40[c] | –.43[c] | – | **.20[c]** | **.15[c]** | **–.06** |
| | 17 | EmEnergetic | .12[b] | .05 | .22[c] | .10 | –.15[c] | –.03 | .04 | .09 | .12[b] | .03 | .21[c] | –.01 | .05 | .06 | –.01 | .30[c] | – | **.73[c]** | **.11** |
| | 18 | EmAlert | .28[c] | .14[c] | .34[c] | .25[c] | –.27[c] | .15[c] | –.02 | .05 | .03 | .06 | .03 | .17[c] | .07 | .37[c] | .29[c] | .01 | .41[c] | – | **.02** |
| | 19 | EmPassive | –.19[c] | .05 | –.18[c] | –.05 | .16[c] | –.10 | .01 | –.09 | .00 | –.01 | .19[c] | .08 | .12[b] | –.09 | –.09 | .36[c] | .00 | –.11[b] | – |

*Note:* Numbers in bold are the correlations for Indian data; numbers in regular font are the correlations for Colorado data.

[a] 1. ContinWrk: Continued what I was doing before the flood (1 = yes, 0 = no); 2. StopStay: Stopped what I was doing but stayed where I was (1 = yes, 0 = no); 3. StopClimb: Stopped what I was doing and went to a higher ground (1 = yes, 0 = no); 4. ProtecOth: Tried to protect other people nearby (1 = yes, 0 = no); 5. ProtectProp: Tried to protect property nearby from the water by lifting it (1 = yes, 0 = no); 6. LeftBldg: Immediately left the building I was in (1 = yes, 0 = no). 7. HmPercep: Perceptions on Home Damage; 8. HmInjPercep: Perceptions on injures at home; 9. ComPercep: Perceptions on Community Damage; 10. ComInjPercep: Perception on injures in Community. 11. EmOPtimistic: Feel optimistic during the flood; 12. EmDepressed: Feel depressed during the flood; 13. EmAnnoyed: Feel annoyed during the flood; 14. EmNervous: Feel nervous during the flood; 15. EmFearful: Feel fearful during the fold; 16. EmRelaxed: Feel relaxed during the flood; 17. EmEnergetic: Feel energetic during the flood; 18. EmAlert: Feel alert during the flood; 19. EmPassive: Feel passive during the flood.

[b] Correlation is significant at the .01 level (two tailed).

[c] Correlation is significant at the .05 level (two tailed).

# 5 Traditional and Contemporary Social Safety Nets in Rural Mozambique

*Miriam S. Chaiken*

## CONTENTS



**Abstract**

Research conducted with Save the Children on social safety nets in rural Mozambique demonstrates that the long era of conflict in the late twentieth century led to the disappearance of traditional safety nets built on kin and religious affiliations. However, programs established by Save the Children now fill that function. Programs that foster new social safety nets rely on high levels of community participation and bottom–up decision making and are important in improving rural incomes, livelihoods, and addressing food insecurity. A better understanding of how individuals and communities respond to stresses and shocks shapes strategies for monitoring the compensatory behaviors, which can gauge vulnerability and circumvent crises. The reliance on communities to be partners in addressing their own problems promotes community buy-in and acknowledges that local people often have unique knowledge of conditions that can inform solutions.

## INTRODUCTION

Save the Children–United States (hereafter, "Save") is one of the leading humanitarian relief and development organizations in the world. In northern Mozambique, they have fostered comprehensive health and development programs. Their programs address conditions of chronic food insecurity and childhood malnutrition in a region where the majority of the children under 5 exhibit stunting, caused by long-term undernutrition. This paper describes programs that were implemented over a decade with the goal of improving child welfare, enhancing food production and access, and improving local livelihoods. The success of these efforts has laid the ground work for the potential implementation of community-based early warning systems (CEWS), which may be the next step in fostering resilience and preparing for shocks in Mozambique.

This paper will document the impact of Save's programs in fostering greater community cohesion and cooperation after decades of conflict. Their programs, which rebuilt collaboration in agriculture, microfinance, and peer learning, largely compensate for the dissolution of traditional kin and religious-based networks that existed prior to Independence. The success of these strategies lays a foundation for the implementation of community-based monitoring of behavioral responses that signal stress. The premise and promise of CEWS approaches are in the ability of communities to monitor and quantify their own vulnerability and, ultimately, to foster greater resilience.

This work occurred in Nampula Province, on the northern coast of Mozambique. Within the province, the coastal districts are most strongly affected by food insecurity. This area was also heavily affected by two decades of conflict that began with a struggle for independence from Portugal (1964–1975), followed by a protracted civil war (1977–1992) that ended with the first free elections in 1994. This long history of conflict seriously damaged infrastructure, including roads, markets, schools, and health facilities, resulting in social disruption and relocations.

The population in Nampula Province is predominantly from the Makhua ethnic group and is largely Muslim. They live by means of subsistence agriculture, cultivating cassava, a root crop, as their primary staple. Maize, beans, and vegetables are secondary cultivars. Most rural households cultivate subsistence gardens. Those closest to the ocean often supplement this with small-scale fishing, some of which is sold in the local markets. Some families supplement their income with day labor in the fields of wealthier landowners or through intermittent sale of charcoal, thatching material, gravel, and other small-scale local enterprises.

Food production levels are chronically insufficient to meet local needs. Nampula farmers face challenges from crop diseases and the effects of global climate change. The area has long been prone to droughts that reduce crop yields and have destroyed entire maize harvests due to insufficient rain. To complicate matters, the staple cassava crop has been affected by the Cassava Brown Streak Virus (CBSV), which spread from Uganda and Kenya southward into Tanzania and Mozambique beginning in the early twenty-first century. This viral disease, much like the historic potato blight that caused the Irish potato famine, results in pulpy, inedible tubers. This double challenge has resulted in severely diminished yields of the two staple foods, maize and cassava, and contributed to low production of other food crops, cashew orchards, and other tree crops.

As part of their humanitarian mission, Save established programs in Nampula Province to address these intransigent problems of low food production, food insecurity, and widespread childhood malnutrition. These include the establishment of farmer's groups to improve agricultural production and the training of *animadoras*, who are village-based peer health educators. Other programs promote collaboration in farming labor and improved microfinance. All program activities were designed to foster high levels of local participation, thereby rebuilding damaged collaborative networks and strengthening local community safety nets. Each strategy will be discussed subsequently.

## FORMATIVE RESEARCH AND PROGRAMS IN NAMPULA PROVINCE

### Research Methods

The programming activities in Mozambique began in the early 2000s. I began collaborating with the in-country staff in 2004, when I designed a community survey to learn more about who participated in Save's programs. Over the next decade, I returned on numerous occasions to support formative research efforts, intended to enhance the efficacy of the program activities, and to support capacity building activities for staff training. I collected some of the data reported in this paper; some is from Save staff, who collected data and did routine monitoring and evaluation for the duration of the project.

Our first collaboration (2004) examined intrahousehold resource allocation, division of labor, pooling of household resources, and factors that affected household food access, including seasonality. This research was conducted in four villages within the coastal districts; we conducted 35 in-depth interviews with local families. To ensure that we did not simply interview those most familiar to the staff or located most conveniently to the road, we conducted transect walks off the main roads on dirt tracks. After a proscribed amount of time, we stopped at the closest house to request their participation. If no one was at home or the respondents were unable to participate, we continued walking an additional allotted time and stopped again. This ensured that there were no "filters" on our access to information or efforts to steer us toward compliant households.

In 2007, we conducted 15 focus group interviews in 15 villages across three of the coastal districts in Nampula (N = 144 participants). The focus groups were convened by Save staff or by the *animadoras* or farmers group members. Participants included members of either farmers groups or mothers groups or both. I facilitated all interviews, and a translator fluent in both English and Makhua assisted. The interviews usually started with a small number of participants, but, as they were conducted outside in full view, other community members felt free to wander over and join the conversation. I believe this helped ensure representative participation in the interviews. Interviews lasted between one and two hours.

We were very mindful of the need to have broad community representation and to include perspectives of both men and women. Our focus groups ranged from 5 to 20 individuals, with 59 men and 75 women participating. As interviews progressed, I made notes indicating when a new person joined the group. I can say with confidence that women's voices were well represented in these data, which is a common challenge in much of rural Africa. The majority of the population in this area is Muslim, as is demonstrated in our sample. However, there were two communities that included Christian families; they participated alongside their Muslim neighbors in both Save programs and in our interviews. All interviews were tape recorded, and I took extensive notes while the interviews were underway. Given the both positive and negative things the respondents related, we felt strongly that we were able to capture unfiltered, representative viewpoints.

## Interviews and Themes

Our goal in the focus groups was to identify the types of support systems currently functioning in the rural communities, with the assumption that these could be the foundation of future program activities. Our research revealed that none of the "indigenous" systems of social support that had been previously documented for this cultural area had survived the social disruption related to the war for independence (1962–1975), civil war (1975–1992), and/or the subsequent period of political turmoil (Bonate 2006; Pitcher 1998). Literature review and information from other groups in the region suggested that we would find various collaborative networks based on kinship, clan membership, shared religious affiliation, shared political affiliation, or membership in community organizations, such as rotating credit or labor societies.

We wanted to better understand the nature of vulnerability and traditional safety nets in the communities served by these programs and ascertain who was participating in Save's programs and why. Our objective was to ensure participation of the poorest and most vulnerable segments of the population and, ultimately, to improve food security and sovereignty (Chaiken 2004, 2007; Chaiken, Dixon, Powers, and Wetzler 2009). When we asked about traditional social networks, several older respondents noted that, in traditional times, prior to Independence (1974), a practice called *stigi* was employed to bring together neighboring households in a rotating credit association; a custom called *mori* united people to work on each other's farms together. At the time of my fieldwork beginning in 2004, neither *mori* nor *stigi* was still being utilized. The loss of these traditional practices occurred during the early years following Independence, when the socialist FRELIMO government imposed compulsory "villagization." This required people to work on collective farms, but they received none of the yield from their labors. Nampula villagers report that they deeply resented the obligatory collective labor. As soon as they were able, they returned to cultivating individual plots, but without the earlier traditional patterns of pooling labor and resources.

The social networks that proved to be the most visible, effective, and utilized were new networks based on secular and voluntary participation in the Save programs. The most poignant example of the importance of these groups emerged during a discussion about food aid distribution that took place in 2005. Our earlier research documented strong evidence of an emerging famine due to drought-induced total crop failure (Chaiken 2004, 2007; Chaiken, Dixon, Powers, and Wetzler 2009). Working with the World Food Program, Save mobilized food aid for more than 50,000 vulnerable people, to support them through the hunger season to the next harvest. Distribution was managed by the groups established by Save, which reinforced ties between community members and the value of the farmers and *animadora* groups (Chaiken, Dixon, and Herminio 2012). In focus group interviews, several respondents noted the importance of these community groups, as they oversaw the critical distribution of food aid and ensured equitable local access to these much-needed resources.

## EARLY PROGRAM IMPLEMENTATION

### Farmers' Groups

Beginning in 2000, farmers' groups were established by Save extentionists, each of whom provided technical assistance to the volunteer members and helped them obtain improved planting stocks. The farmers' groups invited interested participants (men and women) to work together to cultivate plots of cassava that had proven resistant to CBSV and learn improved agricultural techniques. The improved planting stock was then distributed among the participants for replanting on their individual farms. Participation was voluntary and without remuneration. Each farmer group oversaw the management of their subsistence farm plot. Today, upward of 45,000 families in six coastal districts are growing disease-tolerant cassava as a direct result of the project, adding tens of thousands of tons of food to the project area (Chaiken, Dixon, and Herminio 2012). Research indicates that the majority of those planting the improved material also pass on cuttings to family members, friends, or neighbors. A survey found that respondents who've had the material for at least a season in their fields subsequently distributed the cuttings to an average of three or four other people, illustrating an indigenous scaling-up of the project (Chaiken, Dixon, and Herminio 2012).

Our focus group interviews demonstrated that local people who belonged to farmers groups valued both the collective enterprise and the training they received. Comments included the following:

> We have learned it is good to work in groups and we share the harvest. Theresa [the extentionist] doesn't take the harvest away from us, we trust her [reference to the seized harvests produced on communal plots during the period of compulsory villagization].
>
> I like to work with the group in our *mashamba* [garden, farm] and I enjoy what I have learned about planting, I receive seed now to plant, and I am even learning about nutrition.
>
> By joining this group I was able to get *nikwahya* [improved cassava variety]. Not everyone joined in the first year, but after they saw the good harvest and the sweet cassava that we grew, others joined our group.

The fact that local people have successfully participated in these groups has helped rebuild trust and collaboration within the communities, where the traditional labor groups had ceased to function.

### Mothers' Groups

The other community-based groups are organized by women (known as *animadoras*), who volunteer to be trained to become the facilitators of women's groups, which focus on healthful practices. These *animadoras* participate in several days of training, where they learn about child feeding practices, treatments for common illnesses, prenatal care, family planning, HIV prevention, oral rehydration techniques, hygiene, and other topics related to the health, nutrition, and well-being of community members, especially children. As in the farmer groups, the women are unpaid volunteers. However, they did receive a baseball cap and *kapulana** as compensation for their service, as well as meals provided during the training period. Each woman then establishes one or more women's groups in their communities, with a dozen participants per group. They meet weekly for a "lesson" on one of the topics that the *animadora* learned about during her training.

Both of these programs rely heavily on community-based participation for activities and recruitment of the next group of participants. This ensures local buy-in and input into the emphases and directions of the program activities. As with the growth in use of improved planting materials, the number of women participating in the Save programs, either as an *animadora* or in a group, grew exponentially as the project became established. Consequently, the funding continued to a second phase. In the first phase of funding, fewer than 200 women were trained as *animadoras*. They recruited about 5000 women to participate in mothers' groups. In the second phase of the project, the number of women participating in training grew to 1800. They, in turn, established 3600 mothers' groups with more than 54,000 participants (Chaiken, Dixon, and Herminio 2012).

*Animadoras* and participants in their groups reported high satisfaction with the program and with what they were learning. Comments included the following:

> I learned to add ground peanuts, sesame, and coconut oil to porridge [which makes] babies fatter, and I learned about growth monitoring to see if a child is growing well.
>
> I see differences now. We used to not establish breastfeeding immediately after birth, but now we know to breastfeed and also how to space children through family planning, so each child will grow well.
>
> We learned many things [listed lessons from *animadora*]...we know these are good practices not just because we learned this from our *animadora*, but because we have observed these ourselves.

While it is impossible to know how many of these improved practices, especially in child feeding, were routinely utilized, in every focus group, the women were able to accurately recite the health messages that had originally been taught to the *animadora*. One particularly encouraging element was the inclusion of grandmothers in the groups. This is important, as they can become allies for young mothers who sometimes face opposition for altering traditional feeding practices in favor of new lessons learned.

## SUCCESSIVE PROGRAM IMPLEMENTATION: BUILDING ADDITIONAL COMMUNITY-BASED GROUPS

The ongoing research made it clear that, while traditional cultural safety nets and cooperation had disappeared, new patterns of collaboration had emerged as a consequence of the programs implemented by Save. Two additional projects were developed to help address economic vulnerability and build on the earlier impact. The first program, *Ajuda Mútua* (*AM*) (Mutual Aid), encourages farmers to establish rotating, reciprocal labor groups to make the most difficult tasks more manageable. One of the key benefits of this program is access to adequate labor at critical junctures in the agricultural cycle. This allows households to cultivate larger tracts of farmland and produce more food, even when they lack assets to hire additional labor.

The program is based on the assumption that the most powerful asset that Mozambican farmers have is their labor power. Thus, the lack of a sufficient labor force is one of the major production

---

* It is common throughout east and southern Africa for women to use a large colorful cloth to cover their clothes, serve as an apron, or to wrap up bundles. Called *kapulanas* locally, these have colorful designs and often display a moral saying or motto. The *kapulanas* distributed to the *animadora* volunteers were all identical and had a message in Portuguese about preventing HIV/AIDS.

constraints. To address this, each group is composed of four or five households. The labor is organized in a rotating system that requires all members to work for one household on a given day, for a different household the following work day, and so forth, until all of the households in the group have been repaid for their labor. Each household retains all of the crops grown on their land and does not have to share with those who helped with the cultivation. This pattern, often called fiesta labor, is similar to the *mori* practices that were common in earlier generations. Within a few years after introducing the *AM* program, the demand to participate increased. By 2011, there were 800 *AM* groups with a total of 4000 participants, of which 60% were women (Chaiken, Dixon, and Herminio 2012).

A second program has established village-based savings and loan programs (VSL) to increase assets. The program provides a mechanism for rural households to save money and receive credit in a transparent, structured, and self-managed environment within their community. There are few, if any, opportunities for rural households in Nampula to obtain credit or save their earnings in banks or formal financial institutions. Credit is necessary for purchasing farming inputs and starting small enterprises. Savings are essential for dealing with shocks and limiting the negative effects of the annual hunger season, which emerges as their farm produce is depleted.

Village Savings and Loan groups consist of 15–30 self-selected individuals who contribute regularly to a savings account for their future use. They also contribute to a fund that makes loans to group members. Each group meets weekly to deposit their pledged amount. The cash is held in a lock box that is owned by the group. Because of the transparency and peer motivation, members continue to make these weekly deposits. The lock box is stored at the home of one of the members; each box requires two different keys to open it, which are held by two different group members. The box can only be opened if both keys are used. Thus, each member has the confidence that their savings cannot be touched by any other member of the group. At a specified time, typically after 6 to 12 months, each member gets back all of the money that they have saved. While participants do not earn interest as they might with a formal financial organization, they do have the peer support to continue to save small amounts of money over a long period. This permits them to accumulate enough of a reserve to make a large purchase or investment.

Save collaborated with the Mozambican national nongovernmental organization Ophavela to expand the availability of VSL groups. Between the two organizations, they have fostered the establishment of more than 4000 of these, with nearly 67,000 people participating (Chaiken, Dixon, and Herminio 2012). In our interviews, participants reported that they made improvements in the quality of their homes and made small purchases to make life more comfortable. Others are using their savings to make long-term investments in the future of their families through education for their children, by establishing small-scale income generating activities and by expanding the size of their farm plots (Chaiken, Dixon, and Herminio 2012).

## POSSIBLE NEXT STEPS

While both *Ajuda Mútua* and VSLs are relatively new approaches, these programs have promise for addressing the needs of these communities by building on local strengths, given that programmatic successes are possible only with strong buy-in and local participation. These accomplishments and the rapid scaling up of these community-based programs suggest that this would provide an ideal context in which to introduce CEWS. These programs are based on the understanding that local people are keenly aware of their own sources of strength and resilience; they are observant of conditions around them that might indicate threats to their wellbeing. Thus, as droughts emerge or crop pests proliferate, local people engage in a wide variety of predictable and observable compensatory behaviors to try to mitigate the impacts of these challenges.

In a CEWS program, as envisioned in the Appendix, local communities determine which compensatory behaviors are most common and indicative of stress. They identify the threshold at which the frequency of such behaviors denotes a low-grade, chronic problem versus an acute crisis. The Appendix includes a wide array of behaviors of individuals, households, and communities that indicate accelerating food stress and vulnerability. These indicators have been derived from extensive fieldwork and design of surveys throughout the developing world. It is intended as a starting point for discussions rather than representing a complete and inclusive list that is appropriate in all contexts. In implementing a CEWS program, each community must decide which behaviors are most relevant to monitor, given local resources, ecology, culture, and climate. Implementation of the CEWS will require extensive community discussion about which variables are the most sensitive indicators of food stress and then designate a team of volunteers to track these key variables. Monitoring can be done at a household or community level, or both.

While this proposal is linked to the specific context of northern Mozambique and the effective program implementation by Save, the principles of CEWS implementation and the list of compensatory behaviors outlined in the Appendix have applicability in a wide range of situations of shock and vulnerability. The goal remains to fine tune our understanding of behaviors indicative of growing vulnerability. By monitoring the emergence of these compensatory activities, we can increase the likelihood of mitigating negative effects.

Raising awareness at the local level of an emerging crisis can help with mitigation. This awareness can encourage locals to link with regional and national governments and other support services in their areas (e.g., nongovernmental organizations and/or faith-based organizations) to address the root causes of this increasing vulnerability. The CEWS approach complements existing bottom–up, grassroots, participatory collaboration within communities to enhance resilience and reduce vulnerability to food shortages. In all of the existing programs, Save provided the needed catalyst for improvements in well-being. However, the ultimate success of these programs is clearly a product of local participation and buy-in. Stated more eloquently, in the words of famed anthropologist Margaret Mead, the people of rural Mozambique are demonstrating that they typify the "small group of thoughtful, committed citizens who are doing their best to change their world" (Mead 2016).

## REFERENCES

Bonate, L.J.K. 2006. Matriliny, Islam, and gender in northern Mozambique. *Journal of Religion in Africa* 36(2): 139–166.

Chaiken, M.S. 2004. Debriefing report. Washington, DC: Save the Children/U.S. Consultancy Report.

______. 2007. Wealth, inequality, vulnerability, and coping strategies: Conditions of hunger and food security in Nampula Province. Washington, DC: Save the Children/US Mozambique Program, Consultancy Report.

Chaiken, M.S., J.R. Dixon, and A. Herminio. 2012. Food sovereignty and safety nets: NGOs in Northern Mozambique. *Bulletin of the Association of Concerned Africa Scholars* 88(Fall): 20–25. http://concernedafricascholars.org/bulletin/issue88/, accessed February 5, 2016.

Chaiken, M.S., J.R. Dixon, C. Powers, and E. Wetzler. 2009. Asking the right questions: Community-based strategies to combat hunger. *National Association for the Practice of Anthropology Bulletin* 32(Supp. 1): 42–54.

Mead, M. 2016. Used with permission from the Mead Trust. Sevanne Kassarjian, Secretary. New York.

Pitcher, M.A. 1998. Disruption without transformation: Agrarian relations and livelihoods in Nampula Province, Mozambique 1975–1995. *Journal of Southern African Studies* 24(1): 115–140.

## APPENDIX: CHECK SHEET OF INDICATORS FOR COMMUNITY-BASED EARLY WARNING SYSTEMS

The behavioral responses to stress summarized here reflect a synthesis of experiences in conducting fieldwork in chronically food insecure and impoverished rural communities throughout East and Southern Africa and Southeast Asia. The specific compensatory behaviors that are most relevant for any given context are to be determined by community members, following discussions of their specific nature of resilience and vulnerability. This list, while substantial, is not exhaustive. It is intended to be a starting place for community-level discussions. Identifying the most relevant trigger indicators to monitor is the first step in creating a CEWS approach; it is effective only when the community can create a follow-on plan of response to address accelerating vulnerability. The CEWS approach is intended to be the first step in creating webs of support within and beyond the community level.

| Trigger Indicator | Behaviors to Monitor: Household Level |
|---|---|
| Reduce demand for food | Are children or elderly dependents being sent to live elsewhere?<br>Is the frequency of meal consumption/day reduced?<br>Are portion sizes altered?<br>Are select food resources directed at some household members (e.g., head of household) and withheld from others (e.g., women)?<br>Are family members participating in activities solely because food is provided (e.g., school lunch provisioning, ritual celebrations)? |
| Reduction in quality of foods consumed | Is there a decline in consumption of foods of animal origin (meat, fish, dairy products)?<br>Are low-status foods consumed more often (root crops, broken or off-color grains, foods that are indicative of poverty)?<br>Has dietary diversity decreased?<br>Are wild and gathered foods replacing cultivated and purchased foods?<br>Are people relying only on what they can produce themselves because they have no cash to purchase desirable market goods?<br>Have people stopped consuming foods that are purchased in the market (sugar, tea)?<br>Are people eating seeds that they had been saving for replanting? |
| Forgoing consumption of high-value crops in favor of sales | Are high-value crops that would normally be consumed at home (e.g., rice, maize) being sold in the market and substituted in home consumption with low value foods (e.g., root crops, bananas, sorghum)?<br>Is land that was formerly used for subsistence crop production being diverted to produce high-value crops for sale?<br>Are farmers forgoing subsistence production and focusing on cash crops exclusively? |
| Loss of traditional risk-sharing mechanisms and social support groups | Are religious or social events that require gift giving being eliminated?<br>Are people who are perceived to be wealthy attempting to hide wealth from fellow community members?<br>Are traditional practices that increase support networks for children (e.g., good parenting) declining in frequency?<br>Is there an increase in divorces or spouses being abandoned?<br>Is there an increase in conducting activities that are illegal, dangerous, or socially unacceptable (e.g., brewing illegal alcohol, prostitution, theft)?<br>Are people begging when it is not the norm? |
| Increase in child labor/ reduction of school attendance | Are children being withdrawn from school to perform labor on farm or for remuneration?<br>Are girls selectively withdrawn from school in favor of allowing male children to attend?<br>Are children withdrawn from school at time when fees are due?<br>Are children not attending school because the family can no longer afford school supplies or uniforms? |

| Trigger Indicator | Behaviors to Monitor: Household Level |
|---|---|
| Indications of increased social stress within community | Have there been instances of accusations of malevolent supernatural acts (e.g., witchcraft)?<br>Have individuals or families developed feuds or tense relations where amicable relations existed in the past?<br>Is there an increase in people consulting shamans, traditional religious practitioners, or diviners?<br>Have men left home in pursuit of wage labor?<br>Are children being taken out of school and used to perform wage labor?<br>Are people who typically save money or food for lean times unable to do so (e.g., cessation of contributions to community savings programs, cessation of rotating credit)?<br>Are people selling livestock?<br>Are livestock being sold at a loss?<br>Are people selling large assets that are important for food production (e.g., draft animals, farm machinery, canoes or fishing boats)?<br>Are people selling small assets due to need for immediate and ready cash (e.g., kitchen items, doors, clothing, chickens)?<br>Have people been seen going through refuse in search of food or saleable items? |
| Loss of traditional food-sharing practices | In many communities, sharing of food, especially wild game, is a traditional practice. Are there accusations of stinginess and failure to share?<br>Do people disguise when they are eating in order to avoid requests for sharing of foods?<br>Do people pretend not to be home so they will not have to provide refreshments to visitors (e.g., coffee or tea with sugar, meals)?<br>Have neighbors and relatives ceased traditional food-sharing practices? |
| Redirection of expenditures away from discretionary items to food | Are household items that are commonly purchased no longer found in households due to cost (e.g., sugar, soap, coffee or tea, tobacco, lantern oil)?<br>Are families avoiding activities that might incur a cost (e.g., attending a religious ceremony that requires a contribution, visiting kin with expectation of bringing a gift)? |
| Indebtedness to family member | Have normal intrafamilial patterns of sharing been stretched to point of family members owing food, money, or labor to other close kin?<br>Have other family members taken a household's major assets as collateral against indebtedness? |
| Indebtedness to non-family member | Have non-family members (merchants, money lenders, traders) given advances to a family with the promise of a significant share of future harvests?<br>Do individuals have obligations for work to non-family members that are paid in food rations during hunger season?<br>Have non-family members taken major assets as collateral against indebtedness? |

| Trigger Indicator | Behaviors to Monitor: Community and Regional Level |
|---|---|
| Changes in patterns of use for communally managed resources | Are there arguments over access to communally managed resources such as grazing areas, wells, forest reserves?<br>Is there greater scarcity of a community managed resource?<br>Has anyone attempted to seize control over a communally managed resource?<br>Have people reduced size of livestock herds, or substituted small animals (goats, sheep) for large animals (cows, oxen, water buffalo)?<br>Has livestock care become onerous due to lack of labor (herders) or grazing areas?<br>Have there been significant changes in the ways technology related to food production is utilized (e.g., changes in rules and access to irrigation water, shared equipment)?<br>Have areas traditionally valued and reserved for communally important activities been converted to food production or been destroyed (e.g., planting food crops on cemeteries or park lands, destruction of sacred groves of trees for fuel wood sales)? |

(*Continued*)

| Trigger Indicator | Behaviors to Monitor: Community and Regional Level |
|---|---|
| Changes in markets and market practices | Are common foods that are usually readily available more scarce? |
| | Has the price of staple foods risen significantly? |
| | Are market vendors being pressured to extend credit or increase credit to customers? |
| | Are people obtaining market products with the promise of repayment with high rates of interest and/or shares of the next year's harvest? |
| | Has there been an increase in people attempting to sell resources that are typically commonly held goods (e.g., increases in firewood or charcoal sales, bundles of fodder)? |
| | Have local people offered to barter their assets in exchange for food items? |
| Local governmental and community responses | Have local leaders been ousted from their positions due to stress over resource availability or become suddenly more powerful due to their influence? |
| | Have wealthy people been elevated in their influence due to local food stress? |
| | Are wealthy people creating patron-client relationships? |
| | Have religious or social groups attempted to marshal resources for the benefit of community members? |
| | Has there been an increase in religious activities intended to invoke divine assistance to address current problems (e.g., praying for rain, exorcisms or sacrifices to defeat malevolent supernatural forces)? |
| | Do local leaders perceive an increase in the length or severity of hunger seasons? |
| | Have political leaders attempted to gain support or raise awareness among regional or provincial governmental agencies that may be called upon for assistance? |
| | Have political leaders attempted to gain support from any humanitarian groups that are active in their area to address local needs? |
| Other community-level responses | Is there a cessation of traditional rotating credit groups or other financial support institutions (e.g., village savings and loan, microfinance)? |
| | Are people depleting assets that had been saved, stockpiled? |
| | Have people stopped using services that were once valued because of costs associated with them (e.g., healers, clinics, craftsmen, builders)? |
| | Have families begun to move away from the area due to resource scarcity? |
| | Is there an increase in migration or transients? |
| | Is there increasing competition for wage or piecework labor that has very low remuneration (e.g., weaving thatch, transporting sand or gravel by hand, collecting wild resources)? |
| | Has there been warfare, conflict in the area? |
| | Have there been kidnappings or extortions when this practice is normally rare or absent? |
| | Have young people joined military or religious orders because it ensures access to food? |
| | Have young people joined militias or separatist/rebel groups due to their dissatisfaction with the current conditions? |
| Monitoring local and regional environmental conditions | Has there been some sort of natural disaster recently that affected food access? |
| | Have new crop pests or diseases appeared in the area in recent years? |
| | Have people shifted the types of crops produced in response to plan disease epidemics or increases in crop pests? |

# *Policy, Evaluation, and "Best Practice" Models*

The chapters in this subsection focus on evaluating existing policies. They take a "lessons learned/ best practice" approach, using case studies to frame policy evaluations and to generate recommendations to build stronger responses and preventative measures at a variety of levels. These recommendations can enhance the pace of recovery and reduce personal, household, and community experiences of trauma by improving communication structures, mitigating risk prior to the occurrence of an event, accounting for cultural factors, including animal companions in response, and protecting culturally unique social groups from exploitation.

# 6 Accessing Disaster Recovery Resource Information

## *Reliance on Social Capital in the Aftermath of Hurricane Sandy*

*Jason D. Rivera*

## CONTENTS



**Abstract**

This chapter explores how disaster survivors with very limited natural disaster experience accessed information about potential recovery resources in the aftermath of Hurricane Sandy. Based on focus groups with New Jersey residents, I find that, despite official reports documenting Federal Emergency Management Agency strategies to disseminate information, many individuals were not reached. Instead, they had to rely on social networks for information. Policy recommendations are offered as a means of promoting social capital development. These can be maximized and utilized to educate the public about their vulnerability to natural disasters and provide the potential resources available to them should they fall victim to a future event.

## INTRODUCTION

Social capital refers to connections between people, such as their social networks, and the norms of reciprocity and trustworthiness that develop alongside or as a byproduct of these connections (Putnam 2001). Bourdieu (1986), Coleman (1988), and Putnam (2001) all maintain that social capital is a resource that community members can utilize to facilitate and pursue mutually beneficial interests. Although there are a variety of advantages that stem from having a diffuse and diverse social network, social capital is of prime importance when individuals are attempting to access information on disaster recovery resources (Rivera and Nickels 2014).

Researchers argue that both dense and diffuse social networks can serve as sources of informational support in disaster settings (Aldrich 2010, 2012; Chamlee-Wright and Storr 2009; Kaniasty and Norris 2000; Peguero 2006; Rivera and Nickels 2014). In these situations, social capital has the ability to increase information diffusion about evacuation orders, response efforts, and vulnerability that can decrease overall losses when traditional government sources of information are inaccessible, not trusted, or generally lacking. Social networks also have the ability to more easily disseminate information about disaster recovery resources and other things that disaster victims and their families might find important (Aldrich 2012; Chamlee-Wright and Storr 2009; Elliott, Haney, and Sams-Abiodun 2010; Hawkins and Maurer 2010; Messias, Barrington, and Lacy 2012; Peguero 2006; Rivera and Nickels 2014). Despite the growing literature on the use of social capital in disaster recovery, most studies pay little attention to how, when, and why disaster survivors in the United States rely on social networks to access information on governmental resources.

According to Katungi, Edmeades, and Smale (2008), social capital enhances information diffusion in two ways. First, it reduces the cost of information acquisition because it can be obtained passively through social interactions or actively by individuals that already know one another. Second, social capital overcomes some questions about the reliability of information, due to dissemination among and between people that typically trust one another. Researchers argue that these informational benefits are particularly evident in communities characterized by a historic lack of governmental concern and marginalization, which has physically and psychologically isolated populations to the point where they distrust information from formal government authorities (Chamlee-Wright and Storr 2009; Elliott, Haney, and Sams-Abiodun 2010; Messias, Barrington, and Lacy 2012; Peguero 2006). Additionally, these researchers maintain that nonmarginalized communities have a greater tendency to rely on governmental sources for information on impending disaster events and recovery resources, placing less reliance on social capital for their particular needs. Individuals who are better positioned to access information, such as those that are more highly educated, have reliable access to the internet, and/or who know individuals that work in public safety professions, stand a higher probability of knowing about and accessing disaster recovery resources. What is suggested across all these studies is that, although access to disaster recovery information differs across segments of society, it is readily available to the public if one were to proactively search for it.

The studies discussed above pay little attention to how, when, and why disaster survivors in the United States rely on social networks to access information on governmental resources. To address this gap in the literature, this research explores how social capital was used to learn about resources available to disaster victims in the aftermath of Hurricane Sandy in New Jersey. First, a brief description of Hurricane Sandy and its impact on New Jersey is presented. A discussion of the information dissemination strategies used by the Federal Emergency Management Agency (FEMA) in the aftermath of Sandy follows, along with the agency's perspective on social capital in disaster recovery. Finally, findings and potential policy recommendations that could be developed to enhance social capital utility in the aftermath of disasters are presented.

## HURRICANE SANDY AND NEW JERSEY

Sandy was the 10th named hurricane during the 2012 hurricane season, developing in the southwest region of the Caribbean on October 22. Before making landfall, Sandy produced severe flooding along the Atlantic Coast from Florida to Maine as it moved north. The storm affected states as far inland as West Virginia, Ohio, and Indiana. The highest storm surges and greatest inundation on land occurred along the coast of central and northern New Jersey, Staten Island, and the southward-facing shores of Long Island in New York, and in Connecticut. On the morning of October 29, the storm's trajectory shifted northeast toward southern New Jersey. By that evening, Sandy made landfall near Brigantine, New Jersey, as a post–tropical cyclone with winds up to 80 miles per hour.

In New Jersey, the highest storm surge was 8.57 feet above normal tide levels. However, according to Blake, Kimberlain, Berg, Cangialosi, and Beven (2013), this is likely a very conservative estimate, with the actual storm surge being much higher. Water levels were highest along the northern portion of the Jersey Shore in Monmouth and Ocean Counties, north of where Sandy made landfall. Barrier islands were almost completely inundated in some locations. Some areas were entirely breached by storm surge, with large waves from the Atlantic Ocean meeting with rising waters from back bays. In the northern part of the state, storm tide measurements ranged from 4 to 9 feet in Monmouth and Middlesex Counties and as high as 2 to 4 feet in Atlantic and Cape May Counties (Blake, Kimberlain, Berg, Cangialosi, and Beven 2013).

The damages inflicted on the New Jersey coast were unprecedented in the state's history. According to Governor Chris Christie, "I've called this experience New Jersey's Katrina because the damage to our state is nothing that we've experienced ever before" (Drewniak 2013, p. 1). Although the entire state was affected, the most severe damage was sustained in Monmouth and Ocean Counties. Entire communities were "inundated with water and sand, houses were washed from their foundations, boardwalks were dismantled or destroyed, cars were tossed about, and boats were pushed well inland from the coast" (Blake, Kimberlain, Berg, Cangialosi, and Beven 2013, p. 17). Power outages lasted for weeks in some communities, affecting about 5 million residents. In February 2013, the Governor's Office reported that 346,000 housing units had either been damaged or destroyed, with 22,000 of those units being classified as uninhabitable. In the private sector, 19,000 businesses sustained damages of $250,000 or more and total business losses were estimated at $8.3 billion. Additionally, Sandy ruptured natural gas lines, causing fires in some areas, contributing to the loss of housing units. Power and gas line repairs were estimated to cost about $1 billion and repairs to waste, water, and sewer services were estimated at another $3 billion. Overall, the Governor's Office estimated the cost of returning the state to normalcy to be upward of $36.9 billion (Drewniak 2013).

## FEMA'S RESPONSE AND INFORMATION DISSEMINATION STRATEGIES

The importance of social networks has been acknowledged by FEMA for many years as a means of disseminating important information among the public. In his statement to the Senate Subcommittee on Homeland Security and Governmental Affairs and the Subcommittee on Disaster Recovery and Intergovernmental Affairs, Craig Fugate (Fugate 2011, p. 2) maintains "The notion of treating the public as a resource rather than a liability is at the heart of our emergency management framework." In line with this perspective, during the aftermath of Sandy, FEMA reports setting up neighborhood task forces and disaster recovery centers (DRCs), arranging 55 town hall meetings, reaching 5000 people, reaching out to third-sector organizations, and supporting Voluntary Organizations Active in Disasters to disseminate information about disaster recovery to survivors (FEMA 2013).

The agency, alongside the American Red Cross and the US Department of Veterans Affairs, created a smartphone application to provide information about the storm and where shelters could be located. According to FEMA (2013), this phone application was downloaded by 55,000 users. Finally, they used Facebook, Twitter, and YouTube to disseminate disaster response and recovery information (FEMA 2013). Their intent was to provide information about disaster recovery to a segment of the affected population on the assumption that it would then be dispersed throughout the survivor population through social networks. However, FEMA admits that the use of these technological platforms was vulnerable to widespread power and cell phone outages that plagued the disaster area (FEMA 2013).

FEMA states that the agency's response to Hurricane Sandy was generally successful, despite several challenges. The first set of challenges was caused by inexperienced staff and insufficient management, which was magnified by the volume of personnel deployed. For example, many of those deployed had only taken a three-hour training course, more than 70% of the personnel were new to their assignments, and half had no prior disaster experience. As a result, many lacked the confidence to perform their assignments, and some were unprepared to answer questions by survivors in reference to FEMA's own programs (FEMA 2013).

The second challenge involved the DRCs, where survivors could go and get information about and register for disaster assistance. They were not oriented to efficiently meet survivor needs. According to FEMA (2013, p. 21), the process of seeking assistance at a DRC required people to repeat the same information to multiple individuals, resulting in frustration and a lengthy process. DRCs were also not consistent in the services they provided to survivors, nor were they effectively placed in locations that were easily accessible by the public. Moreover, FEMA (2013) reported that many DRCs were not specifically customized to the needs of the local community. As a result, disaster assistance seekers occasionally encountered language barriers, variation in the quality of information provided to them by disaster recovery personnel, and even an inability to get to where DRCs were located due to transportation being compromised by flooding. All of these factors contributed to individuals being further inhibited from understanding FEMA's disaster recovery programs and how to apply for assistance.

Finally, FEMA provided services to survivors through three National Processing Service Centers. These were responsible for answering questions about and registering individuals for disaster assistance. Even though the call centers processed over half a million assistance applications, the agency reports that the centers could not keep up with the pace of survivors' requests for information. Immediately after the storm, there were more than 235,000 call attempts. However, 38% of these calls were deflected by an automated message instructing callers to refer to FEMA's website for information or to call back at a later time (FEMA 2013, p. 21). This left many people in a situation in which they had neither access to information about potential resources nor any historical experience to help guide them on how to recover from a disaster (Rivera 2014). This raises the following question: through whom did survivors learn about disaster recovery resources?

## METHODS

To explore the process of how Hurricane Sandy survivors gathered disaster recovery information, two regional focus groups were conducted (Belzile and Öberg 2012; Marková, Linell, Grossen, and Salazar-Orvig 2007; Morgan 1997): one for northern New Jersey and one for southern New Jersey. To increase the probability of contacting an individual being affected by Sandy, the sampling frame was confined to three municipalities in the north (Long Branch, Asbury Park, and Ocean Township) and three municipalities in the south (Atlantic City, Brigantine, and Pleasantville). These cities were chosen because they are located on the coast, and they all experienced similar disaster affects, such as damages due to flooding, storm surge, and windshear. The Eagelton Institute of Politics was hired to help recruit participants for the focus groups. Random digit dial (RDD) samples were developed independently for the northern and southern focus groups, including both cell phone and landline numbers. To the extent possible, the RDD samples were developed within the communities that were identified for investigation. Once a household was reached, a random process was used to identify one adult in the household to speak with. After expressing willingness to be interviewed, potential participants were screened for (1) living in the same community when Sandy hit, (2) having experienced damage to owned or rented property during Sandy, and (3) having filed a FEMA claim. This ensured that they had some level of experience with the FEMA aid process and had learned about FEMA assistance in some way. Those meeting all three criteria were solicited for participation in a focus group. Those who agreed were asked for detailed contact and demographic information.

Calling continued until at least 25 potential participants were identified for each focus group. A total of 6239 phone numbers were dialed; 685 of these resulted in respondents willing to begin the screening survey. Among those beginning the screening, 68 were not in an appropriate zip code, 249 reported no Sandy damage, 186 did not live in the location during Sandy, and 100 had not filed a FEMA application. This left 56 potential participants for focus group recruiting. In the northern region, 25 individuals expressed interest in participating in the project and 31 expressed interest in the southern region.

Throughout the recruiting process, every effort was made to attract a diverse set of individuals to participate. To incentivize participation, a $30 cash stipend was offered. Prior to the focus group administration, 11 individuals, 6 self-identified as white and 5 as African American, confirmed their attendance in the northern region. In the southern region, 16 confirmed attendance, with 10 self-identified as white and 6 as African American. The northern focus group was held at the Long Branch Free Public Library in Long Branch, New Jersey, and the southern focus group was held at the William J. Hughes Center for Public Policy at Stockton University in Galloway Township, New Jersey. These locations were chosen due to their centrality within each study area and their ease of accessibility by public transportation.

A hybrid of scoping (Belzile and Öberg 2012; Morgan 1997) and theory-building (Jarrett 1993; Marková, Linell, Grossen, and Salazar-Orvig 2007; Morgan 2012) focus group administration techniques were utilized. Aspects of scoping focus group techniques include using a stimulus survey, then developing structured questions prior to the meetings to guide group discussions. Some questions used to stimulate discussion among participants included the following: "Could you please briefly tell us how Hurricane Sandy affected you?" and "Could you provide a rough estimate of the damages inflicted on your home by Hurricane Sandy?" Focus group questions were structured. However, once discussion on a topic was initiated, the moderator allowed the conversation to be fluid among participants, only guiding the discussion if the participants strayed too far from the initial topic.

Participants were encouraged to express themselves in their own words. When the moderator was unclear about meaning, the participant was asked to explain and provide examples. Each focus group lasted approximately one and a half hours. Both focus groups were audio recorded for future transcription and analysis. A framework analysis (Ritchie and Spencer 2002) was used to analyze the data. Thematic categories were identified, based on the statements made by participants. The data were then indexed by highlighting and sorting out quotes within each thematic category to make comparisons among and between the focus groups. Finally, the charting of data was performed, which entails moving participants' quotes from their original context and re-arranging them under the thematic categories developed in the second step of this analytical approach (Krueger 1994).

## ANALYSIS

Table 6.1 documents the descriptive statistics of the focus group participants. The day the northern focus group was held, 90% of the participants were African American and only one participant was white. This composition was unexpected, based on previous confirmation. In the southern focus group, although 16 individuals had confirmed attendance, only 6 participated. The southern focus group was more racially balanced than the northern group, with half the group self-identifying as African American and the other half self-identifying as white. Since the topics under discussion were not of a sensitive or controversial nature, the group composition was perceived to minimally skew the generation of data (Morgan 1997).

Participants were asked how they had heard about FEMA's assistance programs. One way was through organized events that were held in respective community centers. A male participant from Atlantic City reports,

> Generally it's the convention centers.... FEMA was in the new convention center. They [FEMA] had at least 30 partners inside the convention center where you would just go in and they would tell you, these are partners of FEMA. Some were not FEMA per se, but because people were looking for different things individuals directed you to different partners.

However, 87.5% of participants indicated that they had learned about the events through their own social networks and neighbors. Only two participants reported learning about these activities over the radio, on television, or through some other type of traditional communication/news media outlet. Roughly 96% of participants, regardless of race and socioeconomic status, emphasized that they had never received any information from FEMA in reference to what to do or how to begin the assistance application process.

**TABLE 6.1**
**Comparison of Focus Group Composition (*N* = 16)**

| Variable | Frequency | | % of Sample | |
|---|---|---|---|---|
| | Northern Group | Southern Group | Northern Group | Southern Group |
| ***Race*** | | | | |
| White | 1 | 3 | 10.0% | 50.0% |
| African American | 9 | 3 | 90.0% | 50.0% |
| ***Age*** | | | | |
| 26 to 34 years old | 0 | 1 | 0.0% | 16.6% |
| 35 to 44 years old | 1 | 1 | 10.0% | 16.6% |
| 45 to 54 years old | 2 | 1 | 20.0% | 16.6% |
| 55 to 64 years old | 2 | 2 | 20.0% | 33.3% |
| 65+ years old | 5 | 1 | 50.0% | 16.6% |
| ***Marital Status*** | | | | |
| Married | 6 | 3 | 60.0% | 50.0% |
| Single | 1 | 2 | 10.0% | 33.3% |
| Divorced/separated | 2 | 1 | 20.0% | 16.6% |
| Refused | 1 | 0 | 10.0% | 0.0% |
| ***Employment Status*** | | | | |
| Unemployed | 3 | 1 | 30.0% | 16.6% |
| On medical or disability leave | 1 | 0 | 10.0% | 0.0% |
| Employed full-time | 5 | 5 | 50.0% | 83.3% |
| Refused | 1 | 0 | 10.0% | 0.0% |
| ***Educational Attainment*** | | | | |
| Some high school | 1 | 0 | 10.0% | 0.0% |
| High school diploma | 1 | 0 | 10.0% | 0.0% |
| Some college, no degree | 4 | 1 | 40.0% | 16.6% |
| Associate's degree | 2 | 1 | 20.0% | 16.6% |
| Bachelor's degree | 1 | 2 | 10.0% | 33.3% |
| Master's degree | 0 | 2 | 0.0% | 33.3% |
| Refused | 1 | 0 | 10.0% | 0.0% |
| ***Household Income*** | | | | |
| Less than $25,000 | 1 | 0 | 10.0% | 0.0% |
| $25,000 to $34,999 | 2 | 0 | 20.0% | 0.0% |
| $35,000 to $49,999 | 2 | 2 | 20.0% | 33.3% |
| $50,000 to $74,999 | 1 | 2 | 10.0% | 33.3% |
| $75,000 to $99,999 | 2 | 2 | 20.0% | 33.3% |
| $100,000 to $124,999 | 2 | 0 | 20.0% | 0.0% |
| ***Gender*** | | | | |
| Male | 6 | 4 | 60.0% | 66.6% |
| Female | 4 | 2 | 40.0% | 33.3% |

Although all participants indicated their reliance on social networks for information on disaster assistance programs, some of the northern participants did hear about FEMA programs over the radio and in the newspaper. However, this information proved problematic. One participant notes,

> Last year, it was in the Asbury Park Press that there was a grant to assist you with repairing your home and you wouldn't have to repay the grant if you stayed in your home for a period of time. However, the day that [this information was in the paper], was the day after the deadline for the grant had passed. 'Cause of this they extended the deadline, but they only extended the deadline from July 30th to July 31st. Now what is that supposed to do for people that have difficulties finding transportation?

In response to this account, another African American participant commented,

> Yeah, and then a lot of the offices where you were supposed to apply to that grant were shut down, and the ones that were left [open] were like in places that you couldn't even get to.

The northern focus group specifically highlighted the ineffectiveness of various media outlets to provide information about where and when to access disaster assistance resources. These sentiments were shared by the southern focus group. One verbal exchange within the southern focus group between an African American participant and a white participant documented this dynamic.

> [African American participant]: By the time you heard that those organizations would be at the [Atlantic City] convention center or at the community center or wherever, on the radio, you had to move heaven and earth to go. They advertised the events publicly at the last minute. It was like they didn't actually want people to show up.
>
> [White participant]: Actually, the [Brigantine] community center placed flyers on their doors about a week before they held their events.
>
> [African American participant]: Ok, yeah, but you had to go there to actually see the advertisement. The public, the actual public wasn't told about when the stuff was happening. You had to go and find the information out yourself. And by the time you found out it was either after the fact or you had to be there later that day.

Participants provided accounts about learning about disaster assistance programs by "word of mouth" through their own family members and/or personal social networks. One white female respondent from Brigantine explained that she had learned about relief organizations in her respective community center through one of her friend's Facebook posts. One male and one female respondent from Long Branch indicated that,

> [Man]: ...believe it or not, my daughter lives in Pennsylvania, she calls me up and tells me, because she works for the state, that I should apply to FEMA for help. I don't know how she [found] out, but she knew about what was going on in New Jersey better than I did.
>
> [Woman]: Yeah, my son was in Ohio and he gave me more information than anything I was able to get a hold of here.

An exchange between two African American participants from the northern focus group continues to illustrate this dynamic:

> [Person 1]: Mainly because people that obtained damages and stuff like that, people kind of like got together and talked about their different facets and the different organizations that were helpful and things like that. So it was through word of mouth...you know what I mean? And so I heard from this person, I could get in touch with this person and that's the way it went, you understand me, and it was like, I guess, a neighborly thing.... Because definitely FEMA certainly didn't tell anybody, 'Hey we got help for you.'

> [Person 2]: Yeah like you were saying, our neighbors, all through word of mouth, I found out about water and food rations and whatever... so that's how we found out about all that stuff.

Although the majority of participants' discussions centered on learning about FEMA's assistance programs, their experiences with finding out about available programs through other organizations were also mentioned. One white female respondent from Brigantine stated,

> I used Helping Hands with the Latter Day Saints because they were doing a lot of clean up for free all over the place. So he helped me clean up my property, and spoke to me about a program that I might want to apply for with them.

An African American woman said, "One of my sons' teachers told me to go to Catholic Charities... it was totally by word of mouth." Another African American woman reported that

> I volunteered [at my church] and did clean up and we went around helping other places. And it was through talking to people where we cleaned up that I learned about some nonprofit organizations allowing people to apply for some kind of assistance.

One African American man noted that he had learned about other disaster assistance programs through his job. He explained,

> Through my job, I learned about New Jersey's Judiciary Superior Court, they connected with New York for assistance funds, anybody who wanted to donate money to the assistance funds could. I applied there. I got like $236 based on them doing that... everybody that applied for that fund, they just [equally] split it [among the applicants].

Out of all of the participants, there was only one white female respondent who reported learning about FEMA's assistance programs from a FEMA representative. However, she quickly made it clear that it was due to her personal relationship with the individual prior to Hurricane Sandy that she was able to approach him and ask for information. She admitted that, had it not been for that, she would not have known about the programs she could have applied to.

## LESSONS LEARNED

The responses above demonstrate that the focus group participants predominately relied upon their own social networks to gain information about disaster recovery programs rather than from FEMA or the traditional media. This illustrates the importance of social capital in the aftermath of disasters. All participants agreed that personal networks are the best, if not only, way to learn about resources. This perception of the utility of social networks for disaster recovery information diffusion carried across all socioeconomic levels and racial categories. Despite contrary reports by FEMA, focus group participants perceived there to be a lack of outreach by official emergency management organizations to inform the public about recovery opportunities. However, these findings may not be generalizable to the entire Hurricane Sandy survivor population because of focus group sampling.

Despite this limitation, FEMA should continue to recognize the value of social networks for the dissemination of information about recovery resources. To enhance this process in the future, FEMA must build stronger relationships with the third-sector and other government organizations in times of normalcy. FEMA should also enhance and extend their collaborative relationships with faith-based organizations (Rivera and Nickels 2014), because these organizations hold important position within social networks that could aid in information dissemination and diffusion.

## CONCLUSION

As acknowledged by FEMA, despite efforts to disseminate information, technological limitations restricted its diffusion. While various face-to-face interactions with the public were facilitated, this research finds evidence that disaster survivors were still not able to receive pertinent information in a timely manner through official lines of communication. Although one policy recommendation would be to create better technological protocols to overcome these limitations, this recommendation is not entirely convincing. There will always be situations when technologies fail to deliver their intended services to the end-user, both in times of normalcy and disaster. If technology is solely relied upon as a means of building community resiliency, then it will only be beneficial when it operates under preconceived operating parameters.

As a result, emergency management agencies should make greater efforts to engage the public in times of normalcy and adhere to principles set forth within the New Public Service paradigm (Denhardt and Denhardt 2000). Specifically, FEMA should engage the public in authentic two-way communication. This will not only educate the public about potential recovery resources but also help FEMA learn more about the public they are serving so that recovery programs and their administration can be more effective. This process of community engagement will provide a direct benefit to the individuals that participate. It will also provide the opportunity for traditionally marginalized populations to positively engage with government institutions, which can lead to decreasing levels of mistrust of government information (Soss 2000; see also Miller and Rivera 2011). Through this process, the public will be able to expand and diversify their social networks through interactions with others, subsequently enhancing their social capital (Bourdieu 1986; Coleman 1988) and their ability to locate disaster recovery resources in the future.

## ACKNOWLEDGMENTS

The author would like to thank the Center for Urban Research, the Department for Public Policy & Administration, and the Graduate School at Rutgers University–Camden, the William J. Hughes Center for Public Policy at Stockton University, and the Long Branch Free Public Library for their support in the completion of this project.

## REFERENCES

Aldrich, D.P. 2010. Fixing recovery: Social capital in post-crisis resilience. Department of Political Science Faculty Publications. Paper 3. http://docs.lib.purdue.edu/cgi/viewcontent.cgi?article=1002&context=pspubs, accessed August 25, 2016.

Aldrich, D.P. 2012. *Building resilience: Social capital in post-disaster recovery*. Chicago: University of Chicago Press.

Belzile, J.A. and G. Öberg. 2012. Where to begin? Grappling with how to use participant interaction in focus group design. *Qualitative Research* 12(4): 459–472.

Blake, E., T. Kimberlain, R. Berg, J. Cangialosi, and J. Beven II. 2013. Tropical cyclone report: Hurricane Sandy (AL182012) 22–29 October 2012. *National Hurricane Center.* http://www.nhc.noaa.gov/data/tcr/AL182012_Sandy.pdf, accessed October 7, 2015.

Bourdieu, P. 1986. The forms of capital. In *Handbook of theory and research for the sociology of education*, ed. J. Richardson, 241–258. New York: Greenwood Press.

Chamlee-Wright, E. and V.H. Storr. 2009. Filling the civil-society vacuum: Post-disaster policy and community response. *Mercatus Policy Series, Policy Comment No. 22*. Arlington, VA: Mercatus Center at George Mason University. http://mercatus.org/sites/default/files/publication/GCP_MPS_CIVILSOCIETYweb.pdf, accessed October 7, 2015.

Coleman, J.S. 1988. Social capital in the creation of human capital. *American Journal of Sociology* 94(Supplement): S95–S120.

Denhardt, J.V. and R.B. Denhardt. 2000. The new public service: Serving rather than steering. *Public Administration Review* 60(6): 549–559.

Drewniak, M. 2013. Christie administration releases total Hurricane Sandy damage assessment of $36.9 Billion. New Jersey: Office of the Governor, Press Release, November 28, 2012. http://www.nj.gov/governor/news/news/552012/approved/20121128e.html, accessed September 27, 2015.

Elliott, J.R., T.J. Haney, and P. Sams-Abiodun. 2010. Limits to social capital: Comparing network assistance in two New Orleans neighborhoods devastated by Hurricane Katrina. *The Sociological Quarterly* 51(4): 624–648.

Federal Emergency Management Agency. 2013. *Hurricane Sandy FEMA after-action report.* Washington, D.C.: FEMA. http://www.fema.gov/media-library-data/20130726-1923-25045-7442/sandy_fema_aar.pdf, accessed October 7, 2015.

Fugate, C. 2011. *Understanding the power of social media as a communication tool in the aftermath of disasters.* Address to the United States Senate Committee on Homeland Security and Government Affairs, Hearing Before the Ad Hoc Subcommittee on Disaster Recovery and Intergovernmental. http://www.gpo.gov/fdsys/pkg/CHRG-112shrg67635/pdf/CHRG-112shrg67635.pdf, accessed October 7, 2015.

Hawkins, R.L. and K. Maurer. 2010. Bonding, bridging and linking: How social capital operated in New Orleans following Hurricane Katrina. *British Journal of Social Work* 40(6): 1777–1793.

Jarrett, R. 1993. Focus group interviewing with low-income minority populations: A research experience. In *Successful focus groups: Advancing the state of the art*, ed. D. Morgan, 184–201. Newbury Park, CA: Sage.

Kaniasty, K. and F.H. Norris. 2000. Help-seeking comfort and receiving social support: The role of ethnicity and context of need. *American Journal of Community Psychology* 28(4): 545–581.

Katungi, E., S. Edmeades, and M. Smale. 2008. Gender, social capital and information exchange in rural Uganda. *Journal of International Development* 20(1): 35–52.

Krueger, R.A. 1994. *Focus groups: A practical guide for applied research.* Thousand Oaks, CA: Sage Publications.

Marková, I., P. Linell, M. Grossen, and A. Salazar-Orvig. 2007. *Dialogue in focus groups: Exploring socially shared knowledge.* London: Equinox Publishing.

Messias, D.K.H., C. Barrington, and E. Lacy. 2012. Latino social network dynamics and the Hurricane Katrina disaster. *Disasters* 36(1): 101–121.

Miller, D.S. and J.D. Rivera. 2011. Guiding principles of rebuilding trust in government in the aftermath of Hurricane Katrina. *Journal of Critical Incident Analysis* 2(1): 22–32.

Morgan, D.L. 1997. *Focus groups as qualitative research.* Thousand Oaks, CA: Sage Publications, Inc.

Morgan, D.L. 2012. Focus groups and social interaction. In *The Sage handbook of interview research: The complexity of the craft*, eds. J.F. Gubrium, J.A. Holstein, A. Marvasti, and K.D. McKinney, 161–175. Thousand Oaks, CA: Sage.

Peguero, A.A. 2006. Latino disaster vulnerability the dissemination of hurricane mitigation information among Florida's homeowners. *Hispanic Journal of Behavioral Sciences* 28(1): 5–22.

Putnam, R.D. 2001. *Bowling alone: The collapse and revival of American community.* New York: Simon and Schuster.

Ritchie, J. and L. Spencer. 2002. Qualitative data analysis for applied policy research. In *The qualitative researcher's companion*, eds. A.M. Huberman and M.B. Miles, 305–329. Thousand Oakes, CA: Sage Publications, Inc.

Rivera, J.D. 2014. Resistance to change: Understanding why disaster response and recovery institutions are set in their ways. *Journal of Critical Incident Analysis* 4(1): 44–65.

Rivera, J.D. and A.E. Nickels. 2014. Social capital, community resilience, and faith-based organizations in disaster recovery: A case study of Mary Queen of Vietnam Catholic Church. *Risk, Hazards & Crisis in Public Policy* 5(2): 178–211.

Soss, J. 2000. *Unwanted claims: The politics of participation in the U.S. welfare system.* Ann Arbor, MI: University of Michigan Press.

# 7 Lessons Learned from Evaluating a Capacity-Building Initiative to Foster Climate Change Adaptation, Mitigation, and Resilience

*Mary Ann Castle, Norma Tan, and James LaGro, Jr.*

## CONTENTS



**Abstract**

This chapter describes our evaluation of an international nonprofit organization's (NGO) capacity-building program to promote locally driven climate change mitigation, adaptation, and resilience (CCMAR) in the United States. Community capacity building can strengthen local and grassroots efforts to reduce greenhouse gas emissions and increase community resilience through effective adaptations to climate change. The NGO's Theory of Change featured intensive sessions where experts and practitioners from several regions exchanged knowledge and other resources to identify promising CCMAR strategies. Local multidisciplinary teams used the sessions to strengthen relationships, share ideas, and explore implementation goals and approaches. We recommended that the NGO expand its Theory of Change to improve (a) team readiness and effectiveness, (b) the leadership development experience, and (c) ongoing communication and technical assistance. Recommendations emphasize continued capacity building and monitoring to inform both the NGO's and local teams' efforts to achieve CCMAR outcomes.

## INTRODUCTION, BACKGROUND, AND CONTEXT

The United States' per capita contribution to global warming is the highest of any country in the world (Friedman 2012). While China is the biggest carbon emitter overall, the United States is cumulatively responsible for almost 27% of all global carbon dioxide emissions (British Petroleum 2013). Global climate change threatens current and future generations with catastrophic environmental and health consequences. These include increased weather-related mortality, loss of sea ice, accelerated sea level rise, longer and more intense heat waves, wildfires, increased salinity of fresh water, radically altered crop yields, reduction of arable land, changed spatial distribution of infectious and respiratory disease and water- and insect-borne diseases and illnesses, and increased morbidities and mortalities due to respiratory and cardiovascular disease and asthma attacks from harmful pollutants (Ayers and Forsyth 2009).

In the United States, the Environmental Protection Agency (USEPA) has developed regulatory strategies and standards under the Federal Clean Air Act (USEPA 2012; White House 2015). New fuel economy standards may be the most significant action to reduce actual greenhouse gas (GHG) emissions. By 2025, automobile manufacturers selling cars and light-duty trucks in the United States must meet an average fuel economy standard of 54.5 miles per gallon, nearly double today's standard.

Power plants are the largest single industrial source of carbon pollution, accounting for about one-third of all domestic GHG emissions from electricity generation, transportation, industry, and residential and commercial heating (United States Energy Information Administration 2011). The EPA promulgated $CO_2$ standards for new coal-fired power plants and limited power plant emissions of arsenic, mercury, sulfur dioxide, nitrogen oxides, and soot. By 2030, power plants must reduce carbon emissions by 32% from 2005 levels (White House 2015).

Congressional opposition and legislative inaction to reduce the United States' GHG contribution make it urgent to promote awareness of good practices in climate change mitigation, adaptation, and resilience (CCMAR). The Federal Partnership for Sustainable Communities, an interagency initiative of the EPA and Departments of Housing and Urban Development and of Transportation, has funded over 40 regional sustainability planning and/or implementation grants since 2010 (Pendall et al. 2013). Because of Congressional and state government resistance to climate change mitigation, local and regional sustainability initiatives are often the context for actions seeking to advance CCMAR. By evaluating capacity-building with sustainability initiatives, we can identify effective strategies and practices for supporting and expanding local community efforts to reduce vulnerability and foster resilience in the face of climate change.

## FOSTERING LOCAL LEVEL CCMAR THROUGH A CAPACITY-BUILDING INITIATIVE

This chapter describes an evaluation of one nonprofit organization's (NGO*) capacity-building process to promote locally driven CCMAR. The NGO's goal is to help practitioners address

* The name of the NGO is not provided because of a confidentiality agreement related to the evaluation.

complex environmental risks to reduce vulnerability and build resilience. The NGO engaged the authors to evaluate their CCMAR interventions, testing their Theory of Change (ToC). A ToC is a strategic framework for collaborative action that describes how and why a set of activities or interventions, as part of a highly focused program or a broader, comprehensive initiative, are expected, over some period of time, to lead to short-, medium-, and long-term outcomes (Anderson 2004; Taplin and Clark 2012). An effective ToC is not only aspirational (pursuing one or more grand challenges) but also inspirational, envisioning a meaningful and shared future (Connell and Kubisch 1998, p. 2).

The NGO's ToC stated that their capacity-building interventions with CCMAR practitioners would lead to improvements in climate change adaptation and mitigation plans. When implemented, these plans would result in measurable changes on regionally relevant metrics, including vehicle-miles traveled per household, percentage of energy from renewable sources (solar, wind, geothermal), and impervious land cover surface percentage. A local transportation initiative might expect to see changes in transit ridership, transit trips per capita, and air quality. The NGO wanted the evaluation to identify specific environmental measures that would demonstrate the "impact" of their capacity building. The NGO asked us to focus on three climate change–specific interventions: green jobs, adaptation and resilience, and transportation. Systematic evaluation methods (Yin 2013) were used to determine whether, and how, the NGO's capacity-building interventions contributed to intended CCMAR policy and program outcomes.

At an NGO site in the United States, 15 teams of CCMAR practitioners were convened for "capacity-building in response to climate change" sessions built around knowledge exchange and planning. Depending on issues addressed, teams consisted of senior municipal and regional officials (e.g., public sector representatives from water, electric, transportation, housing departments, the Port Authority, the Mayor, or City Council members), civic leaders, private sector representatives (e.g., development, construction, transportation firms), unions, community advocates, and non-profit conservation agencies. Over three consecutive days, teams composed of 5 to 10 members each engaged with one another and practitioners from other localities, including faculty experts, to develop local and regional CCMAR strategies and become effective change agents in their communities.

Capacity building incorporates and strengthens the ability of individuals, groups, and organizations to collaborate to create change. Collective impact is possible when stakeholders have a common agenda, a shared measurement system, mutually reinforcing activities, continuous communication, and a bridging or backbone support organization (Easterling 2013). A major challenge for regional sustainability initiatives is to overcome the compartmentalization of knowledge and responsibilities and to increase the sharing of best practices through coordinated decision making (Geels and Schot 2007; Markard, Raven, and Truffer 2012). Focusing on specific topics and contexts as part of a broader, long-term strategic vision will likely produce better capacity-building outcomes (Eade 1997). This may include exposure to new CCMAR ideas and skills, fostering personal relationships and networking, engaging in political dialogue, shaping public communication strategies, and developing leadership that inspires or adds resources. Inattention to capacity building often impedes regionally coordinated planning, policy-making, and investment (Hedger et al. 2008).

## EVALUATION RESEARCH METHODOLOGY

### Questions and Approach

The NGO wanted to assess the effectiveness of its capacity-building program on energy codes for structures, green jobs, adaptation and resilience, land and water use, and low carbon transportation. The evaluation addressed whether participation in capacity-building sessions led attendees to take more effective local action on climate change. It also aimed to identify the best indicators for testing whether the NGO's ToC was appropriate and realistic.

Our evaluation reviewed program records and participant demographics, specializations, experience, and other factors to clarify program inputs, processes, and outputs and to develop data collection methods. We assessed the NGO's initial ToC to refine the model based on empirical data. We identified process indicators, such as social capacity, which are distinct from climate change outcomes, such as reduction in GHG emissions.

## DATA COLLECTION

We conducted initial interviews with a small sample of session participants (*n* = 7) to identify relevant issues from their perspectives. Participants were from different geographic areas and confronted different environmental challenges. Subsequent in-depth interviews and surveys investigated knowledge transfer of promising practices and collaborative learning and problem solving on relevant issues resulting in CCMAR actions by participants and others whom they may have influenced. These elicited participants' thoughts regarding metrics selection, which provided information on environmental indicators useful for monitoring progress.

Questionnaires were sent to all 292 participants who attended capacity-building sessions at 15 sites between 2009 and 2011. An in-depth, qualitative examination of three specific cases enabled us to see the process of capacity building in its early stages. This approach (Yin 2013) allows for rich description of the behavior of actors embedded in situational contexts before, during, and after participation in the sessions. Three teams from different geographic regions, with different focus areas, were selected: low carbon transportation (South Atlantic), regional climate adaptation and resilience through emergency preparation (Rocky Mountains), and green jobs (Pacific Coast). We conducted in-depth interviews (*n* = 25) and reviewed the NGO's capacity-building session curricula and online materials for specific CCMAR topics. We also examined team plans and written materials. Interviews and documents yielded participant accounts illustrating linkages between short-term and intermediate capacity-building outcomes. These are necessary precursors to the achievement of long-term environmental outcomes.

Ninety-four of the 292 session participants completed an online survey (32% rate of return). The percentage of returns was inversely related to the amount of time elapsed between attending a capacity-building session and receiving the survey. The more recent the event was, the higher the rate of return. Participants were asked about their satisfaction with the capacity-building experience, whether they continued to gain knowledge by accessing the workshop networks, whether the experience promoted capacity-building and leadership activities in their communities, and whether they developed metrics to track progress and outcomes at the local level. The survey offered a snapshot of attendees' post-participation attitudes and behaviors.

## TESTING THE ToC

The NGO's ToC postulated that the knowledge and skills that team members gained by participating in capacity-building sessions would empower them to promote CCMAR leadership in their communities and lead to more evidence-based CCMAR plans and interventions. It affirmed the influence of factors such as the external environment, previous program experience, scientifically generated knowledge, and stakeholder insights on outcomes. Our evaluation aimed to clarify the processes by which participants (individually and in teams) benefited from the sessions and how they applied what they learned. We examined how the new knowledge, skills, and connections enabled participants to exert leadership and advance CCMAR planning and program development. We sought to uncover evidence that CCMAR activities, once implemented, led to desired outcomes. We assessed the ToC to determine if it was specific and complete enough for an evaluator to use to observe progress in credible and useful ways. We wanted to determine if the needed economic, technical, political, institutional, and human resources were available to carry out the initiative.

### Identifying Process Indicators and Environmental Outcome Metrics

Building on the interview and survey data, we identified "process indicators" to assess the quality of partnerships and movement along a continuum of progressive activity toward implementation of CCMAR plans. These regional "upstream" process indicators sharply contrast with "hard" "downstream" measures of environmental change, such as reductions in GHG emissions, reduction in per capita energy demands, or the percentage of energy used from renewable sources.

The NGO hoped we could identify "hard" outcome measures to demonstrate direct effects of their capacity-building initiative. In reality, both sustained collective effort and substantial time are needed for impact on such measures. Recognizing this, the evaluation contributed a process model by which the NGO could track measurable social and organizational indicators of progress toward the adoption of practices expected to ultimately influence long-term environmental outcomes.

## EVALUATION FINDINGS

### Early Indicators of Success

Almost 66% of respondents reported adjusting or creating relevant policies and programs when they returned home from the sessions. They reported promoting the importance of climate change issues more intensively (61%), engaging in action planning with others (56%), and building teams to do the CCMAR work (48%). Roughly 75% mobilized community groups, advocates, union representatives, and businesses to participate in CCMAR activities, including advocating for CCMAR at legislative levels. Two teams held postsession conference calls with other teams, sharing information about how to collect data showing progress implementing CCMAR activities.

Cross-fertilization led one city's team to collect new metric data, while another team and a public agency formed an important new collaboration. Two teams shared ideas to analyze traffic flow, with incentives for truck drivers to work off-peak to minimize congestion. They created community engagement strategies to improve bus service and attributed their CCMAR efforts to participation in peer exchange during and after the sessions.

Table 7.1 shows changes in participants' plans and interventions consequent to capacity building that could ultimately minimize the negative effects of climate change. Each example demonstrates progress toward CCMAR implementation outcomes. Teams composed of decision makers and community representatives had greater success in enhancing plans and implementing CCMAR activities, resulting in real local level changes. For example, in the Pacific Coast region, Green Jobs participants strengthened prior collaborations by expanding team membership to the Workforce Development Board, Department of Water and Power, an Electrical Workers Union local, and a Technical College. That team influenced City government to adopt low energy codes for new buildings and retrofit existing ones. The Western Alliance Adaptation and Resilience team used research data on the need for emergency responses to climate change (e.g., floods, droughts, and landslides) to expand plans and to attend a Sustainability Directors Network meeting armed with greater knowledge of best practices.

### Developing Trust through Continuous, Reciprocal Learning

CCMAR issues are complex. Teams identified several common impact challenges across cities and regions, including effective involvement of community representatives or "beneficiaries," financial instability, interjurisdictional complexity and variations in scalability of projects, and lack of comprehensive, multiple sector team composition, including legislative authority. Failure to include community "beneficiaries" can increase existing conflicts or social tensions. Consequently, marginalized groups may feel patronized and become resistant to CCMAR teams that fail to communicate the potential benefits of changes as a result of new energy options.

**TABLE 7.1**
**Evaluation Findings from Qualitative Methods**

| | Pacific Coast Mega-City: Green Jobs | South Atlantic City: Transportation | Western Alliance: Adaptation and Resilience |
|---|---|---|---|
| | **1: Team as Primary Learning Unit** | | |
| Composition | Cross-sector team, including top decision maker(s) | Some, but not all, necessary roles/agencies on team | Adequate representation; suggestions on representatives to be invited next |
| Immediate learning outcomes | Increased awareness of peer models, green jobs, procurement process; good practices | Peer success stories: light rail; expanding charrettes; ongoing team activities in county; relationship with other city reps; information and idea exchange | Paradigm shift—changed city's emphasis from Adaptation and Management to Adaptation and Resiliency<br>Directors' discussions to create collaborations outside their specific cities |
| | **2: Importance of Team Preparation—Continuity and Readiness for Peer Information Exchange** | | |
| Continuity | Formation of team before session<br>Trusting team relationships established<br>Postsession continuation of teamwork<br>Initial exposure to Green Jobs concepts | No presession teamwork, no postsession continuation of teamwork | |
| Peer information exchange | | Conference call with another major city on how to calculate GHG baseline and benchmark measures<br>Information sharing between expressway and transportation directors | Gelling of prior ideas about regional collaboration with those of other states at session |

*(Continued)*

**TABLE 7.1 (CONTINUED)**
**Evaluation Findings from Qualitative Methods**

| | Pacific Coast Mega-City: Green Jobs | South Atlantic City: Transportation | Western Alliance: Adaptation and Resilience |
|---|---|---|---|
| | **3: Capacity-Building Benchmarks** | | |
| Knowledge transfer | Integrated Plan for green jobs and energy efficiency<br>Goals and standards<br>Research to identify high growth areas<br>Research and funding for sectors with greatest possibility of green job expansion<br>Adapting another team's curriculum for use<br>Entry-level 18-month training program<br>Approval of pre–civil service certification<br>Retrofitting of city owned buildings<br>Research in high-growth areas | Postsession discussion on taking comprehensive Zone Master Plan from policy to implementation<br>Plans to analyze flow of traffic, consider Stop and Stand, incentivize truck drivers; build tunnel from seaport to highway | Adaptation and Resiliency integrated across sector plans<br>Research to train department directors to increase flexibility on emergency preparedness<br>Risk assessments<br>Procurement of federal grant |
| Short-/medium-term outcomes | Investment of $14 million in public funds for retrofit jobs<br>452 fully trained; 225 employed in retrofit projects at time of evaluation interview<br>Passing of ordinance requiring all city buildings to be retrofit<br>15 city buildings retrofitted or almost completed at time of evaluation interview<br>More rigorous standards for privately owned buildings<br>Long-term targets for city<br>Design of pre–civil service certification program<br>Search for private investment | New collaboration between seaport and expressway authorities | Use of Regional Report road map for cities and states in alliance to educate intrastate and interstate decision makers<br>Routine communication between states<br>Research to train directors to increase flexibility for emergency preparedness<br>Convening of regional alliance on inter-state climate strategies affecting all Western states |

Lack of team inclusiveness can result in opposition by union members who negatively interpret certain changes. For example, might the adoption of low-energy construction codes by the city government result in fewer construction jobs? Multiple sector teams, which include municipal buildings departments, community, and union members, have come to understand that, although new green jobs may replace some older construction jobs, retrofitting existing buildings will require union workers. Beneficial changes to heating, ventilation, and air-conditioning systems; lighting retrofits; and microcontrols substantially reduce energy usage in individual buildings. Similarly, if urban streets are modified to support bicycling, taxi drivers who cannot pick up/discharge passengers at curbside, and disabled pedestrians who must cross bicycling lanes to get to transportation can become disgruntled and block further efforts to reduce carbon-intensive modes of transportation. Such issues require inclusive teams, pre- and post-CCMAR planning sessions, and continuous capacity building to address these complex challenges.

In the United States, as elsewhere, power is concentrated among elites who often do not support CCMAR actions. Those opposing CCMAR include legislators who deny climate change or owe their positions to corporations who benefit financially from maintaining the fossil fuel status quo. Thus, teams must be committed to CCMAR goals to overcome obstacles posed by vested interests. Fiscal decisions associated with CCMAR interventions may also inadvertently decrease economic opportunities or supports for those who need them. Misperceptions create barriers, such as the belief that mitigation and adaptation threaten the economy and require "all pain, no gain" responses (McCright and Dunlap 2011). In the words of one participant,

> Having a key decision maker join us at the sessions (our City Manager) was perhaps the best strategic move of the entire workshop. It helped us get a sense of his perspective, helped him to see some of the realities of the situation, and gave us face time with someone with whom we rarely have significant face time.

Team members must be open to information exchange and resource sharing to enhance their capabilities for mutual benefit and a common purpose. They must build trust, share risks and responsibilities, function interdependently, and weather failure and success. Respondents reported that the sessions provided a "safe place" for team members to address the professional risks inherent in working toward CCMAR goals in environments with strong negative attitudes on the part of local governments. Respondents highlighted the benefit of learning in a neutral, nonpoliticized setting with senior administrators from different sectors who formerly opposed CCMAR goals. One participant described how an agency representative built a better relationship with the city's water department, a key connection for dealing with serious threats to water supply. Clearly, an important benefit of the sessions was the chance for team members to establish a common vision and a basis for mutual trust.

## Evaluating Capacity-Building Outcomes: The Big Picture

Our evaluation provided guidance to this CCMAR capacity-building initiative by equipping the NGO with a realistic framework for tracking progress in building capacity. This is the necessary prerequisite to effect policy reforms and, ultimately, more sustainable and resilient built environments. In-depth interview and survey data demonstrated evidentiary links between session inputs (peer learning, networking, teamwork, planning, and access to expertise) and subsequent behavioral learning and application outcomes.

Participants reported greater knowledge of issues, policies, and programs as a result of attending the sessions. For example, five participants noted that low-density population and suburbs present barriers to local low carbon transportation strategies. The sessions provided "great insight" on "redeveloping nodes in a way that is transit-supportive" for a low-density area and for smaller urban areas. Others learned about financing tools and best practices to overcome "local skepticism."

Sessions emphasized cross-sector team CCMAR configurations as an important factor in success. Upon returning home, participants expanded their teams to include an appropriate mix of members from their city/region. Emergent themes included the need for greater team diversity from industry, universities, labor, elected officials, transit agencies, and for greater "equity" via inclusion of advocacy or community groups.

### NGO's Role in Continuing to Build Capacity by Sharing and Coordinating Knowledge and Resources across Networks

Teams requested NGO assistance with securing fiscal resources, developing strategies for fiscal sustainability, communicating with key decision makers and private sector businesses, and incentivizing environmental change. They wanted advice from the NGO on addressing the political culture's unwillingness to plan and its calamity-driven approach to crises. Overcoming these obstacles requires scientific evidence and effective messaging to diverse stakeholders who influence policy. Respondents requested more success/failure stories, including best practices, assistance in consensus building, and national policy convening.

Survey respondents suggested greater information dissemination, including NGO-sponsored conference calls, webinars, facilitating working groups, online tools, and developing list serves. Specific suggestions included: "...peer to peer best practice leaders in EE [Energy Efficiency]... have the best learn from each other...no one has yet to crack the code (but we're getting close)." Team members also emphasized outreach to other stakeholders, planning next steps, focusing on policy change, and developing or further implementing local plans and programs. Participants working together after returning home demonstrate the catalytic role of the sessions for subsequent organizing, planning, and implementation.

Ongoing evaluation efforts should demonstrate how team learning and action contribute to increased commitment of decision makers and stakeholders in addressing climate and sustainability issues and initiating CCMAR policies and programs. Team commitment is necessary to measure the contribution of policy and institutional indicators on longer-term social, economic, and environmental results. Comparisons with CCMAR teams that did not participate in sessions would also help to demonstrate impact.

## RECOMMENDATIONS

### Team Selection and Preparation

We recommended that the NGO enhance the preparatory component of its capacity-building initiative by advising teams in advance about good practices in selection and composition of members, i.e., cross-sectoral, interjurisdictional, and community representation. Inclusive teams have a collaborative advantage as they seek to actualize their goals. Stakeholders most affected by climate change and CCMAR interventions should have representation or, minimally, have their priorities and opinions incorporated into planning. Similarly, individuals and groups with the power to generate or obstruct change should be consulted as teams are formed.

### Conceptualizing a ToC to Guide Action Research and Evaluation

We enhanced the NGO's ToC to include the team's degree of "readiness" to cooperate and its representative composition, noting the value of team diversity and the inclusion of community voices. We proposed process indicators to identify team commitment and effectiveness, hypothesizing that team sustainability for some duration would be a crucial intervening factor linking program participation and CCMAR action and outcomes. The NGO, with selected cities or regions, could then collect baseline data to document progress using agreed-upon benchmarks and milestones (Taplin and Clark 2012). We encouraged the NGO to collect cross-discipline and cross-jurisdictional data to understand specific organizing needs of localities and regions. The NGO, partnering with multiple participant teams, would be able to gather and compare data across different CCMAR issues, strategies, and situational contexts. Teams could then share results and methods and present evidence to others. This allows for building on lessons learned.

### Helping Local Teams Develop and Communicate Their ToC

Without a sustained approach to track local teams' post-CCMAR planning sessions, neither the NGO nor the local teams would be able to offer convincing evidence of connections between leadership development and intended policy, institutional, and environmental change. Systematic observation of "what works" is necessary for participants to understand and communicate how the NGO's interventions, and participants' subsequent actions as a team, result in CCMAR outcomes. We recommended that the NGO support networking of local-, regional-, and national-level sustainability practitioners to create evaluation partnerships with committed teams. The NGO and local teams would thus continue to exchange information and develop CCMAR leadership and collaborative social action while sharing responsibility for implementation and data gathering.

Strategic communication is also essential to promoting positive dialogue that creates support among conflicted citizens and officials, broadens appeal through themes that resonate with diverse groups, and maintains enthusiasm among those who are already proactive. Thus, teams need help finding the appropriate language to reach and motivate stakeholders and gain their support for CCMAR actions. The NGO could advise on communication campaigns targeted to specific challenges by helping with media messaging and tools and by coaching on answering tough questions.

### Providing Leadership for Collaborative Fundraising

Our recommendations include strategies to help the NGO and local teams use an evaluation framework and evidence to make the case for funders' investment in capacity building (Bours, McGinn, and Pringle 2012). The NGO could coordinate fundraising efforts with follow-up assistance to maximize the impact of smaller grants. With such funding, teams would be better able to overcome local barriers to change. For example, the Obama Administration has earmarked substantial funding for CCMAR work. We recommend that the NGO, various teams, and their elected legislators advocate for some of this funding to be distributed to support local capacity building.

## DISCUSSION AND LESSONS LEARNED

We know of no other work that reports on an evaluation of capacity building involving so many local CCMAR practitioner teams in one country. We found that participation, leadership, and evidence are crucial. Our evaluation yielded valuable lessons, discussed here, that are also applicable to highly industrialized countries and to sustainable development projects in the Global South.

### Lesson 1: Participation Matters

Climate change adaptation occurs when people cooperate in new ways, across multiple boundaries, including social and professional roles, professional discipline, geography, and political jurisdiction. CCMAR evaluation must describe and measure the effectiveness of organizing across boundaries, the extent to which different actors participate, the tensions that arise, and how conflicts are resolved within a participatory process. "Participation is both a right and a principle that undergirds human rights-based development" (Musembi 2014, p. 318).

Participation, however, is not always equitable (Hanchett 2015). Social hierarchies and status differentials exist between men and women, the landed and the poor, the marginalized and members of different classes and castes, traditional leaders and government officials, and executives of nonprofit agencies or private firms. These are challenging differences, particularly when the more powerful dominate participatory processes, making outcomes less equitable.

When diverse social segments from the community are represented, a team can better understand the complexities of CCMAR interventions and their collective impacts on different groups. Effective CCMAR practitioners strive to ensure the rights of all affected by changes. Meaningful participation sees that the less powerful are not silenced and that the more powerful are persuaded to listen and collaborate. Mutual learning, knowledge-building practices, and collaborative decision making provide opportunities for discussion of local perceptions and priorities. In this evaluation, the case study of the Green Jobs CCMAR initiative included labor union and local community representatives (through an advocacy organization). These representatives were meaningfully engaged in capacity-building sessions and, later, in the decision-making process as part of a comprehensive team including technical experts, political, and public and private sector representatives.

CCMAR practitioners, working with anthropologists possessing knowledge of local social structures and cultural frameworks, can learn from differing viewpoints and ensure mutual exchange in framing decision-making (King, Feltey, and O'Neill 1998). Community advocates may also play this role. CCMAR practitioners foster trust when they demonstrate understanding and respect for diverse values and concerns.

### Lesson 2: Leadership Matters

Local agents of change are unlikely to have neither the resources nor the expertise to incorporate evaluation strategies into planning and implementation activities in the absence of supportive coordination. This includes outside technical assistance. Local champions, who can assist in implementing CCMAR plans and interventions, are essential for success. They can identify opportunities to influence people in positions of authority. They can also anticipate how cultural, gender-based, and other social differences are likely to influence responses to new ideas and technologies. Champions from outside the community can also bring new expertise and resources and facilitate participatory learning.

### Lesson 3: Evidence Matters

Over the long-term, successful social action should result in measurable environmental change. For the ToC to have explanatory power, it must posit the relationship between progress in social learning indicators and in environmental change indicators. To test the ToC, it must generate evidence that demonstrates whether and how the intervention "works" in achieving climate change mitigation, adaptation and resilience. Evaluation of interventions designed to effect social action through knowledge exchange, skill-building, and leadership development should seek real-world evidence to test the program developers' implicit ToC. Tested against real-world data, the evaluation can help to refine, enhance, confirm, or refute the ToC. This activity improves the quality of evidence-based implementation of CCMAR policy and planning interventions.

## CONCLUSION

Capacity-building programs can help communities translate their commitment to climate change mitigation and adaptation by giving them access to the best available tools and resources and helping them collaborate with their city, state, regional, and federal counterparts. Our research helped refine the NGO's CCMAR initiative by suggesting ways to monitor and evaluate outcomes, focusing on capacity building and collective impact. Our research shows the critical importance of collaborative activities, such as peer-to-peer learning, coordinated teamwork, and intercity networking, for putting sustainability theory into practice.

## REFERENCES


Anderson, A. 2004. *Theory of Change as a tool for strategic planning: A report on early experiences.* New York: The Aspen Institute Roundtable on Community Change.

Ayers, J. and T. Forsyth. 2009. Community-based adaptation to climate change: Strengthening resilience through development. *Environment* 51(4): 22–31.

Bours, D., C. McGinn, and P. Pringle. 2014. Guidance note 3: Theory of Change approach to climate change adaptation programming. http://www.seachangecop.org/node/2933, accessed August 20, 2015.

British Petroleum. 2013. *BP statistical review of world energy 2013.* London: British Petroleum. http://www.bp.com/content/dam/bp/pdf/statistical-review/statistical_review_of_world_energy_2013.pdf, accessed August 20, 2015.

Connell, J.P. and A. Kubisch. 1998. *Applying a Theory of Change approach to the evaluation of comprehensive community initiatives: Progress, prospects, and problems.* Aspen, CO: The Aspen Institute. http://dmeforpeace.org/sites/default/files/080713%20Applying%2BTheory%2Bof%2BChange%2BApproach.pdf, accessed January 8, 2016.

Eade, D. 1997. *Capacity-building.* UK and Ireland: Oxfam.

Easterling, D. 2013. Getting to collective impact: How funders can contribute over the life course of the work. *Foundation Review* 5(2): 67–83.

Friedman, L. 2012. China greenhouse gas emissions set to rise well past U.S. *Scientific American On-line.* http://www.scientificamerican.com/article/china-greenhouse-gas-emissions-rise-past-us/, accessed August 20, 2015.

Geels, F. and J. Schot. 2007. Typology of sociotechnical transition pathways. *Research Policy* 36(3): 399–417.

Hanchett, S. 2015. Sustainability and Society. In *Envisioning sustainabilities in times of disasters*, eds. F. Murphy and P. McDonagh, 100–125. Newcastle upon Tyne, UK: Cambridge Scholars Publishing.

Hedger, M.M., T. Mitchell, J. Leavy, M. Greeley, A. Downie, and L. Horrocks. 2008. *Desk review: Evaluation of adaptation to climate change from a development perspective.* Brighton, UK: Institute of Development Studies. http://www.preventionweb.net/files/7845_GEF20final20report20Oct20081.pdf, accessed August 20, 2015.

King, C.S., K.M. Feltey, and S.B. O'Neill. 1998. The question of participation: Toward authentic public participation in public administration. *Public Administration Review* 58(4): 317–326.

Markard, J., R. Raven, and B. Truffer. 2012. Sustainability transitions: An emerging field of research and its prospects. *Research Policy* 41(6): 955–967.

McCright, A. and R. Dunlap. 2011. The politicization of climate change and polarization in the American public's views of global warming: 2001–2010. *The Sociological Quarterly* 52(2): 155–194.

Musembi, C.N. 2014. How participation as a right enhances realization of the rights to water and sanitation. *Waterlines* 33(4): 317–336.

Pendall, R., S. Rosenbloom, D. Levy, E. Oo, G. Knaap, J. Sartori, and A. Chakraborty. 2013. *Can federal efforts advance federal and local de-siloing? Lessons from the HUD–EPA–DOT Partnership for Sustainable Communities.* Washington, DC: Urban Institute.

Taplin, D. and H. Clark. 2012. *Theory of Change basics: A primer on Theory of Change.* New York: ActKnowledge.

United States Energy Information Administration. 2011. Emissions of greenhouse gases in the U.S.: Report DOE/EIA-0573 (2009). http://www.eia.gov/environment/emissions/ghg_report/ghg_overview.cfm, accessed August 15, 2015.

United States Environmental Protection Agency. 2012. *Overview of final amendments to air regulations for the oil and natural gas industry—Fact sheet.* http://www.epa.gov/airquality/oilandgas/pdfs/20120417fs.pdf, accessed August 20, 2015.

White House. 2015. President Obama's plan to fight climate change. https://www.whitehouse.gov/climate-change, accessed August 20, 2015.

Yin, R.K. 2013. *Case study research: Design and methods.* Thousand Oaks, CA: Sage publications.

# 8 Let's Talk Oil Spill Risk
## *Lessons Learned from Coastal Communities in British Columbia, Canada*

*Shona V.Z. de Jong*

## CONTENTS



**Abstract**

According to the Constitution of Canada Act 1982, §35(1), the Canadian Government ("the Crown") has the legal obligation to fulfill its "duty to consult" with Aboriginal (First Nations, Metis, Inuit) peoples on issues that may potentially effect Aboriginal territories, well-being, and environments. There is increasing evidence that Transport Canada Transport Safety Review Panel (TSRP 2013–2015) did not consider the needs of Aboriginal people in the Phase 1 consultation process. After examining two submissions to the TSRP, I suggest that Northwest Coast First Nations' experiential, technical, and science-based knowledge of oil spill response and recovery science contains fundamental information required to build a new regulatory framework for future hydrocarbon transport activities. However, because legislative and regulatory requirements to insert First Nations into the existing British Columbian disaster management frameworks are nonexistent (Kirk 2015), there have been challenges to including this knowledge. I recommend that a planning, evaluation, and proactive risk communication research initiative be developed to prepare coastal communities for a catastrophic oil spill.

## INTRODUCTION

Federal transportation review processes, such as the Transport Canada Tanker Safety and Spill Prevention Initiative, Transport Safety Review Panel (TSRP 2013–2015), fulfill an extremely valuable mandate. They provide an opportunity for Canadians, particularly Aboriginal (First Nations,

Metis, Inuit) people, to contribute to the new regulatory environment pertaining to hydrocarbon shipping activities in Canada (de Jong 2015). Through experience with First Nations of British Columbia, the Government of Canada (hereafter, the Crown) has developed a sophisticated understanding of the dimensions of the legal requirement of the "duty to consult" with First Nations as rights-bearing communities for the purpose of the Constitution of Canada Act 1982, §35(1) (Kirk 2015; Kuhn and Murphy 2006; McFadgen 2013). Chrétien and Murphy (2009, p. 1) maintain that environmental initiatives have increasingly acknowledged "the legal obligation to consult with Aboriginal peoples" about the "potential effects on Aboriginal environments, territories and well-being." These include strategic planning, such as the lengthy review of the Canadian Environmental Assessment Act; project specific environmental impact review processes, such as the Western Canadian Sedimentary Basin (WCSB) development proposals; and federal transportation review processes, such as the Transport Canada TSRP 2013–2015.

Despite the legal duty to consult Aboriginal peoples, past processes have often marginalized First Nations' knowledge of environmental emergency management (Kirk 2015; Kuhn and Murphy 2006). First Nations' perspectives on their roles and responsibilities in emergency management are beginning to be explored (Auditor General of Canada 2013). Only recently has the need for explicit legislative requirements for the inclusion of First Nations voices in British Columbian emergency management been recognized. The importance of "First Nations seek[ing] an enhanced role in protecting and restoring their respective territories in anticipation of, and in the wake of, disaster" (Kirk 2015, p. ii) is being stressed. Kirk (2015) maintains that consultation should be undertaken with First Nations in British Columbia, who continue to be impacted by these challenges.

However, this paper argues that not all First Nations' environmental emergency knowledge is acknowledged or included in developing the TSRP consultation processes, which creates challenges for including it in the recommendations. This paper will determine if Northwest Coast First Nations' experiential, technical, and science-based knowledge of oil spill response and recovery science was taken into account by examining their TSRP submissions. This paper builds on oil spill risk communication leadership research (Walker, Pavia, Bostrom, Leschine, and Starbird 2015) and disaster response participatory action research (de Jong 2015; de Jong et al. 2011).

## BACKGROUND

### ENBRIDGE NORTHERN GATEWAY PROJECT AND THE CROWN'S OBJECTIVES

> Taxes and revenues from the oil and gas sector contributed $22 billion last year to government revenues....However, [because our resources are landlocked, we're]...losing some $50 million every single day—$18–19 billion every year. We have to connect our pipeline infrastructure to our ports on the east and west coast.
>
> **The Honorable Joe Oliver (2012)**

The Harper Era (2006–2015) concluded when Canadian Prime Minister Stephen Harper lost his seat in October 2015. The quote above reveals how the Canadian economy was being driven with oil and gas export initiatives. TransCanada, Kinder Morgan, and Enbridge (companies in the Canadian energy sector) put forward WCSB development pipeline proposals to connect the oil and gas fields in western Canada with refineries and ports on the west, east, and Gulf coasts. Canada's ambitious WCSB "Alberta oil sands" energy export projects would link western Canada to the global supply chain. These projects envision two tidewater terminal hydrocarbon transportation facility sites in Burnaby (the Kinder Morgan Trans Mountain Expansion Project) and Kitimat (the Enbridge Northern Gateway [ENG] project; de Jong 2015; Sears 2015).

The $6 billion ENG project proposed two pipelines. Both run 1178 kilometers from Bruderheim, Alberta, to a marine terminal in Kitimat, British Columbia. One pipeline would take 525,000 barrels per day (bpd) of heavy crude oil to the west coast for export. The other would bring 193,000 bpd of condensate back east to thin Alberta's land-locked bitumen (Sears 2015). Both pipelines would run across northern British Columbia, predominately on First Nations' lands. According to West Coast Environmental Law (2009, p. 2), the ENG hydrocarbon shipping proposal included

> ... approximately 225 condensate and crude oil-laden tankers a year...approximately 18 condensate and crude oil tankers per month, including four to five Very Large Crude Carriers (VLCCs) with a capacity of 2 million barrels of oil or more per VLCC. Each of these ships is about 350 metres long—the length of 3.5 football fields—and 60 metres wide ...

Engineers and mariners agree that the coastline route of the WCSB/ENG proposal was high risk. The route follows great fjords, deep inlets, straits and sounds, narrow channels, hundreds of small islands, and complicated island shorelines. This route, hundreds of kilometers long, is known for its gale-to-hurricane force winds, heavy fog, deep straits, submarine landslides, seismic activity, and paleotsunamis. Locations lacking the shelter of Vancouver Island would face ocean storms, energized by the rugged coastal mountains that hasten weather systems and outflow winds along the coastline (Concerned Professional Engineers 2013; de Jong 2015; West Coast Environmental Law 2009).

The WCSB/ENG development proposal could affect "the traditional territories and rights of at least 31 inland and 10 coastal First Nations, and many more First Nations...in the Fraser, Skeena and Mackenzie river basins" (West Coast Environmental Law 2009, p. 3). Northwest Coast First Nations would be disproportionately exposed to oil spill risk. For the past decade, they have challenged the WCSB/ENG proposal with legal bans, judicial reviews, and appeals. They are acutely aware of how a catastrophic spill in the Northwest Pacific region would impact spiritual, cultural, and harvesting activities in traditional village sites, recreational activities, and travel routes (de Jong 2015; West Coast Environmental Law 2009).

I find that, because the Crown would not engage with oil spill risk-related questions, judgments were formed (de Jong 2015). These often deem the Crown to be untrustworthy. As a result, the WCSB/ENG has not been granted social license to proceed, and the Crown has lost millions of anticipated energy export revenue and taxes. To explore how risk perceptions impact the financial ambitions of the oil and gas sector and the Crown, I isolated oil risk perceptions. Evidence details how many Canadians provided expressions of nonconfidence in the oil and gas export spill planning and preparedness activities to meet international compliance standards (de Jong 2015).

This earlier paper highlights three events that altered how the Canadian public perceives hydrocarbon export project preparedness for a catastrophic oil spill. First, the Harper government supported significant legislative changes that removed many provincial and federal barriers to project proposals. These changes reshaped the Crown's decision-making processes, with the Crown granting veto power to the Harper Cabinet. This allows the Cabinet to make the final decision on energy sector projects rather than regulators (i.e., the Canadian Environmental Assessment Agency and the National Energy Board). Other strategic efforts to advance the proenergy export sector initiatives include building concurrent timelines of the Crown-led WCSB/ENG proposal review and the TSRP.

The Crown built the TSRP process to refine hydrocarbon transportation risk reduction regulations for the very large crude carrier's activity in the WCSB/ENG proposal. The TSRP was tasked with evaluating response organizations, planning, and resources in three phases. The three phases were Phase I (marine oil spill regime currently in place south of 60° N latitude), Phase II (Arctic), and Phase III (hazards and noxious substances). Each phase of the TSRP focused on reviewing the response capacity of a geographically defined area (de Jong 2015; Transport Canada 2013).

Second, the Crown-led WCSB/ENG proposal review was supposed to serve the Canadian public interest and solicit submissions from Aboriginal people, particularly those identified as potentially affected by its cumulative impacts. However, the Crown cut participant funding allocations for complex project proposal reviews, removed oral cross-examination from hearings, and failed to consult and engage with First Nations. During this time, First Nations and their allies (e.g., municipalities, conventional citizen groups, environmental groups, and alternative media groups) used the media and social media (Facebook) to publically disagree with the WCSB/ENG review process, rigorously detailing how the Harper era proenergy export sector initiatives had been woven into the Crown's initiatives, regulatory laws, policies, and operational practices (de Jong 2015).

My analysis of the structural relationship between the Crown and opponents of the WCSB/ENG proposal, which include grassroots social movement organizations, municipalities, First Nations, and the Province of British Columbia reveals that many Canadians believed that the credibility of the WCSB/ENG proposal review process was damaged. For example, as the WCSB/ENG proposal moved through the review process, a coalition of 160 First Nations said "no" to the project. They signed the "Save the Fraser" Declaration. Additionally, the Union of British Columbia Municipalities, 31 municipal governments, two regional districts, and six unions passed resolutions against the project. Ninety-six percent of the 9500 public submissions to the Crown's review of the WCSB/ENG development proposal were opposed to the project. Further, the expedited timelines of 15–18 months undermined the quality of the conclusions and recommendations from this review. The WCSB/ENG project was approved in June 2014 (see de Jong 2015 and Environmental Defense 2015 for further detail).

Third, the Crown was aware that oil risk perceptions were a multibillion dollar issue. The Crown became proactive, however, when the financial, ecological, health, and public safety consequences of the 2010 Deepwater Horizon Oil Spill in the Gulf of Mexico gained prominence in research agendas of academics and nonprofit organizations. To appease the general public, the Crown built the Transport Canada's Marine Oil Spill Preparedness and Response Regime and formed the TSRP. The TSRP focused on five key topics: liability and compensation issues, risk-based area response planning, prevention, losses, and damages associated with worse case scenario modeling, and industry's new leadership role in tanker safety. The TSRP engagement model used these five topics to create an identified stakeholder list (e.g., Enbridge, First Nations, and the provincial government) to be included in workshops and written communication. Use of these specific topics ensured that the TSRP process would create a policy framework for Industry (i.e., the energy sector, including TransCanada, Kinder Morgan, and Enbridge) to follow the Private–Public Partnership model (de Jong 2015; Transport Canada 2013).

Since the 1990s, industry-funded response organizations were expected to lead in preparing for and responding to an oil spill in the public-private response model. Drawing from the financial analysis of the 2010 Deepwater Horizon Oil Spill, the proposed 2015 revision of the national 1990s "Polluter Pays" principle meant that industry would adopt a new leadership role in tanker safety. They had to adopt the Risk-based Area Response Planning Framework. This is requires that they tailor preparedness efforts specific to regional and local conditions, environmental sensitivities, and marine activity risk profiles. Proposed revisions to the Private–Public Partnership model ensures that polluters would pay for the response to oil spills and compensate coastal communities for environmental and property damages (de Jong 2015).

## Duty to Consult in British Columbia

Jurisprudence associated with the duty to consult with Aboriginal people began in 1990s with the 1997 case *Halfway River First Nation* v. *British Columbia (Minister of Forests)*. In the 2004 *Haida Nation* v. *British Columbia (Minister of Forests)* case, the Court determined that federal and provincial governments of Canada have a constitutional obligation to fulfill their duty to consult (McFadgen 2013). A decade late, the question of how to consult with First Nations involved in managing disaster risk reduction continues to be discussed (Auditor General of Canada 2013; Kuhn and Murphy 2006). Kirk (2015, p. 154) argues that this role has been effectively superseded by the question of how to deal with First Nations' right to have a clear role and responsibility in "managing emergencies within their territories." Kirk notes that the legislative and regulatory requirements to insert First Nations into the existing British Columbia disaster management frameworks are nonexistent. The specific issues identified with the TSRP process follow from this standard. Because there is a "suspension of First Nation constitutional rights in all four phases of emergency management in British Columbia, and most glaringly during a declared state of emergency" (Kirk 2015, p. 155), Northwest Coast First Nations' concerns raised about the TSRP process need to be carefully considered. They will be exposed to WCSB/ENG oil spill risk more than other Canadians.

### Northwest Coast (South of 60° North Latitude)

Empirical evidence revealing Aboriginal concerns includes their written submissions to TSRP. These provide a more complete understanding about the "duty to consult," Crown's objectives, and the needs of Aboriginals, particularly Northwest Coast First Nations, in the TSRP consultation process. Of the 78 written Phase I TSRP submissions, two were from Northwest Coast First Nations: the Haisla Nation Council (including the Coastal First Nations and the Gixaala Nation) and the Gitga'at First Nation with Coastal First Nations. The Coastal First Nations organization is composed of the Council of 10 First Nations. These two submissions represent 14 of the 19 Northwest Coastal area First Nations (*Canadian Encyclopedia* 2016; Coastal First Nations 2016). Built upon systematic information collation, these submissions reveal numerous deficiencies in the roles and responsibilities of industry and government agency experts tasked with protecting their shorelines.

## METHODS

This paper originates from a multimethodological, 18-month research project based in British Columbia. This project brought together First Nations, including Musqueam, Squamish, and Coastal Salish, community land use planners, academics, nongovernment organizations, government agencies, and others, to address hazard, risk, and vulnerability in British Columbia. The project has a specific focus on coastal communities' knowledge. It uses Yin's (2014) qualitative case study methodology and Miles and Huberman's (2014) stages to complete a meta-analysis of existing natural science and social science reports, key informant interviews, and 12 months of participatory notes (de Jong 2015). This project highlights the value of local disaster risk management knowledge in a Canada-wide social movement against the WCSB/ENG proposal (de Jong 2015). In total, over 350 sources were analyzed to triangulate and validate the empirical evidence.

This project is composed of three research components. First, a review of multihazard risk management legislative requirements in British Columbia (Struik, de Jong, Shoubridge, Pearce, and Dercole 2015) and in-depth conversations with two members of Coastal Salish First Nation, employed by the Crown, confirmed Kirk's (2015) evaluation that First Nations lack designated disaster risk management roles and responsibility within their territories. Second, workshops, discussions, and thematic assessment of 200 peer-reviewed journal articles and over 100 Canadian coastal vulnerability studies were completed in the context of a Marine Environmental Observation Prediction and Response Network (MEOPAR) project to identify a set of vulnerability indicators for the development of resilience networks (Chang, Yip, de Jong, Chaster, and Lowcock 2015). Third, participatory observer notes were made during the organization of and participation in a MEOPAR Strait of Georgia Marine Hazards Workshop. At this workshop, I administered surveys and held discussions with marine hazard experts from Musqueam First Nation, Squamish First Nation, and other organizations.

These notes guide the comparative content analysis of TSRP submissions from Enbridge, municipalities of British Columbia, and Northwest Coast First Nations. Content analysis of Northwest Coast First Nations TSRP written submissions was completed with an emphasis upon technical, science-based, and experiential knowledge of oil spill response and recovery science provided by First Nations. Analysis included coding relevant data, sorting by temporal bracketing, interpretation, and integration. Thematic analysis was ranked in terms of importance based on nonenergy sector risk perceptions (de Jong 2015; Miles and Huberman 2014).

## CROWN'S INTERESTS, FIRST NATIONS' TERRITORY, AND DISASTER RISK MANAGEMENT

While the TSRP stakeholder engagement process stated that First Nations would be consulted (Transport Canada 2015), Northwest Coast First Nations clearly identify the challenges they encountered with this process. They encountered barriers such as time constraints for providing "…input to the Expert Panel and the lack of any capacity assistance to facilitate the participation of the Haisla Nation in this process" (Haisla Nation Council 2013, p. 2). Municipalities and non-government organizations have also criticized this process for inadequately notifying stakeholders of its consultation schedule, dismissing their need for capacity and capability assistance, utilizing a weak consultation guidance document in the TSRP communication strategy, and adhering to an unrealistic timeline (de Jong 2015).

The Gitga'at First Nation/Coastal First Nations (2013a) were alarmed by the "lack" of "…oversight, stewardship, investments, and leadership by regulatory agencies and the shipping industry over the past two decades." Therefore, the Northwest Coast First Nations were determined to profile the value of their knowledge in the TSRP process. To deal with competing interests of the Crown, they employed three strategies. The first was to cite Coastal First Nations in the both TSRP submissions. For example, the Haisla Nation Council submission included the Coastal First Nations and the Gixaala Nation; Gitga'at First Nation also aligned with the Coastal First Nations. The support of Coastal First Nations broadens these two submissions to represent 14 of the 19 First Nations in the Northwest coastal area, whose "unceded Traditional Territory" is a vast geographic expanse that extends "from the Alaskan border in the north to Vancouver Island in the south" (Coastal First Nations 2016, p. 1).

The second strategy is to ask if the TSRP is adding value to public safety. For example, the Haisla Nation Council raised the question of why Transport Canada was targeting only tanker safety, given that there are several origins of spills, including offshore pipelines, coastal terminals, offshore platforms, and oil pipeline infrastructure (de Jong 2015). This line of inquiry reveals two key issues: what are the benefits of the TSRP, and how does the TSRP process help stakeholders identify their knowledge gaps and information needs of oil spill response processes? The second question raises issues regarding exposure (sources and pathways) but also effects (socioeconomic and ecological health). Given the aforementioned natural hazards in First Nations territory, these questions highlight the vulnerability of Northwest Coast First Nations to a variety of potential spill scenarios (de Jong 2015).

Cognizant that the mandate of the TSRP was to investigate industry's knowledge of international and national regulatory excellence for oil and gas transportation and, thus, refining the Private–Public Partnership model (de Jong 2015), Northwest Coast First Nations used a third strategy. To create a critical dialogue with the Crown, they effectively inserted culture-specific information, knowledge of response planning, and risk analysis into their submission. As will be discussed, the Haisla Nation Council and contributing First Nations (2013) provide a comprehensive baseline of contemporary scientific studies with which to understand how a potential oil pollution incident might affect the northwest coastal area. These reports, commissioned by First Nations or nongovernmental organizations, originated from long-standing relationships with government organizations (Union of British Columbia Municipalities), nongovernmental organizations (Living Oceans Society), legal specialists (West Coast Environmental Law), academics, technical experts, and others.

### Technical and Experiential Knowledge

Northwest Coast First Nations provided valuable location-specific information to the TSRP process. For example, the Gitga'at people note that they have thousands of years of local knowledge of surface waves, currents, bathymetry, and wind fields in their marine territory. Because of their experience with ship-source oil spills (the Queen of the North and the M.G. Zalinski), they would be the first responders during an environmental emergency, pushing information forward to the response teams. Based on knowledge of their territory and previous impacts, they highlight that the energy sector would be unable to provide full compensation for the response to and the recovery from a catastrophic oil spill incident. Thus, Northwest Coast First Nations would be exposed to increased financial risk because,

> … [the new Private–Public Partnership model has] shortcomings related to how marine emergencies including major vessel casualties are funded and damages compensated. There is a high likelihood that a ship owner will reach its limits of financial responsibility for emergency management and response well before the incident's closure. This legal threshold can happen much sooner than publicly expected, resulting in a transfer of command to the federal government. There is a high financial risk and vulnerability to those coastal First Nations that have invested services and resources towards providing or augmenting the response efforts of not getting complete cost recovery and/or not being fully compensated for natural resource damages and business losses. (Gitga'at First Nation/Coastal First Nations 2013b, p. 5)

The Gitga'at First Nation/Coastal First Nations (2013) and the Haisla Nation Council (2013) question how national maritime transportation policies and plans would ensure that the energy sector have the insurance to remain financially accountable to local and regional response and recovery operations to protect the long-term interests of residents in the vicinity of the spill. Further, they requested clarification of roles and responsibilities that define who will clean up the air, water, and soil contamination resulting from organic and inorganic pollutants, such as petroleum hydrocarbon contamination, heavy metals, and polycyclic aromatic hydrocarbons. Specifically, they wanted to know who will be building models for funding preparedness costs for an oil spill and emergency funds during an ongoing response. They also wanted it specified who would be responsible for paying for the response to a spill and for the air, water, and soil pollution recovery.

## Science-Based Knowledge

Valuable economic, natural, and social science-based information can be found in the Northwest Coast First Nations TSRP submissions. These detail the work of university researchers and technical experts who examined the acute effects of diluted bitumen toxins upon ecosystem health and public safety. They also raise conceptually and mathematically complex concerns regarding the quantification and qualification of marine transportation oil spill risk assessments. Specifically, because the TSRP relied on the results of "worst case scenario" modeling to determine if the hydrocarbon export projects' financial planning standards would be adequate to compensate affected communities for losses and damages incurred by a large-scale oil spill, numerical oil spill modeling was discussed in length throughout the TSRP process. Based on the results of the Crown-commissioned risk assessment, oil and gas companies were required to make financial adjustments in planning to respond to a marine oil spill accident. First Nations' TSRP submissions reveal the uncertainty of numerical oil spill modeling and that the WCSB/ENG proposal was being advanced

> … without adequate scientific knowledge concerning the fate and behavior of oil sands products in the marine environment; without clear parameters regarding the challenges and capacity requirements needed to maintain and deploy effective containment and clean up of spills…and without effective technology designed to respond to sunken or submerged oil. (Haisla Nation Council 2013, p. 1)

In sum, Northwest Coast First Nations TSRP submissions provide a status report of Canada's most vulnerable area in relation to potential oil pollution incidences, based on the comprehensive review of key natural and social science studies (de Jong 2015). Results indicate that First Nations were leading the future of Canadian oil spill response planning via their use of information provided through complex political alliances and provision of analytical reports that include hazard, risk, and vulnerability assessments. Their questions regarding Crown and industry readiness to respond reveal that they are deeply engaged in exploring issues related to the current status of scientific knowledge regarding oil spill outcomes and acute toxic effects. As will be discussed, First Nations also made recommendations to prepare adequate emergency plans and recovery measures.

## SEEING VALUE: LESSONS LEARNED

Improvements to future TSRP processes might include acknowledging First Nations' need for capacity and capability assistance, building a strong consultation guidance document for the First Nations/TSRP communication protocol, and providing First Nations with consultation schedules and realistic response timelines. Unfortunately, the 2013–2015 TSRP may be viewed as a strategic move by the Crown to absolve itself of its responsibilities to Aboriginal peoples and the Canadian public to engage in a meaningful manner regarding their concerns about the very large crude carriers in WCSB/ENG development proposal. This interpretation echoes Kirk's (2015, p. 154) conclusion, which maintains that the Crown assumes

> … First Nations will … play a passive role as "the consulted"… if they are consulted at all. [This] overwhelmingly positions non-First Nation organizations to manage emergencies on behalf of First Nations and further acts as a barrier to First Nations who seek to manage emergencies within their own territories.

Nonetheless, there is much to be learned about how the Haisla Nation Council and the Gixaala, Gitga'at, and other First Nations respond to a federal review process when they lack confidence and trust in the Crown and the energy sector to adequately respond and manage an oil spill (de Jong 2015). Key themes suggest how First Nations may be able to contribute to the future Private–Public Partnership model and oil spill disaster management frameworks. First, the Gitga'at First Nation/Coastal First Nations (2013b) TSRP submission provides local administrative and practical solutions in anticipation of a catastrophic marine oil spill. This report focuses on oversight and capacity, emergency planning and response standards, offshore response operations, onshore response operations, financial considerations, and research and development. It provides 150 recommendations to promote a dialogue to achieve higher level of protection for British Columbia's northern coastal waters. They include an example of an ideal model for environmental incident management and response.

To address regional challenges of a 100% "Polluter Pays" model, the Gitga'at First Nation (2013b) recommends building the capacity of local response experts and cooperative information sharing. They suggest that the Province of British Columba and the Crown empower their people through building up emergency response capacity. The Gitga'at people must be trained and then allowed to "… participate effectively in command, operations, and planning positions of emergency response" (p. 7). Overall, these First Nations have asked important questions regarding as how regulations and standards that evolve from the TSRP might address the context-specific response needs should an incident occur.

Second, this evaluation provides valuable lessons for future Crown initiatives that seek to advance other WCSB energy export proposals. First Nations' TSRP submissions add value. They provide empirical evidence of First Nations' perceptions, judgments, and reflect a variety of types of knowledge. This paper acknowledges valuable details presented to the Crown. However, key questions remain: is the Crown ready to investigate why First Nations and west coast municipalities have aggressively exercised their power to delay the implementation and operation of oil and gas projects with judicial reviews and appeals (de Jong 2015)? Is the Crown ready to acknowledge that the key barrier to hydrocarbon-led economic development is oil spill perceptions and judgments? Has the Crown thoughtfully considered the question of how the risks associated with hydrocarbon transport could be communicated to different Aboriginal people, who are concerned about the unique geographic location of the proposed oil export sea route?

Third, because marine industry safety policy and practice tend to exclude First Nations' knowledge, the Northwest Coast First Nations TSRP submission information collation can provide a model for future submissions to the Crown. Inspired by the work of Eykelbosh (2014), careful gap analysis of these TSRP submissions demonstrates that First Nations need to build information collection tools for oil spill response and recovery teams within a broader preparedness planning project and evaluation initiative. Such tools would allow First Nations to develop baseline surveillance programs for communities in residential proximity to contaminated coastlines and plans for participation in clean-up work. This would allow them to identify potential short- and long-term impacts of oil spills on humans and the environment. It would also help them determine how best to monitor vulnerable groups during the postevent phase.

Relatedly, they must identify how to monitor short- and long-term health problems that result from air, water, and soil pollution in resident communities and among volunteers and clean-up workers. Finally, if a Crown-led oil spill risk communication initiative for First Nations is developed, it could be used to identify objectives, classify issues, and formulate oil disaster recovery management plans that consider the positive and negative implications of compensation provided by the energy sector to affected communities. This would allow for better collaboration among stakeholders and potentially reduce mistrust of Crown initiatives.

## REFERENCES


Auditor General of Canada. 2013. *Fall report of the Auditor General of Canada*. Ottawa, Ontario, Canada: Office of the Auditor General. http://www.oag-bvg.gc.ca/internet/English/parl_oag_201311_06_e_38800.html#hd4a, accessed January 24, 2016.

*Canadian Encyclopedia*. 2016. http://www.thecanadianencyclopedia.ca, accessed January 24, 2016.

Chang, S.E., J.Z.K. Yip, S.V.Z. de Jong, R. Chaster, and A. Lowcock. 2015. Using vulnerability indicators to develop resilience networks: A similarity approach. *Natural Hazards* 78(3): 1827–1841.

Chrétien, A. and B.L. Murphy. 2009. *Métis indigenous knowledge, environmental impacts and the "duty to consult": A discussion document*. Ottawa: Federal Métis Interlocutor Office, Governance Institute. http://iog.ca/en/knowledge-areas/aboriginal-governance/aboriginal-policy-research-initiative, accessed January 24, 2016.

Coastal First Nations. 2016. Who we are. http://www.coastalfirstnations.ca/who-we-are, accessed January 24, 2016.

Concerned Professional Engineers. 2013. Flawed risk analysis. http://www.concernedengineers.org/flawed-risk-analysis/, accessed March 25, 2015.

de Jong, S.V.Z. 2015. Seeking social license to move energy: Tackling supertanker safety risk in the Enbridge Northern Gateway proposal. In *Environmental considerations in energy production*, ed. J.R. Craynon, 99–121. Englewood, CO: Society for Mining, Metallurgy, and Exploration, Inc. http://toc.proceedings.com/27722webtoc.pdf, accessed January 24 2016.

de Jong, S.V.Z., D. Dominey-Howes, C.E. Roman, E. Calgaro, A. Gero, S. Veland, D.K. Bird, T. Muliaina, D. Tuiloma-Sua, and T.L. Afioga. 2011. Process, practice and priorities—Key lessons learnt undertaking sensitive social reconnaissance research as part of an (UNESCO-IOC) international tsunami survey team. *Earth-Science Reviews* 107(1–2): 174–192.

Eykelbosh, A. 2014. Short- and long-term health impacts of marine and terrestrial oil spills: A literature review prepared for the Regional Health Protection Program, Office of the Chief Medical Health Officer, Vancouver Coastal Health. https://www.vch.ca/media/VCH-health-impacts-oil-spill.pdf, accessed January 24, 2016.

Environmental Defense. 2015. Letter to Prime Minister Trudeau and Minister McKenna. Joint Letter from Greenpeace Canada, Environmental Defense Canada, and the Georgia Strait Alliance. http://georgiastrait.org/wp-content/uploads/2015/11/Joint-KM_EE-letter-to-PM-Trudeau.pdf, accessed November 15, 2015.

Gitga'at First Nation/Coastal First Nations. 2013a. Written submission of the Gitga'at First Nation and the Coastal First Nations to the Tanker Safety Expert Panel, Phase one. Cover letter. https://www.tc.gc.ca/media/documents/mosprr/Gitga_at_First_Nation_cover_letter.pdf, accessed February 4, 2016.

Gitga'at First Nation/Coastal First Nations. 2013b. Written submission of the Gitga'at First Nation and the Coastal First Nations to the Tanker Safety Expert Panel, Phase one. Issues and Solutions Statement.

Haisla Nation Council. 2013. Written submission of the Haisla Nation to the Tanker Safety Expert Panel, Phase one. https://www.tc.gc.ca/media/documents/mosprr/Haisla_Nation_Council.pdf, accessed March 25, 2015.

Kirk, C. 2015. The sound of silence: First Nations and British Columbia emergency management. Master of Laws (LL.M.) Thesis. Saskatoon: University of Saskatchewan. http://hdl.handle.net/10388/ETD-2015-08-2241, accessed January 24, 2016.

Kuhn, R. and B. Murphy. 2006. *Developing a siting strategy for a nuclear fuel waste management facility*. Toronto: Nuclear Waste Management Organization, NWMO SR-2006-01. https://www.nwmo.ca/~/media/Site/Files/PDFs/2015/11/04/17/31/466_SR-2006-01_Developing_a_Siting_Strategy.ashx, accessed January 24, 2016.

McFadgen, R.A. 2013. Beyond the duty to consult: Comparing environmental justice in three Aboriginal communities in Canada. Master of Arts Thesis. Halifax, Nova Scotia: Dalhousie University. http://www.collectionscanada.gc.ca/obj/thesescanada/vol2/NSHD/TC-NSHD-35396.pdf, accessed January 24 2016.

Miles, M. and A. Huberman. 2014. *Qualitative data analysis: An expanded source book*, 3rd edition. Thousand Oaks, CA: Sage Publications.

Oliver, J. 2012. Canada's natural resources: Prosperity for all Canadians. https://www.nrcan.gc.ca/media-room/speeches/2012/3369, accessed 24 Jan 2016.

Sears, A. 2015. Need and resistance: A review of the status of major Canadian pipeline projects in 2014. Stikeman Elliot LLP, *Canadian Energy Law Blog*. http://www.canadianenergylaw.com/2015/01/articles/pipelines-and-storage/need-and-resistance-a-review-of-the-status-of-major-canadian-pipeline-projects-in-2014/, accessed April 11, 2015.

Struik, L.C., S.V.Z. de Jong, J. Shoubridge, L.D. Pearce, and F. Dercole. 2015. *Risk-based land-use guide: Safe use of land based on hazard risk assessment.* Ottawa: Geological Survey of Canada, Open File 7772. http://geoscan.nrcan.gc.ca/starweb/geoscan/servlet.starweb?path=geoscan/downloade.web&search1=R=295981, accessed April 21, 2015.

Transport Canada. 2015. Tanker safety and spill prevention. http://www.tc.gc.ca/eng/marinesafety/menu-4100.htm, accessed March 21, 2015.

_____. 2013. *A review of Canada's ship-source oil spill preparedness and response regime—Setting the course for the future*. Ottawa: Tanker Safety Panel Secretariat. www.tc.gc.ca/eng/tankersafetyexpertpanel/menu.htm, accessed October 17, 2014.

Walker. A., R. Pavia, A. Bostrom, T.M. Leschine, and K. Starbird. 2015. Communication practices for oil spills: Stakeholder engagement during preparedness and response. *Human Ecology Risk Assessment* 21(3): 667–690.

West Coast Environmental Law. 2009. Keeping tankers out of BC's north coast: Preventing the next Exxon Valdez. http://wcel.org/resources/publication/keeping-tankers-out-bc%E2%80%99s-north-coast-preventing-next-exxon-valdez-2009, accessed April 14, 2015.

Yin, R.K. 2014. *Case study research: Design and methods*, 5th edition. Thousand Oaks, CA: Sage Publications.

# 9 Imagining Culture

## *The Politics of Culturally Sensitive Reconstruction and Resilience Building in Post–Wenchuan Earthquake China*

*Qiaoyun Zhang and Roberto E. Barrios*

## CONTENTS



**Abstract**

This article examines the way culture is imagined and materialized over the course of state-sponsored community reconstruction programs in Sichuan Province, China, in the aftermath of the 2008 Wenchuan Earthquake. Using evidence collected during a 15-month ethnographic project, we make the case that "culturally sensitive" community reconstruction programs served as a mechanism through which state institutions articulated hegemonic ideas about the qualities and nature of Chinese ethnic minority groups. We also argue that these reconstruction programs served as a spectacle for reasserting the legitimacy of a centralized paternalistic state whose national development programs are implicated in greenhouse gas emission–related climate change and the earthquake disaster itself. Consequently, "culturally sensitive" community reconstruction initiatives have operated as a form of power that perpetuates the disaster as historical–political–ecological process rather than mitigating it.

## INTRODUCTION

Anthropologists often emphasize that for postcatastrophe recovery and resilience-building programs to be successful, planners and managers must take "local culture" into account (Faas and Barrios 2015). But what happens when "culture" is taken seriously by state agencies in reconstruction projects? How is culture imagined, by whom, for what reason, and to what effect? On May 12, 2008, a 7.8-magnitude earthquake took place in Wenchuan County, A'ba Tibetan, and Qiang Autonomous Prefecture (A'ba Prefecture hereafter) within China's southwestern Sichuan Province. With a death toll of almost 70,000 and economic losses exceeding $120 billion, the Wenchuan Earthquake is the most destructive seismic movement since the establishment of the People's Republic of China in 1949. The disaster was particularly catastrophic to the Qiang, 1 of the 55 officially recognized Chinese ethnic minorities. More than 80% of the Qiang lived in the earthquake-stricken areas. About 10% of the Qiang population died and thousands more were injured or reported missing. The earthquake had a tremendous impact on the livelihoods, natural resources, infrastructure, and political institutions of Qiang communities.

In response to widespread social disruption and material destruction, the Chinese government funded a series of reconstruction projects focused on the "culturally sensitive" recovery of Qiang communities. This chapter explores the motivations, assumptions, tensions, and effects of these reconstruction projects. We conclude that, while the Chinese state's focus on "culture" may initially seem promising, it amounts to a representational strategy on the part of governmental agencies that, rather than addressing the political ecological relationships that engendered the disaster, actually buttresses them. Consequently, we call into question the long-term sustainability of this particular brand of culturally sensitive recovery.

To conduct our analysis, we present a review of current anthropological understandings of the culture concept and contrast these perspectives with the way culture figures into the practices of Chinese state-sponsored recovery programs. We review the political–ecological context within which the Wenchuan Earthquake took form and magnitude as a disaster and contextualize state-sponsored, culturally sensitive disaster reconstruction projects as a spectacle-dependent mechanism for diffusing critiques of vulnerability-engendering development policies. We also make the case that the governmentally assisted reconstruction of Qiang communities provides an important window into the ways Chinese state agencies figure and handle cultural difference in the context of china's state-controlled political economy.

## RESEARCH METHODS

To understand the impact of the earthquake and the reconstruction process, Zhang conducted ethnographic fieldwork in China for 15 months between 2011 and 2015. The main research sites are two villages, Dongmen and E'er. These are Qiang settlements located in Longxi Township, Wenchuan County, A'ba Prefecture, Sichuan Province. By living in Dongmen, Zhang obtained most of the data through participant observation and interviews. She also made trips to Beijing, the capital of China, and Chengdu, capital city of Sichuan province, for interviews. Zhang conducted 50 structured interviews with Longxi villagers, government officials, planners, experts, and scholars about their perceptions of and practices regarding earthquake relief and reconstruction. More than 100 informal interviews were carried out throughout the fieldwork, focusing on the transformation of life of the villagers. Two surveys with 40 Dongmen villagers were conducted on their perception of local disasters and the reconstruction, respectively. All ritual and festival practices were visually documented when permitted. All names used in this chapter are pseudonyms to protect the identity and privacy of the informants.

## THE CULTURE CONCEPT

The term "culture" can have a variety of meanings depending on who uses it and why. In the mid-19th Century, the term was used primarily to denote elite Western European art and etiquette, a usage that accompanied ethnocentric judgments of the practices and values of populations in colonial domains and subaltern working classes (Stocking 1966). Through scholarly efforts, the term came to be applied in a broader, nonhierarchal sense to grasp the varying ways people structure their societies, invest bodies and environments with meanings, develop mythological explanations of the world and its origins, and create unique technologies and examples of material culture.

Over the course of the twentieth century, anthropologists gained popular acceptance of this new definition, but their success did not come without complications. Culture, in some instances, came to mean a collection of values or "beliefs" of colonized populations that stood in the way of national development and compared unfavorably to the "rationality" of politically dominant groups (Povinelli 1995). The "culture" of subaltern peoples also became associated with "unchanging tradition" (Fabian 1983). In other instances, culture came to be represented as a superficial veneer of different textiles and staged rituals that could be mobilized as a commodity for a globalizing capitalist tourism industry, not a profound difference in embodied subjectivity (Comaroff and Comaroff 2009).

The ethnographic record has allowed further refinement of the culture concept. Today, anthropologists understand that "cultures" feature internal heterogeneity and multiple levels of subalternity with contestations and power struggles (Ortner 1996). Cultures are not neatly bounded entities with impermeable boundaries but are open-ended phenomena subject to foreign forces and influences (Fischer 2007; Gupta and Ferguson 1992; Way 2012). It is also the result of interpretive processes where people refashion local and foreign ideas, discourses, institutions, technologies, and forms of expression, making sense of them from the vantage point of their cosmologies and systems of category making (Appadurai 1996; Arce and Norman 2000; Brightman 1995).

Concerns with human–environment relations have revealed the emergent and ecologically relational quality of culturally distinct practices, meanings, and values (Biersack 1999; Ingold 2000). The practices and values embodied in the culture concept influence disaster response and recovery efforts on the part of those people who are directly affected by catastrophes (Browne 2015; Button 2010). At the same time, the culture concept lends itself to manipulation on the part of state agents in postdisaster scenarios in the ways these actors define the elements of the culture of affected populations (see Gamburd 2013; Hastrup 2011; Makley 2014). The previous discussion of the culture concept contrasts with the assumptions embedded in state-sponsored earthquake recovery projects in Sichuan. This sheds light on the forms of power at play in "culturally sensitive" community reconstruction.

## "CULTURE," EARTHQUAKES, AND DEVELOPMENT

The twentieth century witnessed a number of struggles between national elites, state governments, and subaltern populations. The former two conceptualized development as the cultural transformation of the latter. Consequently, resulting national development processes upset meaning-laden relationships between people and environments. In some instances, it transformed rural self-sustaining agricultural and pastoralist populations into urbanized wage laborers for an expanding global system of capitalist production (Ferguson 1999; Mitchell 2002).

China's integration into this global network has brought about significant economic prosperity for the country, the rapid execution of monumental development projects, and growing urbanization. This has come at a high environmental cost. In some instances, rapid but haphazard development projects have been implicated in technological and geophysically triggered disasters. The impact of the Wenchuan Earthquake was exacerbated by poorly executed development projects such as the construction of state schools, which resulted in the deaths of many young students (Wong 2008). The earthquake is suspected of having been triggered by a hydroelectric dam project in the Minjiang River Valley; the water reservoir placed 300 million metric tons of pressure on the Beichuan thrust fault, which was responsible for the seismic movement (LaFraniere 2009).

The relationships between people, policy, and environment that engendered the Wenchuan earthquake placed the Chinese State in a predicament. The government's response to the disaster's sociopolitical repercussions has featured a spectacular outpouring of resources for devastated families and communities (see Makley 2014). We argue that this has not addressed the policies and practices that shaped the disaster; rather, it has attempted to reinforce the legitimacy of a paternalistic state. In effect, the focus is on ensuring the continuation of the political and ecological relationships that engendered the catastrophe in the first place.

The reconstruction of Qiang communities presents a similar scenario. Before the earthquake, rural Qiang populations experienced decades of socioeconomic neglect from state institutions. The emphasis on cultural preservation in the reconstruction of Qiang villages provides state agencies with an opportunity for political power-consolidating, spectacular benevolence. It also articulates specific meanings of the culture concept in which Qiang communities do not play a role in/as the future of China. Rather, they represent a "traditional" past that is best put to use as a "consumable other" for the growing tourism appetites of the urban middle class.

## CULTURAL RECONSTRUCTION AS STATE POLICY

Comprising only 0.02% of the Chinese population (roughly 300,000 people) and occupying mostly remote mountain valleys, the Qiang have long remained marginal in the gaze of state institutions. The 2008 earthquake brought Qiang communities to national attention. Less than two weeks after the catastrophe, then Chinese Prime Minister Wen proclaimed that Qiang culture had to be protected, given the disaster's effects on Qiang communities (Cheng, Li, and Chen 2008). In the state-issued "Overall State Planning for Post-Wenchuan Earthquake Restoration and Reconstruction" (hereafter, "Overall Planning") published four months later, one of the eight basic principles of disaster recovery is to "inherit and carry forward local culture and protect ecology" (Chinese State Council 2008, pp. 19–20).

The post-earthquake recovery of Qiang communities became exemplary of what the Chinese government termed "miraculous reconstruction," referring to the state-directed swift and massive transformation of most of the affected areas. State and private agencies completed more than 40,000 reconstruction projects nationwide in three years, with an enormous government-led investment of over 1 trillion renminbi (US$157 billion). The state's spectacular benevolence toward the Qiang helped frame the earthquake relief and recovery as an opportunity to strengthen national unity and patriotism. It also served to reassure the nation that their destiny would continue to be prosperous under the leadership of the Communist Party, despite the national and international condemnation regarding the state's negligence of and military crackdown on many Chinese ethnic minorities throughout the 20th and early 21st Centuries (see Makley 2014).

"Overall planning" elaborates on the mechanisms to restore and preserve culture and ecology. This is to be accomplished by insuring infrastructure reconstruction, especially of rural housing. Also included is rescuing and recovering natural and cultural heritage by repairing historic Qiang structures, building Qiang cultural museums, and constructing the "spiritual homeland" of the Qiang through the establishment of a Cultural Ecosystem Experimental Conservation Area. This will contribute to rebuilding local industry by developing tourism and Qiang craft production such as embroidery (Huang and Bonschab 2010).

These mechanisms reveal the state's particular assumptions about culture, development, and homeland for the predominantly rural Qiang. First, the Qiang culture is reduced to a few physical features, such as traditional houses, symbolic architecture (i.e., watch towers and stone pagodas), ethnic clothing, and ritual performances. These, collectively, constitute stereotypical representations of "traditional" Qiang communities as held by many urban Han (China's hegemonic majority ethnic group, comprising 91% of the national population). Second, the cultural "reconstruction" aims to market the "restored" Qiang culture for ethnic tourism, making it a vital economic development method. Finally, by ignoring the spiritual dimension of the Qiang culture and designing the villages for tourism, the rebuilt village represents anything but a culturally sensitive home for project beneficiaries. Nevertheless, government-hired tourism companies designed and implemented a number of Qiang "cultural recovery" projects that were guided by these exact principles.

## "CULTURALLY SENSITIVE" RECONSTRUCTION OF DONGMEN VILLAGE

Dongmen Village is an agricultural community of about 300 households. Longxi is widely recognized as the Qiang *shibi* culture's place of origin. *Shibi* are the Qiang ritual specialists. They are responsible for leading worship rituals, exorcisms, healing the sick, and officiating weddings and funerals. Located in a remote mountain valley with limited arable lands and means of transportation, Longxi was characterized as a poverty-stricken township by the A'ba Prefecture government before the earthquake.

Roughly 70 kilometers north of the epicenter, Longxi was decimated by the earthquake; 96% of the households were affected and most of the public infrastructure was destroyed. Although only two people died in Dongmen, many of the houses collapsed and landslides buried roads and farmland. Dongmen's living conditions and public service facilities were notably improved through the reconstruction. Most villagers reconstructed their houses, following Qiang architectural style, in less than a year's time, with the help of state subsidies. Some of them were further subsidized by the Hong Kong Red Cross to add antiseismic supports. For the first time, underground electricity and water lines reached every rebuilt house, cables and solar water heaters were installed, and landscaping designs decorated the villages with new trees, flowers, and wall paintings.

After Dongmen's initial reconstruction in late 2009, all the newly erected buildings were painted yellow and decorated with light brown concrete/imitation stone pieces. However, according to the then village head, Donglin Tang, such decoration failed to retain Qiang-ness. Instead, it looked like "a Han village." This refers to the fact that the reconstruction was planned by an outside, government-hired firm, all of whom were Han and had little knowledge of the Qiang culture.

In 2010, then Party Secretary of Wenchuan County, Lidong Qing, suggested that transforming Longxi into a Qiang heritage tourist destination could help restore the culture while developing the local economy. Longxi went through a culturally oriented reconstruction costing over 50 million renminbi (US$8 million). After the project, it was advertised as the Qiang People's Valley and designated as a national, top-notch travel destination. Seated at the entrance of Longxi and surrounded by steep mountains and a clear creek, Dongmen become a highly promoted tourist attraction.

### Physical Transformation of Dongmen

The cultural reconstruction plan, according to Donglin (the former village head), purposely modeled Dongmen as a historic Qiang settlement. State planners made aesthetic choices that played on the nostalgic imaginings of urban, middle-class, predominantly Han tourists about rural, ethnic life. This, in turn, contributed to the exoticization of Qiang villagers by representing them as the opposite of the urban Han. On the newly established square at the front of the village, nine concrete pillars summarize Qiang "culture" for both visitors and residents. Each is carved with an image of origin stories, festivals, food, dance, ritual ceremonies, mythical characters, farming lives, and embroidered clothing. Before the disaster, Qiang structures were made of locally available grey stone, yellow dirt, and wood. To reflect such style, every reconstructed building in the village was painted in grey cement and decorated with grey concrete imitation stone pieces and wooden frames to make them look "traditional."

The few old stone houses left intact after the earthquake were preserved and reinforced from the inside. These family houses are usually three-stories high, with a flat roof. An outside tourist company renovated two of these houses into a bar and a restaurant. The company kept the original dirt floors, stone walls, and wooden beams instead of covering them up. Some rusty Qiang family furniture and kitchen utensils were placed inside to create a sense of "authenticity." Qiang embroideries, made by local women, hang on the walls, enhancing the "exoticness" of this minority group. Qiang dishes are served. At the door of the restaurant, an advertisement states, "Thousand-year-old Qiang ancient house welcomes you to rest, eat, drink, and have fun inside," despite the fact that these houses are only decades-old. Common Qiang household items, such as bamboo baskets, single wooden ladders, and wooden and steel farm tools are variously displayed in the newly established gardens, fish pond, and along the village roads.

## Political Representation of the Cultural Heritage

After the 2010 cultural reconstruction project, a Wenchuan government-sanctioned and Chengdu-based tourism planning company introduced aspects of Qiang cultural heritage into this newly made "historic" community. State planners and tourism agency project managers effectively reduced a complex culture into a simplified commodity that could be transformed into a tourism product (see Zhang 2012). Examples of cultural grafting include the construction of two Qiang-style "stone" watch towers, made of concrete but decorated with imitation stone pieces. While watch towers are widely found in many Qiang villages for defense and storage purposes, there wasn't one in Dongmen before the earthquake. The newly built ones are mainly for decoration, although they are opened occasionally to visiting government officials, journalists, and tourists.

The *shibi* practice is also prominently represented in Dongmen, yet no *shibi* ever lived in the village before the earthquake. Most of the *shibi* are from the E'er Village of Longxi, high in the mountains. Upon entering the township gate, visitors are welcomed by bronze sculptures of a dancing group, led by an elder *shibi*. These sculptures demonstrate the Qiang's sheepskin drum dance, a nationally recognized Qiang intangible cultural heritage. A *shibi*, wearing a fur hat, a long gown, and gripping a cane with a carved human head on one end and a bell on the other, leads the dance. These sculptures seem to announce that *shibi*, the quintessential representatives of the mysterious Qiang, are the very first thing that Longxi wants to offer to curious outsiders.

An extreme form of hegemonic representation of Qiang culture is the *shibi* worship and sheepskin drum dance performances organized by the local government. During major holidays and events, *shibi* and their apprentices from E'er Village are asked by the township government to travel to Dongmen to perform. All of them are required, by the local government officials, to wear blue hemp, long gowns decorated with feathers, animal bones, and embroideries to look "authentic." Their performances, however, are taken out of context. Historically, this ritual was only conducted at the annual god mountain worship. It is now performed almost every month and is introduced as a ritual to bring peace and happiness to the visitors. The solemn sheepskin drum dance, traditionally performed only during funerals to send dead souls back home, is repeatedly organized in the village square to showcase Qiang's traditional dance. Many villagers find these acts ironic and disrespectful. A villager once said, "How is it okay that we welcome tourists with sculptures of the sheepskin drum dance, which is only performed for the dead?" Nevertheless, such performances become the most famous cultural commodities of the "exotic and mysterious" Qiang.

This process of commodification presents the newly rendered Qiang "culture" as "authentic traditional Qiang culture in itself," hiding the sociopolitical relations of reconstruction that produced it. A well-established body of literature deals with these issues in the context of ethnic tourism in China and elsewhere (see Chao 2012; Comaroff and Comaroff 2009; Notar 2006). There is also a robust literature on the way political and socioeconomic elites use disasters and related states of emergency to further develop agendas that would otherwise face significant resistance from grassroots groups and affected communities (Barrios 2010; Button 2010; Gamburd 2013). This case, resulting from the Wenchuan earthquake, brings these sociopolitical concerns into a broader conversation about the analysis of disaster tourism development.

## Rebuilding Local Industry through Tourism

Zhang stayed at Linhua Tang's home hostel (Qiang Scent Garden) throughout her fieldwork. Linhua is an open and energetic lady in her late 50s. Her family opened the hostel with a small subsidy from the local government after the earthquake. Six rooms on the second floor were renovated into guest rooms, each equipped with a bathroom, wooden beds, and a television. Their original living room on the first floor was turned into a big dining room. Linhua's son, Jiafu, who used to work at construction sites in nearby cities, became the manager and chef. His wife, Xueli, gave up her job at the township hospital and dedicated herself to managing the new business's logistics.

Qiang Scent Garden is 1 of the 20 or so home hostels that opened up after the earthquake. Throughout China, this kind of tourism business is often called "peasant family happiness" (Chinese: *nong jia le*). Rural villagers change their own homes into restaurants/hostels to host mainly urban tourists, who are eager to enjoy an imaged idyllic country life (Chio 2014). In Dongmen, "peasant family happiness" centers on promoting and selling Qiang-related services and products. Tourists, many from the surrounding cities, stay in the simply furnished Qiang-style houses, learn the Qiang's circle dance at bonfire parties, and enjoy the cultural and natural sceneries of the village.

Part of this experience includes enjoying local food such as corn, potatoes, and wild vegetables. Linhua often commented, "It's funny that the tourists love the corn and potatoes. I have had enough of them in my life. I never want to eat them again." The representation of Qiang cuisine as a static and reduced "tradition" of corn and potatoes brings up, once again, the phenomena of culture commodification and commodity fetishism that characterizes tourism development projects. The ethnography of disaster reconstruction, in turn, shows how the Qiang villagers are routinely troubled by the fetishization of their culture and culinary practices.

Another attraction of Dongmen is the process of reconstruction itself. Contrasting pictures of the village before and after the earthquake are displayed on the walls of the watch towers. Along with the pictures are texts recording the financial resources invested in Longxi's reconstruction and the major agricultural, economic (tourist), and environmental changes in the township. Zhang observed many visitors commenting on how much money they donated for the recovery and whether or not they were satisfied with the results. Visits to the earthquake-affected Qiang areas not only help arouse national solidarity and common sympathy towards disaster-affected communities, they also reassure the visitors that their donations are appropriately spent and recognized.

## DISCUSSION

The ethnography of Dongmen's reconstruction reveals a number of things that are at stake in the "culturally sensitive" community recovery projects that followed the 2008 earthquake. First, in China, non-Han ethnic minorities are historically targets of the "civilizing project," a process of improving the economic and educational conditions of the minorities as members of the Chinese state, which also raise their awareness of being different and at the periphery (see Harrell 1995). Ethnic cultures are often commodified and advertised as tourism attractions by the local governments, becoming major means of income for ethnic groups with limited industrial or agricultural resources (see Chio 2014).

As the market economy gradually replaces subsistence agriculture patterns, many Longxi villagers' livelihoods are now at the mercy of the "invisible hand" of the market. The "culturally sensitive" projects impacted villagers' relationships to the local environment, as well as their culturally specific practices of space (what is done and where) and time (what is done and when). Much of the village's already limited farmland was expropriated to build tourism-related facilities and sceneries. In China, all rural land is owned by the peasant collectives, while villagers only have use rights. One-time compensation is paid to the villagers when land is used by the local government for public affairs. However, villagers lose the stable income from farming, making them vulnerable to the financial vagaries of the tourism industry. As one villager poignantly said, "We peasants must have land of our own. There is no guarantee of life without land."

Furthermore, no villager was ever consulted or included in the planning of reconstruction projects. Yet, their absolute compliance with the planning was expected and sometimes forced. In addition to losing property rights to land, they were also asked to allow the outside construction workers decorate their houses with a unified design and to perform at the government-organized events for little payment. The reconstruction subjected villagers to the authoritative power of state institutions, perpetuating the political and economic vulnerability which caused their plight in the first place.

The government-sanctioned reconstruction project focused only on restoring the external features of the Qiang culture. In Dongmen, it locked the village into a collection of ritual practices and architectural styles that freeze community life in an idealized past that never actually existed. This encourages a state-sponsored memory of Qiang villages that denies decades of sociopolitical marginalization at the hands of the contemporary Chinese state. The idealized landscape of reconstructed villages, in turn, becomes an exoticized "culture" that stands in stark contrast to the city life of urban visitors. Such officially organized theater is "ethnicized in the language of officialdom, as 'minority nationality' practices" (Schein 1999, p. 367). In this design, the Qiang are made to represent a "traditional" past that is best put to use as a "consumable other" for the growing tourism appetites of the urban middle class.

Finally, this "cultural reconstruction" does not consider the sustainable growth of places like Dongmen and China as a whole. Locals and tourists complained that aid money was wrongly used to transform the village into a nice-looking tourist site. "Decoration" is the word constantly used by the villagers, emphasizing that the reconstruction only manages to change the appearances of their communities. It fails to fully address their predisaster condition of political and economic marginality or acknowledge their constructed dependency on the national tourism market. There is very limited funding to maintain the high-cost tourism facilities after the reconstruction. Neither local officials nor the villagers had prior experience in tourism development. Due to lack of funding, training, and management experience, officials and villagers are finding it difficult to sustain tourism over the long-term.

## CONCLUSION

Faced with public critiques incited by poor planning and negligence in the construction of public schools and nearby dam projects, the Chinese government has paid tremendous attention to previously marginalized Qiang communities, showcasing its spectacular benevolence in an effort to strengthen its legitimacy and authority. Cultural differences, in this case, are managed to reinforce the government's leadership of the multiethnic nation. Cultures of subaltern peoples are figured as the nation's past, the preservation of which is only meaningful in the form of tourism development.

Using the veil of "cultural sensitivity," the Chinese state's overwhelming power allows it to create a representation of the restored Qiang culture that best suits its own purposes. The state and institutional definitions of "culture" bear a number of critical differences from anthropological understandings of the concept. The Qiang villagers highlight the implications of reducing "culture" to physical structures, selective symbols, or staged performances. Culture, as it is lived and practiced, is a dynamic process mutually influenced by historical conditions and contemporary changes that cannot be "preserved." At the same time, the sense of cultural continuity, especially in a postdisaster context, can be of great importance to disaster survivors (Barrios 2010; Browne 2015), even if the catastrophe brings about changes that guarantee the past can never be identically rebuilt (e.g., radical transformations of the environment, loss of loved ones, and population displacement).

The imposition of state interpretations of "traditional culture" seen in the reconstruction of Dongmen guarantees that disaster survivors experience a sense of displacement, as Han imaginings of their culture are represented to them in their own villages. The unsustainable use of the land, misrepresentation and improper "invention" of tradition, and unchecked marketing of the "culture" for tourism further destroy the cultural life of the people. It increases their vulnerability, while leaving the monumental projects that gave the disaster its form and magnitude unaddressed.

The critical examination of Qiang post–earthquake "culturally sensitive recovery" has great potential for informing disaster research and reconstruction practitioners. This case highlights the need for intervention to consider the human–environment relationships within which "cultures" manifest and take on meaning. Peoples like the Qiang, who have a history of being represented by state actors and urban populations as "primitive" or "barbaric" (a term still in use to refer to ethnic minority groups in China today) and either "developmentally delayed" or outside the trajectory of teleological developmental history altogether, usually engage their local environments through meaning-laden practices that comprise the heart of the culture concept. This falls dismally short of understanding culture from an anthropologically informed vantage point and may imperil the long-term socioeconomic sustainability of disaster-affected communities.

An anthropologically informed approach to culturally sensitive reconstruction would prioritize the voices and experiences of Qiang villagers, giving local knowledge equal if not prioritized status in relation to the decisions, development ideals, and knowledge of state planners and reconstruction experts. It is foolhardy to assume that Qiang communities were idyllic "cultures" that existed independent of state development projects prior to the disaster and that their cultures manifested in relation to a pristine and monistic human ecology before 2008. Certainly, Qiang villagers existed in relation to China's urban and manufacturing centers, either through the effects of government development policies that limited their access to natural resources or in the form of migrant labor to support the state-controlled political economy. Nevertheless, state reconstruction programs failed to consider how the Qiang themselves envisioned how their practices of agricultural production and human–environment relationships should relate to China's industrial juggernaut. This leaves much work in disaster reconstruction to be done from an anthropological perspective.

## ACKNOWLEDGMENTS

This research was supported by National Science Foundation, Association for Asian Studies, Chiang Ching-kuo Foundation for International Scholarly Exchange, and Tulane University, with grants to Qiaoyun Zhang.

## REFERENCES

Appadurai, A. 1996. *Modernity at large: Cultural dimensions of globalization*. Minneapolis, MN: University of Minnesota Press.

Arce, A. and L. Norman. 2000. *Anthropology, development, and modernities: Exploring discourses, counter-tendencies, and violence*. New York: Routledge.

Barrios, R. 2010. You found us doing this, this is our way: Criminalizing second lines, Super Sunday, and habitus in Post-Katrina New Orleans. *Identities: Global Studies in Culture and Power* 17(6): 586–612.

Biersack, A. 1999. From the "new ecology" to the new ecologies. *American Anthropologist* 101(1): 5–18.

Brightman, R. 1995. Forget culture: Replacement, transcendence, relexification. *Cultural Anthropology* 10(4): 509–546.

Browne, K.E. 2015. *Standing in the need: Culture, comfort, and coming home after Katrina*. Austin: University of Texas Press.

Button, G. 2010. *Disaster culture: Knowledge and uncertainty in the wake of human and environmental catastrophe*. Walnut Creek: Left Coast Press.

Chao, E. 2012. *Lijiang stories: Shamans, taxi drivers, and runaway brides in reform-era China*. Seattle, WA: University of Washington Press.

Cheng, W.D., Y. Li, and D.B. Chen. 2008. Jiabao Wen: The Qiang culture and civilization must be well protected. *Minzu News*, May 27. http://www.mzb.com.cn/html/node/30316-1.htm, accessed February 27, 2016.

Chinese State Council. 2008. The State overall planning for post–Wenchuan earthquake restoration and reconstruction. http://www.china-un.org/eng/hyyfy/P020080918842779362472.pdf, accessed February 27, 2016.

Chio, J.T. 2014. *A landscape of travel: The work of tourism in rural ethnic China*. Seattle, WA: University of Washington Press.

Comaroff, J.L. and J. Comaroff. 2009. *Ethnicity, Inc*. Chicago: University of Chicago Press.

Faas, A.J. and R.E. Barrios. 2015. Applied anthropology of risks, hazards, and disasters. *Human Organization* 74(4): 287–296.

Fabian, J. 1983. *Time and the other: How anthropology makes its object*. New York: Columbia University Press.

Ferguson, J. 1999. *Expectations of modernity: Myths and meanings of urban life on the Zambian copper belt*. Berkeley and Los Angeles: University of California Press.

Fischer, M.J. 2007. Culture and cultural analysis as experimental systems. *Cultural Anthropology* 22(1): 1–65.

Gamburd, M.R. 2013. *The golden wave: Culture and politics after Sri Lanka's tsunami disaster*. Bloomington: Indiana University Press.

Gupta, A. and J. Ferguson. 1992. Beyond "culture": Space, identity, and the politics of difference. *Cultural Anthropology* 7(1): 6–23.

Harrell, S. 1995. *Cultural encounters on China's ethnic frontiers*. Seattle, WA: University of Washington Press.

Hastrup, F. 2011. *Weathering the world: Recovery in the wake of the tsunami in a Tami fishing village*. New York and Oxford: Berghahn Books.

Huang, C. and T. Bonschab. 2010. *Evaluation of the implementation of the "State overall planning for post–Wenchuan Earthquake restoration and reconstruction."* Beijing: Social Science Academic Press.

Ingold, T. 2000. *The perception of the environment: Essays on livelihood, dwelling and skill*. London and New York: Routledge.

LaFraniere, S. 2009. Possible link between dam and China quake. The *New York Times*, February 6. http://www.nytimes.com/2009/02/06/world/asia/06quake.html?pagewanted=all, accessed February 27, 2016.

Makley, C. 2014. Spectacular compassion: "Natural" disasters and national mourning in China's Tibet. *Critical Asian Studies* 46(3): 371–404.

Mitchell, T. 2002. *Rule of experts: Egypt, techno-politics modernity.* Berkeley: University of California Press

Notar, B.E. 2006. *Displacing desire: Travel and popular culture in China*. Honolulu, HI: University of Hawai'i Press.

Ortner, S.B. 1996. *Making gender: The politics and erotics of culture*. Boston: Beacon Press.

Povinelli, E.A. 1995. Do rocks listen? The cultural politics of apprehending Australian Aboriginal labor. *American Anthropologist* 97(3): 505–518.

Schein, L. 1999. Performing modernity. *Cultural Anthropology* 14(3): 361–395.

Stocking, G.W., Jr. 1966. Franz Boas and the culture concept in historical perspective. *American Anthropologist* 68(4): 867–882.

Way, J.T. 2012. *The Mayan in the mall: Globalization, development, and the making of modern Guatemala.* Durham: Duke University Press.

Wong, E. 2008. China admits building flaws in quake. The *New York Times*, September 4. http://www.nytimes.com/2008/09/05/world/asia/05china.html, accessed August 27, 2016.

Zhang, Q. 2012. Phoenix out of the ashes: Convergence of disaster and heritage tourism in Jina Qiang Village, Sichuan Province, China. *Practicing Anthropology* 34(3): 24–28.

# 10 The Shared Vulnerability and Resiliency of the Fukushima Animals and Their Rescuers

*Seven Mattes*

## CONTENTS



**Abstract**

Domesticated animals are perhaps the most vulnerable living beings in a disaster. They are entirely reliant humans for their needs. There is a dearth of research on animal vulnerability during disasters or their resilience in the aftermath. Japanese emergency response plans during the March 11, 2011, catastrophe illustrate the problems inherent in ignoring the strong bonds between people and animals. The evacuation required by the Fukushima nuclear disaster mandated that domesticated animals remain behind. With little government aid, their fate lay with a handful of nonprofit animal rescue organizations across Japan, who worked tirelessly to connect with those emotionally distraught about the fate of their companions. Following 12 months of multispecies ethnographic research within animal rescues in Japan, this paper explores the sociopolitical vulnerability of companion animals who were abandoned in the Fukushima no-go zone in 2011. This paper provides an argument for the consideration of human–animal bonds and the inclusion of domesticated animal care in emergency response policies.

## INTRODUCTION

The disaster that struck Japan on March 11, 2011, was a catastrophic combination of a 9.0-magnitude earthquake, a tsunami, and a damaged and malfunctioning nuclear power plant. This resulted in the death and displacement of thousands of humans and animals. The disaster led to the initial displacement of over 470,000 residents. As of November 2015, Japan's Reconstruction Agency (2015) has reported that only 180,000 evacuees remain, awaiting housing reconstruction and/or relocation plans. The temporary shelters did not always allow companion animals to accompany their people or were unclear about their pet guidelines. In some shelters, it was reported that pets were allowed only outdoors, leading evacuees to sleep in their vehicles to accommodate them. In many cases, companion animals were banned primarily due to community disapproval. Even if there was no official ban at the premises, it would be considered discourteous to others present to have them. As a result, many animals faced abandonment, starvation, and euthanasia.

All elements of 3-11 affected both human and animal residents of Tōhoku. However, it was the conditions following the damaged Fukushima Daiichi Nuclear Power Plant that resulted in the highest fatalities and large-scale of abandonment of domesticated animals. While animal rescuers aided in offering shelter and resources to those in the wider earthquake- and tsunami-affected areas, the bulk of the problem and the rescue efforts were in the 20-km evacuation zone.

Due to the radioactive leakage, residents within a fluctuating zone had to evacuate. Temporary shelters were established for the human residents. Officials told evacuees that they would be gone from their homes for a few days. Unfortunately, the situation worsened, leading to further evacuations and the shelters becoming temporary housing. In the urgent days and weeks that followed, direct actions were not taken by officials to provide for the large population of domesticated animals in the no-go zone, resulting in mortality on a large scale. Dogs had been chained up outside with only a few days' worth of food and water; some cats were locked inside homes awaiting their people's return. Agricultural animals perished from starvation or were executed, released, or, rarely, were rescued by a nonprofit organization (NPO) or individual.

Prior to this disaster, there were nearly 6000 dogs and a comparable number of cats, around 3400 cows, 31,500 pigs, and 630,000 chickens (Biddle 2011) in what became the no-entry zone surrounding the Fukushima nuclear site. Relatively few were rescued. The residents were not allowed to return to their homes for weeks, and then only for two- to five-hour visits to collect select family belongings. Those who had pets within the zone returned to find them lost, dead, or otherwise suffering from the neglect. Some used this opportunity to leave bags of food and large amounts of water to last until their next potential visit. Sadly, these bags of food would also attract feral or wild animals and lead to the unforeseen death of the often chained-up pet. Others were able to transport their companion to a shelter, relative, or other arrangements. Signs were placed in front of homes or in neighborhoods stating the presence of animal others, asking for someone to help them.

Those companion animals who survived in Fukushima and the wider Tōhoku region, and were not rescued by intervening NPOs, currently roam the deserted area searching for food, becoming increasingly feral. As many were not neutered or spayed prior to 3-11, they continue to reproduce, worsening the problem. Individuals and local NPOs have set up feeding stations within the no-go zone. They continue to leave and collect traps to take as many as possible out and get them into shelters or homes.

The following sections are drawn from the collected experiences of key informants during my fieldwork at animal rescues in 2014–2015. First, I introduce the consideration of domesticated animals in disaster-related research and provide cultural context. Next, I discuss the sociopolitical vulnerability of animal rescue NPOs, who volunteered to aid animal others during the 3-11 aftermath, and their rescues. Finally, I introduce resiliency tactics and recommendations expressed to me by informants who have lived through a multitude of disasters in Japan, to better plan for the next catastrophe.

## LITERATURE REVIEW

### Human–Animal Relationships

The social sciences are increasingly addressing and exposing those areas of academia in which animals are significant, despite being previously marginalized (DeMello 2010; Noske 1989). As this new focus turns a scholarly gaze to human–animal relationships, the significance of animals in the lives of humans becomes increasingly apparent. These range from emotional ties to food dependencies. Animals are prevalent in human societies, with a variety of meanings, values, and perceptions attached to them, differing by culture and context.

This chapter specifically focuses on domesticated animals, primarily those we call "pets." The definition of "pet" can be traced back to singling out individual animals for special treatment (Grier 2006). Companion animals, or pets, are prevalent in cultures around the world. They enjoy special attention by their individual people and, in some nations, legal protections. The perceptions of pets range from living burglar alarm to trendy and temporary fashion accessory to lifelong family members residing within homes. Companion animals are often legally considered property of their humans, commodities who can be bought and sold or disposed of when desired. As Hurn (2012, p. 98) states, "... the sociocultural (and legally sanctioned) expectation is that pets belong to individual humans who have certain responsibilities towards these animals, but also the power over the animal's life and death." The emotional connection we may have with these living beings is not always reflected in our legal systems or policies. Like many sociopolitical vulnerabilities, this certainly becomes strikingly apparent during disasters.

## Companion Animals in Disasters

Oliver-Smith (2009) argues that there is no such thing as a "natural" disaster. Disasters are the result of vulnerable social conditions and the onset of a man-made or biophysical problem. They are the actualization of historically rooted social vulnerability produced via sociopolitical systems (Davis 2001). Therefore, preexisting social inequalities shape the size and degree of impact and the recovery process. Domesticated animals are some of the most vulnerable of living beings in a disaster situation, as they rely entirely on their human caretakers for basic needs and are rarely legally or politically protected.

Humans have the power to cause or prevent disaster for animals by lessening vulnerabilities (Irvine 2009). Irvine (2009) asks, "When a disaster strikes, who should enter the ark?" This calls into question how we decide which animals are protected during a disaster and what this says about how given cultures value certain species. Emergency response policies reiterate and reflect values that give preference to human lives and potentially ignore the strong emotional and social connections between humans and animals, leading to disasters within disasters. For example, during Hurricane Katrina, the residents were forced to evacuate without their animals, as in Japan. This led some to risk their lives to remain with their pets. "According to a Fritz Institute survey, approximately 44% of the people who did not evacuate for Hurricane Katrina stayed, at least in part, because they did not want to leave their pets behind" (Department of Homeland Security [DHS] 2007). These were often those who were already vulnerable, who did not already have the resources to evacuate the area with animals.

As animals could not accompany humans during evacuation, a large-scale animal rescue took place. However, this rescue effort was limited to companion animals. Irvine (2009, p. 3) explains,

> The effort was a disaster-upon-a-disaster, as animal welfare groups struggled to find ways to feed, house, and care for the endless stream of dogs and cats brought out of stricken areas. Yet, as rescuers roamed the streets of New Orleans, breaking into homes to rescue dogs, cats, birds, and other companion animals, millions of farm animals died because of Katrina...the media reports these, and the deaths of other animals used for food, as "losses" for the producers. Their lives are not noted.

Due to the value of these animals in American culture and the resulting backlash that occurred following Hurricane Katrina, and because of the safety risk for both the animals and city from leaving them behind, the Pets Evacuation and Transportation Standard (PETS) Act was enacted. This represents a start to addressing the needs of animals in a disaster (Irvine 2009). The Act requires companion animals to be included in disaster planning.

In Japan, the disaster aftermath reflected the values placed on the variety of animals residing in the Tōhoku region. Despite agricultural animals being present in large numbers, the majority of the rescue efforts were focused on companion animals. The value of companion animals has grown in the past three decades, as Japan's pet boom has continued to usher them into the home. In many cases, they are considered animal friends or "fuzzy kin" (Hansen 2013), sometimes serving as an alternative to children or a remedy for an "empty nest." Values and perceptions of companion animals are highly regional in Japan, however. For example, dogs in the disaster-ravaged Tōhoku region are commonly kept outdoors as *banken*, or guard dogs, rarely entering the family home. In comparison, it is just as common to find a dog snoozing in a stroller and dressed as a child within the Tokyo area.

## METHODS AND INFORMANTS

I conducted 12 months of multispecies ethnographic fieldwork at a variety of NPOs who continue to support the ongoing 3-11 disaster aftermath from 2014 to 2015. Multispecies ethnography considers not only the human as a subject but also other species. It recognizes that that our social world is composed of, and affected by, a multitude of interspecies relationships (Kirksey and Helmreich 2010). This chapter contributes to the fieldwork's broader purpose of understanding the changing human–animal relationships during and following a disaster.

This project was carried out with qualitative research methods (Bernard 2005), including participant observation (DeWalt and DeWalt 2002), semistructured interviews (Oakley 1981), and questionnaires. To gather data, I volunteered at four key animal rescue NPOs in Japan, becoming acquainted with both the humans and animals who experienced the 2011 event. There were 64 interviewees, including 6 directors of NPOs, 25 staff members at these organizations, and 29 volunteers. Interviews were conducted in English and in Japanese, with 18 requiring the use of a translator. While 27 participants were Japanese, 13 more were long-term expatriates. Thirteen others were volunteering short-term (less than a year) and came from all corners of the world, from Iceland to Australia. Roughly 68% of participants interviewed, and significantly more who volunteered alongside me, were women. All participants in this study volunteered or worked in animal rescue efforts following the triple disaster and/or took in companion animals who were rescued. Some continue these efforts, entering the 20-km no-go zone to help the animals still beyond the blockades.

The animal rescue NPOs in this study have small staffs (1–30). As they rely on donations, they are often consistently underfunded and stretch resources as far as they possibly can. This is typical of NPOs in Japan, especially animal welfare–related ones (Ahonen 2012; Kawato, Pekkanen, and Tsujinka 2012). A few were well established prior to 2011, but many rose out of the disaster aftermath when registration of new NPOs was streamlined to encourage disaster relief efforts (Avenell 2012). Western foreigners largely initiated these NPOs. These were often expatriates who brought in their own cultural brand of animal welfare. However, it is becoming more common for Japanese-run organizations to sprout up and flourish (Ahonen 2012).

Rather than working together for a larger cause, these groups are often fragmented and factionalized, working for their local area alone (Interview, Director of NPO, 3/23/2015). While there were a number of nonprofits, individuals, and other organizations that aided in the disaster aftermath, this study focuses on those organizations with which I conducted my fieldwork. These include, but are not limited to, Animal Refuge Kansai (ARK), Heart Tokushima, Animal Friends Niigata (AFN), and Japan Cat Network.

## FINDINGS

### Vulnerability of Animal Rescuers

Japan is no stranger to catastrophic events. Despite the multitude of failures in properly handling the Fukushima Daiichi situation, internal disaster response operations reacted quickly and smoothly.

This is especially true when compared to the infamous government failures of the major earthquake (Hanshin-Awaji) in Kobe in 1995 (Avenell 2012). However, these improvements were largely only in human-oriented disaster response.

The initial decision to leave domesticated animals behind during the evacuation, combined with the lack of institutional aid for animals in the wider Tōhoku region, set the stage for the situation that followed. Due to the lack of initial official support, as their focus was on human need, the majority of the animal rescue efforts fell into the hands of a number of small NPOs. In the case of the Japan-based groups, resources were already tight. Elizabeth Oliver of ARK (1999) reported a similar situation during the 1995 earthquake.

> As the days passed and the scale of the tragedy unfolded it became clear what a huge task for us lay ahead. Priority is of course on rescue but then what? We had at ARK facilities for perhaps a hundred dogs at a pinch and fifty cats but how to cope with the potentially thousands of animals made homeless in the quake? In other countries with established animal welfare systems, there is a built-in evacuation mechanism to rescue and save animals in cases of natural disasters, with facilities to care for them, and trained people to treat them. In Japan, there are no facilities for holding animals except the *hokensho* which are geared only for killing. Veterinary clinics and pet hotels have limited facilities for short-term stays where animals are invariably confined to tiny cages.

Despite nearly a decade passing, little has changed. This disappointing fact was noted by all of those interviewed who had also experience the earthquake in 1995.

Isabella Gallaon, director of AFN, heard about the abandoned animals in the 20-km no-go zone. She decided to head in 10 days after the earthquake, which required entering illegally, as there were checkpoints that would not permit entrance for animal rescue. She asserts, "as far as I'm concerned, I'm in animal rescue, this is what I do. There is an animal, if not animals, who needs rescuing and I've just got to do it." She describes the situation as dangerous in a personal interview (3/9/2015).

> The roads were really bad, ten days after the disaster...That was actually quite scary as there was no phone signal and if we get stuck in one of the cracks, or something, we just have to walk out of here somehow... There was a stench of death. There were putrefying bodies throughout, you could smell it...and there were loud explosions in the background from the nuclear plant. We did take a Geiger counter in, but we couldn't get hold of a decent one. It was a shaky old thing with a dial that was just going berserk. We had no idea of the radiation, but probably it was better not to know. I can imagine that was what going into war is like. Because you're just concentrating on what you've got to do. You don't even have time to think about it.

Gallaon's volunteers, as the geographically closest NPO in an animal rescue coalition called JEARS (Japan Earthquake Animal Rescue and Support), were responsible for bringing out the majority of the companion animals rescued in the 20-km zone in those critical first few weeks after the disaster, using traps for cats and treats to lure dogs into crates.

Official support was noticeably lacking. Despite a large amount of donations coming in to the Dobutsu Kyuen Honbu (Headquarters for the Relief of Animals in Emergencies), animal rescue nonprofits saw little of these funds, despite ongoing efforts. According to Hiro Yamasaki, who set up a spay/neuter clinic in Fukushima Prefecture in the aftermath of 3-11,

> [The Dobutsu Kyuen Honbu] was set up after the Hanshin-Awaji earthquake in 1995 with the intention of helping in future emergencies. In reality, it has done nothing of the kind... poor investment decisions have so far led to losses of ¥8.4 million after the purchase of mutual funds in 2006. A massive ¥200 million currently sits in the organization's account with no designated purpose. (*The Japan Times* 2013)

All five directors of animal rescue NPOs shared fears that this money would be either lost or otherwise misused before the next disaster. Yamasaki explained to me in an interview (2015), "There are no lobbyists of animal rights or welfare." All the weight falls on the shelters, and the shelters lack political power. In fact, they are barely known by the public.

### Animal Vulnerability

The animals suffered a myriad of afflictions. As one volunteer notes, "It wasn't fluffy dogs and cute kitties, these animals had psychological problems." The rescued companion animals had been traumatically separated from their humans. In addition to the usual afflictions accompanying rescue animals, such as a lack of socialization or dog aggression, these pets could have depression, posttraumatic stress disorder, and anxiety from their experiences (Tuber et al. 1999; Wells and Hepper 1992). The stressful life in a crowded and chaotic shelter compounded these issues, as weeks, months, and years went by. As a staff member at ARK explained, "Some dogs will stop eating or will become aggressive when previously friendly." Many dogs could not handle the other dogs' smells and sounds or the multitude of unknown humans coming and going. Cats had trouble with overcrowding and the proximity to nearby barking dogs. Combining these conditions with a large influx of new volunteers, some of whom had never handled a dog before, created sometimes chaotic conditions (Veterinary Nurse, Animal Rescue NPO, Interview 8/5/2014).

Furthermore, many animals arrived unvaccinated, not yet neutered or spayed, and/or requiring often-costly vet care due to injury or sickness. Microchipping has only recently become a mainstream practice for companion animals; thus, information on their medical or social issues was difficult to obtain. As some pets were found wandering or otherwise trapped away from their home, contacting their previous caretakers for this information or for reuniting them was difficult.

The difficulty of reuniting companion animals with their humans was compounded by the fact that residents remained in temporary housing for years. Those who were able to move had to deal with relatively strict housing rules regarding pets. Thus, many of the rescued animals required rehoming. This process often takes a long time for a number of reasons. First, the majority of pets in Japan are purchased from pet shops. Animal shelters are scant and often unknown to the typical pet shopper. Furthermore, informants explained that a rehomed animal is considered a "used" animal, having belonged to someone else. As the Japanese do not often use "preowned" items, they similarly purchase "new" animals.

Rescuing animals is becoming more common, according to the directors of these shelters, but rehoming animals, especially dogs, can still take years. An exception to this was the initial desire to adopt a "disaster" pet during the immediate aftermath. This occurred after the Kobe Earthquake in 1995 and again after 3-11. Having a dog or cat who survived the disaster became temporarily trendy, both in Japan and abroad. This may represent a materially obtainable, and perhaps socially recognizable, form of contributing aid to address the large-scale problem.

## BUILDING RESILIENCY

### Carrying Capacity

The various NPOs employ a number of tactics to remain resilient. The most important, and most emotionally difficult, one is the use of foresight and rationality. As Elizabeth Oliver of ARK warns (personal communication, 2015), "I think we have to avoid burnout. We cannot save everything. We should aim to be compassionate and avoid sentimentality." A staff member echoed this, noting, "You want to save as many dogs as possible, but there is a certain capacity." With the sheer number of retrieved animals, the rescue efforts have long-term consequences. As Susan Mercer of Heart Tokushima explained (2015),

> Before the earthquake our max number of dogs was only 40 or 50. After the earthquake we took in almost 100 dogs and basically our numbers have stayed about the same…it's 3 or 3.5 years now and of course everyone's forgotten about the earthquake. Donations, volunteers and adoptions have decreased. Now is the most difficult point for us, as opposed to before when everyone was willing to help.

Hundreds of these pets still reside within shelter walls originally meant to be temporary; disaster-related funds have largely run dry. As people turn toward other news items or a new disaster in another part of the world, it is difficult to obtain financial support for an indeterminate period of time or to rehome such a massive amount of pets. As difficult as it is to turn away when there are still animals who need to be saved, it is essential to both human and animal well-being to avoid overcommitment.

## Pet-Friendly Shelters

An important recommendation that comes out of my fieldwork is the need to permit pets in evacuation shelters or temporary housing facilities or to have accessible government-run shelters adjacent to the human-only facilities. "The best situation would be that there would be evacuation shelters where they could have pets, and others where pets are not allowed—just as in apartment complexes," argued one ARK staff member. Allowing pets to accompany their people during an evacuation or when seeking shelter is about more than preserving the lives of the animals. It is also an issue of emotional well-being for their people. As Oliver (1999) learned in the aftermath of the 1995 Kobe earthquake,

> For single elderly people especially, having a pet to look after would relieve their loneliness and stress. Without the pet they held nearest and dearest to them they would be more likely to suffer depression and illness. This in reality became the case. More than a hundred elderly people were to take their own lives or die alone in the temporary housing units over the next year. But at the time the local governments actively discouraged pets in temporary housing or outright banned them, despite the fact we urged these cities to consider the importance of keeping pets and owners together.

In the 3-11 aftermath, informants observed the positive emotional impact of those evacuation shelters that allowed, or tolerated, the keeping of companion animals. The presence of pets can be therapeutic. Hurn (2012) argues that pets aid in physical health benefits such as lowering blood pressure. They also provide "ice breakers" with fellow humans, encouraging communication and perhaps brief distractions in an otherwise monotonous atmosphere. One volunteer who participated in animal rescue in the Fukushima region noted that those few companion animals who were kept near or even within evacuation shelters, against regulations, became a sort of community mascot, especially for the children. The companion animals provided purpose and reciprocated affection to those who cared for them (volunteer, interview, 2015).

In the United States, the allowance for pets in evacuation procedures and accepting them in temporary shelters and housing have precedent. Pet-friendly temporary shelters are being encouraged, as the PETS Act is addressed by each state. For example, the Mississippi Board of Animal Health (n.d.) integrated this into its emergency programming. Pet-friendly sheltering is defined as

> …a public human emergency shelter that is located within the same area or facility as an emergency shelter for pets. These shelters typically allow pet owners to take care of their own animals, reducing the shelters' logistical and staffing requirements (DHS 2015).

Such shelters are designed with the advice and collaboration of local Animal Control or Animal Rescue institutions. They make use of public spaces, such as parks and fairgrounds. They prearrange veterinary services and other key resources prior to a disaster occurring. Such measures are an extension to other human services considered necessary during and following major disasters.

## Volunteer Infrastructure

The Kobe earthquake of 1995 displayed a lack of volunteer infrastructure; there were willing volunteers, but little coordination of them. They would show up with no arrangements for sleep or food. Rather than accomplishing anything worthwhile, they took resources from those they hoped to help (Avenell 2012). By the time 3-11 occurred, Japan was far more prepared to provide training to and coordination of volunteer efforts. Learning from Kobe, there was a system that connected the state to the individual volunteer. This brought people to where they were needed, with the proper accommodations and training to make a difference. This structure rose above traditional volunteer arrangements that were disjointed and community based. As Avenell (2012, p. 70) explains,

> After the triple-disaster in Tohoku we have witnessed the operation of a highly organized, professionalized, networked, and financed volunteer infrastructure, involving extensive cooperation and collaboration among state authorities, quasi-governmental organizations, NGOs and NPOs, corporations and business organizations, and voluntary groups.

However, despite these vast improvements for human aid, key interviewees who experienced both disasters noted no improvement for the volunteer infrastructure within animal rescue efforts. As there was no order, no hierarchy of command, and no standards and regulations, it was a chaotic process. Including volunteer coordination alongside human and structure-based volunteering for animal rescue efforts would have contributed to a more orderly rescue effort. The infrastructure already exists; it merely needs to be extended to the NPOs working for animals.

Furthermore, volunteers from abroad often lacked proper cultural and linguistic training to carry out their activities. For example, I spoke to several international volunteers who believed the owners of the abandoned pets did not deserve them or believed that they would be better off in their care. They displayed ignorance regarding the conditions that led to leaving behind often-beloved pets. Further, their interaction with authorities sometimes proved difficult and frustrating for all parties, as native Japanese speaker would not always accompany them. Unfortunately, due in part to these types of culturally insensitive actions, entry into the no-go zone proved more difficult over time. This forced legitimate and respectful organizations to explore other options to rescue animals. Proper training for international volunteers, such as by the organization that recruits them or establishing a partner system that assures that a Japanese-fluent and culturally knowledgeable person accompanies these volunteers during rescue activities, could greatly help overall community relations and support of animal rescue efforts.

### Spay/Neuter and Microchipping

When interviewed, Hiro Yamasaki of Animal Rescue System Fund explained the need to push for spay/neuter practices in Japan as a way to enhance future disaster resiliency. He notes, "You have to decrease the number of animals that need to be rescued before the disaster" (2015). Yamasaki initially ran a spay-neuter clinic following the 1995 Kobe disaster, greatly reducing the feral population in the years that followed. He continues to run a clinic in Fukushima Prefecture, which has already lowered the number of reproducing feral animals significantly. Residents in that area did not typically spay/neuter their pets. As spay/neuter practices were highly priced and not valued, it was a common practice to simply drown unwanted litters of kittens or puppies. Several interviewees noted that this was considered "bringing them back to nature." Had spay/neuter practices, such as "Trap, Neuter, and Release" programs, been more common and accessible prior to 3-11 and used to control feral populations already present, the disaster aftermath would have required significantly less resources.

This is also the case with microchipping. According to those interviewed, this has only recently become a recommended practice by veterinarians in Japan. Most companion animals in Fukushima Prefecture were not microchipped. Had it been the norm, they note, many pets could have reunited with their people.

## CONCLUSION

Addressing the response for animals in disaster situations is a global and urgent need. Although this chapter focuses on companion animals, including the plethora of other species who exist in our care carries the same urgency. This chapter serves as one example of the consequences of not fully preparing for the nonhuman aspect of a disaster. Failing to account for the human–animal bond that exists between human and companion animal in modern Japanese culture created additional emotional and physical health and recovery issues. Further, it exacerbated long-term economic and livelihood problems, especially as related to farmers and their herds. A number of farmers, for instance, committed suicide in the 3-11 aftermath due to the death of their animals and/or from the inability to sell their products in any foreseeable future due to the radiation contamination (Herrmann 2011; *The Japan Times* 2013).

For companion animals, basic prevention strategies, such as planning pet-friendly emergency shelters, microchipping, and an increase in spay/neuter programs, are globally applicable. Their implementation can result in greatly reducing the amount of resources needed following a disaster. Furthermore, extending volunteer infrastructure to account for culturally significant animals in a given location, be they cats or cows, can serve to aid humans emotionally and financially postdisaster. Vulnerabilities can be lessened, and resiliency strengthened, for humans and animals. As illustrated in Japan, their fate is often entangled.

## REFERENCES

Ahonen, P. 2012. *Relievers, bridge-builders and watchdogs: Framing and civil society construction by Japanese pro-animal organizations in the Kansai and Tokyo Areas*. Turun yliopisto, Finland: University of Turku, Studies on Contemporary East Asia.

Avenell, S. 2012. From Kobe to Tōhoku: The potential and peril of a volunteer infrastructure. In *Natural disaster and nuclear crisis in Japan: Response and recovery after Japan's 3/11*, ed. J. Kingston, 53–77. New York: Routledge.

Bernard, R.H. 2005. *Research methods in anthropology: Qualitative and quantitative approaches* (4th ed.). Lanham, MD: AltaMira Press.

Biddle, S. 2011. The lost animals of Fukushima. *Gizmodo*. http://gizmodo.com/5801749/the-lost-animals-of-fukushima, accessed May 20, 2011.

Davis, M. 2001. *Late Victorian holocausts: El Niño famines and the making of the Third World*. London: Verso.

DeMello, M. 2010. Anthropology's animals. In *Teaching the animal: Human–animal studies across the disciplines*, ed. M. DeMello, 387–393. Brooklyn, NY: Lantern Books.

Department of Homeland Security. 2007. Shelter operations: Pet-friendly shelters. http://www.ready.gov/sites/default/files/documents/files/FEMAPetShelteringbestpractices2007.pdf, accessed November 2, 2015.

DeWalt, K.M. and B.R. DeWalt. 2002. *Participant observation: A guide for fieldworkers*. Walnut Creek, CA: AltaMira Press.

Grier, K.C. 2006. *Pets in America: A history*. Chapel Hill, NC: University of North Carolina Press.

Hansen, P. 2013. Urban Japan's "fuzzy" new families: Affect and embodiment in dog–human relationships. *Asian Anthropology* 12(2): 83–103.

Herrmann, L. 2011. Suicide in Japan on the rise after Fukushima disaster. *Digital Journal*. http://www.digitaljournal.com/article/308815, accessed July 6, 2011.

Hurn, S. 2012. *Humans and other animals: Cross-cultural perspectives on human–animal interactions*. London: Pluto Press.

Irvine, L. 2009. *Filing the ark: Animal welfare in disasters*. Philadelphia, PA: Temple University Press.

Kawato, Y., R. Pekkanen, and Y. Tsujinaka. 2012. Civil society and the triple disasters: Revealed strengths and weaknesses. In *Natural disaster and nuclear crisis in Japan: Response and recovery after Japan's 3/11*, ed. J. Kingston, 77–93. New York: Routledge.

Kirksey, E. and S. Helmreich. 2010. The emergence of multispecies ethnography. *Cultural Anthropology* 25(4): 545–576.

Mississippi Board of Animal Health. n.d. *MBAH companion and animal sheltering plan*. Jackson, MS: Mississippi Board of Animal Health. http://www.mbah.state.ms.us/emergency_programs/companion_animal_sheltering_plan.htm, accessed November 2, 2015.

Noske, B. 1989. *Humans and other animals: Beyond the boundaries of anthropology*. London: Pluto Press.

Oakley, A. 1981. Interviewing women: A contradiction in terms. In *Doing feminist research*, ed. H. Roberts, 30–61. London and New York: Routledge.

Oliver, E. 1999. *Best friends*. Translated by M. Mimura. Tokyo, Japan: Shobunsha Publications, Inc.

Oliver-Smith, A. 2009. Understanding Hurricane Mitch: Complexity, causality, and the political ecology of disaster. In *The legacy of Hurricane Mitch: Lessons from post-disaster reconstruction in Honduras*, ed. M.O. Ensor, 1–21. Tucson: The University of Arizona Press.

Reconstruction Agency. 2015. Efforts for the reconstruction of Tohoku. http://www.reconstruction.go.jp/, accessed November 15, 2015.

*The Japan Times*. 2013. Tepco admits culpability in Fukushima farmer's suicide. http://www.japantimes.co.jp/news/2013/06/07/national/crime-legal/tepco-admits-culpability-in-fukushima-farmers-suicide/#.VeXidLxVikp, accessed June 7, 2013.

Tuber, D.S., D.D. Miller, K.A. Caris, R. Halter, F. Linden, and M.B. Hennessy. 1999. Dogs in animal shelters: Problems, suggestions, and needed expertise. *Psychological Science* 10(5): 379–386.

Wells, D. and P.G. Hepper. 1992. The behavior of dogs in a rescue shelter. *Animal Welfare* 1(3): 171–186.

# *Section II*

## *Impacts on Resilience and Vulnerability*

# *Food Security and Livelihoods*

This section takes a more focused look at social dynamics that can contribute to both vulnerability and resilience. Social, political, religious, and economic inequalities structure levels of vulnerability and predict the likelihood of food insecurity. Food security is a major predictor of resilience and recovery, so it is explored in depth. It is intimately linked with livelihood systems, which integrate strategies and coping mechanisms for physical and economic survival (e.g., agriculture, pastoralism, fishing, petty trading, wage labor, or a combination). These systems are shaped by local contexts, such as agro-ecological zones and climate, social, economic, and political environments, and by access to assets including human, social, natural, physical, and financial capital.

# 11 Understanding Child Nutrition Preservation after an Extreme Weather Event Disaster

## *Lessons from Tropical Storm Ketsana and Typhoon Parma (2009) in the Philippines*

*Erlidia F. Llamas-Clark and Cathy Banwell*

**CONTENTS**

**Abstract**

Seasonal tropical cyclones and consequent flooding expose Filipinos to food insecurity, hunger, and endemic malnutrition despite existing health and nutrition policies and programs. After the 2009 extreme weather events (EWEs) Tropical Storm Ketsana and the Typhoon Parma flooding disaster in Luzon, Philippines, we examined the experiences of local officials and community health workers to identify practices that impact child health and nutrition and to develop the EWE/Disaster Food and Nutrition Security Conceptual Framework. This incorporates vulnerability, resilience, and disaster management to understand the basic causes of undernutrition. Preflooding investments in child nutrition determinants had been established but were inadequate over the long-term after the flood. Strengthening resources and child nutrition preservation initiatives with sustainable livelihood assistance, social welfare support, and gender-sensitive disaster risk reduction strategies are needed to prepare for a changing climate and for future mitigation and adaptation measures.

## INTRODUCTION

Extreme weather events (EWEs) are predicted to increase in frequency and intensity, with global environmental change compromising the food and nutrition security of vulnerable sectors of society, particularly children. The widely accepted climate–health pathway illustrates that one of the direct impacts of climate change is the increase in EWE frequency and severity, which impact food and nutrition security (McMichael 2013). The impact of EWEs can also trigger indirect health pathways leading to undernutrition, such as loss of jobs and livelihoods and displacement (McMichael and Lindgren 2011; McMichael, Nyong, and Corvalan 2008). Pathways through which global climate variability and EWEs influence human nutrition operate at national level and on smaller scales in local communities.

There is a growing body of literature on tropical cyclones and flood-related health impacts (Alderman, Turner, and Tong 2012; Bich, Quang, Ha, Hahn, and Guha-Sapir 2011; Doocy, Daniels, Murray, and Kirsch 2013; Doocy, Dick, Daniels, and Kirsch 2013). Studies of severe storms and floods in South Asia, Latin America, the Caribbean, and Africa suggest an increased prevalence and risk of malnutrition postflood (Baez and Santos 2007; Barrios, Stansbury, Palencia, and Medina 2000; Cairncross and Alvarinho 2006; Choudhury and Bhuiya 1993; del Ninno and Lundberg 2005; Omitsu and Yamano 2006; Portner 2010). However, studies in Dominica and Tonga indicate lower postcyclone malnutrition prevalence attributed to food relief and quick responses (Finau 1986; Wit and Gooder 1981). These areas share prevailing underdevelopment, deprived socioeconomic conditions, and prevalence of childhood illnesses, all factors that contribute to vulnerability to malnutrition.

An understanding of the social context is required for fuller assessment of the exposure to, and outcomes of, EWEs. Attributing undernutrition as a direct outcome of an EWE is complex. Many biological and socioeconomic factors, such as age, gender, health status, dietary intake, socioeconomic status, food security, caregiving practices, and cultural attitudes, affect nutritional status (Anderson, Bignell, Winful, Soyiri, and Steiner-Asiedu 2010; Ricci and Becker 1996).

In the Philippines, government and nongovernment organizations (NGOs) from different sectors have tackled undernutrition. Interventions include nutrition promotion, nutrient fortification, food production initiatives, and feeding programs. Basic food and rice subsidies and multisectoral food security programs have also been implemented (Ravanera and Emata 2012). With the prediction of an increase in climate- and weather-related events, the importance of such interventions at the community level needs to be assessed periodically to determine if they address the people's needs.

Seasonal tropical cyclones and consequent flooding have always been part of Filipinos' way of life, particularly in Luzon and Eastern Visayas, exposing them to food insecurity, hunger, and endemic malnutrition despite existing health and nutrition policies and programs. Past events have prompted adaptation strategies, allowing them to manage losses and cope with health and other problems. However, more frequent occurrence of EWEs and widespread flooding suggests that public health could be increasingly compromised, particularly in marginalized sectors. Accordingly, existing adaptation strategies need to be enhanced in order to reduce the impact of future exposure to such events.

In this chapter, we discuss mixed-methods research to determine the relationship between exposure to EWEs and children's nutritional status. We hypothesize that exposure to EWEs contributes to child undernutrition and current disaster risk reduction initiatives and programs may not be adequate in future EWE threats. We use interviews with key informants (KIs), such as government officials and health workers, to identify practices at the community level that support or undermined child health and nutrition preservation.

## EWEs IN 2009: TROPICAL STORM KETSANA AND TYPHOON PARMA

In 2009, tropical storm (TS) Ketsana brought an unusually high volume of rain in a short period (450 mm recorded at the Manila Observatory in 12 hours on September 26, 2009). This caused widespread flooding in Manila and 25 provinces in Luzon. A week later, typhoon (TY) Parma's heavy rain (exceeding 1000 mm in some areas) added large amounts of water to areas already affected by TS Ketsana, resulting in extensive flooding.

While many communities are familiar with, and have adapted to, this type of exposure, thousands of Filipinos in low-lying flood-prone areas were unprepared for the amount of rainfall and the sudden rise in flood water. The agricultural sector of Luzon incurred serious damage and losses to rice crops and fishing, which threatened the food security of the country. Around two months post-disaster, the World Food Program reported children aged 0–59 months had high rates of sickness and vulnerability to diseases that could lead to malnutrition and mortality (World Food Programme [WFP] 2010). We therefore investigated whether there was an association between flooding disaster exposure and undernutrition and asked how this happened.

## UNDERSTANDING THE IMPACTS OF EWEs ON CHILD UNDERNUTRITION

This EWE highlights the need for in-depth knowledge of the development of child undernutrition, as well as the effects of current nutrition and health policies and programs. Because of the impact of TS Ketsana/TY Parma on the Philippines, this EWE was selected as a case study. We adapted a socioecological model for our study that demonstrates the interrelationships and multiple influences on health, including sociopolitical and cultural factors and the physical environment (Mude, Barrett, McPeak, Kaitho, and Kristjanson 2009; Sallis, Owen, and Fisher 2008).

Based on this theoretical understanding, an EWE/Disaster Food and Nutrition Security Conceptual Framework was developed, incorporating the concepts of vulnerability, resilience, and disaster management to understand the basic causes of undernutrition. It also combines elements from a number of existing conceptual frameworks (Engle, Menon, and Haddad 1999; Food and Agriculture Organization 2008; Gregory, Ingram, and Brklacich 2005; Jason et al. 2010; Schmidhuber and Tubiello 2007; United Nations Children's Fund 1990). The new framework incorporates different nutritional status determinants, with a practical approach suited to local contexts. It provides a basis for explaining the link between EWEs and the interactions of demographic and socioeconomic factors that contribute to food insecurity leading to poor nutritional outcomes.

## METHODS

### SURVEY OF DISTRICT IV OF LAGUNA PROVINCE, PHILIPPINES

Our research site is an important geographical area. It consists of 16 municipalities, covering 45.6% of the land area of the province. It includes Santa Cruz, the capital of Laguna, which has regulatory mandate over the province's municipalities and jurisdiction over the biggest public hospital. It is the economic growth center due to its developed infrastructure and social services.

A mixed method research design is used to illuminate food security vulnerability. A brief summary of the results of the quantitative component of our research provides context for the detailed discussion of the results of interviews with KIs. The study was conducted between May 2011 and February 2012, commencing 18 to 24 months postflooding disaster. It consisted of a face-to-face, cross-sectional survey with a "before and after" section to include temporality in analyzing the impact of the disaster on child nutritional status (CNS). The National Disaster Coordinating Council (NDCC) Report on affected "barangays" (smallest local government units, equivalent to a village) guided the multistage cluster sampling from the provincial, district, municipality, and barangay to the household level. Households with children aged 18–108 months and their mothers participated in this study. The sampling frame was based on the local village *Operation Timbang* (the local growth monitoring and surveillance program) list of children aged 0–71 months and immunization records of all children.*

The research team, composed of medical practitioners, local government barangay health workers, and barangay nutrition scholars, implemented three locally validated, translated questionnaires: (1) the Philippine National Demographic and Health Survey questionnaire combined with the Emergency Food and Nutrition Assessment Survey; (2) the Household Food Security Survey, and the (3) standard pediatric health and medical history questionnaire and examination (National Statistics Office [Philippines] and ICF Macro 2009; Radimer, Olson, Greene, Campbell, and Habicht 1992; WFP 2010). The time reference period was modified to capture disaster-related health information and food and nutrition insecurity experiences of mothers, children, and households.

Participants included 1088 children and their mothers, who provided demographic, child nutrition and health, and household food insecurity status data. Analyses with SPSS 20 were conducted using current weights and heights of children aged 0–5 years and historical data from monitoring records. The analysis of responses was used to estimate the extent of household food insecurity as a result of an EWE/disaster.

### KI Interviews

The lead author conducted in-depth interviews with local officials and community health workers engaging in health and nutrition-related activities during and after TS Ketsana/TY Parma to better understand their experiences of the event in the context of child nutrition preservation. They were asked about the state of children's nutrition during and after the flood, community nutrition and health programs, changes in food production, access to food, disease outbreaks, and other health concerns. The analysis of the interviews is guided by the disaster management cycle (Parihar 2011), to assist in navigating the complex events within the flooding disaster and to assign temporal relationships to identified themes and by standard thematic analyzes strategies (Corbin and Strauss 2008; Pope, Ziebland, and Mays 2000). The qualitative data analysis software Atlas.ti 5.7 provides systematic data management.

## RESULTS AND DISCUSSION

There were 946 children recruited from the 13 flood-affected villages of six Laguna District IV municipalities. These municipalities are heterogeneous in socioeconomic distribution, reflecting a transitioning rural to urban economy. The majority of households rely on the wages of husbands engaged in the service industry (50.6%). Most families (67.4%) belonged to a middle-income group, earning 5000–19,999 Philippine pesos per month (roughly 106–424 USD). Around 22% were from

* The health workers and nutrition scholars of each barangay had existing data or records of children at the time of exposure to the EWE, which were available at the start of the study.

the low-income group, and only 10.2% were from the high-income category. Participants experienced different levels of flooding during the EWE. Around 43.4% were in the low-exposure group (ankle–knee flood level), 38.8% in the moderate (thigh–waist level), and 17.8% in the high-exposure group (chest and above).

The overall prevalence of underweight was 27.3% and stunting was 36.7% in this population. The prevalence of underweight and stunting is higher than the national estimates of 26.2% and 27.9%, respectively. A comparison between scores demonstrates that there were more children with normal weights before the flood who became underweight postflood (18.6%), compared to those who were previously underweight and who attained normal weight thereafter (11.1%). This result shows a statistically significant underweight change between the preflood and postflood periods ($p < .001$). Most of the children (56.8%) were in good health, while 43.2% suffered some form of illness since the flood.

Factors associated with underweight and stunting include children who were aged >24 months, had a higher number of siblings, and whose households had no water within their premises. Flood exposure did not have any association with child underweight. Child stunting was associated with a child being ill, low level of maternal education, having a water source outside household premises, and low flood level of less than 2 weeks duration.

Around 18–24 months postflood, the children exhibited a change in weight for age *Z* scores indicative of underweight and slow growth. This may be due to the existence of several assistance programs in the first 6 months postflood ranging from food aid to cash for work incentives. These immediate and intermediate interventions could have provided a buffer against the lack of food and resources for food procurement that can affect dietary intake. As time passed by, assistance became less and eventually stopped. This resulted in child underweight, but children <24 months remained protected. Child stunting, a time-dependent indicator, manifested and was associated with flood exposure. A household's steady recovery from the calamity can prevent this. If this does not occur, chronic malnutrition can appear.

Interviews with local officials provide additional insights into the way in which the EWEs were managed. They illustrate the dynamics of nutrition vulnerability and resilience of affected communities. They also present the different initiatives and reflections during and after the disaster that contributed to child nutrition preservation.

## During the Flood (Disaster Phase): Staying at Home

According to informants, based on previous flood experience and perceptions of their own risk, many people chose to remain in their homes, irrespective of their construction and location, to keep the family together and protect belongings. Anticipated poor conditions in temporary relocation sites were also a factor. Such decisions posed difficulties for search and rescue efforts and also for aid distribution during and after the event due to lack of human resources, food supplies, and equipment.

## After the Flood (Response and Recovery Phases)

### Maintaining Nutrition and Preventing Disease

After the flood, a number of public health services were introduced in keeping with health and disaster protocols (World Health Organization [WHO] 2014). To assist with maintaining child nutrition, the Department of Health banned formula-feeding for babies (WHO 2009), encouraging breastfeeding in accordance with WHO protocols during calamities (American Academy of Pediatrics 2007; NDCC 2009). Breastfeeding missions in evacuation centers encouraged and supported mothers and babies through breast milk donations and milk-banking in designated hospitals (Dedace 2009).

In the initial stages, families rationed their food supplies while awaiting assistance. The distribution of food packs in evacuation centers eased this situation, but only two villages had regular feeding programs for children continued. Vitamin A supplementation, as part of a nationwide campaign, was continued during the time of the disaster and was provided to children in affected areas (NDCC 2009).

### Provision of Safe and Clean Drinking Water

Water supply was of particular concern in villages and evacuation centers. In some areas, it was difficult to get deliveries of clean water, as water supplies were rationed to ensure availability and to prevent diarrhea outbreaks. In some villages, people also bought bottled water for drinking. Well water was generally used only for washing and bathing due to concern about its cleanliness.

### Sanitation and Waste Disposal

During the flood, maintaining cleanliness was a challenge. Public health reminders about handwashing before handling food and after toilet use were promoted. Solid waste disposal and provision of toilet facilities were implemented to decrease the spread of illness. In one area, the sanitation unit collected human waste daily and treated it with lime and chlorine before putting it in landfills. Several villages took this disaster as an opportunity to increase awareness and implement recycling through segregation of home garbage. NGOs and local health providers worked together to address sanitation and hygiene issues using the WHO water, sanitation, and hygiene program (Ansari and Montague-Brown 2010; WHO 2015).

### Evacuation Centers

Despite the establishment of 24 evacuation centers during and after the flood, overcrowding promoted common diseases such as upper respiratory illness, fevers, and diarrhea. It became apparent that people needed safe water sources and adequate toilet facilities to assist with prevention of malnutrition and more serious disease outbreaks. While locally managed evacuation centers provided steady food supplies from local and international aid and development organizations, regular feeding programs for children were disrupted. As a result, additional supplementary feeding programs were initiated by local civic-minded organizations and community leaders through the centers. It was observed that, after this assistance stopped, children's weights started to fall.

### Aid and Support

Institutions, including local churches, municipal and provincial government agencies, and private donors quickly provided assistance during and immediately after the flood. Food and water packs came with other basic needs, such as clothes and hygiene kits. While there were sufficient food aid packs, there was a need to improve the aid distribution system to ensure that aid also reached those who had remained in, or returned to, their homes. A good distribution network system ensures that all affected people will be given appropriate assistance (Smilowitz and Dolinskaya 2011; Sobel and Leeson 2007).

### Food and Nutrition Security Concerns

Following the flood, the main concern was to prevent food insecurity, especially in villages where agriculture was the primary source of income. According to KIs, 70% of households in the villages of Linga and Sto Angel relied on year-round rice production. Thus, people felt the immediate impact of the flood, because their crops were destroyed. It was many months before they were able to start planting again. Even in more urbanized villages where household income is derived from employment, the rising cost of food supplies led to issues with food access. Informants observed that high food prices impacted negatively on the amount and quality of food bought by households.

After the flood, a reduced variety of food choices was available. While most markets in affected communities remained open and temporary markets were created, it was difficult for some people to access them due to their limited mobility and the added expense of boat transportation in areas where flood waters remained for as long as three months. In lakeside and riverside villages, fresh vegetables were expensive, forcing households to purchase tinned food.

In municipalities where food aid was available (e.g., the villages of Santa Cruz), food insecurity was not apparent for the first six months after the flood. However, in the rest of the villages in Pila, Pagsanjan, Pangil, Pakil, and Siniluan, signs of food insecurity appeared once food aid stopped. Rising food prices affected many families who needed to work to pay for food and nonfood needs. When asked about food insecurity after flooding, KIs indicated that many people experienced food scarcity due to devastated agriculture, but not necessarily hunger. They also observed that some people had substantially reduced their dietary intake, as they could only afford to purchase enough food to eat twice a day. This experience substantiates the results of the Household Food Security Survey, which showed 62% of households were food insecure postflood and around 36% of mothers and 28% of children were experiencing food insecurity. The agricultural devastation and food insecurity are consistent with reports from other flooding disasters in countries such as Bangladesh (Ninno, Dorosh, Smith, and Roy 2001).

## After the Flood (Rehabilitation Phase)

### Livelihood and Entrepreneurship

People dependent on agriculture and affected by the flood looked for other means of livelihood, such as construction work, helping on other farms, or getting jobs in towns and cities to generate income. Long-time farmers, who relied on their indigenous knowledge and practices, had to wait for a better time to plant rice. They adapted by planting cash crops such as eggplant, watermelon, and string beans to supplement earnings from the one or two cropping seasons disrupted by the flood.

Government, NGO, and private agencies provided training seminars and technical support to introduce new entrepreneurial skills, such as soap and dishwashing liquid-making, new crop farming, food preservation, street food vending, and slipper making. However, for many, opportunities to use these skills were limited by lack of finances. Some municipalities provided microcredit, loans, and financial support for small industries such as piggeries, home-based retail stores, and other livelihood projects targeting the production of nutritious food. However, budgetary constraints, particularly in the more underdeveloped municipalities, meant that ongoing support for community-driven livelihood initiatives was limited.

### Feeding Programs and Other Nutrition-Related Projects

A month after the disaster, some nutrition-related projects and campaigns were implemented to complement national feeding programs. For example, a WHO program provided corn–soya food packs to boost the availability of nutritious food. Initially, children did not like the food due to its unfamiliar taste and texture. Worried that they would become wasted, local health and nutrition officers suggested that WHO use these packs in combination with familiar cooking recipes, such as sautéed mung beans and sautéed vegetables in coconut milk, without changing the nutrient quantity requirements. This improved food intake, which resulted in increases in children's weights during a three-month assessment. After the program finished, mothers continued to seek similar food products, with local government nutrition staff providing innovative ways to cook meals in a manner similar to when using the corn–soya food packs.

### Barriers to the Health and Nutrition Program

The complexity of activities from the national to the provincial governments, through to the municipality and the barangay, demonstrates a top–down approach with a lack of coordination among agencies. For example, national agencies implemented social welfare programs with little or no coordination with local health and nutrition offices. At the local government level, there was a lack of understanding of what constitutes an effective nutrition program and a lack of connection with other local agencies.

Another barrier to full implementation and sustainability of programs is the lack of community ownership. Nearly all policies and programs were nationally or regionally driven, which may overlook local contexts related to practicality and logistics. Many of the programs were outcomes based. Local people needed to understand the objectives of these projects and programs to ensure their effective implementation and ownership of projects. The intended beneficiaries were busy trying to make a living and therefore would not attend workshops that showed no immediate results. Lack of incentives for implementing programs was also an issue. For example, volunteer nutrition workers with local governments were not allotted proper wages.

### Postflood Disaster Prevention and Nutrition Preservation

Nutrition preservation in disasters is intricately linked with preparedness and prevention. Reducing community exposure to flood hazards in the local environment can decrease infectious diseases and mental health issues and contribute to achieving better CNS. In Bagong Pook, Pila, the evacuation of people was hampered by a lack of equipment such as life jackets, power sources, protective clothing, and shoes for disaster operations. Subsequently, village officials improved their disaster preparations to make it easier to evacuate people when needed. A multipurpose covered hall was constructed on higher ground, which is used as an evacuation center during emergencies.

In Lingga, Pila, disaster preparedness was considered an individual responsibility. People usually relied on families and social networks for support rather than government assistance. KIs emphasized that people try to save some money for when there are calamities. A cooperative was established to provide seed money (a "loan" with very little interest compared to a bank) to initiate recovery programs and help residents apply for livelihood projects. However, people still struggled to keep up with promised payments.

Santa Cruz is prone to flooding; long-time inhabitants are aware of this risk. The municipality has a strong preventive stance in their overall health and nutrition policies and disaster preparedness programs, with all relevant departments involved. The municipal health officer indicated that they actively implement all national preventive health programs, and financial support for health and nutrition programs from private organizations are encouraged. During the flooding, early warning and surveillance mechanisms were activated. Health staff looked after the evacuation centers. Postflood, additional barangay disaster risk reduction activities were implemented to train village staff to respond to different types of calamities, in addition to strengthening backyard planting and teaching mothers good food cooking practices.

In Pagsanjan, ongoing local development programs through livelihood generation and national assistance efforts to rebuild homes have been effective in helping families recover and preserving child nutrition. In Pangil, the emphasis is on maintaining existing nutrition projects related to feeding and weight surveillance of children, while incorporating food livelihood strategies, such as planting malunggay (a leafy vegetable rich in nutrients) to provide a cash crop.

## BEST PRACTICES/LESSONS LEARNED

People have heightened expectations of local government officials and community health workers in times of calamity. The TS Ketsana/TY Parma event provided an opportunity for these workers to reflect upon and learn how to protect people's health during future EWE-related flooding disasters. The experiences of community leaders and the village workforce were, and are, important for reducing casualties, improving nutrition and health provision of children during the crisis, and making the transition back to normalcy easier. Minimum standards for addressing these issues have recently been addressed by the Sphere project, and its use is encouraged by the global community (Young, Taylor, Way, and Leaning 2004). Strengthening resources and child nutrition preservation initiatives with sustainable livelihood assistance, social welfare support, and effective disaster risk reduction strategies are needed to prepare for a changing climate and for future mitigation and adaptation measures.

## CONCLUSION

Most KIs agreed that preservation of child health and nutrition could be achieved during and after a flooding disaster if preflood policies and programs are established, continuously financially supported, and effectively implemented, monitored, and evaluated. We found that preflooding investments in child nutrition had been established but were inadequate to maintain children's nutrition 18–24 months after the flood. Most of the KIs agreed that the mutual assistance and cooperation across all sectors of the community is needed to reduce reliance on reactive measures.

Since this research, changes have been instituted. Climate adaptation strategies and health and nutrition programs have been organized as part of the national disaster risk reduction agenda. Local governments have instituted natural hazards mapping in coordination with the National Disaster and Risk Reduction Coordination Center. Coordination of local government units within the Departments of Social Welfare and Development, Health, Environment and Natural Resources, Agriculture, and other relevant agencies predisaster and postdisaster has been improved and strengthened. However, the concept of prevention and risk reduction needs to permeate the cultural Filipino psyche more fully. Climate and health education in schools and communities through multidisciplinary collaboration among experts and locals is needed. Importantly, a reorientation of perspective toward a socioecological model of health is urgently needed to ensure the well-being of future generations.

## REFERENCES

Alderman, K., L.R. Turner, and S. Tong. 2012. Floods and human health: A systematic review. *Environment International* 47: 37–47. doi:10.1016/j.envint.2012.06.003.

American Academy of Pediatrics. 2007. *Infant feeding in disasters and emergencies: Breastfeeding and other options*. http://www2.aap.org/breastfeeding/files/pdf/InfantNutritionDisaster.pdf, accessed March 10, 2011.

Anderson, A.K., W. Bignell, S. Winful, I. Soyiri, and M. Steiner-Asiedu. 2010. Risk factors for malnutrition among children 5-years and younger in the Akuapim-North District in the eastern region of Ghana. *Current Research Journal of Biological Sciences* 2(3): 183–188.

Ansari, A. and B. Montague-Brown. 2010. *The WASH factor: Oxfam's experiences with humanitarian coordination for water, sanitation, and health*. Oxford: Oxfam.

Baez, J.E. and I.V. Santos. 2007. Children's vulnerability to weather shocks: A natural disaster as a natural experiment. New York: World Bank.

Barrios, R.E., J.P. Stansbury, R. Palencia, and M.T. Medina. 2000. Nutritional status of children under 5 years of age in three hurricane-affected areas of Honduras. *Pan American Journal of Public Health* 8(6): 380–384.

Bich, T.H., L.N. Quang, L.T.T. Ha, T.T.D. Hanh, and D. Guha-Sapir. 2011. Impacts of flood on health: Epidemiologic evidence from Hanoi, Vietnam. *Global Health Action* 4: 6356.

Cairncross, S. and M. Alvarinho. 2006. The Mozambique floods of 2000: Health impact and response. In *Flood Hazards and Health: Responding to Present and Future Risks*, ed. R. Few, 111–127. London: Earthscan.

Choudhury, A.Y. and A. Bhuiya. 1993. Effects of biosocial variables on changes in nutritional status of rural Bangladeshi children, premonsoon and post monsoon flooding. *Journal of Biosocial Science* 25(3): 351–357.

Corbin, J.M. and A.L. Strauss. 2008. *Basics of qualitative research: Techniques and procedures for developing grounded theory* (3rd ed.). Thousand Oaks, CA: Sage Publications.

Dedace, S. 2009. *PGH to embark on breastfeeding mission in 'Ondoy' evacuation centers*. http://www.gmanetwork.com/news/story/173571/news/nation/pgh-to-embark-on-breastfeeding-mission-in-ondoy-evacuation-centers, accessed March 10, 2011.

del Ninno, C. and M. Lundberg. 2005. Treading water: The long-term impact of the 1998 flood on nutrition in Bangladesh. *Economics and Human Biology* 3(1): 67–96.

Doocy, S., A. Daniels, S. Murray, and T.D. Kirsch. 2013. The human impact of floods: A historical review of events 1980–2009 and systematic literature review. *PLOS Currents* 5: doi: 10.1371/currents.dis.f4deb457904936b07c09daa98ee8171a.

Doocy, S., A. Dick, A. Daniels, and T.D. Kirsch. 2013. The human impact of tropical cyclones: A historical review of events 1980–2009 and systematic literature review. *PLOS Currents* 5: doi: 10.1371/currents.dis.2664354a5571512063ed29d25ffbce74.

Engle, P., P. Menon, and L. Haddad. 1999. Care and nutrition: Concepts and measurement. *World Development* 27(8): 1309–1337.

Finau, S.A. 1986. Health and nutritional status of Tongan pre-school children after Cyclone Isaac. *New Zealand Medical Journal* 99(808): 630–632.

Food and Agriculture Organization. 2008. *Climate change and food security: A framework document.* Rome: FAO, Interdepartmental Working Group on Climate Change.

Gregory, P.J., J.S. Ingram, and M. Brklacich. 2005. Climate change and food security. *Philosophical Transactions of the Royal Society* 360(1463): 2139–2148.

Jason, S., A.D. Curiel, D. Liddle, F. Chizea, U.M. Leloglu, M. Helvaci, M. Bekhti, D. Benachir, L. Boland, L. Gomes, and M. Sweeting. 2010. Capacity building in emerging space nations: Experiences, challenges and benefits. *Advances in Space Research* 46(5): 571–581.

McMichael, A.J. 2013. Globalization, climate change, and human health. *New England Journal of Medicine* 368(14): 1335–1343.

McMichael, A.J. and E. Lindgren. 2011. Climate change: Present and future risks to health, and necessary responses. *Journal of Internal Medicine* 270(5): 401–413.

McMichael, A.J., A. Nyong, and C. Corvalan. 2008. Global environmental change and health: Impacts and inequalities and the health sector. *BMJ* 336(7637): 191–194.

Mude, A.G., C.B. Barrett, J.G. McPeak, R. Kaitho, and P. Kristjanson. 2009. Empirical forecasting of slow-onset disasters for improved emergency response: An application to Kenya's arid north. *Food Policy* 34(4): 329–339.

National Disaster Coordinating Council (NDCC). 2009. *NDCC update: Final report on Tropical Storm Ondoy and Typhoon Pepeng Sept 30–Oct 10, 2009.* Quezon City: NDCC.

National Statistics Office (Philippines) and ICF Macro. 2009. *Philippines national demographic survey.* Calverton, MD: National Statistics Office and ICF Macro.

Ninno, C.D., P.A. Dorosh, L.C. Smith, and D.K. Roy. 2001. *The 1998 floods in Bangladesh: Disaster impacts, household coping strategies, and response.* Washington, DC: International Food Policy Research Institute.

Omitsu, M. and T. Yamano. 2006. The impacts of Hurricane Mitch on child health: Evidence from Nicaragua. *International Association of Agricultural Economists Conference.* Gold Coast, Australia: International Association of Agricultural Economists.

Parihar, R. 2011. Disaster nursing: Disaster management cycle. https://pariharraj.wordpress.com/2011/01/20/disaster-nursing/, accessed February 22, 2012.

Pope, C., S. Ziebland, and N. Mays. 2000. Analysing qualitative data. *British Medical Journal* 320(7227): 114–116.

Portner, C.C. 2010. Natural hazards and child health. http://www.portner.dk/archives/2010/05/02/natural-hazards-and-child-health/#.USyvBzDDCSo, accessed May 10, 2011.

Radimer, K.L., C.M. Olson, J.C. Greene, C.C. Campbell, and J.P. Habicht. 1992. Understanding hunger and developing indicators to assess it in women and children. *Journal of Nutrition Education* 24(1, Supplement 1): 36S–44S.

Ravanera, R.R. and C.H.B. Emata. 2012. *Food and nutrition security in the Philippines: An overview.* Cincinnati, OH: Xavier Science Foundation, Inc.

Ricci, J.A. and S. Becker. 1996. Risk factors for wasting and stunting among children in Metro Cebu, Philippines. *The American Journal of Clinical Nutrition* 63: 966–975.

Sallis, J., N. Owen, and E. Fisher. 2008. Ecological models of health behavior. In *Health behavior and health education: Theory, research, and practice* (4th ed.), eds. K. Glanz, B.K. Rimer, and K. Viswanath, 465–485. San Francisco: Jossey-Bass.

Schmidhuber, J. and F.N. Tubiello. 2007. Global food security under climate change. *Proceedings of the National Academy of Sciences* 104(50): 19703–19708.

Smilowitz, K., and I. Dolinskaya. 2011. *Decision-making tools for distribution networks in disaster relief.* Evanston, IL: Center for the Commercialization of Innovative Transportation Technology, Northwestern University.

Sobel, R.S. and P.T. Leeson. 2007. The use of knowledge in natural-disaster relief management. *The Independent Review* 11(3): 519–531.

United Nations International Children's Fund. 1990. *Strategy for improved nutrition of children and women in developing countries.* New York: UNICEF. http://www.ceecis.org/iodine/01_global/01_pl/01_01_other_1992_unicef.pdf, accessed October 31, 2010.

Wit, J.M. and P. Gooder. 1981. Nutritional status of hospitalized pre-school children in Dominica, before and after Hurricane David. *Disasters* 5(2): 93–97.

World Food Programme. 2010. *Emergency food security assessment: Philippines: Luzon typhoons and floods.* Manila: World Food Programme, DSWD, Government of the Philippines, FAO, Save the Children, OXFAM, World Vision, ADRA, Christian Aid, CFSI. http://documents.wfp.org/stellent/groups/public/documents/ena/wfp220033.pdf, accessed September 15, 2010.

World Health Organization. 2015. *Improving nutrition outcomes with better water, sanitation and hygiene: Practical solutions for policies and programmes.* Geneva: World Health Organization. http://apps.who.int/iris/bitstream/10665/193991/1/9789241565103_eng.pdf, accessed December 31, 2015.

_____. 2014. *Flooding and communicable diseases fact sheet.* http://who.int/hac/techguidance/ems/flood_cds/en/, accessed March 8, 2014.

_____. 2009. *WHO backs the DoH over ban on milk products for Ondoy children.* http://www.wpro.who.int/mediacentre/releases/2009/20091005/en/, accessed March 10, 2011.

Young, H., A. Taylor, S.A. Way, and J. Leaning. 2004. Linking rights and standards: The process of developing 'rights-based' minimum standards on food security, nutrition and food aid. *Disasters* 28(2): 142–159.

# 12 Food Insecurity and Health Disparity Synergisms

## *Reframing a Praxis of Anthropology and Public Health for Displaced Populations in the United States*

*Preety Gadhoke and Barrett P. Brenton*

## CONTENTS



**Abstract**

Addressing public health nutrition vulnerabilities and resiliency in displaced US urban populations requires a livelihood model that places food insecurity and health disparity synergisms at its core. It also necessitates the integration of a rights-based and life-course approach for understanding risk and resiliency. This chapter will review specific field-based examples from displaced urban populations to highlight challenges for applied community-based interventions. Drawing from ethnographic fieldwork with women, who are primary caregivers, and their children living in transitional housing in New York City, an analysis is provided of how opportunities and constraints shape their agency in responding to and confronting food security risk. Understanding the coping strategies utilized and the expressions of resiliency realized in these populations is critical for implementing effective public health nutrition interventions.

## INTRODUCTION

> And so, our present perilous plight in the United States, with the many pockets of rural unemployment, city ghettos, ethnic enclaves, where Americans are starving... must be viewed not only in its consequences for ourselves, as a viable political community, but also in its consequences for the world. (Mead 1970, p. 178)

This statement by Margaret Mead, published over 45 years ago, still speaks to concerns that have yet to be fully addressed in the United States. This issue is reflected in the global consequences of inaction and inadequate support structures at home and abroad. Her statement highlights a system that links consequences and responsibility for US poverty to ourselves and a larger international community.

Our overall approach is best summarized by the title of the Food and Agriculture Organization's (FAO) report "Healthy People Depend on Healthy Food Systems" (FAO 2013). In this chapter, we call for a rights-based, life-course approach for the application of international development livelihood models to reduce the vulnerability and bolster the resiliency of internally displaced, marginalized populations in the United States, specifically applying them to families living in transition in New York City. Livelihood frameworks provide a systematic process of rapid assessment for programmatic monitoring and evaluation. We propose a modified sustainable livelihood model for comprehensive public health interventions and programs that address the needs of internally displaced populations, who reveal the state of the health of the nation. We conclude with implications for future research and practice, as they relate to these vulnerable populations.

### World Food Systems Crises

The convergence of climate change with the increased globalization of world food production, consumption, and waste is impacting food systems, food security, and health equity. Food insecurity has become a protracted global crisis, witnessed through the heightened vulnerabilities and acts of resilience in marginalized populations. For example, successful emergency responses to the 2011–2012 Greater Horn of Africa and the Sahel drought and food security crisis focused on food production and employment programs that built assets and minimized the risk of shocks. Although complicated by poverty traps, populations that could utilize a "human capital first" strategy were successful in a household's ability to cope and bounce back with increased crop production and food security (Maxwell, Vaitla, Tesfay, and Abadi 2013). The future of sustainable global food systems requires a commitment to international, national, regional, and local accountability and a realization that long-term food security crises will be the rule, not the exception, in the face of climate change. Food insecurity cycles that seemed acute at first have become persistent and chronic (Maxwell, Russo, and Alinovi 2012).

In terms of response and accountability, there is a clear need to integrate and revisit the temporal dimensions of programmatic objectives. Simply put, cycles of poverty support protracted systems of food insecurity (Maxwell, Russo, and Alinovi 2012). These discussions must be framed by a rights-based approach to food systems security. We argue that this includes anthropologically informed food policy decisions that contextualize the global food security crises, climate change, disasters, and cycles of poverty.

## BACKGROUND

### Rights-Based Approaches to Food Security

While the right to food was a passing mention in Article 25 of the 1948 United Nations Declaration of Human Rights, a much more encompassing rights-based approach for responding to food system globalization can be found in key elements of the United Nations framework for the Human Right to Food developed by the United Nations Office of the High Commission for Human Rights (2010). To conform to that right, foods must be available, accessible, and adequate in a manner that is safe, and nutritious and leads to active and healthy lives. This declaration forges a link between food security and food justice. Protracted systems of food insecurity, resulting from poverty and made more acute by disasters and climate change, require a degree of accountability to all parts of the food system grounded in these rights by individuals, communities, governments, and corporations.

This approach necessitates assessments and interventions, which shift the focus from short-term emergency food insecurity frameworks to more sustainable food security responses.

In the United States, food insecurity is defined by the US Department of Agriculture (USDA) as a "household-level economic and social condition" of having limited or uncertain access to adequate, available, appropriate, and nutritious food (Coleman-Jensen, Rabbitt, Gregory, and Singh 2015). It is important to note that, in 2006, the specific labels were changed to remove the words "food insecurity" and "hunger." While the actual methods for measuring food security did not change, it became clear that the semantic alteration was the product of a very contentious political debate surrounding the stigma of documenting "hunger" in the United States and around defining the concept of hunger (Himmelgreen and Romero-Daza 2010).

While livelihood models for integrating the dynamics of climate change, food insecurity, and health are common in the field of international development (e.g., Ashby and Pachico 2013; FAO 2015), this is missing or underdeveloped in the United States and for local New York City strategies. For example, a report by the US Centers for Disease Control and Prevention assessing health vulnerability to climate change (Manangan et al. 2014) does not consider food insecurity. A report by USDA on climate change, global food security, and the US food system (Brown et al. 2015) does not consider the health impacts.

Relevant to our work, a New York City Council (2013) vision to improve the city's food system does not explicitly consider climate change or related health outcomes. At the same time, a report on building a knowledge base of climate resilience for New York City (Rosenzweig and Solecki 2015) considers health concerns, but it does not directly consider food insecurity. Interagency responsibilities aside, a lack of integrated holistic models creates programs and strategies that do not fully address the impact of climate change on food security and health. Thus, the lack of coordination across these agencies to address such paramount concerns and inability to create a more integral and effective plan of action further marginalizes the needs of displaced populations.

## A Life-Course Approach

A life-course approach is a leading interdisciplinary theoretical and practical method for understanding transitions, turning points, and trajectories in an individual's life across time. In the context of vulnerabilities and resiliency for climate change, this approach is informative for understanding adaptation to external (environmental) events, individual decisions, and opportunities and constraints regarding adaptation and choices (Wethington 2005). Given that approximately 80% of all deaths worldwide are attributable to noncommunicable diseases (NCDs), a sizable body of literature suggests that the development, treatment, and prevention of NCDs are applicable early and across the lifespan (World Health Organization 2011). Risk factors for NCDs are indicative of disease processes that progress from birth until later adult years (Darnton-Hill, Nishida, and James 2004).

This approach has been traditionally applied in epidemiology to quantify longitudinal differences in risk (Ben-Schlomo and Kuh 2002). Moreover, this approach can be applied to ethnographically understand the way individuals interpret and construct their life experiences or through the use of mixed methodology (Devine 2005). Strengths of the life-course approach for public health are that it addresses issues of social and environmental inequalities in health and has helped bridge biological, psychological, and social models of disease causation (Ben-Schlomo and Kuh 2002).

## Livelihood Models

A livelihood approach takes into account the capabilities, assets (including both material and social resources), and activities required for a means of living. They are usually based at the household level. Livelihood models are useful for mapping out strategies and resources for coping and recovering from stress and shocks and the ability maintain or enhance capabilities and assets both now and in the future (Chambers and Conway 1991). In the context of complex emergencies and displaced populations (e.g., natural disaster, famine, forced displacement), livelihood models have been used to document vulnerabilities and resiliency to stressors, although responses to crises have often been ineffective (Lautze, Bell, Alinovi, and Russo 2012). For urban US settings, we are explicitly embedding a rights-based and life-course approach in our proposed livelihood models that incorporates intergenerational risk and resiliency in the context of food insecurity and health disparities.

An emphasis on assets and resources is a primary strength of livelihoods models, which helps to move public health and nutrition policies, interventions, and programs away from its traditional needs-based and "risk factor" epidemiological roots (Galea and Putnam 2007; Krieger 2001). Today, public health researchers and practitioners agree on the importance of understanding and modifying these larger macrosocial forces, taking away the burden from the individual who is at risk of being sick (Galea and Putnam 2007). Our proposed framework takes into account the structure and agency of displaced populations through the complex and synergistic relationship between food insecurity and health disparities in the context of climate change.

Patz, Frumkin, Holloway, Vimont, and Haines (2014, p. 1565) provide evidence of the adverse health outcomes in the United States related to climate change over the past 20 years. They argue that the past, present, and future negative health outcomes include

> …heat-related disorders, such as heat stress and economic consequences of reduced work capacity; respiratory disorders, including those exacerbated by air pollution and aeroallergens, such as asthma; infectious diseases, including vectorborne diseases and waterborne diseases, such as childhood gastrointestinal diseases; food insecurity, including reduced crop yields and an increase in plant diseases; and mental health disorders, such as posttraumatic stress disorder and depression.

Clearly, these conditions already exist among marginalized populations. In the United States, they are particularly acute in homeless individuals and families living on the streets, emergency shelters, and in transitional housing, if they are lucky to qualify for social services (National Alliance to End Homelessness 2015). Thus, climate change and disasters exacerbate the impact of these conditions and vulnerabilities, leading to the "troubling paradigm" of longer-term patterns of even more "internal displacements," which require even greater efforts to address the structural inequities that perpetuate them (Amster 2012). Ramin and Svoboda's (2009) work on the health of the homeless and climate change supports this view. However, their work makes no reference to food insecurity. This is not uncommon and has been discussed previously.

## Homelessness as Displacement

A home to call one's own is not only a sanctuary for individuals and families, but it is also a space that provides one with basic human necessities and a feeling of safety, security, tranquility, and dignity. UNOHCHR (2015) recognizes the right to adequate housing as interdependent with a number of other human rights: rights not only to health, to education, to employment but also to nondiscrimination and equality, to freedom of association or freedom from violence, and ultimately, to the right to life. Appropriate governance, including national and local housing strategies, is necessary in order to provide adequate housing to all constituents.

Yet, adequate housing is rarely treated as a human right, and according to the United Nations Special Rapporteur, the gap is getting larger and wider globally. Populations such as children, women, pregnant women, the elderly, those with disabilities, migrant workers, indigenous peoples, and individuals living in poverty are particularly at risk for being homeless and therefore need special attention and assistance. It is the "obligation" of national, subnational, and local governance structures to address this widening gap through appropriate and equitable resource allocation and nondiscrimination framed in human rights to provide adequate housing to all constituents. Still, adequate housing continues to be an unmet need across all regions of the world for men, women, and children (UNOHCHR 2015).

Today's myriad global political economic crises, warfare, violence against women and children, and environmental (manmade/natural) disasters continue to widen social inequalities and leave populations at risk of being homeless. According to a United Nations Special Report (UNOHCHR 2015, p. 1), over 1 billion people are living in "precarious conditions in slums and informal settlements threatening their health and even their survival, including 100 million people who are homeless on any given day." In the United States, the face of homelessness is changing, especially after economic and housing crises and the recent natural disasters, but still remains unseen to the larger society (Amster 2012). In 2008, a survey reported that 83% of US cities observed an increase in homelessness (Amster 2012).

The invisibility of the poor becomes more poignant and prominent given the multiple stressors that poverty-stricken households must adapt to while simultaneously avoiding risks and facing competing priorities within a life of changing demands and constraints. This adds an additional layer to the complexity of the vulnerability of societies facing climate change and disasters. We emphasize displacement as being framed as living in spaces and places that are borrowed and not owned by households at risk. This adds to the effect of marginalization through degrees of invisibility (Amster 2012).

## Research Focus

This chapter provides narratives of women, who are primary caregivers, and their children, who are living in marginalized and displaced settings. These can be used to learn about the assets, opportunities, and constraints for coping and adaptation. The narratives elaborate the reality of transitional lives and vulnerabilities of poverty, along with their resiliency. Our focus is on the relationship between food insecurity and health disparity synergisms that sit at the core of our proposed conceptual livelihoods framework (Gadhoke and Brenton 2015b). The research is centered on understanding the profound everyday vulnerability and resiliency of households faced with food insecurity, disability, and hope. These homeless households exhibit a type of displacement that can manifest itself in any number of degrees of "invisibility." Their displaced lives result from having lost social standing through unemployment, housing, and greater exposure to institutional settings such as prisons and foster homes (Hoch 2000).

## Methodology and Research Design

Our proposed livelihood model was informed by an ongoing small pilot study on food insecurity, resiliency, and health disparities at a transitional shelter in New York City. The overall goal is to inform the development, implementation, and evaluation of a pilot public health intervention engaging caregivers and their children. In this chapter, we report on select findings applicable to the discussion of internally displaced urban US populations. Therefore, our methods are specific to women as primary caregivers and their children, who are particularly vulnerable among the homeless. We discuss our results in terms of the key dimensions of our proposed livelihoods model. These include individual choices, coping strategies, and opportunities and constraints and derived from the voice of the women and children who participated in our project.

Key methods and the research design of our ongoing ethnographic fieldwork project at a transitional housing facility in Queens, New York, are described in detail elsewhere (Gadhoke, Daravi, Patel, Sam, and Brenton 2016). The location offered apartment-style housing for displaced households with independent living units from studios to two bedrooms with bunk beds, a fully equipped kitchen with an electric stove and oven, and a bathroom. Our research team is composed of the principal investigator (Gadhoke), coinvestigator (Brenton), and graduate students in the Masters in Public Health program. We obtained informed consent from the adults and both child assent and parental consent from their caregivers prior to children's participation. Nine in-depth interviews with mostly single women as primary caregivers were conducted, with repeated follow-ups. Two focus groups with primary caregivers (five women per focus group) between ages 18 and 54 and representing African American, Asian American, European American, Caribbean American, and Native American ethnic identities were also conducted. Eighteen youth (9 boys, 9 girls, through September 2015) between ages 10 and 17 also attended ongoing weekly workshops (Gadhoke and Brenton 2015a). All interviews, focus groups, and workshops were audio taped, transcribed, and analyzed using Atlas.ti software.

What follows is an overview of select emergent themes. These highlight the challenges that paradox and synergisms of food insecurity and health disparities pose for this population. Through that process, we ascertain some key messages about vulnerability, resiliency, and health from women and children's perspectives.

## FINDINGS

Listening to poignant life stories over a shared meal with both the women and their children has given us a glimpse into the episodic nature of food insecurity that is otherwise lost amidst the sea of "snapshots" of food insecurity surveys. Homelessness, unemployment, food insecurity, chronic diseases, and their associated social suffering reinforce dependency on a welfare system and social structure of poverty that supports a form of structural violence that impacts access to basic needs (Kleinman, Das, and Lock 1996). It became clear that the unmeasured, accumulating, and long-term stress of this structural violence, self-perpetuating as it is, contributes to further worsening health and social disparities. Key themes that emerged from the narratives inform the ongoing development of our proposed livelihood model and include structural violence, transgenerational poverty, coping strategies, food deserts, episodic food insecurity, social vulnerability, and sources of resiliency (social support, social capital).

The face of displacement represents a microcosm of the diversity of suffering and healing in New York City. Some women were homeless for a few days to weeks, others were trapped in a perpetual state of displacement for years, and some have been displaced intergenerationally, having been homeless as children themselves. Women spoke of the unique and manifold reasons for becoming homeless. They spoke of social suffering from disabilities, preventing them from seeking employment and protracting social welfare dependence for programs that are altogether insufficiently addressing household needs and expenditures. Because the shelter is located in a high-income neighborhood, groceries and provisions are too expensive. Thus, it is a food desert as defined by both limited economic and spatial access. Only having access to expensive foods makes the food as inaccessible to the homeless families living at the shelter as having no access at all. The women must walk, take public transit, or obtain a ride to other neighborhoods that are farther away from the shelter in order to locate affordable foods. Even with support from SNAP (Supplemental Nutrition Assistance Program, formerly known as "food stamps") and WIC (Women, Infants, and Children—a need-based supplemental nutrition and education program) programs, the women and their children describe living in a food desert as contributing to the nearly constant frustration of being unable to achieve a pattern of healthy eating for their family and themselves on a limited budget.

Running out of money is anticipated monthly, with the women regularly depending upon supplementing their household food with nonperishable items from the small food pantry at the shelter and sometimes leaning upon the generosity of family members for money. Transportation can be both expensive and limited in New York City. The women can neither afford a vehicle nor public transit around their local area for grocery shopping and errands, including laundry and access to food. Suffering from preexisting chronic health conditions, several women spoke of their forced dependence upon taxis for bringing back groceries to the shelter out of necessity and survival.

Interviewees generally speak of staff at the shelter as being helpful. At the same time, they express frustrations with the larger body politic within which the shelter is positioned. They stated that, while the homeless shelter may help them with some methods for short-term coping, it is neither sufficient aid for survival on a daily basis nor is it sufficient for obtaining enough aid to get out of the vicious cycle of poverty. They are caught in the middle of the gray interstitial spaces between the homeless shelter and independent housing.

Women's modes of coping include heuristics or experiential insights for cooking healthy foods. They modify typically unhealthy foods by adding healthy components; self-learn about dietary principles and being more diet conscious; take advantage of the food pantry at the homeless shelter to supplement food in anticipation of insufficiency at the end of the monthly food assistance cycle; skip meals, particularly breakfast; and cut down portions for themselves in order to feed the children. A middle-aged, single mother of two teenagers explained that she enhances mashed potatoes with cauliflower without her children noticing a difference in the flavor and adds fresh tomatoes to canned pasta sauce. A young single mother described how she taught herself to read nutrition labels. All caregivers described going to their case workers and requesting access to the in-house food pantry when food runs out near the middle to the end of the month. The pantry includes basic emergency shelf-stable canned and dried goods, such as pasta, ramen, rice, and dried beans.

When food runs out, caregivers rely on staple, nonperishable foods stashed at home, such as beans and rice, for this purpose. Most women and children describe fast foods as rare treats because they are pricey. Respondents unanimously acknowledge the difficulty of traversing the local food landscape and requested assistance in the form of information, training, and workshops beyond the resources provided to them by the shelter.

Adaptive food shopping heuristics include identifying grocery stores for their competitive advantage and shopping selectively. This often means going to a particular grocery store for meats, another one for seasonal vegetables and fruits, another for nonperishables, and shopping at a dollar store for other types of household items. Heuristic mechanisms for coping with food insecurity include tapping into the food pantry and preparing nonperishable foods with high shelf lives (e.g., ramen and rice and beans). Social support heuristics include using a taxi and family members driving them to/from grocery store.

Most women spoke of the importance of social support through these difficult times, including family, friends, community, and their religious groups. They emphasize the importance of maintaining hope, eating together, engaging in activities together, giving a helping hand to other homeless families, and intrapersonal sources of resilience such as forms of self-motivation and self-care. Caregivers spoke of their children as the primary motivation for waking up every day and facing this violence of poverty.

## CONCLUSION

Our proposed livelihood model includes options for coping and resiliency that are much more complex, holistic, and integrative than those currently applied to the context of relative poverty in displaced urban United States populations. The bureaucratic structures that are available, yet generally difficult to navigate and access by these populations, create a complex system that requires additional internal models within the broader framework. In our conceptualization of livelihoods models, we observe the need to have an action-oriented anthropological model centered within these frameworks.

We recognize the fact that findings from our small study of homeless women's heuristics are not generalizable to the larger body of diverse displaced populations. In fact, the purpose of this brief review of our ethnographic fieldwork with one such population in New York City is to apply broad brush strokes to the canvas of livelihood models. We believe that this establishes a starting point for anthropologists and other academics to enter into a dialogue about how best to inform interventions designed for displaced and homeless households living with children.

Drawing from these illustrative narratives, we reveal the embodiment of poverty as a component of larger reinforcing systems of structural violence and its consequences. We argue that, while the existing welfare system does give limited benefits, it provides neither the structure nor resources to allow displaced households to be freed from the system. Ultimately, it does not fully provide the opportunity or rights to live with dignity. Because of their invisibility, these sentinel populations continue to be understudied, underresearched, and underresourced. Our focus on food insecurity and health disparity synergisms highlights the need for a rights-based approach to human dignity and social justice that embodies the right to food and a call of food justice.

In this way, public health recognizes the importance of sustaining momentum towards cross-disciplinary prevention and a holistic approach. This must also entail a continuing movement away from the reductionist medical gaze on the population's health toward a critical lens toward the past and future. While we did not directly measure perceptions of climate change and disasters from the respondents, a body of research points to the added vulnerability that homeless populations have faced following Hurricanes Katrina and Rita (Sims-Muhammad 2012) and Super Storm Sandy (United Nations News Centre 2012) in the United States. City Harvest of New York City reported that, a year after Super Storm Sandy devastated the City, it delivered "more than seven million pounds of food in direct response to the storm, in addition to our regular deliveries" (City Harvest 2013).

Although not fully evident, the narratives of women caregivers and their children discussed exemplify food insecurity and health disparity synergisms that may be rapidly heightened by disasters and climate change (Ramin and Svoboda 2009). Certainly, ethnographic research is desperately needed among homeless and displaced US populations to ascertain the direct impact of climate change and disasters upon the existing local food systems and food insecurity. Such research can strengthen the call for a shift in focus from acute to more sustainable long-term responses for existing and future displaced, homeless households.

The larger political and economic structures within which the homeless services operate miss the mark for providing a robust structure for households to truly move out of displacement and relative poverty (Amster 2012). In the end, the most valuable asset to any population is their sense of hope, self-efficacy, and motivation to move through challenging spaces and places and attain wellbeing. What is beginning to emerge out of these women's narratives is their intrinsic ability to identify their needs and assets and maintain hope for a promising future for their children and themselves to live with dignity. We promote the application of ethnographic methods to informing the construction of livelihoods models in order to more fully understand the vulnerability and resiliency of displaced populations. How else will we be able to respond to the inevitability of the impact of climate change across disparate spaces in the United States and beyond?

## REFERENCES

Amster, R. 2012. Homelessness as "internal displacement": Scholarship and activism in post-Katrina New Orleans. In *Professional lives, personal struggles: Ethics and advocacy in research on homelessness*, eds. T. Valado and R. Amster, 131–138. New York: Lexington.

Ashby, J. and D. Pachico. 2013. *Climate change from concepts to action: A guide for development practitioners*. Baltimore, MD: Catholic Relief Services. http://www.crsprogramquality.org/storage/pubs/agenv/climate-change-from-concepts-to-action.pdf, accessed October 15, 2015.

Ben-Schlomo, Y. and D. Kuh. 2002. A life course approach to chronic disease epidemiology: Conceptual models, empirical challenges and interdisciplinary perspectives. *International Journal of Epidemiology* 31(2): 285–293.

Brown, M.E., J.M. Antle, P. Backlund, E.R. Carr, W.E. Easterling, M.K. Walsh, C. Ammann, W. Attavanich, C.B. Barrett, M.F. Bellemare, V. Dancheck, C. Funk, K. Grace, J.S.I. Ingram, H. Jiang, H. Maletta, T. Mata, A. Murray, M. Ngugi, D. Ojima, B. O'Neill, and C. Tebaldi. 2015. *Climate change, global food security, and the U.S. food system*. Washington, DC: United States Department of Agriculture. http://www.usda.gov/oce/climate_change/FoodSecurity.htm, accessed October 15, 2015.

Chambers, R. and G.R. Conway. 1991. Sustainable rural livelihoods: Practical concepts for the 21st century. Brighton: Institute of Development Studies, Discussion Paper 296. https://www.ids.ac.uk/files/Dp296.pdf, accessed October 15, 2015.

City Harvest. 2013. Hurricane Sandy relief: A report on City Harvest's response to the storm. http://www.cityharvest.org/images/uploads/site/A_Report_on_City_Harvests_Response_to_Hurricane_Sandy_-_July_2013.pdf, accessed October 15, 2015.

Coleman-Jensen, A., M.P. Rabbitt, C. Gregory, and A. Singh. 2015. *Household food security in the United States in 2014. ERR-194*. Washington, DC United States Department of Agriculture, Economic Research Service. http://www.ers.usda.gov/media/1896841/err194.pdf, accessed February 16, 2016.

Darnton-Hill, I., C. Nishida, and W.P.T. James. 2004. A life course approach to diet, nutrition and the prevention of chronic diseases. *Public Health Nutrition* 7(1A): 101–121.

Devine, C.M. 2005. A life course perspective: Understanding food choices in time, social location, and history. *Journal of Nutrition and Education Behavior* 37(3): 121–128.

Food and Agriculture Organization. 2015. *Climate change and food systems: Global assessments and implications for food security and trade*. Rome: United Nations Food and Agriculture Organization. http://www.fao.org/3/a-i4332e.pdf, accessed October 15, 2015.

_____. 2013. *Healthy people depend on healthy food systems: Sustainable food systems for food security and nutrition*. Rome: Food and Agriculture Organization. http://www.fao.org/fileadmin/templates/getinvolved/images/WFD_issues_paper_2013_web_EN.pdf, accessed October 15, 2015.

Gadhoke, P. and B.P. Brenton. 2015a. Children in transition: Visual methods for capturing impression of food landscapes, family, and life among homeless youth. *NEOS: Publication of the Anthropology of Children and Youth Interest Group* 7(2): 8–9.

_____. 2015b. Food insecurity and health disparity synergisms: Implications for understanding public health nutrition vulnerabilities and resiliency in displaced U.S. populations. Paper presented at the Society for Applied Anthropology 75th Annual Meetings. Pittsburgh, PA.

Gadhoke, P., K. Daravi, B. Patel, R. Sam, and B.P. Brenton. 2016. "I lost my dignity": Embodiment of syndemic suffering among ethnically diverse women living in a precarious state of being. *Ethnicity & Health*. Under Review.

Galea, S. and S. Putnam. 2007. The role of macrosocial determinants in shaping the health of the population. In *Macrosocial determinants of population health*, ed. S. Galea, 1–26. Ann Arbor, MI: University of Michigan.

Himmelgreen, D.A. and N. Romero-Daza. 2010. Eliminating "hunger" in the U.S.: Changes in policy regarding the measurement of food security. *Food and Foodways* 18(1–2): 96–113.

Hoch, C. 2000. Sheltering the homeless in the US: Social improvement and the continuum of care. *Housing Studies* 15(6): 865–876.

Kleinman, A., V. Das, and M. Lock. 1996. *Social suffering*. Berkeley: University of California Press.

Krieger, N. 2001. Theories for social epidemiology in the 21st century: An ecosocial perspective. *International Journal of Epidemiology* 30(4): 668–677.

Lautze, S., W. Bell, L. Alinovi, and L. Russo. 2012. Early warning, later response (again): The 2011 famine in Somalia. *Global Food Security* 1(1): 43–49.

Manangan, A.P., C.K. Uejio, S. Saha, P.J. Schramm, G.D. Marinucci, C.L. Brown, J.J. Hess, and G. Luber. 2014. *Assessing health vulnerability to climate change: A guide for health departments*. Atlanta, GA: Centers for Disease Control and Prevention, Climate and Health Technical Report Series, Climate and Health Program. http://www.cdc.gov/climateandhealth/pubs/assessinghealthvulnerabilitytoclimatechange.pdf, accessed October 15, 2015.

Maxwell, D., L. Russo, and L. Alinovi. 2012. Constraints to addressing food insecurity in protracted crises. *Proceedings of the National Academy of Sciences* 109(31): 12321–12325.

Maxwell, D., B. Vaitla, G. Tesfay, and N. Abadi. 2013. *Resilience, food security dynamics, and poverty traps in northern Ethiopia: Analysis of a biannual panel dataset, 2011–2013*. Somerville, MA: Feinstein International Center, Tufts University. http://reliefweb.int/sites/reliefweb.int/files/resources/Ethiopia%20Resilience-Food-Security-Dynamics.pdf, accessed February 16, 2016.

Mead, M. 1970. The changing significance of food: A discussion of the interrelationship between the diet of Americans and their capacity to provide for the poor and starving at home and abroad. *American Scientist* 58(2): 176–181.

National Alliance to End Homelessness. 2015. *The state of homelessness in America 2015*. Washington, DC: National Alliance to End Homelessness. http://www.endhomelessness.org/page/-/files/State_of_Homelessness_2015_FINAL_online.pdf, accessed February 16, 2016.

New York City Council. 2013. *FoodWorks: A vision to improve NYC's food system—Accomplishments and new ideas, Fall 2013*. New York: New York City Council. http://www.council.nyc.gov/html/action/acpdfs/foodworks_report_update_2013.pdf, accessed October 15, 2015.

Patz, J.A., H. Frumkin, T. Holloway, D.J. Vimont, and A. Haines. 2014. Climate change challenges and opportunities for global health. *Journal of the American Medical Association* 312(15): 1565–1580.

Ramin, B. and T. Svoboda. 2009. Health of the homeless and climate change. *Journal of Urban Health* 86(4): 654–664.

Rosenzweig, C. and W. Solecki. 2015. Building the knowledge base for climate resiliency: New York City panel on climate change 2015. *Annals of the New York Academy of Sciences* 1336.

Sims-Muhammad, T.Y. 2012. After the storms: South Louisiana sustainable food system assessment in light of environmental natural disasters Hurricanes Katrina & Rita. *International Journal of Humanities and Social Science* 2(3): 129–135.

United Nations News Centre. 2012. Food insecurity major concern after Hurricane Sandy strikes Haiti—UN Official. http://www.un.org/apps/news/story.asp?NewsID=43393#.VifnQk2FPoo, accessed October 15, 2015.

United Nations Office of the High Commissioner for Human Rights. 2015. Special Rapporteur on adequate housing as a component of the right to an adequate standard of living, and on the right to non-discrimination in this context. http://www.ohchr.org/EN/Issues/Housing/Pages/HousingIndex.aspx, accessed October 15, 2015.

_____. 2010. Fact sheet no. 34: The right to adequate food. http://www.ohchr.org/Documents/Publications/FactSheet34en.pdf, accessed October 15, 2015.

Wethington, E. 2005. An overview of the life course perspective: Implications for health and nutrition. *Journal of Nutrition and Education Behavior* 37(3): 114–119.

World Health Organization. 2011. *Global status report on noncommunicable diseases, 2010.* http://www.who.int/nmh/publications/ncd_report_full_en.pdf, accessed October 15, 2015.

# 13 The Dynamics of Vulnerability and Adaptive Capacity in Southern Ethiopia

*Logan Cochrane and Yishak Gecho*

## CONTENTS



**Abstract**

Agriculture accounts for more than 40% of the Ethiopian economy, 85% of all employment, and is driven primarily by rural smallholders. Those living in rural areas face a range of short-term, seasonal, annual, and long-term vulnerabilities. This chapter analyzes the range of dynamic, and sometimes unpredictable, challenges in Wolaita Zone, southern Ethiopia. We explore how individuals proactively manage vulnerabilities and seek means to enhance their adaptive capacity. These findings demonstrate that smallholders are engaging in change, highlighting the important role of their agency in understanding vulnerability and resilience.

## INTRODUCTION

The largest contributor to the Ethiopian economy is agriculture, accounting for almost half of the gross domestic product. It is also the primary livelihood activity for more than 80% of the population (Loening, Durecall, and Birru 2009). The vast majority of national agricultural activity is conducted in rural areas: smallholders farm more than 90% of the cultivated land in the country, with 60% doing so on less than a hectare of land (Taffesse, Dorosh, and Gemessa 2012). Although smallholder livelihoods and yields are crucial for national food security and the Ethiopian economy, those living in rural areas face a range of seasonal, annual, and long-term vulnerabilities.

This chapter explores smallholder vulnerabilities using a case study from Wolaita Zone, located within the Southern Nations, Nationalities and Peoples' region in southern Ethiopia. We use broad and inclusive measures of adaptive capacity and vulnerability that encompass livelihood choices and coping mechanisms to contextualize resilience. These are outlined in the first section. An examination of local vulnerabilities and an analysis of how individuals are engaging with change follows. The concluding discussion reflects upon the role of agency within the context of vulnerability and adaptive capacity and explores how academics and professionals can enhance their understanding of resilience by better incorporating agency into analyses.

## CONTEXTUALIZING RESILIENCE

Smallholder farmers have long practiced approaches to manage their vulnerabilities and enhance their capacity to adapt to change. Resilience-based perspectives in the academic literature are a recent phenomenon, much of which stems from systems research in ecology (Holling 1973). Walker and Salt (2006, p. 1) define resilience as "the ability of a system to absorb disturbance and still retain its basic function and structure." Viewing change from this foundational paradigm enables new phenomena, technology, and processes to be assessed in terms of direct impact, as well as how the community and/or individual is able to respond so as to maintain the function of the system processes and structure.

One of the ways in which community and individual resilience is evaluated is through adaptive capacity, which Ludi, Tesfaye, and Levine (2011, p. 7) define as the "potential of individuals and societies to respond to change." In order to understand the capacity of individuals and communities to adapt, assessments must take into account system-wide impacts and identify change that is manageable and absorbable or disruptive. To do this, an investigation into uncertain and/or unknown potential must be conducted to identify the ways in which individuals and communities will respond to new phenomena, technologies, and processes. Therefore, aspects of adaptation may not be "possible to directly measure" (Ludi, Tesfaye, and Levine 2011, p. 7). Consequently, rather than a specific methodology or set of measurements, we use resilience-based perspectives, which provide a lens through which the changes can be understood.

New phenomena, technologies, or processes that occur within the functionality of a system are considered managed and manageable by existing adaptive capacity; those beyond that threshold can result in an "irreversible new state" (Resilience Alliance 2007, p. 1; see also Walker and Salt 2006). Applying these concepts to smallholder contexts suggests that individuals and communities have thresholds within which they can adapt to change and a point beyond which entire livelihood(s) will be disrupted. This does not necessarily relate to size or scale; minor changes can be disruptive and major changes can be managed.

Resilience-based perspectives include an evaluation of the likelihood that any change might disrupt the functionality of the entire system, such as when new crop species or seed types are introduced or when large-scale infrastructure projects are proposed. One of the unique contributions of this framework is the system-wide, long-term evaluation of potential impacts, in addition to yield, cost, suitability, and other factors common to economic models.

New phenomena, technologies, or processes that cannot be absorbed and disrupt system functionality can be causes or manifestations of vulnerability. An insufficient capacity to adapt, for example, may be a result of poverty and the agro-ecological setting and negatively affect the resilience of an individual and/or community. Assessments of resilience can use vulnerability as a proxy measure of adaptive capacity, while recognizing limitations and avoiding equating resilience with the absence of vulnerability. Evaluations of this nature provide a means to assess the limits of individuals and communities as well as their strengths (Department for International Development 2003; Sen 1988; World Bank 2005). The substantial literature describing vulnerability provides insight into how these assessments can be applied in practice (e.g., Moser 1998; Scaramozzino 2006).

Resilience-based perspectives can also include components of renewal and reorganization (Folke 2006). One example from ecology research is ecosystem restoration, which "aims to enhance the resilience and sustainability" (Allen et al. 2002, p. 1421) of an ecosystem to a state where it is within its "natural range" of variability (Landres, Morgan, and Swanson 1999, p. 1181). In this context, resilience-based perspectives seek to strengthen the stability of a renewing or reorganizing system so that it is better able to absorb change, such as by enhancing the genetic diversity among and within species (Harris, Rhodes, and Martin 2013). For individuals and communities, this also includes fostering a diversity of knowledge and skills. Turner, Davidson-Hunt, and O'Flaherty (2003) describe this as "cultural capital"; a collective asset that enhances resilience by enabling the utilization of a larger range of options during times of change.

## METHODOLOGY

The case study from Wolaita Zone draws upon qualitative and quantitative research conducted by the authors from 2013 to the present. Gecho (2014) completed a survey of 300 households in four districts, purposefully selected to represent different agro-ecological zones. Households were randomly sampled following a community-wide wealth ranking exercise. In 2015, the authors completed a second household survey, covering 450 households, purposefully selected from three districts to compare the influence of access to services, infrastructure, and irrigation. Following the second survey, Cochrane conducted focus group discussions, which act as a feedback and triangulation mechanism for the survey findings, as well as 31 interviews within smallholder households in Wolaita Zone.

## CASE STUDY OF WOLAITA ZONE

Residents of Wolaita Zone confront a range of dynamic and unpredictable challenges. These include high population density, variable rainfall, limited land availability, shrinking land size holdings, land degradation, crop diseases and pests, volatile commodity prices, chronic food insecurity, limited access to services, and high levels of poverty (Rahmato 2007). Household surveys conducted by the authors in 2015 indicate that, on average, households are food insecure for two to five months per year, depending upon rainfall and yields. Within the focus group discussions, participants explained that lack of yield due to poor, inconsistent, or too heavy rainfall, which reduces income, pushes families into debt, and results in an inability to feed everyone in the household. This, residents state, is a primary reason why youth drop out of school and leave the household for labor work in towns. Although numerous challenges continue to confront the residents of Wolaita, this research demonstrates that individuals have been proactively managing vulnerabilities and have been engaging in means to enhance their adaptive capacity.

Ethiopia is home to four main agricultural systems: pastoralism, root crop-based, cereal crop-based, and shifting agriculture. Within Wolaita, root crops are of primary importance, particularly as a means to overcome seasonal food insecurity. These crops include enset* (*Ensete ventricosum*, native to Ethiopia), sweet potato, Irish potato, and taro. Cereals are also grown in the region, with maize as the most common. Locally grown fruits include bananas, mangos, and avocados. Small-scale production of coffee, an important cash crop, is common in certain parts of the region.

Livestock holdings are a vital part of livelihoods: cattle for plowing fields, donkeys for transporting goods and people, and sheep and goats for household and market purposes. Two breeds of poultry are also raised. Animal byproducts are used as fertilizers to replenish essential nutrients in the soil. Due to the limited amount of protein in many root crops, animal products are an important component of local diets.

### LONG-TERM

The greatest long-term challenge faced by smallholders in Wolaita is the lack of irrigation infrastructure, combined with a vulnerability to climate change (Center for Global Development 2012; Central Statistical Agency of Ethiopia [CSAE] 2009). The residents of Wolaita also experience declining landholding sizes. As Rahmato's study notes (2007, p. 10), the land "holdings [in Wolaita]

* Enset is a crucial contributor to the root crop-based agricultural system. It is considered one of the most sustainable crops in Africa, particularly for densely populated areas (Brandt et al. 1997).

have always been small relative to other parts of the country." Rahmato found that, in 1976, the average landholding size was 0.7 hectares. This dropped to 0.5 for most smallholders by 1989. In some areas within Wolaita, average landholding size has since fallen below 0.25 hectares (data provided by the Damot Gale District Agricultural Office, Wolaita Zone, Ethiopia on May 14, 2015). Smallholders note that land size is not sufficient; many face chronic food insecurity.

The government has set aside communal grazing land, protected forest areas, and developed a "land bank" system for unused land to be redistricted. In Wolaita, 57% of the land is used for crops, 19% is forest and bush area, and 11% is for grazing. The remaining 13% is classified as "other"; it is uncultivable or cultivated but not distributed (Gecho 2014). The majority of cultivated land is owned and inherited. The division of land is largely a product of inheritance, whereby a number of children share the land of their household.* This results in smaller plots with each generation. Within Wolaita, the size of landholdings is compounded by population density, which is one of the highest in Ethiopia (CSAE 2007). Therefore, there is practically no unused cultivatable land for new generations. The land shortage has compelled the government to create resettlement programs multiple times over the last 50 years, moving residents to different parts of the region and throughout country.

### Annual

According to the 2015 surveys, the most common input used in Wolaita is fertilizer (91%). Farmers also utilize improved seed varieties (72%). Both resources are acquired annually through government channels. There are two key access barriers: poverty and irregular supply. Although the government subsidizes inputs and facilitates access through the provision of credit (with a percentage of the initial cost paid at the outset), many of the poorest households still cannot afford it. This is the product of entrenched poverty and is experienced by households on an annual basis. The majority (50%) rely on formal loans and credit. Gecho (2014) finds that 68% of surveyed households said that the cost barrier was too high for fertilizer and 41% said that it was too high for improved seeds.

The irregular supply of inputs deters farmers from relying upon them. For example, rapid fluctuations in fertilizer distribution have continued from at least the 1970s (Rahmato 2007) until the present (data provided by the Damot Gale District Agricultural Office, Wolaita Zone, Ethiopia on May 14, 2015), with doubling and halving of distributions occurring on a year-to-year basis. Not knowing if inputs will be available and in what quantities influences decisions about adopting and relying upon them. In focus group discussions, farmers expressed appreciation for the new drought tolerant varieties developed at regional agricultural research centers. However, they explained that availability, cost, and accessibility prevent adoption.

### Seasonal

Rainfall data are typically presented in an annual and averaged format. This gives the impression that rainfall is seasonally consistent (see Figure 13.1). Contrary to these data, farmers cite variable rainfall as being a major seasonal challenge. Gecho (2014) finds that 79% of smallholder farmers mentioned rainfall as their greatest problem.

The challenge of rainfall volatility is clear in Figure 13.2, which shows a range of minimum–maximum rainfall from 2003 to 2013, highlighting significant fluctuations. The difference of rainfall peaks and troughs, as well as irregular and out of season rainfall, confirm farmers' experiences and challenge the conventional narrative about seasonal rainfall. For farmers who are entirely dependent upon rainfall for their agricultural livelihoods, the determination of when to prepare fields and plant seed is much more difficult as a result; incorrect timing can have negative, multiyear impacts.

* Land tenure has shifted significantly in the last century. The introduction of land certification is the most recent attempt to enhance tenure security (Deininger, Ali, Holden, and Zevenbergen 2008). The traditional patrilineal system of inheritance has been legally altered, giving equal rights to sons and daughters. However, much more progress is needed to align legal rights with lived realities (Holden 2008).

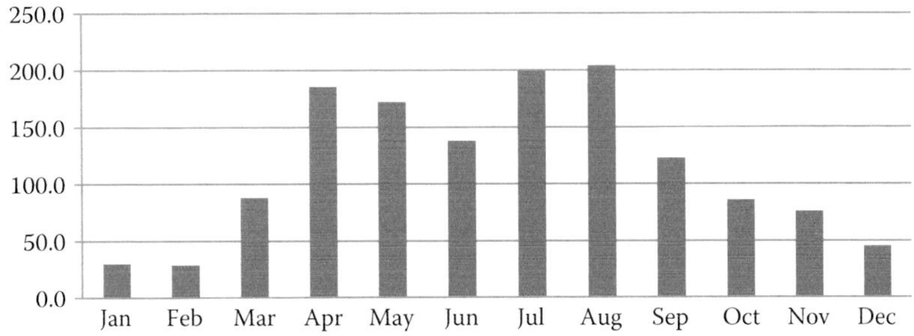


**FIGURE 13.1** Average rainfall in Wolaita Sodo (2003–2013).

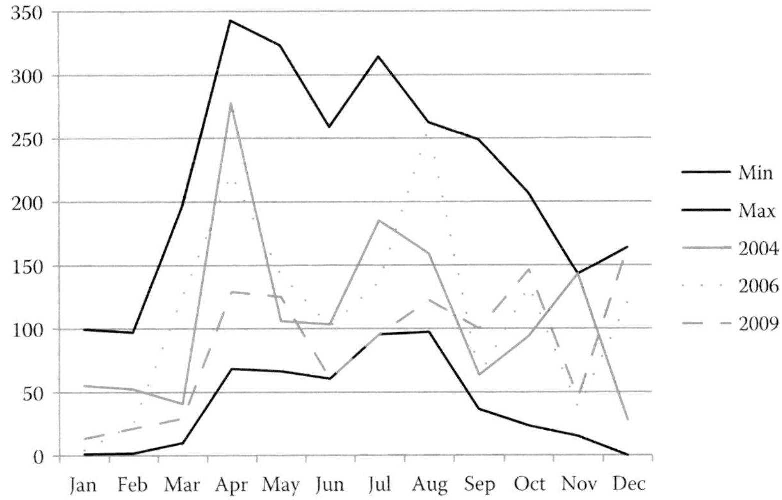


**FIGURE 13.2** Rainfall variability in Wolaita Sodo (2003–2013), selected years shown.

Throughout much of Ethiopia, the "hunger season" ranges from one to four months, depending upon the rainfall of the previous year. In Wolaita, this averages two to five months, creating seasonal food insecurity and malnutrition. Each year, there is a rise in diagnosed malnutrition cases toward the end of the "hunger season," which slightly overlaps with the planting of the first seasonal rains (see Figure 13.3). The rise in malnutrition indicates the severity and annual nature of these seasonal

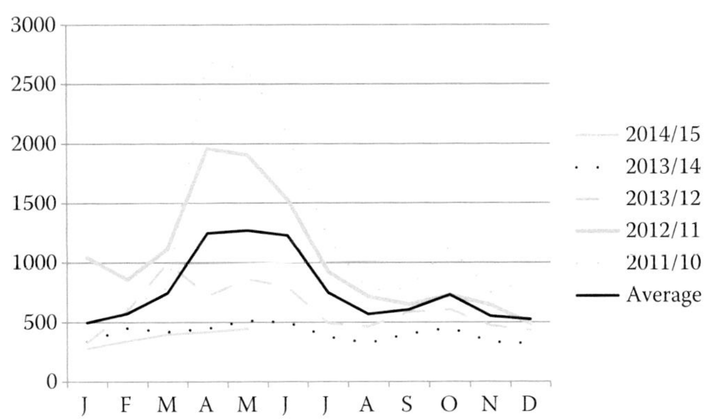


**FIGURE 13.3** Seasonal child malnutrition in Wolaita Zone (new intake of outpatient malnutrition cases).

challenges. It should be noted that the cases shown in Figure 13.3 are only children diagnosed at a health extension post and do not capture undiagnosed cases or convey the impact of reduced and less diverse food intake during these months.

## ENGAGING CHANGE

Residents of Wolaita engage with their long-term, annual, and seasonal vulnerabilities in proactive and informed ways. This agency demonstrates the ways in which individuals, households, and communities understand their vulnerabilities, seek to enhance their capacity to adapt to change, and become more resilient. Some of the responses to change explored below are unconventional. Indeed, some are chosen as the best option amongst an array of limited and relatively unfavorable choices.

### LONG-TERM

Long-term responses to declining land size include family investment in child education. If unable to send all children to school due to the cost, families strategize to ensure at least one child completes tertiary education. In Wolaita Zone, almost 90% of children begin primary school, but less than 16% continue into grades 11 and 12 (see Table 13.1). The dropout rates in primary and secondary school are due to high costs of education and the indirect costs of lost household labor and pressures faced from the inability to provide basic needs for all members of the household.

In the 2015 household surveys, we found that households facing fewer risks, such as those with access to irrigation, felt they had sufficient income to send all their children to school (61%) when compared to those without such access (41%). Individual interviews and focus group discussions within all communities consistently highlighted the idea that supporting as many children as possible through secondary school raises the potential future household income. In most cases, however, graduates relocate to nearby towns or cities for employment. This negatively impacts households, as they lose agricultural labor. With aging parents and school-aged children remaining, this strategy also creates short-term challenges.

A second response to long-term vulnerabilities in the household is the domestic migration of youth for unskilled work opportunities in towns and cities (e.g., domestic work and labor at construction sites). Insufficient resources within the household often drive this choice; in interviews and focus group discussions held throughout Wolaita, households consistently cited insufficient food as a primary reason pushing youth to make this decision. Even though such work is low paid and

**TABLE 13.1**
**Educational Enrollment Rates in Wolaita[a]**

| Grades[b] | School-Aged Population[c] | Enrolled[d] | Percentage Enrolled |
|---|---|---|---|
| 1–4 | 301,687 | 270,726 | 89.7 |
| 5–8 | 187,505 | 143,590 | 76.6 |
| 9–10 | 102,961 | 43,387 | 42.1 |
| 11–12 | 79,470 | 12,580 | 15.8 |

[a] These figures are approximated. Community members explained that dropout rates are primarily understood as a product of limited resources, but that is not the only cause.

[b] The grouping of grades follows the cycles of education in the Ethiopian education system.

[c] Data obtained from the Wolaita Zone Administration Office for 2012.

[d] Data obtained from the Wolaita Zone Administration Office for 2013. We recognize that the different comparison years do not allow for exact percentages. Due to data availability limitations, we present approximate figures to demonstrate the extent of dropout rates.

irregular, for many, these jobs are the best available option. Dropout rates reflect the high levels of youth leaving education (see Table 13.1). In one district where food insecurity was higher (average 4.3 months food insecure) than the surrounding ones (average 3.7 months), community members estimated that 70% of the youth had left for work.

Those who leave for skilled or unskilled work feel an obligation to support their families; however, most are unable to do so due to the low salaries they receive. In the 2015 household surveys, 29% of families in one district received financial support from family living elsewhere in the country; domestic remittance in a neighboring district was much lower (8%). In focus group discussions, community members explained that this was due to the types of work commonly undertaken by people from different locations: some migrate for long-term work in more distant parts of the country, others remain nearby.

Obtaining education and employment are long-term responses. Employment results in members of the household semipermanently or permanently leaving their communities; it requires investment over time to acquire education. A significant percentage of households engage in these off-farm work options. In Wolaita, 20% of surveyed households had at least one member engaging in off-farm employment. Sixteen percent of households had at least one member who migrated domestically (Gecho 2014). Work migration is a direct response to the long-term challenges of high population density, declining land size, and chronic food insecurity.

### Annual

Farmers in Wolaita typically planted a limited number of primary crops in the two planting seasons. In the shorter of the two rainy seasons (*belg*), maize and beans were grown. In the second rainy season (*meher*), sweet potatoes and taro were commonly planted. Most households planted enset, referred to as "the enemy of hunger," an important perennial crop that is relied upon during times of food insecurity (Tsegaye and Struik 2002, p. 292). Farmers recognize that relying upon fewer crops enhances vulnerabilities. Having a wide variety strengthens their ability to adapt to changing rainfall, as well as reducing the risk of pests and diseases devastating an entire crop. Thus, many farmers have purposely diversified the types of crops they grow. New root and cereal crop varieties, as well as fauna, have been introduced. Most of these have been made available through agricultural extension workers, with some hybrids being the result of work done by government-run regional agricultural research centers. Recent diversification is not a result of a newfound appreciation of vulnerabilities; rather, it is related to improved access to new seeds, seedlings, and livestock.

It is traditional practice in Wolaita for households to partition their land into six small areas, within which different crops are grown. These may also be intercropped (Rahmato 2007). Diversification within these plots has been supported through agricultural extension workers, regional agricultural research centers, and government-supported nurseries. As part of this process, farmers maintain important perennial crops, such as enset but have introduced new types of crops, including fruit trees, vegetables, and improved varieties of root crops and cereals. These meet household needs first. In the case of surplus, they are sold in local markets. They have also introduced new animals, such as hybrid chickens for improved egg production.

The types of diversification vary, influenced by location, land size, and household income. Household surveys conducted by the authors in 2015 found that those with irrigation, who experience less risk due to regular water access, had less crop diversity (averaging 5.8 crops) than those without it (averaging 6.7 crops). The greater diversification reflects the level of risk and efforts to mitigate potential negative outcomes, even if some choices result in lower yields. However, higher-cost diversifications were more common in the community with irrigation than those without. These include planting avocado trees (average 2.3 trees versus 1.5 per household) and purchasing egg-producing poultry (average 0.5 versus 0.1 per household).

When exploring these differences in focus group discussions, the more remote communities reported that they knew about other means to diversify but were unable to access them. For example, tree seedling nurseries were located too far away or vaccinations for hybrid chickens were not available in their communities, resulting in poultry loss and a discouragement of this form of diversification. As a result, the ability to enhance adaptive capacity is affected by access to irrigation and transportation infrastructure, nearness to livestock health facilities and towns, as well as household capacity to invest in diversifications.

### Seasonal

The challenge of variable seasonal rainfall makes its impact on malnutrition inconsistent and unpredictable. There can be too much rain, too little, or it may come at the wrong time in the planting cycle. Therefore, it is difficult for households to engage in proactive ways. In theory, the establishment of irrigation infrastructure would enable households to manage these risks. The few communities in Wolaita that have irrigation infrastructure do not experience these challenges in any significant way. In one such community, household members explained that, instead of one or two yields per year, they now have three or four. As a result of increased and consistent yields, seasonal food insecurity had largely been overcome. Households experienced an increase in their income from improved yield and from the ability to plant new crops, particularly vegetables.

In interviews and focus group discussions, smallholders stated that surplus yields and selling to the markets was not a common practice in the past. In our 2015 household surveys, however, the majority of all households sold at least some of their yield (65%). Those with access to irrigation infrastructure engage in this practice much more (91%) than did those without it (56%). Transportation infrastructure enables those crops to reach the market. Although the community with irrigation infrastructure was far from the nearest town market (approximately 20 km), it had access to an asphalt road. Thus, the vast majority (91%) sold crops at the market. Households in a community equally far from the market town but without transportation infrastructure sold significantly less (46%).

The introduction of improved seeds, the diversification of crops and livestock, as well as the development of irrigation and transportation infrastructure have strengthened the importance of weekly markets within towns and expanded their scale. The high cost of infrastructure, however, is beyond the capacity of individual communities. Therefore, households focus upon new crops and diversification in response to seasonal vulnerabilities.

For those without irrigation, the responses to variable rainfall are more localized and focus on diversifying livelihood options. When harvests are poor, household members may overcome seasonal food insecurity by engaging in nonfarm and off-farm options, such as selling milk or butter, collecting firewood or grass, or engaging in petty trade. The collection of firewood and grass is practiced by those without livestock or the financial capacity to buy and sell goods, which are sold in nearby towns. This activity, however, does not fully provide for the needs of the households and is a last resort option.

Choices such as these are ones of necessity rather than proactive engagement. Households that were relatively poor relied upon these nonfarm income sources to a much greater extent. Fifty-two percent of the poorest households engaged in nonfarm activities, while only 16% of relatively better-off households did (Gecho 2014).

## LESSONS LEARNED

This chapter explored vulnerabilities that exist in Wolaita and the ways in which community members engage with new phenomena, technology, and processes. The experiences demonstrate that change is dynamic and multidirectional. The findings outline the immediate and long-term challenges posed by declining land holdings, irregular supply of inputs, malnutrition, and volatile rainfall. In order to address challenges, policies and programs can enhance the adaptive capacity of individuals and communities. For example, this research highlights the positive impact of irrigation and transportation infrastructure, as well as market access.

This research also demonstrates that individuals and households engage with change, proactively enhancing their own adaptive capacity and taking advantage of opportunities available to them. The exercise of agency is a key finding here, and one that is often under emphasized. The importance that households place upon education, employment, and diversification demonstrates that they are not averse to change. Rather, they make calculated choices, sometimes between limited and relatively unfavorable options.

Many households continue to struggle with chronic poverty and seasonal food insecurity. While external changes, such as rainfall and irrigation, are important, this research highlights the role of individuals and households as agentic change makers. Programs and policies can be strengthened if the vulnerabilities are addressed in tandem with strengthening opportunities. This is particularly critical for those opportunities that community members themselves have prioritized.

## REFERENCES


Allen, C.D., M. Savage, D.A. Falk, K.F. Suckling, T.W. Swetnam, T. Schulke, P.B. Stacey, P. Morgan, M. Hoffman, and J.T. Klingel. 2002. Ecological restoration of southwestern Ponderosa Pine ecosystems: A broad perspective. *Ecological Applications* 12(5): 1418–1433.

Brandt, S.A., A. Spring, C. Heibisch, J.T. McCabe, E. Tabogie, M. Diro, M.G. Wolde, G. Yntiso, M. Shigeta, and S. Tesfaye. 1997. *The "tree against hunger." Enset-based agricultural systems in Ethiopia.* Washington, DC: American Association for the Advancement of Science.

Center for Global Development. 2012. *Mapping the impacts of climate change vulnerability.* http://www.cgdev.org/section/topics/climate_change/mapping_the_impacts_of_climate_change, accessed September 19, 2015.

Central Statistical Agency of Ethiopia. 2009. *Large and medium scale commercial farms: Samples survey 2008/09 (2001 E.C.).* Statistical Bulletin 446. Addis Ababa: Central Statistical Agency of Ethiopia.

Central Statistical Agency of Ethiopia. 2007. *Population and housing census.* Addis Ababa: Central Statistical Agency of Ethiopia.

Deininger, K., D.A. Ali, S. Holden, and J. Zevenbergen. 2008. Rural land certification in Ethiopia: Process, initial impact, and implications for other African countries. *World Development* 36(10): 1786–1812.

Department for International Development. 2003. *Social protection, in policy planning and implementation.* http://www.odi.org/sites/odi.org.uk/files/odi-assets/publications-opinion-files/3185.pdf, accessed September 19, 2015.

Folke, C. 2006. Resilience: The emergence of a perspective for social-ecological systems analyses. *Global Environmental Change* 16: 253–267.

Gecho, Y. 2014. *Livelihood strategies and food security of rural households in Wolaita Zone, Southern Ethiopia.* Doctoral Dissertation submitted to the College of Agriculture and Natural Resource Management, Haramaya University.

Harris, M., T. Rhodes, and A. Martin. 2013. Taming systems to create enabling environments for HCV treatment: Negotiating trust in the drug and alcohol setting. *Social Science & Medicine* 83: 19–26.

Holden, S. 2008. From being property of men to becoming equal owners? Early impacts of land registration and certification on women in southern Ethiopia. Oslo: Norwegian Mapping and Cadastre Authority, Centre for Property Rights and Development. http://mirror.unhabitat.org/downloads/docs/10768_1_594333.pdf, accessed September 19, 2015.

Holling, C.S. 1973. Resilience and stability of ecological systems. *Annual Review of Ecology and Systematics* 4: 1–23.

Landres, P., P. Morgan, and F.J. Swanson. 1999. Overview of the use of natural variability concepts in managing ecological systems. *Ecological Applications* 9: 1179–1188.

Loening, J.L., D. Durevall, and Y.A. Birru. 2009. *Inflation dynamics and food prices in an agricultural economy: The case of Ethiopia.* Policy Research Working Paper 4949. Washington, DC: The World Bank.

Ludi, E., K. Tesfaye, and S. Levine. 2011. *Preparing for the future? Understanding the influence of development interventions on adaptive capacity at local level in Ethiopia.* http://community.eldis.org/.5a35bbfb/Ethiopia_Synthesis_Report.pdf, accessed September 19, 2015.

Moser, C.O.N. 1998. The asset vulnerability framework: Reassessing urban poverty reduction strategies. *World Development* 26(1): 1–19.

Rahmato, D. 2007. *Development interventions in Wollaita, 1960s–2000s: A critical review*. Addis Ababa: Forum for Social Studies, Monograph No. 4.

Resilience Alliance. 2007. *Assessing and managing resilience in social-ecological systems: A practitioner's workbook*. http://www.resalliance.org/workbook/, accessed September 19, 2015.

Scaramozzino, P. 2006. *Measuring vulnerability to food insecurity*. Agricultural Development and Economics Division (ESA) Working Paper No. 06-12. Rome: Food and Agriculture Organization.

Sen, A. 1988. The concept of development. In *Handbook of development economics Vol. 1*, eds. H. Chenery and T.N. Srinivasan, 9–26. New York: Elsevier.

Taffesse, A.S., P. Dorosh, and S.A. Gemessa. 2012. Crop production in Ethiopia: Regional patterns and trends. In *Food and agriculture in Ethiopia: Progress and policy challenges*, eds. P. Dorosh and S. Rashid, 53–83. Philadelphia: University of Pennsylvania.

Tsegaye, A. and P.C. Struik. 2002. Analysis of enset (*Ensete vventricosum*): indigenous production methods and farm-based biodiversity in major enset-growing regions of southern Ethiopia. *Experimental Agriculture* 38: 291–315.

Turner, N.J., I.J. Davidson-Hunt, and M. O'Flaherty. 2003. Living on the edge: Ecological and cultural edges as sources of diversity for social-ecological resilience. *Human Ecology* 31(3): 439–461.

Walker, B. and D. Salt. 2006. *Resilience thinking: Sustaining ecosystems and people in a changing world*. Washington: Island Press.

World Bank. 2005. *Afghanistan: Poverty, vulnerability and social protection*. Human Development Unit, South Asia Region, No. 29694-AF. Washington, DC: The World Bank.

# 14 The Production of Material Goods as Resilience Adaptation by Impelled Migrants in Malawi

*Michèle Companion*

## CONTENTS



**Abstract**

Framing impelled displacement resulting from ecotourism promotion and development as a form of sociocultural and economic disaster, this study investigates the challenges faced by this new class of environmental refugees. Interviews conducted in Malawi with 153 local craftspeople and vendors show that the portability of human capital helps to ease the rural to urban transition and reduce the impact of anomie. Through the production of material goods, impelled migrants forge connections with their past while reinventing their sense of self. This contributes to disaster literature that focuses on transition processes in the aftermath of disasters and provides suggestions to improve resilience amongst displaced populations.

## INTRODUCTION

This study examines the process of identity maintenance and reconstruction that occurs after involuntary displacement. With the designation of the southern arm of Lake Malawi as a national park and UNESCO World Heritage site, there has been a proliferation of private, upscale venues along the lakeshore. Local access to the shoreline, once considered a communal right, is now being restricted as private property. Similar situations are occurring along the outskirts of other national parks throughout southern Malawi, where occupants have been displaced by the expansion of amenities and infrastructure to generate ecotourism dollars. This creates a new class of impelled environmental refugees.

As noted by Cox and Perry (2011), economic, material, and symbolic losses and changes are associated with displacement. Displacement "refers to both physical removal of people from their homes and restrictions on their resource use and access to places which prevents them from pursuing their livelihoods" (Schmidt-Soltau and Brockington 2007, p. 2183). Involuntary displacement and loss of access to traditional resources forces communities and individuals to alter livelihood strategies and to migrate to other areas, where they must integrate into new communities and economic structures. Migrants experience forms of displacement trauma, confronting grief over their loss of place, status, community identity, traditional knowledge, relational networks, and social capital. They express anger at the government and resentment of the wildlife and park workers. In many cases, this anger remains years, even decades, after displacement.

In this study, environmental displacement is framed as a disaster (Schmidt-Soltau 2003). Impelled migrants must adapt to new economic, social, cultural, and political situations while establishing new forms of personal identity, community, and livelihoods. This necessitates a reorientation and reroutinization process to build a "new normal." This study explores the process of reroutinizing everyday life by framing the production of material goods as a means of identity maintenance and reconstruction, as well as an income generating activity.

The ability to recreate and maintain identity after or in anticipation of social, cultural, economic, and physical disruption is a form of community and personal resilience. Borrowing from Gaillard (2007), while vulnerability only focuses on susceptibility to harm, resilience addresses capabilities to respond and adapt in order to prevent or minimize harm. This study shows that impelled migrants carry their human capital with them and adapt their skill sets to new environments and social conditions, demonstrating resilience. The production of material goods allows them to maintain a connection to existing skills and previous identity markers (continuity theory), while enhancing those best suited to adaptation and niche positioning in their new environment (complexity theory). This contributes to discussions of the impact of tourism expansion on local populations and to the broader disaster literature about community resilience and recovery after catastrophic events.

## BACKGROUND

After Malawian independence in 1964, tourism came to the fore to help diversify economic development plans. Political changes in 1994, combined with the establishment of the Department of Tourism as a Ministry, resulted in the launch of a national tourism policy in 1995. The "Warm Heart of Africa" campaign was designed to capitalize on friendly local people and a stable government to encourage foreign visitors. By 2003, numerous facilities in protected areas were privatized to improve services to tourists and promote eco-, ethnic, and adventure tourism (Magombo 2011). The 2008–2013 Tourism Strategic Development Plan (Government of Malawi 2008) prioritized eco-lodges and leisure accommodations, along with infrastructural improvements, to propel this sector forward as a replacement for the declining tobacco industry. Consequently, it is a major component of the Malawi Growth Development Strategy (Government of Malawi 2006, 2012).

A quick perusal of Malawi's official tourism website (www.visitmalawi.mw) highlights casinos and theater entertainment, alongside cultural and ethnic experiences (e.g., traditional/sacred/cultural dances and festivals, initiation ceremonies, installation ceremonies for traditional chiefs). Thanks to well-funded reintroduction programs, many of the wildlife preserves now feature a wider array of species. This was designed to increase demand for adventure tourism (horseback riding, safaris) (Government of Malawi 2012). However, Lake Malawi is the focus of most development activity, including water sports (diving, snorkeling, windsurfing, kayaking, pleasure boating), cycling, and, of course, lounging.

The impact can be seen in the geographic spread and increased number of accommodation establishments. Sandy beaches, perfect for attracting tourists, line the southeast arm of Lake Malawi.

Hotels, guest houses, and private or corporate owned cottages and holiday homes, built on customary land obtained from local chiefs, have rapidly appeared over the last two decades. By 2011, there were over 40 of these along the southeast arm (Donda, Hara, Ngocherea, and Berge 2014). On Cape Maclear, in Lake Malawi National Park, numerous facilities have sprung up in a very compact area.

The expansion of tourism has created conflicting demands for space. The beaches valued by tourists are also the busiest fishing and trading sites. Traditionally, small-scale fisherman kept their boats at the beach. As tourism increased, hotels and resorts have cleared lakeshore and in-water vegetation to improve beach recreation space for sun bathing, walking, swimming, and launching kayaks and wind surfing boards. Conflicts over processing fish along the beach (sight, smell, smoke, and noise) caused resorts to fence off beach areas and privatize use, affecting launching and landing and processing and trading areas to the detriment of local men and women involved in all aspects of the fishing industry (Chilembwe 2014; Derman and Ferguson 1995; Magombo 2011). This also prevents local people from accessing the lake for bathing and washing (Chilembwe 2014).

Mdulumanja Village represents an extreme example of the outcome of such conflicts. This fishing community was located along the shores of Lake Malawi near Salima. At the behest of the Grand Beach Hotel owner (Dutch), the entire village of 70 homes and businesses was razed in 1991 to make way for hotel expansion. The owner argued that the village was "unsanitary, unsightly, and harbored thieves." In addition, he was losing business to the village restaurants and tour guides. Families received less than $20 compensation and no effort was made to relocate them (Derman and Ferguson 1995, pp. 132–133).

Similar situations can be found near Liwonde National Park, south of Mangochi. The park was gazetted in 1973, resulting in the expulsion of all local residents from within the boundaries. Consequently, the park periphery has the highest population density in the country (Novelli and Scarth 2007, p. 64). These boundary areas do not generate enough physical resources or job opportunities, leaving residents feeling that they have no option but to illegally use materials from the park, such as grasses and fuelwood. Local residents continue to express resentment over this situation, commenting that the government favors animals and foreigners over them (Novelli and Scarth 2007).

## THEORETICAL FRAMEWORK

Continuity theorists argue that material goods become a form of narrative that reproduces identity by creating a biographical flow and allows a consistent self to be maintained (Tuohy and Stephens 2012). As Murray (2000) notes, "the process of creating narrative enables the person to give meaning to the constant change in his or her life, to bring order to disorder" (p. 338). Baker and Hill (2013) extend this to the production of material goods, noting that people find ways to "protect and propagate" things that are valued, including cultural ideals, personal and group identity, and group and individual differentiation. "In conditions of material disruption, people value material objects for their role in simultaneously reconstructing collective and individual identities" (p. 284).

Complexity theorists argue that this process of identity re-negotiation also presents opportunities for change (Morrison 2005). Complexity theory is a theory of adaptation and development that facilitates survival in a changing environment (Morrison 2005). The process is "marked by increasing differentiation and niche location or positioning" (Morrison 2005, p. 321).

These processes become relevant when the production of material goods are necessitated by the loss of access to previous livelihood practices as a result of displacement and migration. Cash-based economies push many migrants into the informal economic sector (Companion 2010a, 2010b, 2015), including petty trading and day labor. As complexity theory argues, this can also create opportunities for vendors to adapt to local demands and carve out a competitive economic niche (Companion 2010a, 2010b, 2015). The commodification of culture and traditional knowledge, such as dances, foods, rituals, and presentation of self, and the production of material objects, such as masks, carvings, jewelry, and figurines, represents an important income-generating activity in areas that attract eco-, ethnocultural, adventure, and disaster tourists and large numbers of nongovernmental organization (NGO) staff (Companion 2015). Gaillard (2007) argues that adaptability is one of the fundamental forms of societal resilience; in this case, adapting material output to meet local demands is essential for economic and physical survival.

Marketing culture and material objects provide a second critical function for impelled migrants: the maintenance and construction of personal and collective identity. Baker and Hill (2013) note that "objects' self-continuity properties facilitate adaptation, development, and preservation, particularly when identity is uncertain or challenged...when self-identity is in flux, through significant changes such as migration...objects may serve to confirm some aspects of self-identity while reconstructing others" (p. 276). This can ease displacement trauma and facilitate transition to a new environment. This will be elaborated upon in the Findings and Discussion section below.

## METHODS

The data for this analysis are an extension of previous work conducted on behalf of the Save the Children Federation (SCF)–Malawi Field Office in 1998. In 2009, members of SCF staff implemented a follow-up survey in Lilongwe, Mangochi, Liwonde, and Zomba to identify household food security threats, focusing on the nature of local markets and marketing structures, the increasing influence of tourism in the area, the displacement of local populations, and how these issues impact gender inequity and HIV/AIDS vulnerability. Semistructured questionnaires were used to gather data from vendors at market locations during the period of June–July 2009. Participants were recruited through targeted convenience samples, with teams identifying and visiting all local market areas. All vendors in that area were approached and asked to participate. Interviews were conducted in English and Chichewa. General characteristics of participants can be found in Table 14.1.

Using SPSS 22, questions from the survey were used to filter responses from the larger participant pool. Through this process, only those who had been impelled to migrate or forcibly relocated at some point ($n$ = 153) were included in this study. Content analysis was performed on the transcripts of open-ended survey answers. Grounded theory (Corbin and Strauss 2008) used to generate theoretical implications of the data.

**TABLE 14.1**
**Vendor Characteristics**

| | | Market Area | | |
|---|---|---|---|---|
| **Participants** | **N** | **Lilongwe** | **Mangochi** | **Zomba** |
| Number of vendors | 153 | 54 | 61 | 38 |
| Male | 63 | 21 | 29 | 13 |
| Female | 90 | 33 | 32 | 25 |
| Vending types | | | | |
| Food—men | 17 | 4 | 11 | 2 |
| Food—women | 48 | 23 | 12 | 13 |
| Wood crafts—men | 24 | 9 | 7 | 8 |
| Tin crafts—men | 9 | 2 | 6 | 1 |
| Tin crafts—women | 2 | 0 | 2 | 0 |
| Batik/art—men | 5 | 4 | 1 | 0 |
| Clothing—men | 8 | 2 | 4 | 2 |
| Clothing/jewelry—women | 32 | 8 | 15 | 9 |
| Self—women | 6 | 2 | 3 | 1 |

## FINDINGS AND DISCUSSION

### Construction of Positive Identity

After conducting a content analysis on the open-ended survey responses, five main findings emerge relating to the impact of the production of material goods on impelled migrants. The first is that the production of material goods is a proactive and positive strategy designed to help migrants integrate into their new communities and economies. Implicit in this orientation is a simultaneous rejection of externally imposed, negative labels. Some of these labels are generated by community members, framing newcomers as beggars, thieves, and job competition with nothing positive to offer (76% of respondents report being called a derogatory term). Others are generated by government agency personnel and NGO staff and involve concepts that categorize and homogenize impelled migrants as potentially problematic. Terms such as "homeless," "refugee," "transient," and "displaced" are viewed by the respondents as negative or limiting. These labels expose recent arrivals to targeting for harassment by local residents, migrants who have been in the area longer, and authorities. Nine respondents (6%) noted that NGO presence in the area makes impelled migrants more of a target because it draws attention to them.

By focusing on the production of material goods that are unique to the area, the respondents strategically fill economic positions that do not place them in direct competition with other local vendors (complexity theory). It also provides them with ability to define themselves as craftspeople, merchants, and vendors, in opposition to the negative, imposed labels. Self-definition, then, represents agency that can be asserted as a form of empowerment. One artist in Lilongwe (male 2) describes the attitude toward new arrivals as follows:

> [Transients/migrants] are viewed as carrying the [rural country] with them [dusty/dirty/lowly]. They have no roots or [stability]. People treat them with suspicion and do not offer them help. As a [merchant/artist], I am not to be viewed this way. I am someone who has come here seeking opportunity... I am not lazy or begging. I am providing a service and earning money.

The ability to adapt human capital to new forms of enterprise provides an essential sense of control that was stripped away in the relocation and struggles to integrate into communities that may not want them. A woodcrafter (Zomba male 6) describes the process of integrating and differentiating imagery in his artwork: "While I use things from my home, I use many things that I see here. I go to markets and look at what others make. I try to use this, too, so I am not easily identified as new here. My [technique or style] helps me stand out to customers, but I am not so different that I am [targeted]." For example, his work features monkeys, elephants, and kudu, but he also carves lions and giraffes. While popular with tourists, these animals were not found in the Zomba area at the time of the survey.

### Link to Place/Narrative Continuity

The second major theme that emerges from the data is that the production of material goods plays a significant role in the reroutinization of everyday life by helping to create and maintain a link to personal historic places and people. All respondents report using the production of foods, jewelry, or craft objects as a way to link them to their ancestral homes and community-derived identities. This allows them to move forward with an economic survival strategy without having to jettison their connections to the past. Thus, the production of material goods represents continuity and a form of reorientation, supporting Baker and Hill's findings (2013).

For respondents ($n$ = 107 or 70%), maintaining links to deceased and/or disbursed family is particularly important. "Pleasance" (Mangochi female 32) emphasizes how craft vending helps her to maintain emotional ties to her family:

> My mother taught us how to make beads out of [found material such as wood and bark] and how to make cord. My sisters and I would...make ourselves pretty. I think of that when I am making things for the sales....my sisters went away to different directions with their husbands. I wouldn't know where to look for them.

"Stan" (Mangochi male 7) cultivates similar connections, noting "My father...taught us...how to use bones to make things...I can make small things for girls and ladies. Because he taught me things, I can find ways to still earn now...Things that I make keep me strong with him and remind me to teach my children things too."

## Identity Maintenance and Formation

The third theme to emerge is that the production of material goods is critical for both identity maintenance and formation for impelled migrants. From a continuity theory perspective, this preserves a connection to existing senses of self. From a complexity theory perspective, it allows for adaptation to the social and cultural environment, easing transition and the formation of new identity elements. This process is facilitated by working in market areas, which increases social participation and builds social capital, or at least allows for exposure to local phrases/slang and gesticulation forms.

All respondents note that impelled migration impacts identity; a broader sense of community and ones place in it are lost until a new one can be created. The vehicle through which this process occurs is the production of material goods. Baker and Hill (2013, p. 278) find that material objects are agents of both communitas ("we") and individualism ("me"). Thus, the creation of material objects can simultaneously generate a sense of connectedness and community and represent personal expression. This can reduce feelings of anomie (normlessness) and the stress of relocation and adaptation to a new environment (Companion 2015).

Baker and Hill (2013, p. 276) find that "...objects' self-definitional properties derive from their abilities to help individuals tell life-stories, contemplate who they are and what they do, designate boundaries among people, places, and times, and foster interconnections." This is supported by the study data. Women engaged in food preparation report that their recipes and cooking styles serve as identity markers that differentiate them from other food vendors in the area. This attracts clientele from their home regions and those looking for new taste experiences, which generates revenue while establishing network connections and increasing social capital. For these women, food production allows for continuity of the familiar, while providing them with a mechanism to integrate into the economic structure of their new home.

This holds true for craftspeople as well. Nineteen (44%) of the 43 craftsmen reported having some renown for talent within their families. They made toys, gifts, and decorative and ceremonial objects. However, they did not engage in this activity as a primary form of income generation. Seven (16%) were recognized by their communities as skilled craftspeople. They were asked to create things for public or communal spaces like religious areas or to craft ceremonial objects. Both sets of respondents carried their local identities as "skilled" to their new locations through the production of a variety of items for sale in the markets.

The female respondents who were making and selling jewelry had transformed a skill that they used for self or family ornamentation for fun or ritual into a new economic venture. This was especially important for the women, as the female respondents are less likely to be literate than men ($n$ = 19 females or 21% vs. $n$ = 27 males or 43%). This limits their wage labor opportunities and decreases the likelihood of obtaining credit. In addition, as impelled migrants, they have neither access to land nor collateral to leverage for credit. The women reported feeling powerless about changing their income-generating options. For them, producing material goods becomes an orienting framework that not only offers a key identity marker (e.g., business person, vendor, or craftsperson) but also shields them from making more difficult choices to generate income. Lack of income-generating activities for women can propel them into the ever-expanding sex trade business, fueled in part by tourism development, which places them at greater risk for HIV infection and rape (Chilembwe 2014; Nagoli, Holvoet, and Remme 2010).

## Coping Mechanism for Displacement Trauma

The fourth theme to emerge was that the production of material goods helps to provide the respondents with an outlet for expressing their senses of loss, grief, and anger. Impelled migrants are more likely to find themselves at higher risk of cultural, economic, social, and political marginalization. Schmidt-Soltau (2003) expands this discussion to include psychological marginalization, which encompasses the loss of special statuses or rights that they had accrued in their premigration communities (e.g., healer, sage elder/holder of traditional knowledge, midwife, mediator). He argues that this is much harder to mitigate than economic marginalization (p. 540). As a result, he finds that the displaced are subject to feelings of alienation, helplessness, and powerlessness (p. 539). This is amplified by the process of grieving and a loss of sense of self, creating a Durkheimian state of "anomie" or normlessness (Companion 2015).

This displacement trauma is expressed in a variety of ways. All respondents report feeling like outsiders, being alienated from social structures and a sense of community, feeling unsure about the social rules and norms, and struggling with a sense of impermanence. Responses reveal a loss of place, with many reminiscing about the landscape, the wild life, gathering wild food or resources, or hunting with family members. This was often expressed in opposition to their lack of familiarity with their new location. "Elizabeth" (Zomba female 11) lamented, "I wouldn't know where to find that type of plant here." "Sister" (Zomba female 24) stated, "I miss the smell of [shrub]. We would pass a stand of them on our way to the [water source]...that smell reminds me of my village...I wonder if I will ever find that again." Others grieve the loss of shared meanings, which makes conversation and jokes difficult to join in on and understand.

However, respondents report channeling energy generated by displacement trauma into creative expression. The production of material goods serves as a coping mechanism, providing an emotional outlet and catharsis. This is done by incorporating images from their previous environments into their artistic output. Carvers mention including local plants or scenes from their memories into tableaus, masks, and chief's chairs (see Figure 14.1). In addition to utilizing more fanciful images driven by the tourist industry (e.g., lions, camels, and other animals not found in area), woodcrafters incorporated chambo fish (a popular local variant of cichlid) into their work. The tin crafters fashioned traditional fishing boats and chambo fish out of scrap metal, along with motorcycles, cars, lions, and other creatures. Batik artists and other painters reorient their senses of loss by drawing on images from their memories to create new works of art. Food "artists" report a similar experience but use recipes and cooking techniques to accomplish this, as discussed previously.

Using continuity theory, it can be argued that this allows them to establish a displacement narrative that links past and present in a coherent fashion to help them move into the future and ease the transition process. This would fall in line with O'Sullivan-Lago and de Abreu's work (2010). They find that improving connections to cultural continuity helps reduce suicide rates and improves a range of other community well-being markers.

## Opportunities to Reinvent Oneself

The fifth and final theme to emerge from the data is that, despite negative consequences associated with impelled migration and identity loss, there are opportunities as well. These stem from the ability to construct new identities and break away from ones that constrained social and economic

**FIGURE 14.1** Malawian chief's chair. (Courtesy of Michèle Companion.)

advancement. With the loss of village structures and social relationships, existing power dynamics between individuals and family groups change. Schmidt-Soltau (2003) frames this social disarticulation (the breakdown of social links within a group and in that group's relationship with other groups) as a negative consequence of impelled migration. Chilembwe (2014) agrees, linking social disarticulation to changes in behavioral culture driven by the expanding tourism industry. He argues that traditions of elder veneration, styles of dress, marriage traditions, and modes of sharing as opposed to individual accumulation are being lost, fostering community dysfunction.

Despite the literature, many respondents (54%) felt that impelled migration provided an opportunity to escape familial obligations or indebtedness or reputation/labels/gossip that influenced social standing and present themselves anew. This was particularly true for the female respondents ($n$ = 65 or 72%; men: $n$ = 15 or 24%). "Fanta" (Mangochi female 2) says, "Yes, I am still poor. But, I am making my own pathway now. I am not bound by my family's history with [another family]."

## The Risks of Commercialization of Culture

It is important to note that, while the study data show a positive link between the production of material goods and coping with the impacts of impelled migration, there are some potentially negative consequences of overreliance on this strategy. Chilembwe (2014) reminds us that "tourism is an opportunity for culture, but at the same time it consumes, contaminates, and ultimately can destroy culture" (p. 62). He points out that the commercialization of aspects of culture and local products can impair their authenticity through modification to meet tourist demands and simplification of forms, which can alter the meaning and importance of representations. For example, elaborately carved Chief's chairs were once in high demand in this area. They not only serve as cultural manifestations of respect for elders and traditional authority but also represent tremendous artistic achievement. Chilembwe finds this art form to be disappearing in highly traveled tourist areas to match the demand for small, easily portable items. As these cultural manifestations are discarded, the traditions and values associated with them are threatened. At its most extreme, this can result in reconstructed ethnicity (p. 82).

## CONCLUSION

The prioritization of tourism as development strategy has had profound consequences on segments of the population in southern Malawi. Particularly impacted are those individuals and communities located around the lakeshore and boundaries of national parks and wildlife reserves. Loss of access to traditional livelihood resources has exacerbated impelled migration.

This study shows that, despite experiencing displacement trauma, impelled migrants demonstrate resilience by elevating facets of their human capital to successfully carve out new competitive niches using the production of material goods as the mechanism for adaptation. This finding supports the application of complexity theory. The ability to shape skill sets and to control the definition of self are shown to be sources of autonomy and empowerment in populations that are experiencing marginalization. Thus, the production of material goods is a form of control over identity that can be asserted (agency) to countermand negative identifiers that are externally imposed (migrant, refugee, unwanted, intruder, etc.).

This study also finds that the production of material goods helps reduce displacement trauma and eases integration into new environments. The act of creating provides a vehicle for impelled migrants to maintain connections to their history while allowing for new identity formation. This contributes to adaptation and demonstrates resilience, supporting the application of continuity theory.

These findings contribute to the broader disaster literature by highlighting processes of adaptation and aspects of recovery. They also illuminate some wide policy gaps. Regardless of the cause, disaster recovery plans must incorporate programming that facilitates the identification of human capital skill sets that can be reoriented to new endeavors. This is particularly relevant for disaster survivors who have no options for returning to their previous homes or livelihoods. Future research needs to explore adaptation phenomenon in a variety of contexts and physical locations. By generating a more encompassing base of knowledge about the recovery and adaptation process, policy makers and responders may be better able to develop programs that improve resilience in the face of displacement.

## REFERENCES

Baker, S.M. and R.P. Hill. 2013. A community psychology of object meanings: Identity negotiation during disaster recovery. *Journal of Consumer Psychology* 23(3): 275–287.

Chilembwe, J.M. 2014. Examination of socio-cultural impacts of tourism in Chembe Village in Mongochi District—Malawi. *International Journal of Business Quantitative Economics and Applied Management Research* 1(1): 60–90.

Companion, M. 2015. Marketing and material goods: The impact of disaster responders on livelihood strategies. In *Disaster's impact on livelihood and cultural survival: Losses, opportunities, and mitigation*, ed. M. Companion. Boca Raton, FL: CRC Press, Taylor & Francis Group, 183–196.

______. 2010a. Commodities and competition: The economic marginalization of female food vendors in northern Mozambique. *Women's Studies Quarterly* 38(3&4): 163–181.

______. 2010b. Information commodification and social capital in local street markets. In *Community disaster recovery and resiliency: Exploring global opportunities and challenges*, eds. D. Miller and J. Rivera, 205–222. Boca Raton, FL: CRC Press.

Corbin, J. and A. Strauss. 2008. *Basics of qualitative research: Techniques and procedures for developing grounded theory.* Los Angeles: Sage Publications.

Cox, R. and K.E. Perry. 2011. Like a fish out of water: Reconsidering disaster recovery and the role of place and social capital in community disaster resilience. *American Journal of Community Psychology* 48: 395–411.

Derman, B. and A. Ferguson. 1995. Human rights, environment, and development: The dispossession of fishing communities on Lake Malawi. *Human Ecology* 23(2): 125–142.

Donda, S., M. Hara, M. Ngochera, and E. Berge. 2014. *Fragmentation of resource management on the south east arm of Lake Malawi: Dynamics around fisheries*. Zürich: Lit Verlag.

Gaillard, J. 2007. Resilience of traditional societies in facing natural hazards. *Disaster Prevention and Management* 16(4): 522–544.

Government of Malawi. 2012. Malawi growth and development strategy II: From poverty to prosperity, 2011–2016. Lilongwe: Ministry of Development Planning & Cooperation.

_____. 2008. *Malawi Tourism Policy*. Zomba: Ministry of Tourism, Wildlife and Culture and National Statistical Office.

_____. 2006. Malawi growth and development strategy: From poverty to prosperity, 2006–2011. Lilongwe: Ministry of Development Planning & Cooperation.

Magombo, A. 2011. The Development of tourism and the accommodation sector in Malawi since independence. MA Research Report, University of the Witwatersrand, 1–133.

Morrison, K. 2005. Structuration theory, habitus and complexity theory: Elective affinities or old wine in new bottles? *British Journal of Sociology of Education* 26(3): 311–326.

Murray, M. 2000. Levels of narrative analysis in health psychology. *Journal of Health Psychology* 5(3): 337–347.

Nagoli, J., K. Holvoet, and M. Remme. 2010: HIV and AIDS vulnerability in fishing communities in Mangochi district, Malawi. *African Journal of AIDS Research* 9(1): 71–80.

Novelli, M. and A. Scarth. 2007. Tourism in protected areas: Integrating conservation and community development in Liwonde National Park (Malawi). *Tourism and Hospitality Planning and Building* 4(1): 47–73.

O'Sullivan-Lago, R. and G. de Abreu. 2010. Maintaining continuity in cultural contact zone: Identification strategies in the dialogical self. *Culture & Psychology* 16(1): 73–92.

Schmidt-Soltau, K. 2003. Conservation-related resettlement in Central Africa: Environmental and social risks. *Development and Change* 34(3): 525–551.

Schmidt-Soltau, K. and D. Brockington. 2007. Protected areas and resettlement: What scope for voluntary relocation? *World Development* 35(12): 2182–2202.

Tuohy, R. and C. Stephens. 2012. Older adults' narratives about flood disaster: Resilience, coherence, and personal identity. *Journal of Aging Studies* 26(1): 26–34.

# *Gender and Social Inequality*

Gender dimensions impact the ability of both men and women to plan for disasters, actively mitigate risks, respond to unfolding events, and rebuild in the aftermath. Gender both shapes and is shaped by levels of poverty and social, political, and economic marginalization. Studies presented in this section explore the benefits of explicit inclusion of gender in policy and in planning and response initiatives.

# 15 Gender Dimensions in Disaster Management

## *Implications for Coastal Aquaculture and Fishing Communities in the Philippines*

*Morgan Chow, Lori A. Cramer, and Hillary Egna*

## CONTENTS



**Abstract**

Women are critical to aquaculture and small-scale fisheries sectors, despite a lack of recognition and access to resources. In the Philippines, the status of women has improved over the last few decades. However, gender issues during disasters still emerge. In 2009, the Asia-Pacific Economic Cooperation (APEC) published a study that indicated a high level of awareness of the importance of gender integration for disaster risk reduction (DRR) in the Philippines, yet gaps remain during disaster plan implementation. This research builds on that study by assessing gender integration in disaster management in fishing and aquaculture communities since recent DRR legislation (2010) and two major typhoons (2013 and 2014). Results reveal that important steps are being taken to integrate gender at the disaster risk reduction and management (DRRM) programmatic level, yet gaps remain at the community level. Addressing these shortcomings and underlying perceptions of gender in disaster management will foster more resilient fishing and aquaculture communities in the Philippines and nations worldwide.

## INTRODUCTION

In the Philippines, roughly one third of the population depends on agriculture and fishing to make a living. Women make up a large proportion of Filipino fishers. However, as one of the most disaster-struck countries in the world (Relief Web 2014), with approximately 75% of the population vulnerable to natural hazards (Relief Web 2012), these resource-dependent communities are left in a constant state of repair. While coastal populations face increased vulnerability, disaster risk also reflects existing social divisions. This is particularly true of social vulnerabilities rooted in gender, class, race, ethnicity, culture, and age relationships. Women's roles as primary household managers, as well as their dependence on natural resource-based livelihoods (e.g., fisheries and aquaculture), are viewed as especially vulnerable to hazardous events that put their families at risk (Cutter 1995).

In November 2013, the Philippines experienced Typhoon Haiyan (Yolanda), one of the largest to make landfall. An estimated 14.1 million people were affected, and over 6000 deaths were recorded (Food and Agriculture Organization [FAO] 2014). The President declared a State of National Calamity for the Category 5 super typhoon (Relief Web 2014). Almost 94% of casualties in the hardest hit cities were caused by the storm surge (Deutsche Gesellschaft für Internationale Zusammenarbeit 2014). Mass displacement and overcrowded conditions raised risks to safety and wellbeing of vulnerable groups, in particular women. A lack of female police officers, scarcity of women-only spaces in evacuation centers, and disrupted maternal and reproductive health services made the challenge of reducing the risks to vulnerable groups even harder (Relief Web 2014). Fishing communities reported losing two-thirds of their fishing equipment (Relief Web 2014). Nearly 30% of fisher folk (Filipino term for fishermen/women) in Haiyan's path were affected, resulting in 24,000 MT of fisheries stocks lost (Office of the Presidential Assistant for Rehabilitation and Recovery 2014) (Figure 15.1).

One year later, the nation was hit again with Super Typhoon Hagupit (Ruby). It arrived in the Philippines on December 6, 2014, as a Category 2, with moderate to heavy rains. It weakened as it moved through the nation (Figure 15.2) (Relief Web 2014). Approximately 227,000 families, or 1 million people, were in evacuation centers before the typhoon hit (Relief Web 2014). FAO (2015) praised the government for a timely response and for protecting the nation's fisheries and agricultural livelihoods. Damages to fisheries and aquaculture infrastructure were much less severe than with Typhoon Haiyan. Still, as many as 800,000 workers were affected, 350,000 of whom were living in poverty (International Labor Organization 2014).

These two major typhoons put the recently passed Philippine Disaster Risk Reduction and Management Act (PDRRMA) of 2010 to the test by providing an up-to-date assessment of gender integration in disaster management in Filipino coastal aquaculture and fishing communities. While numerous studies have examined gender issues in disaster management (see Enarson, Fothergill, and Peek 2007 for a review), few have focused on them in fishing and aquaculture communities. Even fewer have compared differing perceptions of gender by disaster managers in these communities.

Research on how disaster management affects women's capacity to recover from Typhoon Haiyan in the Philippines provides critical information for building resilience to future events. Resilience in this context is defined as "the capacity of social, economic, and environmental systems to cope with a hazardous event or trend or disturbance, responding or reorganizing in ways that maintain their essential function, identity, and structure, while also maintaining the capacity for adaptation, learning, and transformation" (Intergovernmental Panel on Climate Change 2014, p. 5). This is critical, because climate change is expected to affect coastal communities with more storms of greater severity, and global aquaculture production is increasing at a disproportionate rate in poorer countries.

Resilience to disasters requires both "bottom–up" and "top–down" strategies (Brose 2015). Bottom–up strategies need to emerge through local people within their social–ecological systems. To better meet the needs of current and future residents of aquaculture dependent areas, a qualitative analysis was undertaken. This work seeks to understand the perceptions of gender integration

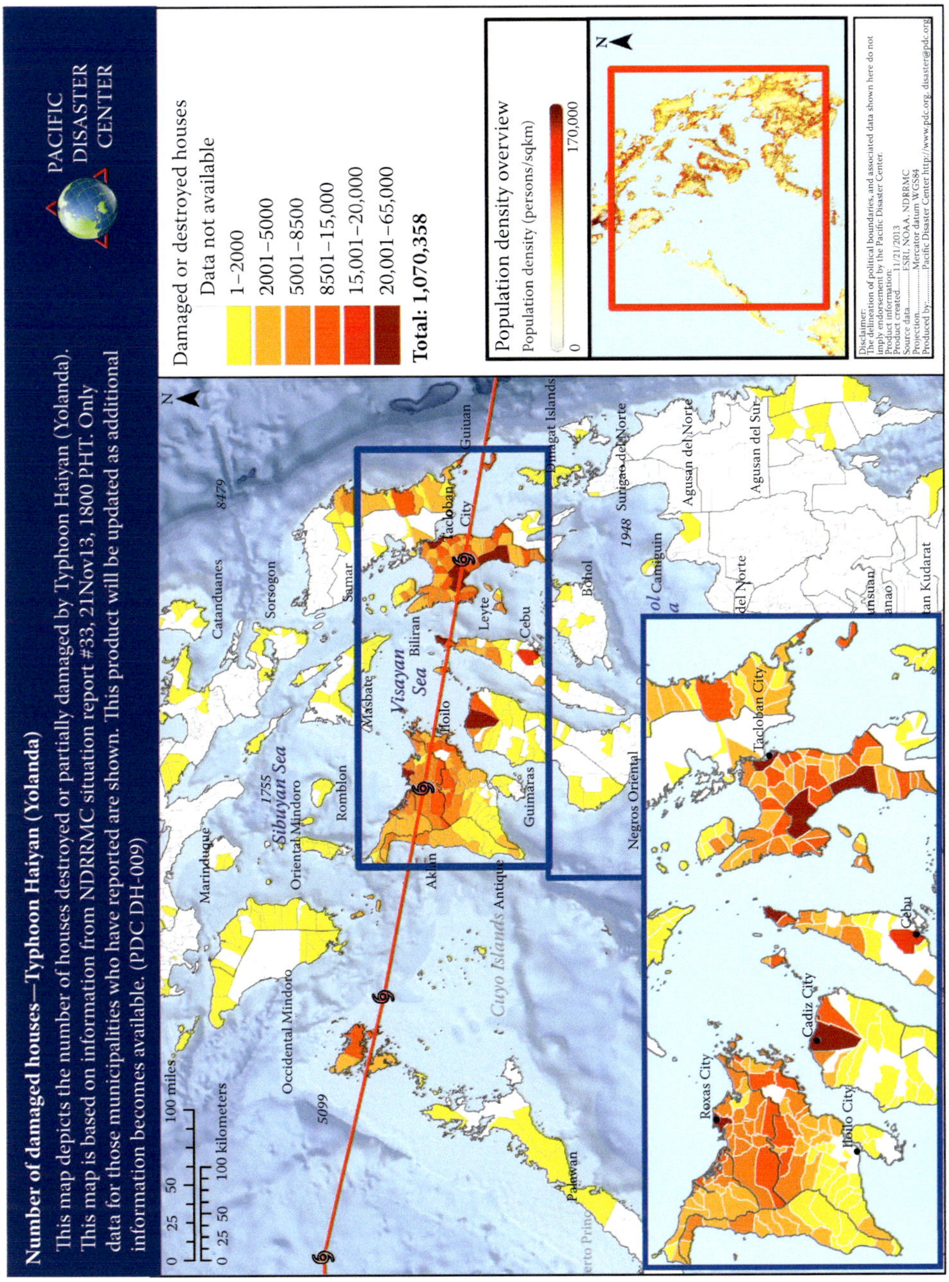


**FIGURE 15.1** Map of Typhoon Haiyan-affected areas: Haiyan's track through the Visayas regions of the Philippines, with provinces color-coded by the number of damaged or destroyed houses. (Source: Pacific Disaster Center.)

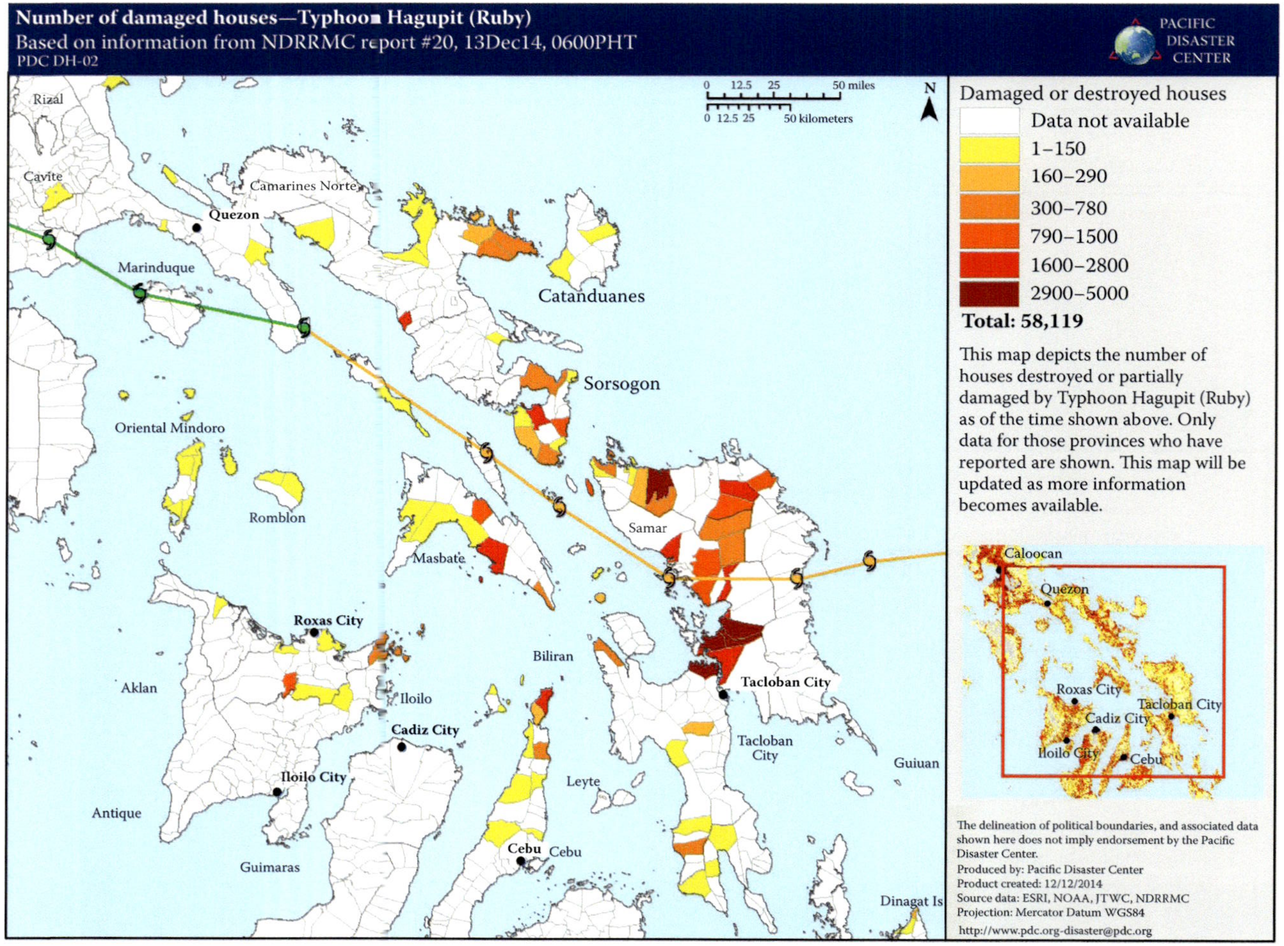


**FIGURE 15.2** Map of Typhoon Hagupit-affected areas: Hagupit's track through the eastern Visayas region, Bicol, and southern Luzon provinces of the Philippines with provinces color-coded by the number of damaged or destroyed houses. (Source: Pacific Disaster Center.)

in disaster management by professionals working at various governance scales set forth in recent "top–down" disaster policies.

## BACKGROUND

Women's work in fisheries and aquaculture is undervalued, perpetuating their limited access to resources such as education, information, technology, financial assistance, and land ownership (FAO 2014; US Agency for International Development [USAID] 2012). However, women participate in almost all activities in the fishing sector including construction of gear, fish sorting and handling, and processing. They are a critical component to the future of the sector. In the Philippines, the participation rates of women in fisheries is underestimated due to their lack of registration with the local government and non-gender-disaggregated data within various subsectors of fishing and aquaculture (Siason et al. 2006). Actions prior to and after disasters that favor an economic value chain which excludes women could further marginalize them in the industry. For example, if fish processing facilities are not protected or if recovery programs do not rebuild facilities that are used by women, then they suffer disproportionately.

Women become more vulnerable during disasters. Research has shown that women are treated differently at every stage, from the initial warning period through the long-term recovery process (Delaney and Shrader 2000; Enarson, Fothergill, and Peek 2007). Studies of major destructive events in the developing world have found that women are more vulnerable to the mortal impact of natural hazards (Neumayer and Plumper 2007), are generally the poorest of the poor (Bradshaw 2001), display different coping strategies in response to disasters, prioritize different needs, and demonstrate clear differences in their perceptions of impacts or risk (Delaney and Shrader 2000). Women are often left out of the disaster planning and decision-making roles, reinforcing "the invisibility of gender" (Delaney and Shrader 2000). These gender biases arise from normative expectations about whose voice matters and a lack of knowledge about the challenges women face (Enarson and Chakrabati 2009). The impacts of disasters on women's paid and unpaid work are well documented (Enarson, Fothergill, and Peek 2007), and livelihood protection is an increasingly important goal of disaster policy, including in the Philippines.

The Asia-Pacific Economic Cooperation study (APEC 2009) examines how gender can be better integrated into disaster management, thereby influencing the PDRRMA. They find that, although there is sensitivity to the critical importance of gender considerations for transforming economies and building resilient communities, clear deficiencies remain. APEC identifies the following disaster management gender issues: (1) lack of coordination of policies due to a lack of understanding of the issues; (2) lack of local actions and a need to mainstream DRRM in local development plans, land use plans, budgets, evacuation plans, and governance; and (3) increasing vulnerabilities because of changing demographic, technological, environmental, and socioeconomic conditions. APEC recommends better promotion of female participation in disaster management at all levels of government. Specified plans of action include investing in training for local leaders, improving facilities at evacuation centers, conducting adequate assessments of impacts on women, and better monitoring and compliance assessments of disaster plan implementation (APEC 2009). These findings guided the research design for this study, as well as interpretation of results.

The PDRRMA was passed in 2010, reshaping Filipino disaster management and explicitly aimed at being "gender responsive." The PDRRMA builds on gender and disaster legislation that had been passed during the previous 20 years. The foundational legislation is Executive Order No. 348 (Government of the Republic of the Philippines 1989), which mandates the creation of a Gender and Development (GAD) focal person at every major agency in the Philippines. The Philippines has also made important strides toward building resilience through community-based programs and federal early warning coordination (Allen 2006; Yumul, Dimalanta, Servando, and Cruz 2013). These formative laws set the tone for gender integration in disaster management for fisheries and aquaculture sectors. Assessing how the PDRRMA and recent super typhoons affected gender dimensions in these coastal communities includes understanding the backbone legislation upon which disaster management and gender integration are founded.

## METHODS

### Site Selection

To examine gender integration into disaster management, fishing regions particularly hard-hit by Typhoon Haiyan were selected. The most affected Eastern Visayas region is the third poorest in the Philippines, with weak infrastructure and fragile agricultural and fishing sectors. Tacloban City, a commerce hub, saw roughly 90% of its infrastructure damaged by Haiyan's storm surge (United Nations Office for the Coordination of Humanitarian Affairs 2013). Northern Iloilo, in the Western Visayas, also experienced severe damage from Haiyan. Northern Iloilo contributes roughly 35% to the nation's fisheries (Relief Web 2014). For these reasons, these areas are the geographic foci of this study.

### Research Approach and Sampling

This research takes a grounded theory approach and applied the appropriate qualitative methodologies to achieve the research objectives (Corbin and Strauss 2008; Maxwell 2013). The research protocol is consistent with literature on gender and disasters, as well as the methodology used in the APEC study, which includes a series of interviews with authorities in disaster management. The interview protocol was pretested and modified to fit with local language patterns. The interviews focused on the respondents' work in DRRM for Typhoons Haiyan and Hagupit. Respondents were asked how and whether DRRM has changed at an institutional, structural, and community level and how changes affect their day-to-day work.

The initial sample consisted of a purposive or criterion-based selection. Participants were chosen to achieve representation within the topical and geographic focus areas, were familiar with Filipino disaster management policies, and were involved with preparatory and/or recovery efforts (Table 15.1) (LeCompte, Preissle, and Tesch 1993). Snowball sampling was used to reach the

**TABLE 15.1**
**Respondent Characteristics**

| | Frequency | % of Total |
|---|---|---|
| Employment scale | | |
| International | 4 | 14.29 |
| National | 6 | 21.43 |
| Provincial | 9 | 32.14 |
| Municipal | 9 | 32.14 |
| Organizational type | | |
| Government | 17 | 60.71 |
| Nongovernment | 11 | 39.29 |
| Employment sector | | |
| Fisheries | 13 | 46.43 |
| Disaster | 11 | 39.29 |
| Women | 4 | 14.29 |
| Gender | | |
| Women | 17 | 60.71 |
| Men | 11 | 39.29 |
| Total *N* | 28 | 100.00 |

remaining respondents (Berg and Lune 2012). A total of 28 individuals participated in semistructured interviews (17 women and 11 men). This sampling method captures heterogeneity in the population, establishing comparisons across sectors and scales (Maxwell 2013). Bias was handled by triangulating themes from interviews with secondary data sources.

### Data Analysis

The analysis process involved transcribing the interviews and line-by-line coding (Corbin and Strauss 2008). Significant phrases were sorted into categories and codes were grouped into themes (Auerbach and Silverstein 2003). Coding was completed in Max QDA, a qualitative data analysis software. Respondents were characterized by their employment scale, organizational type, employment sector, and gender (Table 15.1). The analysis focuses on respondent perceptions of gender as a function of their occupational role, rather than comparing responses by gender. Due to the small number of respondents per occupational category, gender of respondents is generally not indicated in the results.

## RESULTS

The research began approximately one year after Typhoon Haiyan shattered the region. Unexpectedly, Typhoon Hagupit formed as the data collection was beginning. Hagupit became a super typhoon one day after the initial warning (December 3, 2015) and was projected to follow the same devastating track as Haiyan. This exposed wounds from traumatic experiences with Haiyan, including who to trust for accurate information. Uniformly, respondents remarked on the poor communication before Haiyan. Almost every respondent shared the issue of confusing terminology used by weather experts, particularly the term "storm surge." Because of this miscommunication, many people did not evacuate the coastal areas and were killed.

The sudden arrival of Typhoon Hagupit complicated original research logistics, including limiting access to respondents, shortening the time frame, and imposing travel restrictions. Yet, it also provided a unique opportunity to observe and listen to real-time experiences. There were commonalities across all 28 responses, particularly regarding changes in disaster management that were implemented after Typhoon Haiyan, and observed during Typhoon Hagupit. Some facets improved, especially warning system coordination, evacuation protocols, and general early preparedness. These changes were a response not only to the destruction from Typhoon Haiyan but also to the PDRRMA, which changed the nation's approach to and regulations regarding disaster management. By the time Hagupit hit, every level of governance had reorganized its disaster management councils, allowing for the potential of improved gender integration.

### Perceptions of Gender Mainstreaming/Integration

Each respondent was asked to discuss the role of gender mainstreaming during the recent disaster events. They shared that women are active in disaster management and hold positions on DRR councils. Respondents reiterated the importance of women in leadership positions in disaster management and discussed the phases of disaster management women tend to occupy. However, many participants did not elaborate on specific ways to conduct gender mainstreaming or mechanisms for improving attention to other socially vulnerable populations during disasters. When asked about specifics, respondents referred to broad, slowly occurring changes such as building the capacity of women in these sectors and encouraging women to participate in trainings. They did not express distinct changes since the new legislation or between the two typhoon events.

When questioned about the level to which gender had been integrated into disaster management, most disaster managers answered that women are encouraged to participate. Women dominate Department of Social Welfare positions and are doing much of the on-the-ground work.

A respondent notes, "In the assessment, more women are involved in going around in the communities." Respondents shared that women are more active and social throughout the communities and do a good job of informing neighbors of disaster protocols. Main concerns for women were at evacuation centers. "It's not just about evacuation, but how to sustain life inside evacuation," notes another respondent.

Those working in the fisheries and aquaculture sectors shared that more groups are working to build capacity of women fisher folk through livelihood projects. Seaweed aquaculture was used as an example of a women-targeted livelihood program by many respondents. One notes, "Seaweeds project is very successful, wherein the women have the primary role in the management." Another shares, "the technologies in aquaculture [are] more women friendly than in capture fisheries." A few respondents highlighted a trend of more women shifting to engaging in aquaculture activities from having previously worked in capture fisheries.

### Perceptions by Employment Scale

Responses are differentiated by occupational scale (international, national, provincial, and municipal). Many of the respondents are government officials at all levels; they were mostly positive about the status of gender integration into Filipino disaster management. At the municipal level, gender is discussed according to women's roles on the DRRM councils and as recipients of aid. At the provincial level, respondents discuss how entire communities are involved in DRRM, including women. "At the evacuation centers, the managers are usually females," says a municipal disaster manager. At the national level, GAD coordinators and initiatives are the focus. Respondents at the national level have the most optimistic perspectives, emphasizing how far the nation has progressed. "Agencies are now particularly aware of GAD. Unlike before, they were in denial that there's no disparity between men and women..." says a national fisheries respondent. Some considerations for future improvements include a need for child- and women-friendly spaces in evacuation centers and support for the mobilization of women's groups.

Despite progress, all respondents remarked on areas that still require improvement. Disaster management respondents point to needing a more substantial shift in focus toward rehabilitation and reconstruction so that gender is integrated into long-term recovery. The functions of the DRRM councils can be improved, as well as preparedness and awareness of gender issues during disasters at the schools. Lastly, the need for more coordinated information processing and record keeping was expressed. A respondent notes that warning information is often broadcasted in English and that technical terms are used that people in the rural communities have difficulty understanding. Fisheries and agriculture respondents commented on needing to improve awareness, preparation, implementation of laws, storage facilities, and communication. At the municipal level, respondents emphasized shifting efforts toward rehabilitation and increasing the number of trainings for the public and DRRM council members on basic protocols and gender issues. At the provincial and national levels, the scope was wider. Respondents mentioned mainstreaming DRRM with other government programs, such as climate change and GAD funds and improving rapid needs assessments to better reach vulnerable populations, including women.

In addition to the aforementioned recommendations, a respondent notes that there will never be enough assistance from within the Philippines for typhoon response, stating, "If we shall rely solely from the local government on the national aid, we'll find it very hard for the people to recover." The complex relationship of international and local aid organizations was a common theme in the interviews. One of the most salient points came from a respondent who says, "The question is how are you going to integrate the culture of preparedness risk reduction into this system of everybody in the community?" The lack of a culture of preparedness for disasters is not unique to the Philippines (Brose 2015) but may be exacerbated by levels of vulnerability and cultural barriers found in this region.

### Perspectives by Employment Sector

Comparisons were also made between respondents working in nongovernment sectors and government employees. The nongovernment employees tended to respond more critically about the state of gender integration in disaster management, while government employees tended to be more optimistic. Respondents at the provincial and national levels were the most critical and willing to bring up issues of inequity. This is illustrated by the following statement: "He gets the registration at the municipality...but what about the women who don't have a husband...even women themselves don't consider themselves as women fishers...they were socialized to think and act that they are only in support of their husband...." Although women are legally able to register as fisherfolk, it is not culturally acceptable in some areas. A nongovernment fisheries respondent states that "women are still delegated along the shorelines...gender sensitivity is quite high, but it has not diffused to the communities...People still think that fishing is a men's role..."

The perceived lack of gender integration identified by respondents strongly correlates with APEC's finding regarding community perceptions of women. As captured by one respondent, "What's lacking right now is how to apply a gender lens." Respondents also commented on persistent gender integration challenges in times of disaster, such as safe spaces for women. For example, a respondent noted, "It's a real challenge for the LGU [local government unit] to invest infrastructure for the evacuation centers." This comment addresses the need for managers to go beyond what they previously believed to be suitable in times of disaster and more purposefully integrate gender-sensitive policies at all phases of disasters.

The perceptions of the status of gender integration described earlier echoed throughout many of the interviews and are corroborated with media and agency reports released after Typhoon Haiyan. Content analysis of these reports reiterated some of the respondents' claims. For instance, according to Oxfam (2013), following Typhoon Haiyan, there needed to be more resources for reconstruction and for vulnerable populations. Oxfam recommends that services to women and children be rapidly expanded, with increased numbers of trained staff and women-friendly spaces in displaced communities. Similarly, the Philippines Shelter Cluster WASH (Water, Sanitation, and Hygiene) Assessment (2013) finds that age and gender should have been more significant factors for informing beneficiaries of shelter assistance. Adjustments also need to be made to restore livelihoods and transition from response to recovery (Inter-Agency Standing Committee 2014), given that 13% of the population with no income after Typhoon Haiyan was in the fishery and aquaculture sectors (Philippines Shelter Cluster WASH 2013). These numbers reiterate the importance of building resilience for coastal communities that frequently bear the brunt of damage from severe weather events.

## DISCUSSION

The initial aim of this study was to address gender integration in long-term recovery from disasters. This was overshadowed by immediate recovery concerns post-Typhoon Hagupit. Many of the interviewees discussed the major changes addressed in the year between Haiyan and Hagupit: disaster preparedness, warning systems, evacuation centers, and communication. For many of the respondents, gender integration was secondary to our discussions. The 2010 PDRRMA restructured a disaster management approach that was clustered according to response types to one that is inherently geographic in scale. The mandated creation of DRRM councils at every scale of governance allows for additional local disaster management oversight and has opened up opportunities for women to participate in disaster management. Results indicate some participation by women, but the assessment of whether this shift is effective is yet to be determined.

From the interviews, it is clear that a lot has changed in Philippine disaster management since the 2009 APEC study and the policy instituted in the 2010 PDRRMA. After Typhoon Haiyan, the DRRM councils became more active. The structure of the councils plays an important role the effectiveness of management at all jurisdictional levels. During the study, changes in disaster management were immediately evident. New mechanisms for preparation were put in place by coordinating warning signal systems and evacuation. The Filipino government showed it can evacuate hundreds of thousands of people before a typhoon makes landfall.

The general trend across responses shows that the perception of gender integration in DRRM is dependent on its integration in other social, cultural, and political settings. Although differences in perceptions emerged across governance levels and organization types, the main concerns for gender integration in DRRM were the conditions at evacuation centers, inclusion in recovery efforts, and overall awareness of gender concerns by managers. These echo findings of the 2009 APEC study, with recommendations for more investment in trainings, better facilities, and improved assessments of DRRM implementation.

Many respondents emphasize how far gender integration in disaster management has come in recent years. There are growing numbers of women's organizations receiving support for livelihood projects. Women are present on the DRRM councils. Generally, government employees tend to be more positive regarding the level of gender integration in disaster management, while nongovernmental employees are more critical of the process. While this study does not go into detail by distinguishing various subsectors of fishing and aquaculture, it addresses the understudied area of managers' perceptions of gender integration in disaster management. Future studies should look at how gender integration varies across subsectors and varying levels of production in fishing and aquaculture.

## CONCLUSION

In this study, respondents shared their perspectives on gender integration in disaster management and what it means for the future resilience of coastal communities in the Philippines. The timing of the interviews, immediately following another super typhoon, provoked thoughtful and reflective responses. The optimistic outlook shared by almost all of the respondents sheds light on the potential for improvement at both the legislative and the community levels. Although the data collected are not meant to be representative of the status of gender integration in disaster management for the entire nation, the information provided by key informants offers valuable insight as to its status and areas for future improvement for enhanced resilience of vulnerable coastal fishing and aquaculture populations. As women will continue to play a critical role in global fisheries and aquaculture production, taking the appropriate steps toward gender integration in disaster management will contribute to improved global food security.

## ACKNOWLEDGMENTS

This research is a component of the AquaFish Innovation Lab, which is supported in part by the USAID (USAID CA/LWA No. EPP-A-00-06-0012-00) and by participating institutions. The AquaFish accession number is 1444. The opinions expressed herein are those of the authors and do not necessarily reflect the views of the AquaFish Innovation Lab or USAID.

## REFERENCES

Allen, K.M. 2006. Community-based disaster preparedness and climate adaptation: Local capacity-building in the Philippines. *Disasters* 30(1): 81–102.

Asia-Pacific Economic Cooperation. 2009. *The study on "Women in times of disaster": The integration of gender issues and gender perspectives in disaster management.* Singapore: APEC Secretariat. Retrieved from http://dspace.africaportal.org/jspui/bitstream/123456789/23785/1/Women%20in%20Times%20of%20Disaster.pdf?1, accessed May 14, 2014.

Auerbach, C.F. and L.B. Silverstein. 2003. *Qualitative data: An introduction to coding and analysis.* New York: New York University Press.

Berg, B.L. and H. Lune. 2012. *Qualitative research methods for the social sciences (8th ed.).* Upper Saddle River: Pearson.

Bradshaw, S. 2001. Reconstructing roles and relations: Women's participation in reconstruction in post-Mitch Nicaragua. *Gender and Development* 9(3): 79–87.

Brose, D.A. 2015. *Developing a framework for measuring community resilience: A summary of a workshop.* Washington, DC: National Academies Press, National Research Council.

Corbin, J.M. and A.L. Strauss. 2008. *Basics of qualitative research: Techniques and procedures for developing grounded theory.* Thousand Oaks, CA: Sage Publications, Inc.

Cutter, S.L. 1995. Race, class and environmental justice. *Progress in Human Geography* 19(1): 111–122.

Delaney, L. and E. Shrader. 2000. *Gender and post-disaster reconstruction: The case of Hurricane Mitch in Honduras and Nicaragua.* New York: The World Bank.

Deutsche Gesellschaft für Internationale Zusammenarbeit. 2014. *Assessment of early warning efforts in Leyte for typhoon Haiyan/Yolanda.* Retrieved from http://www.preventionweb.net/files/36860_36860gizassessmentofearlywarningyol.pdf, accessed April 2, 2015.

Enarson, E. and P.D. Chakrabati. 2009. *Women, gender, and disaster: Global issues and initiatives.* New Delhi, India: Sage Publications.

Enarson, E., A. Fothergill, and L. Peek. 2007. Gender and disaster: Foundations and directions. In *Handbook of disaster research*, eds. H. Rodriguez, E.L. Quarantelli, and R.R. Dynes, 130–146. New York: Springer Press.

Food and Agriculture Organization. 2015. *FAO praises government for early typhoon warnings to Philippine farmers and fishers.* Retrieved from http://www.fao.org/philippines/news/detail/en/c/271479/, accessed March 5, 2015.

_____. 2014. *FAO in emergencies: From prevention to building back better.* Retrieved from http://www.fao.org/fileadmin/user_upload/FAO-countries/Phillippines/Docs/Exec_brief_17Dec_2014.pdf, accessed February 15, 2015.

Government of the Republic of the Philippines. 1989. Executive Order 348: Approval and Adoption of the Philippine Development Plan for Women for 1989–1992. Philippines. Retrieved from http://www.pcw.gov.ph/law/executive-order-no-348, accessed January 10, 2015.

Inter-Agency Standing Committee. 2014. *IASC inter-agency humanitarian evaluation of the Typhoon Haiyan response.* New York: United Nations Office for Coordination of Humanitarian Affairs. Retrieved from http://www.unicef.org/evaldatabase/index_78200.html, accessed September 10, 2014.

International Labor Organization. 2014. *Philippines: Typhoon Haiyan aftermath.* Retrieved from http://www.ilo.org/manila/typhoon-haiyan/lang—en/index.htm, accessed February 15, 2014.

Intergovernmental Panel on Climate Change. 2014. Summary for policymakers. In *Climate change 2014: Impacts, adaptation, and vulnerability. Contribution of Working Group II to the fifth assessment report of the Intergovernmental Panel on Climate Change*, eds. C.B. Vields, V. Barros, D.J. Dokken, K.J. Mach, M.D. Mastrandrea, T.E. Bilir, M. Chatterjee, K.L. Ebi, Y.O. Estrada, R.C. Genova, B. Girma, E.S. Kissel, A.N. Levy, and S. MacKraken, 1–32. Cambridge and New York: Cambridge University Press.

LeCompte, M.D., J. Preissle, and R. Tesch. 1993. *Ethnography and qualitative design in educational research.* New York: Academic Press.

Maxwell, J.A. 2013. *Qualitative research design: An interactive approach.* London: Sage Publications.

Neumayer, E. and T. Plumper. 2007. The gendered nature of natural disasters: The impact of catastrophic events on the gender gap in life expectancy, 1981–2002. *Annals of the Association of American Geographers* 97(3): 551–566.

Office of the Presidential Assistant for Rehabilitation and Recovery. 2014. *Yolanda rehabilitation and recovery efforts.* Bonifacio Global City: OPARR. Retrieved from http://president.gov.ph/wp-content/uploads/2014/08/Revised-DraftYolanda-Rehab-Briefer-as-of-1-Aug-2014-w-status-report.pdf, accessed March 10, 2014.

Oxfam. 2013. *Typhoon Haiyan: The response so far and vital lessons for the Philippine recovery.* Oxford: Oxfam International. Retrieved from https://www.oxfam.org/sites/www.oxfam.org/files/bn-typhoon-haiyan-philippines-response-071213-en.pdf, accessed March 1, 2014.

Pacific Disaster Center. 2014. *Philippines: Number of damaged houses—Typhoon Hagupit (Ruby) based on information from NDRRMC Report #20, 12 Dec 14, 0600 PHT.* Retrieved from http://reliefweb.int/map/philippines/philippines-number-damaged-houses-typhoon-hagupit-ruby-based-information-ndrrmc-0, accessed January 10, 2015.

_____. 2013. *Typhoon Haiyan response.* Retrieved from http://www.pdc.org/weather/index.php/2013/11/21/hazard-highlights-18/, accessed February 5, 2014.

Philippine Disaster Risk Reduction and Management Act of 2010. 2010. PDRRMA S. No 3086 11 No 6985. Philippines: Republic of the Philippines, Congress of the Philippines Metro Manila Fourteenth Congress Third Regular Session. Retrieved from http://www.lawphil.net/statutes/repacts/ra2010/ra_10121_2010.html, accessed May 15, 2014.

Philippines Shelter Cluster WASH. 2013. *Shelter and WASH rapid assessment. Typhoon Haiyan, Philippines.* Retrieved from http://www.reach-initiative.org/wp-content/uploads/2013/11/Haiyan-Typhoon-Shelter-WASH_assessment_Final-Report_validated-formatted.pdf, accessed March 10, 2015.

Relief Web. 2014. *Typhoon Haiyan.* Retrieved from http://reliefweb.int/disaster/tc-2013-000139-phl, accessed February 10, 2014.

Siason, I.M., E. Tech, K.I. Matics, P.S. Choo, M. Shariff, E.S. Heruwait, T. Susilowait, N. Miki, A.B. Shelly, K.G. Rajabharshi, R. Ranjit, P.P.G.N. Siriwardena, M.C. Nandeesha, and M. Sunderarajan. 2006. Women in fisheries in Asia. In *Global symposium on women in fisheries: Sixth Asian fisheries forum, 29 November 2001*, eds. N.H. Chao-Liao, K. Matics, M.C. Nandeesha, M. Shariff, I. Siason, E. Tech, and M.J. Williams, 21–28. Kaohsiung, Taiwan: Worldfish.

United Nations Office for the Coordination of Humanitarian Affairs. 2013. *Multi-cluster/sector initial rapid assessment.* Retrieved from http://reliefweb.int/sites/reliefweb.int/files/resources/MIRA_Report-Philippines-Haiyan_FINAL.pdf, accessed January 10, 2014.

United States Agency for International Development. 2012. *Gender equality and female empowerment.* Washington, DC: USAID. Retrieved from http://www.usaid.gov/sites/default/files/documents/1865/GenderEqualityPolicy_0.pdf, accessed May 5, 2015.

Yumul, G.P., C.B. Dimalanta, N.T. Servando, and N.A. Cruz. 2013. Abnormal weather events in 2009, increased precipitation and disastrous impacts in the Philippines. *Climatic Change* 118(3–4): 715–727. doi:10.1007/s10584-012-0661-8.

# 16 Women's Leadership in Texas Forest Fires and Recovery

## *How Gender Roles and Assumptions Empower and Constrain Women and Men Postdisaster in a Rural Southern Town**

*Josephine Nummi and Kathryn Henderson*

## CONTENTS



**Abstract**

This chapter analyzes the ways in which gender and gender assumptions empower and constrain women and men during and in the aftermath of the 2011 Bastrop County Complex Wildfires. Based on over 100 interviews and three years of participant observation, this research uses grounded theory to voice and analyze the perspectives of fire survivors. Women took leadership roles in this southern, conservative, rural community through a variety of service organizations, while simultaneously rebuilding and reprovisioning for their own families. In the private sphere, women's voices and labor potential were often ignored or discouraged. Men, too, were constrained by gender assumptions, as they dealt with inability to accept needed help or to express extreme emotions. Analysis of the ways in which gender roles and gender assumptions on the part of organizations and individuals both facilitated and hampered short- and long-term fire response suggests changing tensions in gender roles and policy implications.

* This study was funded by a Tier One Program Grant from Texas A&M University.

## INTRODUCTION

Gender norms affect how individuals relate to themselves, their relationships, and their surroundings. Therefore, gender affects how individuals and communities cope during and after a disaster, as recognized by the increasing emphasis on gender in disaster studies (Anderson 2000; Callaghan et al. 2007; Pacholok 2013; Tobin-Gurley, Peek, and Loomis 2010). This paper builds on this literature to examine how gender empowered and constrained men and women during and after the 2011 Bastrop County Complex Wildfires, the most destructive forest fires in Texas history (Huffman 2011). We recognize that gendered behaviors are neither "good" nor "bad." We hope to shed light on them in a situated context to help mitigate the tensions among individuals and agencies.

The Bastrop wildfires started on September 4, 2011 and were not declared extinguished until October 9, 2011. Contributing conditions included the worst drought in Texas history (Vertuno and Graczyk 2011) and Tropical Storm Lee. The fires burned 34,000 acres (16,200 acres were state forest) and destroyed over 1600 homes, killing two people. The estimated losses were \$2822 per person, making it the worst per capita loss in the nation's history (Gray et al. 2012; Huffman 2011).

Even before the fires, Bastrop was a community of contrasts and transition. Bastrop is a traditional, small, southern town of hard-working people with pre-Civil War ties to the land and to gendered and racial attitudes. Ties to the land may be generational (inherited family property), economic (cattle or horse ranching), or nature oriented, given that people choose the area because of the forest or to have room for large animals. Today, Bastrop retains some vestige of its history along with modern attitudes, while undergoing tourist and commercial development. The Lost Pines forested area is so much a part of the local identity that establishments from garages to laundromats incorporate it into their names, as do businesses geared to forest visitors. The recent influx of commuters from nearby metropolitan Austin has spawned multiple chain-store shopping plazas, which are slightly removed from Bastrop's quaint nineteenth century downtown.

## METHODOLOGY

Researchers' interaction with fire survivors was facilitated through various agencies providing services to those in need. Agencies ranged from permanent institutions, such as the local library, workforce offices, and a tree-planting organization to grant-funded relief organizations that came into being post-wildfire, such as the Bastrop Disaster Recovery Center and the Bastrop Long Term Recovery Team. Representatives of these organizations coordinated the volunteer projects and introduced us to survivors. In turn, we used a snowball technique (Atkinson and Flint 2004; Biernacki and Waldorf 1981) to reach additional fire survivors, revealing neighborhood networks and allowing us to provide additional volunteer assistance.

The wildfire burned public and private land in the Lost Pines forest, where many landowners had inherited homesteads or purchased homes because of love of the trees. Given historical class and race privilege in Texas and because most minorities lived elsewhere in Bastrop County, our interviewees were mainly white. Over 100 interviews were conducted between the Fall 2012 to Spring 2015 semesters by teams of sociology graduate and undergraduate students and the authors. Interviews lasted from approximately 60 to 90 minutes and were spatially and contextually situated in postwildfire conditions, as interviewers helped fire survivors to clear or rebuild. Detailed field notes were kept along with interview transcripts.

This study utilizes grounded theory, which develops coding and themes using the respondents' own words and perspectives, recognizing that respondents create their own reality through their interactions. Thus, theory generating and gathering data are one and the same (Charmaz 2014; Strauss and Corbin 1998). Situational analysis (Clarke 2005; Clarke, Friese, and Washburn 2015) was integrated with grounded theory's systematic and rigorous constant comparative method. Situational analysis incorporates the multiple perspectives that Haraway (1988) stresses are so important for addressing the highly critiqued notion of "objectivity" through providing a set of partial perspectives, grounded in specific situational context. The analysis process was assisted by Atlas TI qualitative software.

## FINDINGS AND DISCUSSION

### Why Is It Important to Talk about Gender?

Ascribing characteristics and roles based on gender creates false assumptions regarding an individual's traits and skills. These socially constructed assumptions impact how people perceive themselves, others, and what they "should" do in any given situation, imposing limitations. Structures reflect and further these gender norms, creating gender stratification and unequal power dynamics between men and women. Gender stratification leads to the undervaluing of work women do and furthers the myths of masculinity and femininity (Lorber 2006). This inequality puts women and their families at a disadvantage before, during and after disasters (Fothergill 1998; Tobin-Gurley, Peek, and Loomis 2010).

Assumptions about masculinity also affect men's disaster relief and recovery paths. Hegemonic masculinity is privileged in respect to other masculinities (Connell and Messerschmidt 2005, p. 832). Although the literature illustrates that men are generally in a better position socially and economically in a disaster, exceptions exist, i.e., men of color (Tobin-Gurley and Enarson 2013). In many cases, ideas privileging white males and masculine behavior and undervaluing women and their efforts hinder disaster recovery and community restoration. These include men not seeking appropriate care and women's lack of social power and financial resources to make decisions (Richter 2011; Tobin-Gurley and Enarson 2013). In rural Texas, we observed a hegemonic rural masculinity quite parallel to that which Tyler and Fairbrother (2013) describe in Australia, with its inclusion of a frontier mentality, a concept of man against nature, the importance of physical strength, and the valorization of risk-taking. Many masculinities are possible; we observed others, such as pastoral leadership in organizations. However, this hegemonic rural masculinity was dominant. It was problematic in that it hindered recovery and impacted the relationships that codefine masculine and feminine roles.

### Strategies of Self

After evacuation, it took weeks before some survivors knew whether their house was lost. Survivors emphasized the emotional trauma of losing their home, their possessions, and the trees but stated that not knowing was even worse. In the wake of the disaster, many developed or changed their "strategies of self" (Sherman 2005, p. 133). Men and women employing these strategies tended toward behaviors based on gender norms. We saw occurrences in Bastrop similar to those Pacholok (2009) describes in a discussion of gendered strategies of firefighters. However, these strategies were less competitive than those Pacholok (2009) describes. We found that a number of men's startegies of self were conflicted; they wanted to give aid but were unable to accept aid or to express deep emotional loss. Women's strategies of self, which had been located within traditional roles as caregiver, were expanded into leadership roles. This included providing fiscal management along with emotional intelligence, i.e., skills in identifying and responding to the emotional needs of individuals and communities (Hochschild 1983).

### Confronting Gender Myths

First responses to the wildfire in Bastrop County tended to be gendered. In several cases, women expressed the desire to evacuate, but the men they addressed often dismissed their concerns (Gladwin and Peacock 1997; Tobin-Gurley and Enarson 2013; Tyler and Fairbrother 2013). In one such situation, Charlie* told of dismissing his wife's desire to leave, telling her: "nahh, don't worry about it, no problem." Then, he shared "...they came by in a little truck and they were telling everybody 'you must evacuate, you must get out'...I convinced my wife, I said 'we gotta go.'" His dismissal of his wife's earlier warning and his later claim to "convince" her of the need to evacuate illustrates the issue. Such undermining of women in the evacuation process was mentioned in several interviews. Another survivor commented that men did not heed the warning to leave and decided to stay and fight the fire while women and children left. Such examples illustrate the gendering of responses to evacuation: men undermine women's warnings to leave and only leave after being ordered to evacuate (Gladwin and Peacock 1997; Tyler and Fairbrother 2013).

After realizing that their house and everything they owned had burned, both men and women were emotional. This is as expected in any disaster, yet was sometimes perceived by men as an assault on hegemonic masculinity. Pacholok (2009) identifies the gendered assumptions: "appropriately masculine men are supposed to (a) remain calm and reliable in a crisis, (b) be aggressive and take risks, (c) repudiate anything even remotely related to femininity and (d) strive for power, success and wealth" (p. 474). While men do not achieve all of these standards, these markers are what other men use to judge them (Pacholok 2009). Hence, in the wake of the disaster, expressing emotions was a struggle for some men. One survivor, Jason, commented, "For me, I was emotional. I don't know why I was. I tried not to be. I tried to do it my own way." His statement illustrates his reluctance to feel or express emotion at the time while acknowledging them in hindsight.

Many survivors commented that the wildfire was emotional for everyone, implicitly allowing men's emotional behavior to be accepted. For some men, it was the first time their wives saw them cry. Everyone was emotional about animals, even firemen. Given the devastation not only to structures but also wildlife, firefighters brought both domestic and wild injured animals to field veterinarians. One shared:

> As we were trying to leave...a fire truck pulled up and a fireman got out and brought us an injured fawn. That tough fireman cried when he handed it off to us and wanted to name it—after his daughter.

Liz is a volunteer firefighter who was on the fire line with the men. Being in a male-dominated field, she said she "keeps a face" when she's in her gear. However, she describes herself as the "little heart" of the department. When she found the body of one of her dogs following the fire, a fellow firefighter came and she noted that they "just held each other and cried." This illustrates the breaking of gender norms in the face of tragedy, especially for men who are in a field which includes toughness and competitiveness and that is defined by masculine standards and rejection of femininity (Pacholok 2009).

As mentioned before, hegemonic masculinity dictates ways for men to behave and roles they should take. Masculinity norms of detachment and independence, in which survivors were disconnected from their family, social networks, and community (Klinenberg 2002), were present in 13 interviews. Examples of this behavior ranged from leaving for remote work for five to six months to men refusing gift cards offered to them to replace necessities. A counselor shared a much-heard survivor statement: "keeping myself busy is the way I take care of myself so I don't have to think about it."

In the aftermath, people were scattered all over the state. Although some local shelters were provided, motels completely filled up. Many people went to towns as far as an hour away seeking housing. Grieving was especially hard for those not surrounded by fellow survivors for support, who could not share their emotions or grief with anyone. While detachment and independence can be a part of overall culture, it was expressly part of male survivors' coping mechanisms and behavior patterns as it is termed the "gender of isolation" (Klinenberg 2002). Men identified the tendency to isolate as part of being "givers"; they wanted to give assistance and often refused help. Thus, Jason

* Names, except those of public officials, are pseudonyms.

helped people to the hotel, Charlie gathered information about donations, and other men would point out they volunteered with various organizations in the relief effort.

Jason, who left for work for several months, identified his own isolation as difficult. His comments suggest that his mental breakdowns on the road could have been due to this and lack of grieving after the disaster. This resulted in physical isolation, a lack of processing grief, and other emotional effects, along with an inability to obtain aid needed for recovery. Jason, who paid hotel expenses for a number of friends during evacuation, explained that he would get clothes at a donation center for everyone else, but not himself. He did not evacuate with any clothes and really needed them. The result was that the manager at the donation center, a woman, retrieved the "nicest clothes" for him. This illustrates the problems of independence and the efforts that it took some men and women to overcome it.

Men helped through formal organizations, such as men's church groups, scouting, and riding clubs, as well as individually. They often described themselves as "givers." Brent shared that "as a guy it's really hard to—you know—not define yourself by what you do." Willey shared, "that's why it was hard for me to accept something because I've always been a giver, you know." This juxtaposes the need to feel strength by fulfilling the needs of the community and emphasizes the individual is giving rather than receiving help. In Bastrop, this often resulted in men gathering information about locations of resources and donation centers to share with other community members, but not for their use or that of their family. Charlie commented on why he went to churches and donation centers:

> They [volunteers] handed me a bag and said 'Here take anything you want'…I felt really self-conscious…I kind of made my rounds. One of the reasons I did that was that if I ever bumped into somebody that ever needed something, I could say well they got some of that over there.

These examples highlight the lengths and roles men take to be independent and self-sufficient yet also demonstrate that men do need help.

Giving rather than receiving also puts men in control. They possess useful knowledge about where the donations are and where to go for aid, thus establishing themselves as information brokers (Sutton, Palen, and Shklovski 2008; Yates and Partridge 2015). This is especially true for men who were physically limited because of health issues or age. Being an information broker provided them the power and control modeled all around them in the military model/command and control structure and through the roles of official disaster responders (Artemova and Korotayev 2003; Pacholok 2013). The behavior of refusing aid illustrates the desire to keep themselves self-sufficient and not be vulnerable. In the wake of Willey not being able to verbalize his needs, Sally, a recovery aid organization coordinator, repeatedly called him to ask him if he needed anything. He described her as being a kindly "pest." When these kinds of behaviors on the part of men did not dissipate, it was most often females in positions to help who stepped in to resolve untenable situations. Such gendered relationships allow men, who may refuse to recognize their own needs, to remain in their masculine comfort zone. However, it creates more work for women.

## Care Work and Women in Leadership

The practice of calling Willey for months is part of a larger phenomenon of women helping others before, during, and after the evacuation. This included strangers, family members, and neighbors. Women's organizations and networks play a crucial role in disaster recovery, sometimes informally (Ganapati 2012). Care work was identified in 31 interviews. Either a survivor was engaged in behavior that we coded as "care work" or they described another's such behavior. Lynn had emergency kits prepared for her family prior to the fires. During evacuation, Heather told her oldest son to notify neighbors about their elderly invalid neighbor: "Even if you have to pick her up because she can be stubborn, don't leave without her." This behavior of preparing for disasters and caring for others during evacuation was emphasized in multiple interviews with women.

Postdisaster, many women performed informal roles, such as serving as the information broker for their neighborhoods. This was done as an act of caring, rather than as power and control. For example, when Anne's mother-in-law refused to live in a trailer, the family decided to stay on their burned-out property. This meant camping with no electricity or running water. For weeks, Anne cooked on an open fire for 15 people. She also took on being the information funnel for her neighborhood and coordinated provisioning, using donated gift cards to buy tents, food, and anything else she and everyone needed to "live comfortably."

Women were resources for helping relatives and friends back on their feet. This often meant finding housing for elderly parents immediately following the fire. Charlie's daughter found them a place to stay following the fire. Due to her own limited resources, she was approached by the Mennonites, who offered to build her a house. Because of this connection, the Mennonites also built a house for Charlie and his wife. Anne reported that, once back in her house, she put on special lights to signal that anyone in the neighborhood was welcome to visit. These examples illustrate the extra, unrecognized care work and networking, crucial to family and community recovery, that women are responsible for following a disaster (Edwards 2004).

The roles women had taken on before the fire also included taking care of treasured family belongings and heirlooms. Liz described herself as "the keeper" of the family. Candice explained, "The first thing I had to do was to forgive myself for losing all the things that my family had trusted [to] me." Such gendered responsibility shows an extra emotional burden that women experienced (Fothergill 1998).

After evacuation, women's caregiving roles expanded to the organizational level, including working at one of the two long-term recovery organizations with which the authors volunteered. One of the organizations was not only headed by a woman, but was also almost completely staffed by women, many of whom were brought back into the workforce after a long hiatus. At the organizational level, these women wrote grants, networked with aid agencies, acquired and handled a large budget from multiple sources, conducted liaison work between fire survivors and volunteers, and coordinated funding, people, and materials with the help of Mennonite, Red Cross, and other volunteers to build over 130 homes for uninsured survivors. Kelly, a recovery organization's rebuild/resource manager, described the many roles women perform in such postdisaster work:

> You just go out to the property and everybody just wants to talk. So end up taking all different kinds of roles out there. Like therapist…best friend…prayer buddy…that's all you can do.

Betty, at the same organization, described her case work along with her professional responsibility:

> It's getting people back in their homes…Part of what we do as case managers is assess where they are, why they're in the position they're in…because before we build them a house, we want to…make sure they can afford it…afford the taxes, afford the insurance.

Another survivor described the extra work volunteers for a local charity undertook for her mother, who needed work clothes. Addressing the emotional and task overload of having to replace every single taken-for-granted item of daily life that resulted in forgetting details, she said:

> …the volunteers were really helpful in that they helped you find shoes, clothes, work clothes or whatever you needed…it saved her hours of time when…time…was critical.

The other long-term recovery organization with which we worked, although headed by a man, was staffed almost entirely by women. They engaged in similar activities, including working on developing, monitoring, and revising criteria for distribution of building and furnishing materials.* Linda shared that Rebecca, who had created a shelter on her own, "did amazing things, and helped

* These were donated by big-box stores that got a tax write-off for slightly damaged goods.

with more than what she had to." Some of the first people back to work after the disaster were school teachers. Sharon estimated that 15 teachers who had lost their homes went back to work when the schools reopened. She stated, "It was pretty bad for a while." This explicit commitment by women illustrates the emotional intelligence and strength that women bring to disaster recovery.

Women in leadership roles before the fires took on even more responsibility afterward. Clara Beckett, District Commissioner for much of the burn zone, explained that the local community had to provide 25% of the estimated $20 billion cleanup cost in order to receive the 75% "matching funds" from the Federal Emergency Management Agency (FEMA). Pointing out that counties are not allowed to take out long-term loans, she asked, "Where are we going to get 5 million bucks?" She then answered her own question: "Several different pots, right?" This demonstrates the challenge and the networking necessary to obtain the matching money for FEMA-funded tree and debris removal. Through her networking, another influential female leader, a Bastrop resident who had been evacuated, ultimately "convinced the board of LCRA (Lower Colorado River Authority) to write a check to Bastrop County for five million dollars."

Liz, the volunteer firefighter, was promoted to assistant fire chief after the fires. She presents a final example of the burdens that women took on. Liz reflected on the community coming together, stating:

> And that's the big lesson here. It ain't about us, as individuals. You know?...You are here for each other. It's the only way you can make it. You can't make it on our own. Most of us out here are proud. It's hard to take a hand for anybody, but you, under certain circumstances, just have to do it. And then to turn around and pay it forward...but you can't get better unless you give back, you can't.

Liz's words contrast with the behaviors of those men, who embraced detachment and independence. Bastrop's resilience and solidarity as a community is due, in part, to the perseverance of such women, who were part of networks, in supporting family, neighbors, and strangers.

In each of these gender strategies, there are drawbacks. Striving for hegemonic masculinity creates consequences for men's relationships (Kaufman 2001; Rubin 2003), negative health outcomes (Sabo 1998), and other negative effects (Pacholok 2009). Pacholok (2009, p. 496) suggests that some "bad effects" on firefighters after a fire result from their use of gendered strategies of competition in trying to achieve superiority. As noted, Jason recognized that his isolation from other fire survivors was difficult, suggesting that this could have led to his mental breakdowns while traveling. Beth, a case worker who helped fire survivors access resources, states, "You immediately take the burdens on as your own and to some extent your frustration with lack of resources now matches that of the survivors you are working with." Such tendencies of women to overinvest and take on extra effort can create stress following a disaster (Morrow and Enarson 1996; Tobin-Gurley and Enarson 2013).

Women were in formal elected and appointed organizational roles and informal neighborhood leadership positions in Bastrop. Beth shared that the disaster recovery organization she worked for "sent out a notice to all of us that you were eligible for the project if you had been unemployed for a certain length of time or you were a victim of the fire." This resulted in an office comprised of 11 women. Women in leadership roles brought with them emotional maturity and intelligence. Beth instructed her volunteers to ask survivors about their stories, knowing they would want to talk about it. Liz represents breaking gender norms as a female firefighter. Her role as the "little heart" of the department represents a combination of gender norms. Her role also allowed the men to cry with her at her house. Clearly, the firefighters needed to express emotion all along, and Liz's leadership gave them an opportunity.

## LESSONS LEARNED AND POLICY RECOMMENDATIONS

### Advantages of Women in Leadership

We have illustrated the skills that women bring to their leadership roles as crucial community members. As Richter (2011, p. 28) states, "Clearly, in disaster and health care, it is better to plan *with* [sic] women—rather than for them." Disaster management should involve women from the beginning. As in this case, it is helpful to implement hiring policies that encourage women to apply for positions, focusing on applicants who are unemployed and/or are disaster survivors. This integration of women into disaster management and the recovery process fosters resilience in any community.

### Supporting Men through Disaster Recovery

Due to how they have been socialized in our culture and, especially in this case, the norms of hegemonic rural masculinity, it is difficult for some men to express the emotions necessary to move through grief and loss and to connect with fellow survivors and community. Men feel the need to act as information brokers and to help others, as opposed to accepting help during recovery. A post-disaster program that facilitates occasions for men to help others *while* helping themselves could fill this void. Such programming could be local, informal opportunities in the community, inviting men to be part of specialized "helping teams." These could be partnered with existing organizations, initially supported by a trained facilitator skilled in generating crucial conversations during work projects. Survivors throughout Bastrop confirmed that those who engaged in some sort of helping work were much better off emotionally at the end of the second and the third post-disaster years than those who did not. Grants and trained personnel to get such groups off the ground would benefit men, women, and communities on multiple levels.

## CONCLUSION

This study documents that gender assumptions impact both men and women. In this case, hegemonic rural masculinity, while not the only masculinity performed, impacts gender relationships in ways that are harmful to men and make more work for women. Where some men left Bastrop for work, some women aided in the recovery by taking on extra, often unpaid, work. Men welcomed the chance to help others, but felt self-conscious in accepting help and expressing emotions. Men's perceptions of women also undermined women's plea to evacuate, resulting in crucial time lost. These should be addressed by making more room for women in leadership and facilitating situations where men can work through grief and loss while helping others. Breaking down normative gendered behavior patterns and gender expectations will diminish the impact natural disasters have on vulnerable populations while fostering the resiliency of individuals, families, and communities.

## REFERENCES


Anderson, W. 2000. Women and children in disasters. In *Managing disaster risk in emerging economies*, eds. A. Kreimer and M. Arnold, 85–90. Washington, DC: World Bank.

Artemova, O. and A. Korotayev. 2003 Monopolization of information and female status: A cross-cultural test. *Cross-Cultural Research* 37(1): 81–86.

Atkinson, R. and J. Flint. 2004. Snowball sampling. In *The SAGE encyclopedia of social science research method*, eds. M.S. Lewis-Beck, A.E. Bryman, and T.F. Liao, 1044–1045. Thousand Oaks, CA. Sage Publications Inc.

Biernacki, P. and D. Waldorf. 1981. Snowball sampling: Problems and techniques of chain referral sampling. *Sociological Methods & Research* 10(2): 141–163.

Callaghan, W., S. Rasmussen, D. Jamieson, S. Ventura, S. Farr, P. Sutton, T. Mathews, B. Hamilton, K. Shealy, and D. Brantley. 2007. Health concerns of women and infants in times of natural disasters: Lessons learned from Hurricane Katrina. *Maternal and Child Health Journal* 11(4): 307–311.

Charmaz, K. 2014. *Constructing grounded theory: A practical guide through qualitative analysis*. Thousand Oaks, CA: Sage.

Clarke, A. 2005. *Situational analysis: Grounded theory after the postmodern turn*. Thousand Oaks, CA: Sage.

Clarke, A., C. Friese, and R. Washburn. 2015. *Situational analysis in practice: Mapping research with grounded theory*. Walnut Creek, CA: Left Coast Press, Inc.

Connell, R.W. and J.W. Messerschmidt. 2005. Hegemonic masculinity: Rethinking the concept. *Gender & Society* 19(6): 829–859.

Edwards, R. 2004. Present and absent in troubling ways: Families and social capital debates. *The Sociological Review* 52(1): 1–21.

Fothergill, A. 1998. The neglect of gender in disaster work: An overview of the literature. In *The gendered terrain of disaster: Through women's eyes*, eds. E. Enarson and B.H. Morrow, 11–15. Westport, CT: Praeger Publishers.

Ganapati, N.E. 2012. In good company: Why social capital matters for women during disaster recovery. *Public Administration Review* 72(3): 419–427.

Gladwin, H. and W.G. Peacock. 1997. Warning and evacuation: A night for hard houses. In *Hurricane Andrew: Ethnicity, gender, and the sociology of disasters*, eds. W.G. Peacock, B.H. Morrow, and H. Gladwin, 52–74. New York: Routledge.

Gray, R., M. Fisher, W. Powell, K. Ridenour, S. Rissel, and J. Sommerfeld. 2012. Bastrop Complex Wildfire case study: The most destructive wildland urban interface wildfire in Texas history. *Texas Forest Service and Bastrop County Office of Emergency Management*: 1–42. http://content.austin.ynn.com/auscontent/documents/BastropReport1-42.pdf, accessed August 19, 2015.

Haraway, D. 1988. Situated knowledges: The science question in feminism and the privilege of partial perspective. *Feminist Studies* 14(3): 575–599.

Huffman, H. 2011. Forest economics and resource analysis: Bastrop Fire, 2011. Texas A&M Forest Service. http://tfsweb.tamu.edu/BastropFire-2011/, accessed August 19, 2015.

Hochschild, A.R. 1983. *The managed heart: Commercialization of human feeling*. Berkeley: University of California Press.

Kaufman, M. 2001. The construction of masculinity and the triad of men's violence. In *Men's lives*, 5th ed., eds. M.S. Kimmel and M.A. Messner, 4–18. Boston: Allyn and Bacon.

Klinenberg, E. 2002. *Heat wave: A social autopsy of disaster in Chicago*. Illinois: University of Chicago Press.

Lorber, J. 2006. The social construction of gender. In *The inequality reader: Contemporary and foundational readings in race, class, and gender*, eds. D. Grusky and S. Szeleny, 276–283. Philadelphia: Westview Press.

Morrow, B.H. and E. Enarson. 1996. Hurricane Andrew through women's eyes: Issues and recommendations. *International Journal of Mass Emergencies and Disasters* 14(1): 5–22.

Pacholok, S. 2013. *Into the fire: Disaster and the remaking of gender*. Toronto: University of Toronto Press.

_____. 2009. Gendered strategies of self: Navigating hierarchy and contesting masculinities. *Gender, Work & Organization* 16(4): 471–500.

Richter, R. 2011. Disparity in disasters: A frontline view of gender-based inequities in emergency aid and health care. In *Anthropology at the front lines of gender-based violence*, eds. J.R. Wies and H.J. Haldane, 19–28. Nashville, TN: Vanderbilt University Press.

Rubin, L.B. 2003. The approach-avoidance dance: Men, women, and intimacy. In *Men's lives*, 6th ed., eds. M.S. Kimmel and M.A. Messner, 409–415: Boston: Pearson Education, Inc.

Sabo, D. 1998. Masculinities and men's health: Moving toward post-Superman Era prevention. In *Men's Lives*, eds. M.S. Kimmel and M.A. Messner, 347–361. Boston: Allyn & Bacon.

Sherman, R. 2005. Producing the superior self strategic comparison and symbolic boundaries among luxury hotel workers. *Ethnography* 6(2): 131–158.

Strauss, A. and J. Corbin. 1998. Grounded theory methodology: An overview. In *Strategies of qualitative inquiry*, eds. N.K. Denzin and Y.S. Lincoln, 273–285. Thousand Oaks, CA: Sage.

Sutton, J., L. Palen, and I. Shklovski. 2008. Backchannels on the front lines: Emergent uses of social media in the 2007 southern California wildfires. In *Proceedings of the 5th International ISCRAM Conference—Washington, DC, USA, May 2008*, eds. F. Fiedrich and B. Van de Walle. Washington, DC: *Information Systems for Crisis Response and Management*. http://www.cs.colorado.edu/~palen/Papers/iscram08/BackchannelsISCRAM08.pdf, accessed October 2, 2015.

Tobin-Gurley, J., L. Peek, and J. Loomis. 2010. Displaced single mothers in the aftermath of Hurricane Katrina: Resource needs and resource acquisition. *International Journal of Mass Emergencies and Disasters* 28 (2): 170–206.

Tobin-Gurley, J. and E. Enarson. 2013. Gender. In *Social vulnerability to disasters*, eds. D.S.K. Thomas, B.D. Phillips, W.E. Lovekamp, and A. Fothergill, 139–165. Boca Raton, FL: CRC Press.

Tyler, M. and P. Fairbrother. 2013. Bushfires are "men's business": The importance of gender and rural hegemonic masculinity. *Rural Studies* 30: 110–119.

Vertuno, J. and M. Graczyk. 2011. Firefighters have yet to control Texas wildfire. *The Seattle Times*, http://seattletimes.com/html/nationworld/2016120900_apustexaswildfires.html, accessed November 23, 2014.

Yates, C. and H. Partridge. 2015. Citizens and social media in times of natural disaster: Exploring information experience. *Information Research* 20(1): paper 659. http://www.informationr.net/ir/20-1/paper659.html#.Vg8QRfRH0-V, accessed August 15, 2015.

# 17 Gender Dynamics and Disasters in Zimbabwe: *A Case of Tokwe Mukosi Flooding*

*Catherine Bwerinofa and Manase Kudzai Chiweshe*

## CONTENTS



**Abstract**

This chapter provides a nuanced analysis of the gendered dynamics of the 2013/14 Tokwe Mukosi flooding in Zimbabwe, assessing the link between gender and disasters. Women are typically more vulnerable than men to the effects of natural disasters and climate change because of socioeconomic differences and inequitable power relations. An intersection of factors, most importantly gender, mediates how people experience flooding because they have different concerns, needs, priorities, and opportunities. In addition, when people are called "flood victims" or "survivors," they are lumped into one homogenous category. Yet, they suffer and find ways to survive differently. The research was conducted mainly in Chingwizi, where the communities were resettled after the floods. Good practices of gender-inclusive disaster risk reduction worldwide provide strong evidence that a gender-balanced approach benefits men and women. The chapter provides an illustration of how gender becomes an important factor in understanding disaster situations in Zimbabwe.

## INTRODUCTION

This chapter presents a contextual analysis, using the case of Tokwe Mukosi flooding in Zimbabwe in 2013/2014, to explore how impacts and experiences of disasters are mediated by gender. The homogenization of flood "victims" or "survivors" into one group falsely paints a picture of an undifferentiated victim who is vulnerable to disasters in the same way and timeframe. Such generalization hides the nuances and vast differences among women who are facing and adapting to disasters across Zimbabwe. As we build a theoretical understanding of the gendered dimensions of resilience, we need to keep in mind Bakare-Yusuf's (2003) assertion. She notes that any intervention focusing on African women requires a theoretical account of embodied gender differences that is grounded in the complex realities of their everyday experiences.

The role of coordinating emergencies and disasters is under the Ministry of Local Governance, through the Department of Civil Protection; the Minister in office leads the process. The current system uses the existing government, private, and nongovernmental organizations whose regular activities contain elements of disaster risk prevention and community development (Betera 2011). There is, however, little regard for gender within this system, as the government treats those impacted as a homogeneous group. Zimbabwe has adopted a militarized approach to disaster response because it is easier to mobilize and control and have strong logistical networks (Betera 2011). Such a system has little regard for people's agency and often relies on force. Thus, women's needs in these situations are rarely met. The case presented here succinctly shows how disaster management in Zimbabwe is not designed to meet their needs.

The Hyogo Framework, endorsed by 168 countries in 2005, states that gender perspectives should be integrated into all disaster risk management policies, plans, and decision-making processes. This includes those related to risk assessment, early warning information management, education, and training. This is complemented by research (Enarson 2000; Enarson and Phillips 2008; Fothergill 2004), which demonstrates that the specific gender issues within a community facing risk or a hazard should be identified and documented and recommendations made in order to minimize losses of life, assets, and livelihoods.

There is a vast amount of literature focusing on gender and disasters. Enarson (2000) argues that there are three critical areas for understanding gender in a disaster situation: (1) women and men have different and specific short-term needs and long-term interests; (2) women are not passive but play a key role throughout the cycle of preparedness, mitigation, relief, and reconstruction; and (3) attention to gender equity is important in interventions to alleviate vulnerability in future events. Exploring everyday experiences of women survivors of flooding in Grand Forks, North Dakota, Fothergill (2004) shows how class, race, gender, sexual orientation, and disability shape impacts and recovery. Her book traces the physical, social, economic, and psychological impacts of disaster on women while also providing a sociological framework to analyze women's roles in disasters. In this chapter, we do the same with women in rural Zimbabwe. Our research contributes to this growing literature by illuminating the intersection of gender, class, age, and disability in disaster situations within African spaces.

Zimbabwean society is largely patriarchal; this has implications for women's experiences of disaster. Women's access to assets and resources that can mitigate loss is mediated through their relationship to men. For example, land access is arbitrated by male relations (Chiweshe, Chakona, and Helliker 2015), placing women in precarious positions when disasters affect land ownership patterns. Rural women in Zimbabwe are largely dependent on natural resources, often impacted by disasters, for their livelihoods. This leaves them vulnerable to food insecurity. Patriarchal norms regarding division of labor place women within the domestic sphere, saddling them with much of the burden of surviving a disaster. This is further entrenched by *roora* (bride wealth payments), which forms the basis of marriages in Shona society. *Roora* reinforces patriarchy, breeding inequality, and widening socioeconomic gaps between men and women, placing women in a subordinate position (Ansell 2001). Because of prescribed social responsibilities, women's burdens are multiplied in disaster situations due to tradition and custom. Any program focusing on disaster risk reduction, response, and/or mitigation should understand these social dynamics and how they impact community experiences of disaster.

## BACKGROUND

The Tokwe Mukosi is a concrete-face/rock-fill dam on the Tokwe River, connecting with Mukosi River about 72 kilometers south of Masvingo, Zimbabwe (Relief Web 2014). It is a dam of great magnitude, with a wall 90 meters high and a back throw over 35 kilometers on land (Chenga 2014).

Zimbabwe has seven water catchment councils; Masvingo Province has five water subcatchment councils, which include Tokwe. Plans to construct the dam were set in 1980 after the country had attained independence, in order to create water storage, irrigation, and fisheries. All of these would improve access to food and income in the drought prone Masvingo Province. Construction of the dam, however, began 12 years later in 1992. It was halted in 2002 due to the economic meltdown (Mugabe 2014).

During the 2013/2014 rain season, the area around the dam was flooded and affected over 6000 households. The event was declared a national disaster, which was supposed to mobilize government and international resources. Engineers constructing the Tokwe Mukosi dam noted that the floods were caused by large volumes of water, due to the unusual, above-normal rainfall. The water was forced to seep through the dam wall, which was still under construction (Mtimba 2014a).

Chivi district usually receives poor rainfall. In early 2014, the area received torrential rains, which contributed to the flooding disaster. The chairperson of the Chivi Civil Protection Department said, "the rains were just too much and for the past three years the area received less than 400 mm of rain per season but this season things changed" (Maponga 2014). The Chivi District administrator identified 13 affected villages: Chekai, Jahwa, Zifunzi, Mharadzano, Chikandigwa, Nemauzhe, Tagwirei, Ndove, Matandandizvo, Mashenjere, Nongera, Chikosi, and Neruvanga. The scale of impact, he pointed out, was why there were too many people within the transit camps and why planning was a challenge.

Affected communities were relocated to Chingwizi, in the controversial Nuanetsi ranch. Parts of the ranch had been occupied during the Fast Track Land Reform Program (FTLRP) in 2002, despite being a black-owned enterprise (see Chiweshe and Mutopo 2014; Mujere and Dombo 2011). The FTLRP was initiated by the Zimbabwean government in 2000 to redistribute land from 5000 white commercial farmers, who owned 29% of Zimbabwe's land area, to black families (Chiweshe and Mutopo 2015).

By mid-2015, most people at Chingwizi were still living in the camp because the government had failed to relocate them as planned. Mazara (2015) argues that authorities have forgotten the people, who had gone for months without food aid. He notes the following:

> With relocation seemingly a pipe-dream, Chingwizi villagers have gone for months without receiving food rations and their salty water sources are quickly running dry. Due to the incessant hunger stalking the villagers, they have turned to unorthodox means of obtaining food, whereby they ransack sugarcane transporting trains passing by, in the process putting their livestock in danger when they come to feed on the residue of sugarcane which they would have thrown around the railway tracks.

The continued suffering of communities at Chingwizi provides evidence of a government that has neither the capacity nor will to ensure livelihoods after disasters. It is a tragic case that highlights the need to build community resilience. Inhabitants were told not to construct permanent structures because they are going to be relocated to other areas by the government. Yet, years later, they are still in the temporary structures, which provide gender-specific challenges discussed later in the paper.

In August 2014, there were violent clashes between the communities and police and army when the government moved the clinic to new plots. The families resisted. The government wanted to move them to a nearby farm, where they would have one-hectare plots, but the families demanded compensation for lost property. A *Daily News* report noted that:

> Armed police last week visited the camp in an unsuccessful attempt to get the displaced families to accept relocation without compensation to one-hectare plots, where they have been told they must grow sugar cane or lose food aid. The relocation was vigorously resisted. The protest saw the villagers overpowering anti-riot police officers, disarming them and setting alight their two vehicles, forcing government to rope in the army from Masvingo's 4 Brigade. The soldiers ransacked the camp and assaulted villagers. The relocated villagers have since deserted the camp. (Mtimba 2014a)

At the time of this research (September 2014), the people were complaining that government was withholding food to force them to relocate. The families have resorted to ransacking sugar cane transporting trains (Mazara 2015).

## RESEARCH METHODOLOGY

The research is based on an exploratory case study design, which utilizes a qualitative research paradigm meant to provide a nuanced understanding of everyday experiences of communities living at Chingwizi. Fieldwork was conducted between September and October 2014. The focus on participants resettled in Chingwizi stems from the fact that villagers relocated to the Chisase and Masangula areas did not experience similar circumstances during and after the floods; they were relocated before the floods. This means that the same findings cannot be applied uniformly to the other relocated communities. In addition, there were more people resettled in Chingwizi (5782 families, making up an estimated population of 20,000) than any other site, thereby increasing diversity of points of view. Masangula had 485 families and Chisase had 126 families, though the exact number of people could not be ascertained.

This study focuses on understanding the experiences of 50 people through in-depth interviews, focus group discussions, key informant interviews, informal discussions, and observation at Chingwizi transit camp. While a sample of 50 is not statistically significant, this exploratory study does not intend to generalize findings or to provide universal facts about Chingwizi. Rather, it explores the emerging gendered experiences of flooding. The respondent population consists of 10 men and 20 women, ages 24–64, and 10 male and 10 female youths, ages 15–21. Sixteen interviews (8 men and 8 women) were conducted. Participants were purposively sampled, with a focus on people with the following characteristics: large households, pregnant women, couples with newborn children, those who had suffered sickness, female-headed households, and community leaders.

This sample, while not representative, provides insights from key informants from organizations working in the areas. In designing the sample, we sought to ensure coverage of people in diverse situations, including different ages and marital statutes. Four focus group discussions were organized separately for men and women. Young people under 21 were separated from adults to ensure that they were free to discuss issues such as sexuality (taboo to discuss with elders). Ten key informants with specialized knowledge on the camp were interviewed, including health workers, civil society organizations, and government ministries and departments.

Informal discussions were done during a week of observation at the camp. The observation was organized as a transect walk through the camp, focusing on location and distribution of resources. This included water points, clinics, living arrangements, livelihood options, and sanitation. The walks also provide an understanding of the social features and landscapes that shape experiences of men and women within the camp.

Women were more eager to participate in the research; men were more circumspect. The majority of men interviewed were afraid of being targeted if they gave out information, given the political nature of the flooding crisis. They shared how the armed forces had victimized them violently and how others were taken into police custody when they had refused relocation to the allocated plots at another farm without compensation. This demonstrates how men and women are not homogenous in these scenarios. Rather, they occupy diverse social positions defined by age, class, location, and background. This is at the heart of understanding how people experience disasters.

The respondents range in age from 15 to 63 years; their experiences illuminate how gender and age intersect within disaster situations. Young people were more willing and likely to use migration, especially to South Africa and Botswana, as a response strategy to the floods. This was made easier by the fact that most of the young people in the sample were not married and did not have children. The study included women who were married, single mothers, divorced, never married, and widowed. Men were widowed and married (see Table 17.1). Some of the female respondents were de facto household heads; their partners are illegal migrants in South Africa, Mozambique, and other parts of Zimbabwe.

**TABLE 17.1**
**Social Differentiation of Research Participants**

| Sex | Male ($n$ = 20) | Female ($n$ = 30) | | |
|---|---|---|---|---|
| Interviews | 8 | 8 | | |
| Age | | | | |
| 15–21 | 10 | 10 | | |
| 22–46 | 7 | 13 | | |
| Over 46 | 3 | 7 | | |
| Marital status | | | | |
| Single | 13 | 11 | | |
| Married | 4 | 10 | | |
| Widowed | 1 | 2 | | |
| Divorced | 2 | 7 | | |
| Household size | No children | One to three children | Four to six children | More than six children |
| | 22 | 13 | 7 | 8 |
| Household health status | Sick at moment | Sick in last 6 months | Sick in last year | |
| | 13 | 37 | 42 | |
| Household with new births | 7 | | | |
| Sex of household head of respondents | Female headed | Male headed | De facto female head | |
| | 7 | 31 | 12 | |

## FINDINGS AND DISCUSSION

### Gendered Impact of Flooding on Communities

The Tokwe Mukosi flooding disaster has had a tremendous impact on the affected communities. Daily life has been disrupted. Resettled villagers in Chingwizi bear the brunt of the flooding, without much assistance from government. Women with children faced multiple challenges in the camp, including inadequate of medical care, as the clinic was underresourced and overwhelmed by the large numbers of people. The nature of the disaster also led to asset stripping, as households have been forced to sell productive resources to survive. Households have lost not only property and savings but also livelihoods. A female participant noted:

> The floods destroyed our way of living and we have been forced to live as refugees at Chingwizi. We have lost our fields and we cannot do much here. The government is promising to move us but what about all that we have lost. Who is supposed to replace the property we lost? The flood had destroyed our community and we are now destitute.

Food, water, and clothing challenges have been eased by donations, but these are not long-term solutions. Building resilience and community livelihood systems requires a sustained program beyond Chingwizi that enhances people's capacity to respond to problems.

Within patriarchal contexts such as Zimbabwe, decision making is a male domain. Married women waited on their husbands to make important decisions about evacuation. Married participants complained that their husbands were, in most cases, adamant about not leaving. This placed women at risk, as they were responsible for children during the evacuation. This is made worse by the nature of women's traditional dress in the region, which hinders mobility. One respondent noted, "Wearing dresses proved problematic when running towards safety. I wish I had jeans or trousers because they are easier to run in." Women were also responsible for ensuring children and the elderly got to safety. This is not to say men were not involved in the process but rather highlights how the productive and reproductive roles of women placed multiple stresses on them during the disaster.

An added complication for the evacuation and for survival in the camps is physical limitation. A report in the national newspaper (Sachiti 2014) highlights the specific challenges facing people living with disabilities in the camp:

> Life is hard; more so for the disabled, pregnant women and children…[male] lives with disability and lived in the Chekai area in Chivi, lost all his extra sets of crutches and the only one he has is now broken. He also lost his orthopedic shoes in the floods and remains with only one pair. He is in for double tragedy.

It is worse for women living with disabilities, who also have to deal with gender discrimination. The toilets and water points at the camp are not designed to meet the needs of such women. According to one woman, "Living here is difficult for me because of shortages especially of water. I cannot wait in the line and no one can do it for me. Moving around in this camp is impossible." The government and donor efforts are largely excluding this group of people, which increases their marginalization. The impact of flooding on women thus depends also on age and their condition of disability.

The floods also had a negative impact on agriculture. This affected women because of their domestic role of food provision. Before the floods, communities were expecting a bumper harvest, given the good rains. According to one male farmer, "the crops were promising a good harvest. Our fields have maize, pumpkins, sorghum and groundnuts but now we live on handouts like beggars." Women's gardens and crops were destroyed, a burden on women who are responsible mainly for preparing food within the home. This is well illustrated by a woman, who narrated her experiences as follows:

> When the children are hungry they run to the mother to ask for food. Fathers do not know about their children's hunger but the mother knows. Even when fathers get hungry they will come to you and ask "my wife is there anything to eat?" So what do I tell my hungry children when all my crops and food is gone with the flood? It is hard to be a mother when your children are hungry.

The flooding impacted small and large livestock during evacuations and while people were in the camp. Most of the respondents in this study lost all chickens, a significant number of goats, and cattle. Large and small livestock are difficult to manage in transit camps; overcrowding worsens the situation. Chickens, guinea fowl, turkeys, and rabbits were affected by crowding within the campsite, and many perished. Women and girls generally take part in small livestock rearing (goats and poultry), while boys and men are responsible for large livestock (cattle). This is critical, because men and boys practice nomadic livestock herding. Grazing areas are far from the camp, due to its proximity to the Nuanetsi Ethanol sugarcane plantation. Before the floods, communities had communal grazing lands where mainly boys were involved in herding cattle. They did not have to move long distances to find grazing. This practice leaves women and girls behind in the camp, with increased workloads within the household.

Women and girls have limited income-generating options. They can only take part in construction jobs where their role is restricted to collecting water or grass for thatching. Men and boys, on the other hand, spent more time in brick molding, garden construction, and crafts making (stools, shelves, and yokes). Boys are mainly involved in working illegally in neighboring countries or panning for gold near their previous settlement areas in Tokwe. Men and boys participate in vending, but it is not profitable due to the increase in poverty levels, as people have no money to buy goods.

## GENDERED DIMENSIONS OF LIFE AT CHINGWIZI

This section discusses issues affecting women at the camp. Sanitation and basic hygiene were problematic at the time of this research. Pit latrines were lacking. They were also dirty, which poses serious health risks for children and pregnant women. Women faced challenges in accessing the toilets at night because of lack of lighting. A local telecommunications company provided solar lamps, but most female-headed households did not get these because they are excluded in most community programs.

Traditionally, women and children are responsible for water provisioning within the household, yet water at Chingwizi remains a difficult commodity to get. Government and civil society have attempted various strategies, including bringing tanks, but water is rationed. Women have to stand in long lines and jostle for water. Sachiti (2014) describes this situation:

> Even the heavily pregnant Chengeto Masocha from Chekai has just discovered that being pregnant is no golden ticket to skip the water queue. "I almost collapsed while standing in the queue. First you have to guard your containers and when the water is delivered, wait some more for your turn," she says. Another displaced woman, Mai Molly said: "Water is a big challenge for breastfeeding mothers. Diapers we are being given are never enough, we end up using nappies which have to be washed." Mai Lucia from Zifunzi area, Chivi, said she did not have enough nappies for her baby. "They gave us sanitary pads and condoms, we want more napkins for our children," said the mother of four.

Our research validates these experiences by highlighting how water remains a gendered challenge at Chingwizi. During the transect walk, we observed that more women and girls were out fetching water before noon (school time).

Access to sexual and reproductive health is still a challenge for men and women, as people rely on one clinic. For those who are the furthest way, there is an average walk of 8–10 kilometers to access health related services. Visits to the clinic are harder for pregnant and lactating mothers. One pregnant woman notes,

> We have at least a semblance of a clinic here but you cannot call it a health center. In such a place you cannot afford to have a complicated pregnancy because there is no doctor or equipment to help you. For those with relatives elsewhere in Zimbabwe it is better to go and live with them until you give birth.

The various hardships faced by women and girls in accessing resources, especially while in the camp, increased their economic vulnerability. They were faced with a weak social safety net, where the presence of a man within a household proved to be important. Getting food or resources at times required physicality. Male heads of households also used their influence to access food and water better than households without adult males. In trying to adapt, women used transactional sex. From the interviews and group discussions, respondents reported to widespread cases of women using sex to access food. Sex work was reported to be rampant, with the women charging as low as US$1 for sex. There were reports of increased participation of children (Mtimba 2014b). Newspaper reports also alleged that government workers involved in distributing food were demanding sex from young girls (*Newsday* 2014). One of the effects has been the increased child and teenage pregnancies (Mtimba 2014c).

Another important gendered dimension is the access to sanitary wear for women and girls. Research participants highlighted that women had to resort to using cow dung, leaves, and newspapers. Individuals and civil society organizations had provided some sanitary pads for women, but during the time of fieldwork, the donations had stopped. Marungwara (2014) highlights how women reported losing their pads to their husbands, who used them to barter for food. It is not only pads that were problematic for women's reproductive health. Our research also found that access to family planning methods was severely affected after the flooding. This is supported by Marungwara (2014), who finds that women lost their contraceptive pills during relocation, leading to some unplanned pregnancies.

The experiences of men are different within the camp, given that they are mainly involved in livelihood activities. The activities include stealing, artisanal mining, and undocumented migration to neighboring countries and other areas in Zimbabwe. Young women (especially single) are also increasingly involved in migrating to neighboring countries, although there were no available statistics of how many had gone.

In their previous location, both men and women were involved in subsistence agriculture of mainly maize. The climatic conditions at Chingwizi, however, cannot sustain maize production. The area was specifically set aside for sugarcane plantations under irrigation, wildlife management, cattle ranching, and crocodile farming. A key informant with agricultural knowledge noted,

> Farmers at Chingwizi have started adopting their old farming practices which include maize production, as compared to drought tolerant crops like sorghum and millet which are common crops grown in Mwenezi district. With the high temperatures and low rainfall characteristics of Mwenezi district where Chingwizi is located, it is advisable to change the type of crops they grow.

The people have to adapt to new crops such as small grains that can be supported by the climatic conditions. Farming will also increase women's work, as they have to work in the fields and at home.

## MULTIPLE ROLES FOR WOMEN AND GIRLS

Women and particularly girls do nearly all of the household chores. Women and girls perform most of the time-consuming tasks, such as child rearing, fetching water and fuel wood, and walking to and from market sources. Distances to and time spent on these activities increases with the growing scarcity of natural resources. They walked about 2 kilometers to fetch water and about 5 kilometers to get to the nearest shops. This means that women have little time to engage in economic and livelihood activities, which further entrenches their vulnerability.

Women and girls look after younger siblings, older people, and ill persons within the family. They risk contracting diseases without the adequate knowledge and training to handle patients. According to a key informant, "Girls have become the face of this disaster. They suffered like everyone else, but the demands on them in this camp are multiple. They work, cook, go to school, care for the sick, go to the fields, get water and do all sorts of things." They also perform agricultural tasks alongside with and similar to other family members. According to key informants and discussion with young people, these multiple tasks often lead to girls dropping out of school in the seventh grade. We were unable to get statistics on the number of drop outs, although schooling within the camp was free at the time.

## LESSONS LEARNED

What emerged from the research was gender dynamics impacting access, ownership, and control patterns in social, cultural, political, environmental, and economic spheres. This has a huge bearing on men's and women's ability to cope and recover after a disaster. The case outlined previously provides four instructive lessons on how gender is an important consideration when understanding vulnerability and when planning responses to disasters.

First, it reinforces the notion that disasters and their impacts are not only gendered but also impact people differently depending on their social position. Women, generally, are impacted more by disasters; their reproductive role means they carry the heaviest burden of disasters. Second, framing survivors and victims of disasters as a homogenous group leads to one-size-fits-all responses. This may entrench gender inequalities and increase the vulnerabilities of women in general and young, disabled, pregnant, and breastfeeding women in particular. Third, responses to disasters need to address issues such as privacy, dignity, and respect, which go beyond providing water, food, and clothes. Flood victims are people with fundamental rights; their condition of destitution does not mean they surrender these rights. Lastly, adaptation processes are also gendered. Women are generally left more vulnerable by their adaptation activities, such as transactional sex, as this may lead to infections and unsupportable pregnancies. Male activities, such as migration, leave women as de facto household heads with double the burden when looking after the household.

## CONCLUSION

The chapter provides insights into the role that gender plays in people's experience of disasters. Using the flooding in a region of Zimbabwe, we highlight how women and men are affected differently. Three key issues emerge from this chapter. First, women and men are not a homogenous group; they occupy different social positions. In the case of Chingwizi, age intersects with gender to make young women bear the biggest burden of the disaster. Pregnant and breastfeeding women also face serious challenges. Young men tend to migrate or embark on gold panning as livelihood options. Second, investing in resilient communities is important, especially in contexts where the national government cannot afford to provide proper assistance to affected communities, such as in Zimbabwe.

Finally, structural gender inequalities are further entrenched by disasters. It is imperative to mainstream gender in all discussions on disaster reduction, responses, and intervention after disasters (Enarson and Phillips 2008; Fothergill 2004). Our research and findings support Enarson and Morrow's (1997) assertion that disaster studies have failed to reflect an understanding of female victims' daily lives and to utilize effectively the knowledge and skills of over half of the population.

## REFERENCES

Ansell, N. 2001. "Because it's our culture!" (Re)negotiating the meaning of *lobola* in Southern African secondary schools. *Journal of Southern African Studies* 27(4): 697–716.

Bakare-Yusuf, B. 2003. Beyond determinism: The phenomenology of African female existence. *Feminist Africa* 8(2): 8–24. http://agi.ac.za/sites/agi.ac.za/files/fa_2_feature_article_1.pdf, accessed May 4, 2015.

Betera, L. 2011. *Overview of disaster risk management and vulnerability*. http://www.itu.int/en/ITU-D/Emergency Telecommunications/Documents/Zambabwe_2011/Overview%20of%20disaster%20management%20and%20vulnerability%20-%20Civil%20Protection%20Unit.pdf, accessed March 5, 2015.

Chenga, F. 2014. Cheap design linked to problems at Tokwe Mukosi. *Nehanda Radio*. http://nehandaradio.com/2014/02/15/cheap-design-linked-problems-tokwe-mukosi/, accessed December 5, 2014.

Chiweshe, M.K., L. Chakona, and K. Helliker. 2015. Patriarchy, women, land and livelihoods on A1 farms in Zimbabwe. *Journal of Asian and African Studies* 50(6): 716–731.

Chiweshe, M.K. and P. Mutopo. 2015. Class and race complexities in understanding large scale land deals as new forms of imperialism in Zimbabwe. In *The Palgrave encyclopedia of imperialism and anti-imperialism*, eds. I. Ness and Z. Cope, 293–307. New York: Palgrave McMillan.

Chiweshe, M.K. and P. Mutopo. 2014. National and international actors in the orchestration of land deals in Zimbabwe: What is in it for small holder farmers? In *International land deals in east and southern Africa*, ed. P. Mihyo, 243–274. Addis Ababa: OSSREA.

Enarson, E. 2000. *A gender analysis of work and employment issues in natural disasters*. Final report prepared for the In Focus Programme on Crisis and Reconstruction of the International Labour Organization. http://natlex.ilo.ch/wcmsp5/groups/public/@ed_emp/@emp_ent/@ifp_crisis/documents/publication/wcms_116391.pdf, accessed September 24, 2014.

Enarson, E. and B.H. Morrow. 1997. A gendered perspective: The voices of women. In *Hurricane Andrew: Race, gender and the sociology of disaster*, eds. W.G. Peacock, B.H. Morrow, and H. Gladwin, 116–140. London: Routledge.

Enarson, E. and B. Phillips. 2008. Invitation to a new feminist disaster sociology: Integrating feminist theory and methods. In *Women and disasters: From theory to practice*, eds. B. Phillips and B. Morrow, 41–74. Philadelphia: Xlibri.

Fothergill, A. 2004. *Heads above water: Gender, class and family in the Grand Forks flood*. Albany, NY: State University of New York Press.

Maponga, G. 2014. The gods must be angry. *The Herald*, February 15. http://www.herald.co.zw/the-gods-must-be-angry/, accessed August 12, 2015.

Marungwara, W. 2014. *The plight of internally-displaced communities: Case of Tokwe Mukosi in Zimbabwe*. Unpublished bachelor of arts honours thesis, Midlands State University, Zimbabwe.

Mazara, G. 2015. The forgotten people at Chingwizi, *Sunday Mail*, July 25. http://www.sundaymail.co.zw/?p=41182, accessed August 20, 2015.

Mtimba, G. 2014a. Lingering hardships after Tokwe Mukosi floods. *Daily News*, February 16. http://www.dailynews.co.zw/articles/2014/02/16/lingering-hardships-after-tokwe-mukosi-floods, accessed June 4, 2015.

Mtimba, G. 2014b. $1 for sex at Chingwizi. *The Weekend Post*. http://www.weekendpost.co.zw/articles/2014/07/11/1-for-sex-at-chingwizi, accessed May 19, 2015.

Mtimba, G. 2014c. 100 Chingwizi school girls pregnant. http://nehandaradio.com/2014/07/27/100-chingwizi-school-girls-pregnant/, accessed June 5, 2015.

Mugabe, M. 2014. *Corruption in Tokwe Mukosi dam disaster.* http://www.changezimbabwe.com/index.php/news-mainmenu-2/1-latest/4917-corruption-fingered-in-tokwe-mukosi-dam-disaster, accessed May 3, 2015.

Mujere, J. and S. Dombo. 2011. *Large scale investment projects and land grabs in Zimbabwe: The case of Nuanetsi Ranch bio-diesel project.* Paper presented at the International Conference on Global Land Grabbing, April 6–8, 2011, University of Sussex, Brighton, United Kingdom. http://www.future-agricultures.org/papers-and-presentations/conference-papers-2/1127-large-scale-investment-projects-and-land-grabs-in-zimbabwe-the-case-of-nuanetsi-ranch-bio-diesel/file, accessed June 4, 2015.

NewsDay. 2014. Sex-for-food at Chingwizi Camp. www.newzimbabwe.com/news-15933-Sex-for-food+at+Chingwizi+camp/news.aspx, accessed May 17, 2015.

Relief Web. 2014. *Update: Flood water over Tokwe Mukosi Dam.* http://reliefweb.int/sites/reliefweb.int/files/resources/UNOSAT_TokweMukorsiDam_20140218.pdf, accessed June 4, 2015.

Sachiti, R. 2014. Tokwe Mukosi: Tale of desolation, hope. *Herald*, February 26. http://www.herald.co.zw/tokwe-mukosi-tale-of-desolation-hope/, accessed June 5, 2015.

# Section III

## Community-Based Factors That Impact Resilience and Vulnerability

In the last section, multiple facets of communities are explored, along with how these dynamics shape and are shaped by disaster events. Community mechanisms for resilience and mobilization and organization building are explored in depth in this section. As will be discussed, emergent groups can hinder or help disaster preparation or mitigation strategies. In addition, scholars look at how dimensions such as faith and the composition of collective memory alter vulnerability and resilience, thereby impacting mitigation planning, emergency response, and rebuilding.

# 18 Vulnerability and Tourism Development

## *Fostering the Capacity of Resilience in the Context of Climate Change*

*Sara E. Alexander*

## CONTENTS



**Abstract**

This chapter examines the paradox of promoting coastal and marine tourism in Belize in the context of climate change. The study offers a comparative research protocol to understand the root causes and spatial distribution of differential vulnerability and the short and long-term effectiveness of various coping strategies that build resilience of local communities. My analysis indicates that vulnerable households respond with strategies that work to strengthen their capacity. The strongest resources indicated are capital assets; less common strategies were evident in the social and emotional arenas. A key ingredient for resilience is resource access and empowerment of marginal groups, yet the resilience of communities depends on the ability to act collectivity in the face of threats posed by climate change.

## INTRODUCTION

Climate variability and change are strongly implicated in the increasingly intense patterns of natural disasters and other climate events in the Caribbean. The El Niño-Southern Oscillation, droughts, and hurricanes, as well as sea level rise, lowered ocean pH, and increases in sea surface temperatures, affect marine species, exacerbate coral bleaching, cause upland and shoreline erosion, and destroy coastal habitats and human infrastructure (Adger, Hughes, Folke, Carpenter, and Rockstrom 2005; Greene and Pershing 2007; Harley et al. 2006). The Intergovernmental Panel on Climate Change's Mitigation of Climate Change Report (Edenhofer et al. 2014) lists small islands, low-lying areas, and river corridors as particularly vulnerable for the next half century. The Caribbean region is projected to experience a minimum 1.5°C increase and a 20% decline in precipitation by 2030 (United Nations Development Programme [UNDP] 2013). In a continuously changing climate, the ecological integrity of the region, particularly the reef and the goods and services it provides, will be further compromised (McField and Bood 2007).

This research focuses on vulnerability as determined by food insecurity, poverty, marginalization, socioeconomic status, ethnicity, household composition, and housing conditions (Adger, Brooks, Bentham, Agnew, and Eriksen 2004). Vulnerability encompasses factors that affect the degree to which a household's livelihood, property, and other assets are put at risk by identifiable events that occur in nature or society. The concept of vulnerability provides the means to measure the ability a household or community has "to anticipate, cope with, resist, and recover from the impact of [the] hazard" (Wisner, Blaikie, Cannon, and Davis 2004, p. 11). Vulnerability is usually juxtaposed against capacity; it refers to the combined strengths and resources available that can reduce the level of risk, or the effects of a disaster (International Strategy for Disaster Reduction 2004).

In this study, I identify four key elements of resilience: capacity for learning and adaptation, ability of a system to self-organize, competence for maintaining functions and feedbacks following stresses, and, at the household level, the means by which households access physical, social, or emotional resources to cope with climate-related events. The resilience of a community to respond to climate change depends on the ability to act collectively in the face of threats. Research in coastal environments demonstrates that security of social networks is an important element for coping with climate variability and hazards (Tompkins and Adger 2004).

Examining the social dynamics and outcomes of adaptation moves beyond accounting for the economic costs and benefits of certain behaviors. Therefore, one objective of this research is to explore the role social connectedness has in fostering resilience. To do this, I address the following topics: (1) the level of dependency that local populations have on natural resources and/or ideal weather conditions for their livelihoods, (2) their understanding of changing weather patterns in Belize, (3) the means by which households cope in crises and how resilience may be affected by their choices, and (4) the status of climate change policy directed towards mitigation and adaptation.

## SETTING THE STAGE

### Climate Change in the Mesoamerican Barrier Reef System (MBRS)

A recent assessment by the Healthy Reefs for Healthy People Initiative (2010) concludes that 30% of the reef in the Mesoamerican Barrier Reef System (MBRS) is in "critical" condition and 40% is in "poor" condition. Attention to the severity of threats was underscored in June 2009 when the United Nations Educational, Scientific, and Cultural Organization (UNESCO) placed the MBRS on the List of World Heritage in Danger, citing uncontrolled tourism development and climate change as major threats (UNESCO 2010). This system is unique in the Western Hemisphere for its size and array of reef types and coral diversity. Extending over 1000 km, the system forms a mosaic of seagrass meadows, lagoons, and mangrove forests, which have recently been threatened by mass bleaching events (Barton and Casey 2005).

An increase in temperature ranging from 2°C to 4°C is projected by 2100 for Belize, as is a 10% decline in annual rainfall. By 2030, reduced precipitation is predicted for the entire country; sea level rise is projected to exceed 10 cm along the coast (UNDP 2013). If the social and ecological systems within the MBRS are to adjust to these environmental changes, wise use, and interaction with resources are critical, as is defining measures to foster resilience within both the natural ecosystems and those communities that depend on them.

### Tourism Development in Belize

Over the last 15 years, Belize has transitioned from an economy dependent on agriculture to one largely reliant on reef-based tourism and associated service industries. Belize's economic growth rate averaged 1.18% from 1994 to 2015, with an all-time high of 13.45% in 2000 (Trading Economics 2015). This growth was stimulated by expansionary fiscal policies, including increased capital and social expenditures. The tourism industry is heavily dependent on the country's natural and cultural assets, particularly the reef resources. Based on a vulnerability assessment of the tourism sector conducted in 2006, 80% of visitors travel to Belize for reef-based activities (Richardson 2009).

The projected expansion of the tourism industry targets destinations along the coast and the reef. After an initial commitment to ecotourism, the government broadened its approach with contracts to international cruise lines. In 1998, the government adopted a strategic vision centered on responsible tourism (Blackstone Corporation 1998), the basic premise of which includes local stakeholder involvement, conservation of resources, dependency on local natural resources, and economic benefits for local residents. Indeed, the tourism sector has grown significantly since this initiative. This is demonstrated by the sheer numbers of cruise tourists. Growth is also related to the Belize Tourism Board's (BTB's) focus on improving soft adventure tourism in biologically diverse areas. Tourist arrivals, documented at all borders and international airports, increased from 176,054 in 1998 to 973,527 in 2013 (BTB 2013). Tourism receipts increased from $248 million in 2011 to $350 million in 2013 (World Bank 2015).

### Tourism and Climate Change Adaptation Policies

While the previous figures appear to be healthy from an economic standpoint, a 2007 Tourism Vulnerability Assessment determined that 45% to 70% of the tourism sector is vulnerable to the effects of climate change (Schneider et al. 2007). Projected impacts include loss of beaches, properties, and public infrastructure; saltwater intrusions, rising water tables, and poor water quality; higher temperatures; intensification in the size and duration of flooding; and damage to transport and other infrastructure. If visitor satisfaction rates decline and tourist arrivals fall, loss of employment would result. Currently, 70.9% of the population works in service industries (Central Intelligence Agency 2015).

While the government has begun initiatives to mainstream climate change into their national development plans, including the establishment of a National Climate Change Office, no formal national policy addressing mitigation and adaptation exists (David Simmons and Associates 2015). The European Union granted funding through the Global Climate Change Alliance to prepare a National Climate Change Policy, Strategy, and Action Plan, the intent of which is to address the adverse effects of climate change on the country's economic and social development. The government specifically identified tourism as a sector for national priority for climate change mitigation efforts.

In light of this, two plans to be revised are the National Sustainable Tourism Master Plan and the National Climate Resilience Investment Plan. Emphasis is to be given to enhancing climate resilience and improving disaster risk management capacities across all sectors (UNDP 2013). The National Emergency Management Organization (NEMO) has been charged to "promote a culture of safety and community resilience, especially regarding climate variability, change and adaptation" (NEMO 2015). NEMO is responsible for disaster mitigation, public preparedness, response, recovery, and reconstruction. They send out three-day early warnings for tropical storms and hurricanes, enforce the forced evacuation regulations for tourists located in areas under threat of a hurricane, and after storms, assist in recovery and rehabilitation (NEMO 2015).

## RESEARCH DESIGN AND METHODS

This research involves a reliable, comparative, and spatially sensitive protocol to assess vulnerability (Adger, Brooks, Bentham, Agnew, and Eriksen 2004; Alexander 2008) with a specific focus on how households respond to climate-related events. The field research extended over a 2-year period, beginning July 1, 2007. The research team was comprised of three field directors (doctoral students in anthropology), two master's students, and nine Belizean field assistants, who were postsecondary students and local residents of respective study sites. Data were collected using empirical and quantitative methods and integrating participatory techniques to map communities, including local-level vulnerabilities (Salkind 2011).

The primary criteria for community selection were matches for economic sectors, shared regional history, local administrative structures, livelihood strategies, physical proximity to protected areas or other key resources, and, because of the relationship between genetic endowment and anthropometric measures, ethnicity (Alexander and Whitehouse 2004). Sites were chosen along the coastal region to illuminate the effects of national-level policies for environmental protection and tourism development. Additional criteria included those variables described by the International Union for Conservation of Nature to establish protected area categories: level of protection, protection rationale, and the types of access allowed (Ceballos-Lascuráin 1996).

All three study communities are located in proximity to transboundary Marine Protected Areas within the MBRS (see Figure 18.1). San Pedro, on Ambergris Caye, is the oldest tourism destination in the country. Since the early 1980s, residents have abandoned commercial fishing and transitioned to reef-based tourism. Placencia is located at the end of a 22-km narrow peninsula and took a direct hit from Hurricane Iris in 2001, resulting in 95% structure loss (Avila 2001). Punta Gorda's economy is more diversified, relying on commercial fishing, shrimping, logging, and Maya-based cultural tourism. These communities are highly susceptible to tropical storms, hurricanes, and resultant flooding. They have also recently experienced rapid socioeconomic change, given tourism

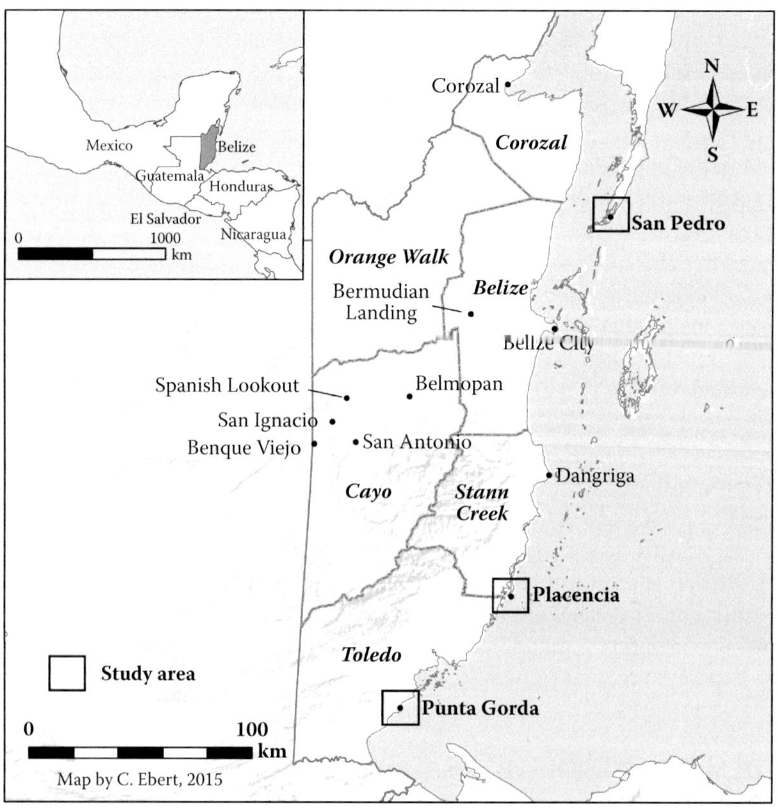


FIGURE 18.1 Study communities in Belize.

expansion and the establishment of Marine Protected Areas regulating certain types of resource access (Stonich 2008).

### Field Methods

Data were first collected using key informant interviews and community mapping techniques to identify households by locally defined levels of security and vulnerability. As part of the survey design process, the field directors interviewed 26 local leaders, business owners, health care workers, and long-term residents, chosen using purposive sampling based on length of residence and occupation (Bernard 2006). This was done to elicit retrospective data about former climate-related experiences and to gauge local participation in response to these crises.

The household survey was designed based on the household livelihood security framework (Chambers and Conway 1992), where baseline data on the capacities, assets, and activities required for a means of living are used to determine a household's degree of livelihood security or vulnerability. Livelihood strategies are the means for understanding the way people cope with crises. Unequal access to resources and possible resulting poverty is one of the factors that drives vulnerability to shocks (Hartmann and Standing 1989). Resources required for people's livelihoods to be secure are rarely distributed evenly in geographic space. In most situations, the spatial inequality of access is a reflection of economic and social inequalities (Wisner, Blaikie, Cannon, and Davis 2004).

The survey sample was chosen using a random number generator based on households identified from the community maps; this method ensures a representative sample of households (Bernard 2006). Sample size was the largest feasible percentage of households in each community given time and financial constraints. A total of 299 households were sampled (104 in San Pedro, 77 in Placencia, and 118 in Punta Gorda). The survey data were used to identify the nature and extent of household dependency on natural resources for their livelihood, to determine awareness levels of recent weather patterns, and to ascertain coping strategies used in response to recent climate events. Economic activities, extent and nature of social networks, and sense of connectedness were also documented, as they influence the type and extent of safety nets available to households.

A neighborhood cohesion analysis was included to measure the "psychological sense of community attraction-to-neighborhood and social interaction within a neighborhood" (Buckner 1988, p. 771). An individual-level variable was constructed; the mean value indicates a measure of the neighborhood's cohesiveness, that is, the feelings of unity and social connectedness that a person has with regard to his/her local community. Eighteen questions were posed, with responses using a Likert scale format. These were summed to create a Neighborhood Cohesion Score. The higher the score, the more connected a person feels with his/her community.

## FINDINGS: WEATHER, CLIMATE, RISK, AND COPING RESPONSES

### Dependency on Natural Resources

Belize is a biologically diverse country with roughly 43% of terrestrial land in protective status and 18 Marine Protected Areas (McField and Bood 2007). Organizations, including, the government, World Wildlife Fund, Belize Audubon Society, along with evolving support from local, community-based not-for-profit organizations, such as Green Reef Belize in San Pedro and Friends of Nature in Placencia, have placed increasing importance on conservation of the region's diverse resources. This is viewed as a key strategy for protecting the tourism industry. Seventy-one percent of adults in San Pedro work for tourism businesses or protected areas, and 82% and 37% in Placenica and Punta Gorda, respectively.

Do respondents understand that their livelihoods depend on a healthy natural resource base? Their acknowledgement of this dependence may contribute to the nature of their coping strategies

**TABLE 18.1**
**Dependence on Natural Resources and Weather**[a]

| | San Pedro ($n$ = 104) | Placencia ($n$ = 77) | Punta Gorda ($n$ = 118) | Total ($n$ = 299) |
|---|---|---|---|---|
| Direct dependence on natural resource(s) for 1° occupation | 52.0 | 62.3 | 21.2 | 45.2 |
| Is weather where you live ever a problem in your life? | 54.6 | 39.2 | 41.2 | 45 |
| Is the work you do to support your household influenced by the weather? | 67.7 | 70.3 | 26.7 | 54.9 |
| Last year, did you experience any weather-related events that affected your ability to earn a living? | 51.4 | 34.2 | 21.7 | 35.8 |

[a] All figures indicate percentage of positive responses.

following a climate-related event. Thus, they would take into account natural resource conditions as they make choices not only regarding their personal recovery but also for the tourism businesses they own or for whom they work. Table 18.1 indicates the acknowledged degree of resource dependency for households and businesses. Residents in San Pedro (52%) and Placencia (62.3%) had the highest level of self-reported, acknowledged dependency on a natural resource for their work.

## Understanding Changing Weather Patterns

Recent weather patterns for Belize indicate the following trends from 1960 to 2006: change of +0.11°C per decade, decline in precipitation by 3.2 mm per decade, and 5-day rainfall patterns increasing by 5.37 mm per decade (Richardson 2009). There was an average of 2.6 hurricanes or tropical storms per decade, with nine hurricanes occurring over the last six years. Between 1995 and 2005, the reef was threatened by three mass bleaching events that coincided with elevated sea temperatures (Barton and Casey 2005).

Approximately 68% and 70% of residents in San Pedro and Placencia, respectively, indicate that their livelihood is influenced by the weather. Slightly over 50% of San Pedro respondents also said they had experienced weather-related problems in their work over the past year. It should be noted that two category 5 hurricanes hit San Pedro within a three-week period in 2007—Dean (August 21) and Felix (September 4).

Recent weather patterns would suggest to local residents that weather is changing. Their knowledge and understanding of these patterns, and whether their knowledge impacts their actual behavior, are critical to the process of fostering resilience after an event. My evidence suggests that, based on personal experience and educational programs provided by local and national organizations, including NEMO, residents recognize recent weather changes; they cite hurricanes, high winds, and tropical storms as the new normal of coastal life. Table 18.2 shows affirmative responses made to statements referring to weather patterns over the last 5–10 years. Of the 10 statements, 7 are factual—false statements were included as a validity check to ensure respondents were reading every statement and not merely checking off the identical response through all of the questions. For the patterns most relevant to tourism businesses, the majority of respondents indicate high levels of accurate understanding. For example, 78.5% correctly report there have been "hotter temperatures," and 74.2% recount that there have been "changes in when it rains."

The weather awareness questions are followed by a section eliciting information regarding behaviors related to the last three major storms experienced by the communities. These were Hurricanes Iris in 2001 and Dean and Felix in 2007. Respondents were asked to reflect on the nature and source of information regarding the imminent risk, the preparations they made prior to

**TABLE 18.2**
**Perceptions of Changes in the Weather over the Last 5–10 Years[a]**

| | San Pedro (*n* = 104) | Placencia (*n* = 77) | Punta Gorda (*n* = 118) | Total (*n* = 299) |
|---|---|---|---|---|
| There has been more rainfall[b] | 50.0 | 31.3 | 48.3 | 43.2 |
| There has been changes in when it rains | 77.1 | 88.1 | 57.4 | 74.2 |
| There have been more hurricanes | 67.1 | 56.7 | 65.2 | 63.0 |
| Hurricanes have been more destructive than before | 66.3 | 75.8 | 57.8 | 66.6 |
| There has been more flooding | 67.5 | 37.3 | 62.1 | 55.6 |
| There has been more drought | 56.6 | 50 | 55.3 | 54.0 |
| We have had hotter temperatures | 86.6 | 71.2 | 77.6 | 78.5 |
| We have had colder temperatures[b] | 62.7 | 52.2 | 39.1 | 51.3 |
| There have been more heat waves[b] | 78.3 | 65.7 | 69.6 | 71.2 |
| More people get malaria, dengue, skin infections, or diarrhea than in the past | 45.7 | 32.8 | 52.7 | 43.7 |

[a] All figures represent percentage of respondents who indicated "I agree" to the statement.
[b] These statements are not true, e.g., there has been less amount of rainfall rather than more as indicated in the statement.

the storm, decisions regarding the physical location they chose for themselves and their household members during the storm, and their means for recovery of any losses incurred.

## Responses to Recent Current Events

This research began in all three communities simultaneously in July 2007 and extended through June 2009. The field research teams were in the study communities before both Dean and Felix hit San Pedro directly and caused damage along the coast of Belize. The survey was constructed such that respondents were asked to provide details of storms they had experienced; Hurricanes Iris, Dean, and Felix were specifically referenced as all of the study communities had experienced impacts from these storms. Given their magnitude and the fact that surveys were conducted shortly after Dean and Felix, I estimate that the responses are highly accurate.

Residents of the communities know that when a climate-related event is forecast, they must assist in the evacuation of tourists, make decisions regarding their own evacuation, lose a number of work days, and perhaps incur significant property loss. All of the study communities experienced significant flooding and a number of tropical storms or hurricanes over the last 10 years. Respondents were asked about their coping behaviors before an event and in the aftermath. These data were collapsed into four broad categories: "secure financial resources"; "build or repair," which includes securing structures prior to the event; "assistance from family or friends"; and "seeking solace—feeling spiritual or emotional." In the discussion of responses here, the percentage indicated is based on the total sample from all three communities. Response categories are not mutually exclusive, as respondents could indicate multiple coping strategies. Also, some activities clearly overlap, such as securing finances for repair and the time and labor spent completing that repair.

Fifty-four percent of households indicate "secure financial resources" as a coping mechanism. These households use savings or borrow from a bank, friends, or family to help meet expenses they have before and after the event. These funds were used to meet basic needs, support costs associated with evacuation, and to purchase physical materials to secure property before the storm and make repairs after the event. Fifty-two percent would evacuate under any circumstances; the remaining 48% make those decisions on a case-by-case basis. Forty-seven percent list to "build or repair" as one of their coping strategies. This indicates that they, family members, or friends have property damage, and physical work and time are invested in repairing structures, such as personal homes, business offices, restaurants, hotels, docks, and/or boats.

Thirty-two percent ask for "assistance from family or friends." The neighborhood cohesion score indicates whether residents feel they can go to family and/or friends for help and vice versa. The average score is 55.16, out of a possible range of 26 to 77, with a standard deviation of 10.6. This score indicates a strong sense of social connectedness. When a major shock, such as a hurricane, occurs to someone in or to the community-at-large, the score indicates a strong tendency toward sharing, cooperation, and a willingness to help those in need. This assistance usually supports meeting basic needs, such as food, clothing, or temporary lodging. These residents had little to no financial safety nets and no immediate plans to rebuild, either because they had no savings, did not qualify for emergency relief, or were unable to secure a loan. Spending time with family or friends provided them a feeling of safety and being confident of protection in a time of insecurity.

Twenty-three percent report "seeking solace—feeling spiritual/emotional" as one of their coping strategies. These responses are kept separate from the social network responses because many respondents did not necessarily want to be with anyone else. Rather, they seek solace in their religious beliefs or reference feeling "emotional." Some talked about being depressed, while others were anxious or stressed. However, they did not want to find employment or begin rebuilding or repairing structures. Their priority was to feel emotionally secure and to make efforts to address any depression or feelings of loss they were experiencing after the storm.

## DISCUSSION

Residents in coastal communities in Belize recognize their dependency on ideal weather and natural resources that are in good condition for their tourism-based livelihoods. Having a healthy resource base along the coastal region to support a thriving marine tourism economy necessitates a healthy reef. Respondents acknowledge the importance of changing weather and increases in surface temperature of the sea, as it affects the health of the coral and general condition of the reef. They also recognize how these trends can ultimately affect their livelihood security. One of the primary mandates of the National Climate Change Policy, Strategy, and Action Plan is to educate the general public and ensure those working in the tourism industry comply with all mandates to conserve and protect the natural resources of the country, as stipulated in the policy. Several dive shop managers, who were survey respondents, relayed efforts that the Belize Tourism Board is making to educate tourists regarding their behavior when they go snorkeling or diving and the impacts they can potentially have on the health of the reef.

The majority of study respondents have an accurate understanding of recent changes in weather patterns, recognize impending climate events as a threat to themselves and their livelihoods, and have, at a minimum, informal preparation plans for when large storms are approaching. Roughly 55% of survey respondents recognize that the work they do to support their household is influenced by the weather; 45% acknowledge that weather where they live is "a problem in [their] life." All of the respondents working directly with tourists in their primary occupations (42%) are committed to enforcing the government's regulations to evacuate all tourists from coastal areas when mandated. Given the NEMO early warnings now in place, most feel safe knowing they will receive this warning and maintain they are prepared for any event. They hear about the forecast, check their devices to receive weather updates, and begin to make decisions as to how they will prepare.

Over the last decade, the significant progress NEMO has made to upgrade warning systems to more effectively reach at-risk populations has proven effective for those working in the tourism industry. Those respondents working in hotels or guesthouses rely on these warnings to evacuate guests in a timely manner, as stipulated by NEMO, by boat from San Pedro and by bus from Placencia and Punta Gorda. All residents who remain in their communities are required to have the physical resources and the time to board up buildings, bring boats on land, and guarantee sufficient food and water stocks.

In reference to coping strategies employed by local residents, evidence indicates that households respond in various ways. Relative to their immediate needs, these strategies demonstrate resilience. The one area indicating more mixed results involves asking for assistance from friends and family. While hesitant to do this, 28% of those engaging in this practice also expressed frustration that they were not able to secure financial resources easily. They were annoyed that they did not qualify for emergency relief and disappointed that they were not able to secure bank loans. Turning to family and friends for help was not necessarily their first choice, but it was an option that helped meet their most immediate needs.

Communities also have inherent capacities to respond to severe climate events, which are manifested in the ability of groups to act collectively. The level of social connectedness, indicated in the neighborhood cohesion score, can influence the ability of these communities to effectively self-organize and to learn from others. A community that indicates closeness may organize more efficiently, both pre- and post Spanish lookout event, as residents work collectively without conflict. Social cohesion, along with information provided by NEMO and local organizations, can also help provide a conducive setting for learning effective coping behaviors that may prove to be more successful in the future.

## CONCLUSION

The capacity of individuals to be resilient in their response to climate events is a function of a number of factors: access to resources and information, possessing the willingness and having the environment that supports a learning process, having households and the communities in which they live be able to act collectively in the face of the threats posed by repeated climate events, and having support mechanisms to allow households to make the choices that they feel allows them to cope in meaningful ways. Examining responses over the course of the three most recent hurricanes in Belize demonstrates that households in these coastal communities have developed a range of strategic coping behaviors that foster resilience in the face of climate events. Evidence shows that communities have "learned" from responses over time. Findings indicate levels of cooperation through the sharing of financial and/or physical resources. They also demonstrate that some members resort to an emotional adjustment period, seeking consolation or spiritual support with little attention paid to rebuilding physical structures.

NEMO, in their charge to develop strategies for residents to feel safe and to focus on improving community resilience, has played an important role in strengthening linkages between residents, local administrative units, and national agencies. Community residents have begun to believe that their government cares about their livelihoods and the resource base on which they depend for economic security. These actions have helped to foster higher levels of trust, in turn, creating an environment where communities can improve their capacity for learning and cooperation in times of crisis.

While most citizens are unaware of the formulation of a National Climate Change Policy, local government leaders know about the goals that the national government is working toward. These include efforts to prepare for the longer-term impacts of climate change that could threaten the viability of the tourism industry. In one study community, the Mayor plans to involve residents in the feedback process when it begins in 2018. These efforts to foster local empowerment can only help to strengthen community ability to self-organize and mobilize, enhance their overall competence, and foster learning and capacity building over time.

## ACKNOWLEDGMENT

I gratefully acknowledge funding support from the National Oceanic and Atmospheric Administration's Sectoral Applications Research Program: NOAA grant number NA070AR4310409.

## REFERENCES


Adger, N., N. Brooks, G. Bentham, M. Agnew, and S. Eriksen. 2004. *New indicators of vulnerability and adaptive capacity*. Norwich: Tyndall Center for Climate Change Research, Technical Report 7.

Adger, W.N., T. Hughes, C. Folke, S. Carpenter, and J. Rockstrom. 2005. Social ecological resilience to coastal disasters. *Science* 309(5737): 1036–1039.

Alexander, S. 2008. The resilience of vulnerable households: Adjusting to neoliberal capitalism in the aftermath of Hurricane Iris. In *Capitalizing on catastrophe: Neoliberal strategies in disaster reconstruction*, eds. N. Gunewardena and M. Schuller, 93–113. New York: Alta Mira Press.

Alexander, S. and J. Whitehouse. 2004. Challenges for balancing conservation and development through ecotourism: Insights and implications from two Belizean case studies. In *Sustainable tourism 2004*, eds. F. Pineda and C. Brebbia, 129–142. Southampton, UK: Wessex Institute of Technology Press.

Avila, L.A. 2001. *Tropical cyclone report: Hurricane Iris*. Washington, DC: National Oceanic and Atmospheric Administration.

Barton, A. and K. Casey. 2005. Climatologically context for large-scale coral bleaching. *Coral Reefs* 24(4): 536–554.

Belize Tourism Board. 2013. *Travel and tourism statistics*. CD. Belize City, Belize: Belize Tourism Board.

Bernard, R. 2006. *Research methods in anthropology: Qualitative and quantitative approaches*. Walnut Creek: Altamira Press.

Blackstone Corporation. 1998. *A tourism strategy plan for Belize*. Toronto, Canada: Blackstone Resource Management and Tourism Consultants.

Buckner, J.C. 1988. The development of an instrument to measure neighborhood cohesion. *American Journal of Community Psychology* 16(6): 771–791.

Ceballos-Lascuráin, H. 1996. *Tourism, ecotourism and protected areas*. Rome: International Union for Conservation of Nature.

Central Intelligence Agency. 2015. World factbook for Belize. https://www.cia.gov/library/publications/the-world-factbook/geos/bh.html, accessed November 5, 2015.

Chambers, R. and G. Conway. 1992. *Sustainable rural livelihoods: Practical concepts for the 21st century*. Institute of Development Studies Discussion Paper 296. Brighton, U.K.: Institute of Development Studies.

David Simmons and Associates, Ltd. 2015. *A national climate change policy, strategy and action plan to address climate change in Belize*. Belmopan: Caribbean Community Climate Change Center.

Edenhofer, O., R. Pichs-Madruga, Y. Sokona, E. Farahani, S. Kadner, K. Seyboth, A. Adler, I. Baum, S. Brunner, P. Eickemeier, B. Kriemann, J. Savolainen, S. Schlömer, C. von Stechow, T. Zwickel, and J.C. Minx. 2014. *Climate change 2014: Mitigation of climate change. Contribution of Working Group III to the Fifth Assessment Report of the Intergovernmental Panel on Climate Change*. Cambridge: Cambridge University Press, Intergovernmental Panel on Climate Change.

Greene, C. and A. Pershing. 2007. Oceans. Climate drives sea change. *Science* 315(5815): 1084–1085.

Harley, C., A.R. Hughes, K. Hultgren, B. Miner, C. Sorte, C. Thornber, L. Rodriguez, L. Tomanek, and S. Williams. 2006. The impacts of climate change in coastal marine systems. *Ecology Letters* 9(2): 228–241.

Hartmann, B. and H. Standing. 1989. *The poverty of population control: Family planning and health policy in Bangladesh*. London: Bangladesh International Action Group.

Healthy Reefs for Healthy People Initiative. 2010. *Report card for the Mesoamerican reef*. Belize City, Belize: Healthy Reefs for Healthy People Initiative. http://healthyreefs.org, accessed November 4, 2015.

International Strategy for Disaster Reduction. 2004. *Living with risk, a global review of disaster reduction initiatives*. www.unisdr.org, accessed October 12, 2015.

McField, M. and N. Bood. 2007. *Our reef in peril—Can we use it without abusing it?* Rome: United Nations Development Programme/Global Environment Facility.

National Emergency Management Organization. 2015. Hurricane tracking. http://site.nemo.org.bz/preparedness-guidelines/hurricane-tracking, accessed November 28, 2015.

Richardson, R. 2009. *Belize and climate change: The costs of inaction*. Belmopan: United Nations Development Programme, Human Development Issues Paper.

Salkind, N.J. 2011. *Exploring research*, 8th ed. Essex, UK: Pearson Education Limited.

Schneider, S., S. Semenov, A. Patwardhan, I. Burton, C. Magadza, M. Oppenheimer, A.B. Pittock, A. Rahman, J.B. Smith, A. Suarez, and F. Yamin. 2007. Assessing key vulnerabilities and the risk from climate change. In *Climate Change 2007: Impacts, adaptation and vulnerability. Contribution of Working*

*Group II to the fourth assessment report of the Intergovernmental Panel on Climate Change*, eds. M.L. Parry, O.F. Canziani, J.P. Palutikof, P.J. van der Linden, and C.E. Hanson, 779–810. Cambridge, UK: Cambridge University Press.

Stonich, S. 2008. (Eco)tourism and marine protected areas in a time of climate change. In *Ecotourism and conservation in the Americas*, eds. A. Stronza and W. Durham, 51–65. Oxfordshire and Cambridge: CABI International.

Tompkins, E. and W.N. Adger. 2004. Does adaptive management of natural resources enhance resilience to climate change? *Ecology and Society* 9(2): 1–14.

Trading Economics. 2015. Economic statistics for Belize. http://www.tradingeconomics.com/belize/gdp-growth, accessed November 2, 2015.

United Nations Educational, Scientific, and Cultural Organization. 2010. List of world heritage in danger. World Heritage Convention. http://whc.unesco.org/en/list/764, accessed March 15, 2011.

United Nations Development Programme. 2013. Draft country programme document for Belize, 2013–2017. http://www.bz.undp.org/content/dam/belize/docs/UNDP%20BZ%20Publications/Country%20Programme%20Document%202013%20to%202017.pdf, accessed October 5, 2015.

Wisner, B., P. Blaikie, T. Cannon, and I. Davis. 2004. *At risk: Natural hazards, people's vulnerability and disasters*, 2nd ed. London: Routledge.

World Bank. 2015. *International tourism, receipts (current US$)*. Washington, DC: World Bank. http://data.worldbank.org/indicator/ST.INT.RCPT.CD, accessed November 3, 2015.

# 19 Why Isn't There a Plan? *Community Vulnerability and Resilience in the Latrobe Valley's Open Cut Coal Mine Town*

*Michelle Duffy, Pamela Wood, Sue Whyte, Susan Yell, and Matthew Carroll*

## CONTENTS



**Abstract**

On February 9, 2014, the town of Morwell in Victoria, Australia, was confronted with several bushfires, resulting in a blaze at the Morwell open cut coal mine adjacent to the Hazelwood power station. For 45 days, the local communities were impacted by smoke, ash, and reports of raised carbon monoxide levels. The duration of the crisis placed an unprecedented strain on the capacity of the community and the authorities to adequately respond. Many see Morwell as vulnerable to future events because it is surrounded by coal mines, power stations, forests, and pine plantations. Drawing on interviews from key stakeholders in the community and a detailed analysis of media reports and social media, this chapter examines the factors that both harm and promote community resilience. It emphasizes the complexity of resilience and the importance of communal narratives as community members react to and recover from traumatic experiences and unknown futures.

## INTRODUCTION

On February 9, 2014, the town of Morwell in the Latrobe Valley, Victoria, Australia, was confronted with several bushfires, which resulted in a blaze at the Morwell open cut coal mine adjacent to the Hazelwood power station. This event became known as the Hazelwood Mine Fire. After 45 days, the mine was declared safe, but smoke emissions continued for some time. The impact was felt across the Latrobe Valley, but Morwell was most impacted and, at times, "overwhelmed" (Hazelwood Mine Fire Inquiry 2014b, p. 257) by smoke and ash.

The township of Morwell is about 150 kilometers from Melbourne and has a population of about 14,000 people. The wider Latrobe Valley has a population of almost 74,000 (Australian Bureau of Statistics 2015). The Latrobe Valley is home to one of the largest brown coal deposits in the world, making the region central to Victoria's power generation (Department of Economic Development, Jobs, Transport, and Resources 2015). Immediately south of Morwell is the Morwell open cut coal mine, which supplies coal to the nearby Hazelwood power station (see Figure 19.1).

Prior to the Hazelwood Mine Fire, the health status of Morwell and the Latrobe Valley was already disadvantaged. A 1996 study into the burden of disease in Victoria showed "the Gippsland region, and in particular the Latrobe Valley, had a higher than state average of healthy years lost due to disease" (Hazelwood Mine Fire Inquiry 2014b, p. 250), with "males in the Latrobe Valley [having] the largest number of years lost to disease of any area in Gippsland" (p. 251). Vulnerable groups include "an ageing population with a high incidence of cardiovascular and respiratory disease" and a high percentage of "low-income households and a higher percentage of residents who have a disability" (Hazelwood Mine Fire Inquiry 2014b, p. 23).

The health of the community is inextricably linked to the power industry; privatization of the industry in 1996 resulted in a significant socioeconomic decline (Department of Education and

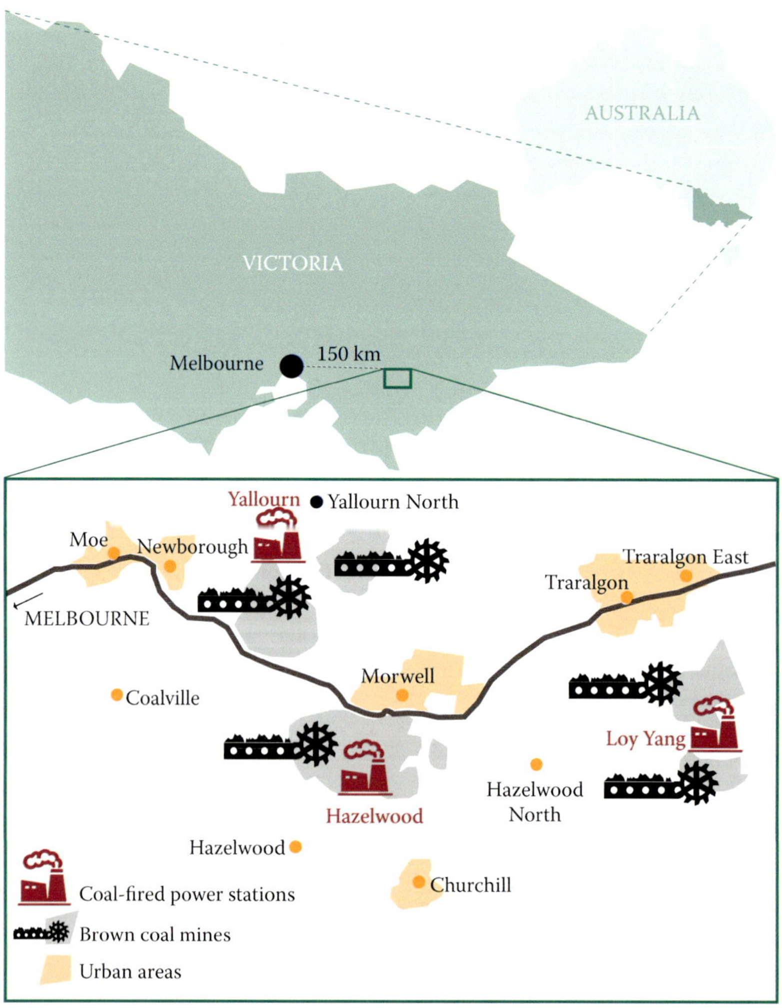


**FIGURE 19.1** Latrobe Valley coal precinct. (Courtesy of Coretex.)

Early Childhood Development 2012). The Hazelwood Mine Fire was the latest in a series of mine-related impacts on the Morwell community (Victorian Council of Social Services [VCOSS] 2015), including a small, but significant, movement that occurred in the northern wall of the Hazelwood Mine following a period of heavy rain in 2011 (Langmore 2013). This led to closure of the major highway running alongside it due to drainage problems. This movement also resulted in cracks forming in residential properties adjacent to the mine (Department of Economic Development, Jobs, Transport, and Resources 2012).

During the fire, health professionals anecdotally reported that residents presented with respiratory and other physical symptoms, along with general health and well-being concerns related to the fire. This small-scale qualitative project investigates the community's perception of the fire's initial impact on its health and well-being. This study is not designed to gather specific health information about individuals. Rather, it contributes to a better understanding of the way the community's resilience is affected and how the community perceived its capacity to respond effectively to any similar event in the future.

## AN OVERVIEW OF RESILIENCE AND VULNERABILITY

Resilience has become an important part of the rhetoric in devising strategies and policy for addressing a diverse range of challenges faced by communities. Yet, there has been little critical engagement with how it has been mobilized beyond the promise of "business as usual…or even business that is better than usual in the face of a threat" (O'Hare and White 2013, p. 275). Resilience may be defined as the capacity of an individual, community, or environmental systems to cope with stress, overcome adversity, and/or adapt positively to change (Maguire and Cartwright 2008). However, the appropriation of resilience from its original use and into a variety of frameworks and disciplines has led to tensions between stakeholders involved in shaping urban and regional environments, as well as within the communities that policy and practice seek to support (O'Hare and White 2013; Reid and Botterrill 2013).

Within government frameworks, protection against individual and community vulnerability has begun to focus on measuring indicators of community well-being. Well-being has been defined as "a state of being with others, which arises where human needs are met…and where one can enjoy a satisfactory quality of life" (McGregor 2008, p. 4). Scholars agree that central to ensuring a resilient community is the need to enable individuals to feel connected such that a stable society is valued and actively maintained (Doyal and Gough 1991; Gough 2004; McGregor, Camfield, and Woodcock 2009). In this framework, social cohesion plays an important role in building a set of shared values, which facilitates a sense that individuals are engaged in facing shared challenges. All communities are different, but at the heart of resilient communities is a sense of belonging, a feeling of being connected, and the capacity to participate in community life. Research into the impact of natural disasters on community resilience also identifies the importance of trust and effective partnerships between communities and official agencies responsible for disaster management and recovery (Sharp, Thwaites, Millar, and Curtis 2009; Thornley, Ball, Signal, Lawson-Te Aho, and Rawson 2015). As this chapter demonstrates, the various formal and informal responses to the Hazelwood Mine Fire and its immediate aftermath point to a more complex set of processes involved in a community's capacity for resilience.

## METHODOLOGY

This study uses qualitative research methodology (Sandelowski 2010), including interviews with key informants and media analysis. Both were designed to capture perceptions of the mine fire's initial impact on community health and well-being. The two sources of research material were analyzed separately in order to identify key themes and then compared. This enables reflexive triangulation of data sources of community concerns and strengthens the findings of the study (Flick 1992; Hammersley and Atkinson 1983).

### Interviews with Key Informants

Semistructured interviews were conducted with key informants from the Morwell community. Purposive and snowball sampling strategies were used to recruit employees or volunteers in organizations working in Morwell in ways that contributed to the community. Potential participants were identified through the research team's networks with the community and through publicly available information about community groups and social organizations. Contact was made directly with individuals, where appropriate, or with the contact person of a service, organization, or group to request participants. Key informants were drawn from health, education, social support agencies and organizations, and community groups. Participants' perspectives as residents, or as people in professional or community roles, enabled them to comment on the initial impact of the mine fire and associated smoke event on the community's health and well-being.

The purposive sampling strategy ensured that a range of viewpoints was obtained. Nineteen key informants, including residents, volunteers, or employees, were interviewed. One interview session was conducted with two people, another with four people. In terms of stakeholder representation, eight interviews were conducted with representatives (most often the chief executive officer, manager, president, or principal) of professional community agencies and seven interviews with representatives from volunteer community organizations. Interviewees were assured of anonymity. This recruitment method and sample size aligns with accepted conventions in qualitative exploratory research (Ritchie, Lewis, and Nicholls 2014; Sandelowski 1995). Interview transcripts were analyzed to identify themes relating to community perceptions of the mine fire's initial impact on community health and well-being.

### Media Analysis

Analysis of the news coverage during the 45-day period of the Hazelwood Mine Fire was undertaken to identify themes regarding the way the health and well-being aspects of the fire were presented and discussed through different media, including social media. Researchers collected all articles mentioning the mine fire between February 9 and March 25, 2014. Data collection focused on locally produced media: the local newspaper (the *Latrobe Valley Express*), the regional radio and online news service, ABC Regional, and the Facebook site for the activist group that formed in response to the crisis (Voices of the Valley, www.votv.org.au/). The findings from the analysis of local news and social media showed an alignment with the findings from the analysis of interviews.

## FINDINGS

Media coverage of the fire and smoke event, community members' responses expressed through social media, and the interviews with key informants provide some of the communal narratives operating in Morwell and the wider Latrobe Valley community. While there was no single, unified communal narrative, there were common themes. Many were negative—mistrust, abandonment, and fear. Some of the differences arise from longer-standing divisions within the community, perceptions of who could speak with authority as representing the community, and different views on the way forward. The perceptions and experiences of the mine fire, as discussed by participants and presented in the media, compound the issues of economic and health disadvantage already faced by vulnerable groups in Morwell. However, three main and interconnecting factors have had a particularly negative impact on both individual and community resilience: perceived failures in the emergency response and the sense of there being no community-wide emergency plan, inadequacy of the information provided and the way it was communicated, and concerns about the impact of exposure to the smoke on future health.

A recurring theme was the belief that the state government, state authorities, GDF Suez (the company that owns the mine), and the community were ill-prepared for such an event. Some respondents believed Morwell was abandoned, that "Melbourne doesn't care about the Morwell community, only about their electricity" (Professional, Organization 1). There was a sense that there was no community emergency plan during the crisis or subsequently:

> I think it would be really good...if there is a clear plan of what the community needs to do if it happens again. That really needs to be well articulated...It's nearly the anniversary and we still have nothing. (Professional, Organization 8)

Contributing to this is the perceived inadequacy of information and communication provided to the community. Terms such as "inconsistent," "contradictory," "inadequate," and "poorly delivered" were used. The Department of Health repeatedly advised that "prolonged exposure to smoke is not likely to cause long-term health issues" for residents (Department of Health 2014; Nelson 2014b, p. 3). They simultaneously advised at public meetings, via the media, and through health alerts on their website that acute exposure was very serious for women and children but was not currently posing a threat to the community (Charalambous 2014). Local general practitioners, Latrobe Regional Hospital, and Ambulance Victoria reported increased numbers of patients with respiratory issues (Charalambous 2014); carbon monoxide levels were reported as fluctuating (ABC News Online 2014). This conflicting advice left a legacy of mistrust toward government at all levels, state agencies, particularly the Department of Health (now Department of Health and Human Services) and the Environment Protection Authority, which monitors air quality, and mine owner GDF Suez.

People were worried about immediate and future health impacts, particularly for their children, and wanted to know what was in the air they were breathing. Local and social media reported that residents were experiencing numerous physical symptoms of smoke inhalation, including itchy eyes, sore throat, bleeding or runny noses, coughing, wheezing, chest tightness, and difficulty breathing (Darroch 2014; Dunstan 2014; Nelson 2014a; Voices of the Valley Facebook 11/03/2014, post 9). Asthmatics and those with heart conditions were warned to avoid breathing the smoke; paper masks, primarily used to filter particulate matter rather than gases, were made available to residents to wear outside on days of poor air quality (Nelson 2014c).

Carbon monoxide exposure was raised by members of the community and emergency and health professionals as a potentially dangerous health risk (Anderson 2014a; Caldwell 2014; Nelson 2014a). There were three key time periods of significantly elevated levels of pollution (primarily particulate matter 2.5 and carbon monoxide) in February: 15–18, 21–25, and 26–28 (Hazelwood Mine Fire Inquiry 2014b, p. 266). The Country Fire Authority (CFA), Environment Protection Authority, and the Department of Health were also alert to the potential risk to public health, although the readings taken "were not considered to be a health concern" (Hazelwood Mine Fire Inquiry 2014b, p. 9). However, local media reported that 20 firefighters were checked into the hospital for exposure to carbon monoxide (Caldwell 2014). A carbon monoxide alert was also issued for Morwell by the CFA via text message to a "defined group of residents located close to the mine" (Hazelwood Mine Fire Inquiry 2014b, p. 332) and reported in the local media (Nelson 2014a, p. 3). Residents heard information via the news media, which was quite alarming, yet this did not correspond with the health messages issued by authorities.

A particular grievance for the community was that health authorities continued to insist for some time that the level of exposure to smoke and poor air quality was not harmful (ABC 7.30 Report 2014). One resident noted that it was simply to keep the public calm, like "stun[ning] cattle before they put them in the knock box" (Voices of the Valley Facebook 03/16/14, post 10). A recurring theme among interviewees was the belief that they were not told the truth about potential health issues. They wanted transparent and honest information and communication. They wanted reassurance that, if there were future health impacts, the community would be looked after. Such concerns were not new to the local community, which has experienced the impacts of exposure to asbestos and a history of misinformation and cover-ups.

> I mean it's like asbestos, it's not going to harm you right at the time you are working with it, it's 20 or 30 years down the track...I think it's still in the back of most people's minds now. (Professional, Organization 8)*

However, in terms of community resilience, the smoke event was not all negative. The mine fire ignited community activism and community groups. Ironically, one of the factors that research has suggested diminishes community resilience—the mistrust and confusion regarding information—led some in the community to take control of information dissemination, calling community meetings and using social media to great effect (Henderson 2014). This was noted by the Hazelwood Mine Fire Inquiry (2014b, p. 403):

> The Board commends those from Morwell Neighbourhood House, the Ramahyuck District Aboriginal Corporation, Asbestos Council of Victoria and Gippsland Asbestos Related Diseases Support Inc., and other community organisations for their efforts in keeping their community as informed and connected as they could be under the circumstances...the Board commends...Voices of the Valley...in disseminating important information to the local community and advocating on their behalf during the emergency.

New community groups were formed, new leaders emerged, and new voices were and continue to be heard in Morwell. For example, the coordinator of the Neighbourhood House ran as a candidate in the State election (Gray 2014). Since the fire, there continues to be a focus on advocacy. For example, Voices of the Valley lobbied for the reopening of the Mine Fire Inquiry to examine whether the mine fire resulted in an increase in deaths in Morwell. Other groups focus on facilitating social connectedness and community building, such as the newly created Latrobe Valley Support Network (LVSN) secured land to create a community garden.† Significantly, the push from the community was instrumental in securing a long-term study to investigate the health impacts of the mine fire on the community (Anderson 2014b).

> ...the biggest bonus out of it [the fire] is we've been able to get the community awake again and alive. Instead of waiting for help to come from outside, we are helping ourselves to get better, and helping ourselves to grow better. (Volunteer, Organization 5)

## DISCUSSION

The Hazelwood Mine Fire demonstrates how differing stakeholders will frame vulnerability and operationalize resilience. We find that the narrative a community tells about an experience shapes their understanding of the event and how they may then react to and recover from that experience. These narratives can have significant positive or negative impacts on the community's recovery. Norris, Stevens, Pfefferbaum, Wyche, and Pfefferbaum (2008, p. 140) argue that narratives offer an "insight into how communities see themselves and others" and give an experience, such as living through the smoke event, a "shared meaning and purpose." This process enables people to tell their stories; framing and reframing their experience is part of recovery and the community's capacity to determine new futures (Chamlee-Wright and Storr 2011; Mutch and Gawith 2014).

Nonetheless, those we interviewed felt a keen sense of abandonment. One individual states "I don't think it's a sense. I think it's a reality—not only were they abandoned but they weren't

* For a detailed report on asbestos in the Latrobe Valley, see Walker and LaMontagne 2004.

† A local television station (WIN News Gippsland) report on the establishment of this initiative can be viewed at www.youtube.com/watch?v=NyRG2eWhpE8.

advocated for" (Professional, Organization 1). Another pointed out, "I think the community here feels a little bit betrayed" (Professional, Organization 2).

The abandonment and betrayal expressed by Morwell communities does raise issues as to what constitutes an adequate response and who should be involved in such circumstances. In Australia, planning policy tends to be based on a strategy of governance focused on hazard management and emergency response. It is one supported by a broader neoliberal framework where responsibilities for risk governance and management have shifted from the state to the private sector and communities (Porter and Davoudi 2012). In this case, government, the private sector, and some service providers proved inadequate to respond to the emergency, leaving members of the community, particularly those that have ongoing experiences of vulnerability, in confusion. This is not to say that local communities do not have the capacity to respond; individuals and groups did seek to address health and well-being issues as best they could. Eventually, these were fundamental to the opening of the 2014 and 2015 Hazelwood Mine Fire Inquiries and the establishment of the Hazelwood Health Study (Hazelwood Mine Fire Inquiry 2015).

Agencies' use of multiple communication methods and the extent to which they provide satisfactory answers and address and resolve perceived negative outcomes have considerable impact on community-agency trust (Sharp, Thwaites, Millar, and Curtis 2009). The breach of trust in Morwell has had a detrimental effect. One of the strong messages from those interviewed was that agencies and government bodies need to talk to the community where they are located, in ways that are appropriate to them, using community organizations that are connected into and trusted by the community.

As noted in our findings, the absence of an adequate response from emergency management agencies, combined with mistrust and confusion, led some in the community to take control by calling community meetings, creating websites, and using social media. As one person explained, the frustration with authorities meant that residents felt they had little choice in addressing the crisis. "That's why we did what we did with Voices of the Valley. It was like, 'hang on, there's something we are not being told'" (Volunteer, Organization 3). Our findings are in accord with Kulemeka (2014), who also studied the use of social media during the Hazelwood Mine Fire, regarding the degree to which the Morwell community engaged through social media. For example, Voices of the Valley developed an online health survey during the smoke event to capture health issues experienced by members of the Morwell community.* Widespread participation in discussion and topical engagement is an important component in facilitating community resilience.

Community resilience is complex. There are many interrelated elements that act upon each other in often unexpected ways. Community resilience is as much about an approach and process as it is about particular strengths or challenges. As McIntosh et al. (2008, p. 6) state, "There appears to be general consensus that resilience emerges 'bottom up' through the independent activities of many elements, resulting in more robust and adaptable systems than those designed 'top down.'" Building on a community's strengths is an effective way of developing a community's resilience, enabling it to take action and respond to change. Community resilience is not achieved by adopting an off-the-shelf recipe of factors.

Strong social networks and social connectedness are important to enhance and develop resilience and as a predictor of resilience in a community (Maybery, Pope, Hodgins, Hitchenor, and Shepherd 2009). It appears that resilience and rejuvenation can occur in the Morwell area by utilizing and developing social resources and connections. Since the fire, many groups have focused on recovery. The Victorian State Government provided a number of early recovery activities as a means to support individual and community well-being. These included the establishment of Respite and Relocation

* The "Online Wellness Survey," conducted March 5–17, 2014, collected information about symptoms by location, according to postcode, within a 10–15-km radius of the mine. The report, produced by Voices of the Valley, is available at www.votv.org.au/community_health_reports.

Assistance Centers, a Community Health and Assessment Centre, a Community Information and Recovery Centre, and free bus and train travel and accommodation assistance (VCOSS 2015).

Despite this, consultation with the Morwell community for the first Hazelwood Mine Fire Inquiry noted that community members were critical of the slow response taken by authorities. Community members cited lack of information about the respite centers in the first few weeks following the fire event and a lack of coordination in relief and recovery services. Respondents reported inoperative contact phone numbers and agencies unaware that they would be contacted by the community for assistance (Hazelwood Mine Fire Inquiry 2014a).

As part of a longer-term strategy for recovery, several community rebuilding activities were set in place. Included were arts-based workshops, such as the 10-week "Journey through the Smoke." This was held from July through September 2014 at the Morwell Neighbourhood House. It was attended by up to 10 people each week and included a trip to the snow, which was attended by more than 400 people (VCOSS 2015).

Groups such as the Disaster in the Valley and Voices of the Valley, who were especially active in trying to establish assistance and clearer communication during the Hazelwood smoke event, joined forces to establish the LVSN. This is a grassroots organization that will "raise community spirit in the Latrobe Valley, to help where there is no help" (www.latrobevalleysupportnetwork.com 2015). LVSN established a community garden. They also recently had a warehouse donated for use as a "free store" to distribute donated goods and as a base for the group to continue to support other projects in the Latrobe Valley (Symons 2014). Such community activism is a marker of the community's resilience (Kirmayer, Dandeneau, Marshall, Phillips, and Williamson 2011; Morello-Frosch, Brown, Mercedes, Cohen, and Krupa 2011).

To further build resilience, a consistent theme that emerged is that authorities need to engage the community in meaningful planning and preparation for different or future forms of disaster (Coles and Buckle 2004). Some members of the community are concerned that there is no plan in place. Others expressed that community consultation about any such plan has, at best, been minimal. Another theme arising from the interviews is the need for more community building activities and engagement to strengthen a sense of belonging and social connectedness. This will facilitate the process of addressing community problems from the ground up. All of these contribute to long-term and sustainable community resilience (McManus et al. 2011).

## CONCLUSION

The Hazelwood Mine Fire had a widespread impact. We find that community members felt disconnected from the broader community and the local and state authorities. At times, they felt entirely forgotten as the smoke event unfolded. People struggled with a range of physical symptoms, but many also experienced anxiety about the fire's long-term health effects. A lack of clear information and a sense of abandonment resulted in fear, confusion, anger, and frustration. This adversely affected community well-being and left a legacy of mistrust.

Nonetheless, our analysis demonstrates an inherent capacity for self-help and agency within vulnerable communities. Use of social media, organization of and participation in public meetings, the formation of new groups, advocacy, and a variety of actions all demonstrate this community's resilience and capacity to respond to the crisis. For example, the strong call for an investigation into the health impacts culminated in a petition with over 21,000 signatures. In response, the Victorian Department of Health funded the 10-year Hazelwood Health Study to identify potential long-term health outcomes. The community was also instrumental in securing an independent inquiry into the mine fire. Despite these successes, considerable work still needs to take place to promote resilience within the Morwell community.

How can a crisis become the starting point for a more fundamental transformation of the community's economic and social well-being? This study suggests the need for a "bottom–up" approach. This would specifically include diverse community groups and agencies. For true resilience and recovery, they must work together to rebuild some of the trust that was lost during the mine fire and develop a dynamic and responsive approach to move the community forward.

## ACKNOWLEDGMENTS

Ethical approval for the study was granted by the Human Research Ethics Committee of Federation University Australia GB14-143. This study was funded by a Federation University Collaborative Research Network small grant.

## REFERENCES

ABC 7.30 Report. 2014. Three week blaze leaves residents angry, sick and demanding answers. Broadcast March 3. http://www.abc.net.au/7.30/content/2014/s3955987.htm, accessed October 24, 2014.

ABC News Online. 2014. Evacuation of Morwell considered over smoke from mine fire. February 20, 2014. http://www.abc.net.au/news/2014-02-20/officials-considered-evacuatin, accessed October 22, 2014.

Anderson, S. 2014a. Hazelwood Mine Fire inquiry: Chief health officer on the defensive over advice to residents. June 4, 2014. ABC News Online. http://www.abc.net.au/news/2014-06-04/hazelwood-mine-fire-inquiry3a-chief-health-officer-on-defensiv/5500388, accessed October 21, 2014.

Anderson, S. 2014b. Hazelwood mine fire health effects examined in 20-year Monash University study. November 5, 2014. ABC News Online. http://www.abc.net.au/news/2014-11-05/monash-uni-to-lead-20-year-study-into-hazelwood-mine-fire-impact/5866204?source=rss, accessed October 23, 2015.

Australian Bureau of Statistics. 2015. *National regional profile, 2009–13*. Canberra: Australian Bureau of Statistics.

Caldwell, A. 2014. Firefighters hospitalised, people told to stay inside, as fire rages through open cut mine. ABC News Online. http://www.abc.net.au/worldtoday/content/2013/s3946193.htm?site=gi, accessed September 20, 2014.

Chamlee-Wright, E. and V. Storr. 2011. Social capital as collective narratives and post-disaster community recovery. *The Sociological Review* 59(2): 266–282.

Charalambous, S. 2014. No long term health worries. *Latrobe Valley Express*. February 20, 2014. http://www.latrobevalleyexpress.com.au/story/2099965/no-long-term-health-worries/, accessed September 16, 2014.

Coles, E. and P. Buckle. 2004. Developing community resilience as a foundation for effective disaster recovery. *Australian Journal of Emergency Management* 19(4): 6–15.

Darroch, S. 2014. Morwell united in anger. *Latrobe Valley Express*. March 3, 2014. http://www.latrobevalleyexpress.com.au/story/2123594/morwell-united-in-anger/, accessed September 13, 2014.

Department of Economic Development, Jobs, Transport, and Resources. 2015. *Lignite/brown coal: Fact sheet*. State of Victoria, Melbourne: Department of Economic Development, Jobs, Transport and Resources.

Department of Economic Development, Jobs, Transport and Resources. 2012. *Summary of Morwell land movement survey and report*. State of Victoria, Melbourne: Department of Economic Development, Jobs, Transport and Resources.

Department of Education and Early Childhood Development. 2012. *A profile of the Latrobe Valley*. State of Victoria, Melbourne: Department of Education and Early Childhood Development.

Department of Health. 2014. Hazelwood open cut mine fire 28 February Community update. http://www.epa.vic.gov.au/about-us/news-centre/news-and-updates/news/2014/february/28/department-of-health-community-update-on-the-hazelwood-fire, accessed October 19, 2015.

Doyal, L. and I. Gough. 1991. *A theory of human need*. London: Macmillan.

Dunstan, J. 2014. Morwell is a health emergency the government is ignoring; Greens leader. ABC News Online. February 17, 2014. http://www.abc.net.au/local/stories/2014/02/17/3946601.htm?site=gipp, accessed September 21, 2014.

Flick, U. 1992. Triangulation revisited: Strategy of validation or alternative? *Journal for the Theory of Social Behaviour* 22(2): 175–197.

Gough, I. 2004. Human wellbeing and social structures. *Global Social Policy* 4(3): 289–311.

Gray, D. 2014. Battle for Morwell heats up as independent Tracie Lund launches campaign. *The Age*. October 7, 2014. http://www.theage.com.au/action/printArticle?id=61754506, accessed September 21, 2014.

Hammersley, M. and P. Atkinson. 1983. *Ethnography—Principles in practice*. London: Tavistock.

Hazelwood Mine Fire Inquiry. 2015. *Hazelwood mine fire inquiry report 2015–2016: Volume I, Anglesea Mine*. Melbourne: Victorian Government Printer.

Hazelwood Mine Fire Inquiry. 2014a. *Morwell community consultation* (summary of discussion). http://morwellnh.org.au/wp-content/uploads/2014/05/Morwell-Community-Consultation-15-April.pdf, accessed September 24, 2015.

Hazelwood Mine Fire Inquiry. 2014b. *Hazelwood mine fire inquiry report 2014*. Melbourne: Victorian Government Printer.

Henderson, J. 2014. Smoke in the Latrobe Valley creates a social media storm. ABC News Online. February 25, 2014. http://www.abc.net.au/local/audio/2014/02/25/3952110.htm?site=gippsland, accessed October 19, 2014.

Kirmayer, L., S. Dandeneau, E. Marshall, M.K. Phillips, and K. Williamson. 2011. Rethinking resilience from Indigenous perspectives. *Canadian Journal of Psychiatry* 56(2): 84–91.

Kulemeka, O. 2014. How people affected by disaster use the internet. *Australasian Journal of Disaster and Trauma Studies* 18(2): 51–56.

Langmore, D. 2013. *Planning power: The uses and abuse of power in the planning of the Latrobe Valley*. North Melbourne: Australian Scholarly Publishing.

Maguire, M. and S. Cartwright. 2008. *Assessing a community capacity to manage change*. Canberra: Australian Government Bureau of Rural Sciences. http://data.daff.gov.au/brs/brsShop/data/dewha_resilience_sa_report_final_4.pdf, accessed October 10, 2014.

Maybery, D., R. Pope, G. Hodgins, Y. Hitchenor, and A. Shepherd. 2009. Resilience and well-being of small inland communities. *Rural Society* 19(4): 326–339.

McGregor, J.A. 2008. *Wellbeing, poverty and conflict*. WeD Policy Briefing 01/08. www.bath.ac.uk/econ-dev/wellbeing/research/bp/bp1-08.pdf, accessed October 22, 2014.

McGregor, J.A., L. Camfield, and A. Woodcock. 2009. Needs, wants and goals: Wellbeing, quality of life and public policy. *Applied Research Quality Life* 4(2): 135–154.

McIntosh, A., R. Stayner, K. Carrington, F. Rolley, J. Scott, and T. Sorenson. 2008. *Resilience in rural communities*. Armidale: Centre for Applied Research in Social Science, University of New England.

McManus, P., J. Martin, N. Argent, S. Baum, L. Bourke, B. Pritchard, T. Sorenson, and J. Walmsley. 2011. The sustainability of towns, livelihoods and nature in Australia's rural heartlands. In *The sustainability of Australia's country towns*, eds. J. Martin and T. Budge, 145–155. Ballarat: Victorian Universities Regional Research Network Press.

Morello-Frosch, R., P. Brown, L. Mercedes, A. Cohen, and K. Krupa. 2011. Community voice, vision, and resilience in post-Hurricane Katrina recovery. *Environmental Justice* 4(1): 71–80.

Mutch, C. and E. Gawith. 2014. The New Zealand earthquakes and the role of schools in engaging children in emotional processing of disaster experiences. *Pastoral Care in Education* 32(1): 54–67.

Nelson, N. 2014a. Dangerous gas threat remains. *Latrobe Valley Express*. February 17, 2014: 3.

Nelson, N. 2014b. Record readings. *Latrobe Valley Express*. February 27, 2014: 1, 3.

Nelson, N. 2014c. Hold your breath. *Latrobe Valley Express*. February 27, 2014. http://www.latrobevalleyexpress.com.au/story/2115399/hold-your-breath/, accessed October 6, 2014.

Norris, F., S. Stevens, B. Pfefferbaum, K. Wyche, and R. Pfefferbaum. 2008. Community resilience as a metaphor, theory, set of capabilities, and strategy for disaster readiness. *American Journal of Community Psychology* 41(1–2): 127–150.

O'Hare, P. and I. White. 2013. Deconstructing resilience. *Practice, Planning Practice & Research* 28(3): 275–279.

Porter, L. and S. Davoudi. 2012. The politics of resilience for planning. *Planning Theory & Practice* 13(2): 329–333.

Reid, R. and L. Botterrill. 2013. The multiple meanings of "resilience." *Australian Journal of Public Administration* 72(1): 31–40.

Ritchie, J., J. Lewis, and C.M. Nicholls. 2014. *Qualitative research practice*, 2nd edition. London: Sage.

Sandelowski, M. 2010. What's in a name? Qualitative description revisited. *Research in Nursing & Health* 33(1): 77–84.

Sandelowski, M. 1995. Sample size in qualitative research. *Research in Nursing & Health*, 18(2): 179–183.

Sharp, E., R. Thwaites, J. Millar, and A. Curtis. 2009. *Factors affecting community-agency trust in bushfire management*. New South Wales, Victoria: Charles Sturt University, Institute for Land, Water, and Society, Report No 51.

Symons, R. 2014. Plenty of room for community spirit. *Latrobe Valley Express*. August 11, 2014. www.latrobevalleyexpress.com.au/story/2478188/plenty-of-room-for-community-spirit/, accessed January 23, 2014.

Thornley, L., J. Ball, L. Signal, K. Lawson-Te Aho, and E. Rawson. 2015. Building community resilience. *Kotuitui: New Zealand Journal of Social Sciences Online* 10(1): 23–35.

Victorian Council of Social Services. 2015. *One year on: Morwell and the 2014 Hazelwood Mine fire.* Melbourne: Victorian Council of Social Services.

Voices of the Valley Facebook. https://www.facebook.com/groups/VOTV1/, accessed on October 26, 2015.

Voices of the Valley. *Community health reports.* www.votv.org.au/community_health_reports, accessed January 23, 2016.

Walker, H. and A. LaMontagne. 2004. *Final report: Work and health in the Latrobe Valley: Community perspective on asbestos issues.* Melbourne: University of Melbourne, Centre for the Study of Health and Society.

# 20 Best Family Rwanda
## *A Case Study on Religious Sources of Resilience*

*Sharon Kim and David Kim*

## CONTENTS



**Abstract**

The 1994 Rwandan Genocide was one of the most brutal episodes in human history, with approximately 800,000 Tutsis slaughtered by the Hutu. In 2001, the organization Best Family Rwanda was established by three survivors who were less than 12 years old during the genocide. The organization served as their new surrogate family. Today, it helps nearly 110 orphans and vulnerable children in Kigali, Rwanda. Forging partnerships with individuals and organizations in the United States and Rwanda, Best Family provides school fees, health care, mentoring, family support, and spiritual development to participants. This case study examines resilience in post-genocide Rwanda, with the aim of identifying the ways in which religious faith shapes individuals' ability to cope with trauma, reconstruct their lives and institutions, extend forgiveness, instill hope for a better future, and use their resources to empower others in their community. This case study describes current programs and the challenges that the organization encounters in empowering and equipping its members.

## INTRODUCTION

Jean Claude Rwagasore was nine years old in 1994 when his father and sister were brutally murdered when fighting erupted between two artificially divided Rwandan ethnic groups, the Hutu majority and the Tutsi minority. In three months, 800,000–1,000,000 Tutsis were slaughtered. According to the Human Rights Watch report, the Rwandan Genocide resulted from the deliberate choice of the Hutu to foster hatred and fear of Tutsis to keep themselves in power (Daly 2002).

On the night of April 6, 1994, an airplane carrying Rwandan president Habyarimana was shot down on its descent into Kigali, killing all on board. Murders began the following day. Soldiers, police, and militia quickly erected checkpoints and barricades and used Rwandans' national identity cards to systematically kill Tutsi. They were joined by Hutu civilians, who armed themselves with machetes, clubs, blunt objects, and other weapons to rape, maim, and kill their Tutsi neighbors.

The government announced that everyone should remain in their homes so that the killers could easily find and murder Tutsis. Jean Claude recalls,

> I saw a group of people coming towards our home. They looked happy and were carrying various traditional weapons such as machetes, clubs, and spears. I was afraid when I saw them coming toward us and went behind the fence to hide. They ordered my father to take off his clothes. When he refused, one of the people immediately cut off his arm with a machete. He started to remove his clothes using his one arm. Immediately, the man cut off his other arm. They put my father on the ground and cut off his legs. They cut off his genitals after that. They killed him like an animal. Then they raped my sister, speared her body numerous times, and stabbed her to death. They had no humanity.

When the men left, Jean Claude rushed to his dying father. He will always remember and carry his father's last words with him: "My son, be a man, seek justice, love everyone, obey your God, and forgive them because they don't know what they are doing. We will meet in heaven."

In the span of 100 days, families were decimated, children were orphaned, and women were left infected with HIV, many of them pregnant and suffering with posttraumatic disorders. Yet, two decades after the genocide, visitors to Rwanda would be amazed at the level of progress, growth, and social change that has taken place. Since 1994, life expectancy has doubled to more than 60 years, economic growth consistently reaches 8% annually, and the number of deaths of children under age 5 has plummeted from 230 per 1000 to 55 (Dixon 2014). Rwanda has completely rebuilt itself in the past two decades.

What are the sources of this remarkable resilience? Studies have pointed to the impact of external factors such as economic and political reforms (Burnet 2008; Kinzer 2014). The post-genocide Rwandan government has taken steps to increase the participation of women in politics by creating a Ministry of Gender, organizing women's councils at all levels of government, and establishing a constitutional quota of reserved seats for women in the national parliament (Burnet 2008). Today, women hold nearly 64% of the seats in Parliament, the highest percentage globally. Economic growth has been primarily driven by liberalization in the agricultural sector, through coffee and tea production, which are the country's main exports. These reforms allow producers to benefit from an export boom, increasing incomes and boosting productivity through capital investments (Booth and Golooba-Mutebi 2014).

It is also important to highlight the role of internal factors such as hope, forgiveness, and faith as sources of resilience. Mooney (2010) finds that religious beliefs and participation in religious rituals instill hope, strength, and self-efficacy among the survivors of the 2010 Haitian Earthquake. Following a stressful event, religious beliefs and practices help people find meaning and develop a sense of control and self-efficacy. Faith also motivates victims to forgive those who've harmed them. Akl and Mullet (2010) find that individuals' capacity to forgive is directly connected to their own conceptualizations of God's forgiveness.

## METHODOLOGY

This case study continues a line of research investigating resilience in Rwanda. We examine the connection between religion and resilience within the context of the local nongovernmental organization Best Family Rwanda (BFR). BFR's mission is to provide vulnerable children access to education, health care, social welfare, entertainment, discipleship, and civic education in the context of a familial community. The organization was birthed by an initiative of three young genocide survivors, who autonomously developed its vision, strategy, resources, and partnerships. We focus on the following question: In what ways does religious faith shape young genocide survivors' ability to cope with trauma, reconstruct their lives and institutions, extend forgiveness, instill hope for a better future, and use their resources to empower others in their community?

We spent the summer months of 2012, 2013, and 2015, in Kigali, Rwanda, conducting participant observation and interviews with the leaders and members of BFR. We conducted in-depth qualitative interviews with the three founders of the organization, 18 members of BFR's Intervention Program (IP), and eight parents of the children in the organization. Of the 29 interviewees, 6 were women and 23 were men. The organization has nearly 30 adult members and 120 children in its sponsorship program. These interviews were in-depth conversations that lasted one to two hours, with a number spanning several interview sessions. Some of the interviews were conducted entirely in English, while others were conducted with one Kinyarwandan interpreter. All were tape-recorded and transcribed. The interviews were conducted in a variety of locations, including homes, offices, villages, and cafes.

We also engaged in participant observation at four Saturday meetings at the three villages (Gikondo, Gashuru, and Nyaragunga) where BFR operates. At these meetings, we observed the programs that they offer to the children in its sponsorship program. We attended one Bible study, held at BRF's office, with approximately 50 parents of the children in the program. Additionally, we attended leadership meetings, one community medical clinic, and other events sponsored by the organization. Field notes and interview transcripts were coded and analyzed according to conventions of grounded theory methods (Glaser 1978; Strauss and Corbin 1990).

## PLANTING THE SEEDS FOR A BRIGHTER FUTURE

In the immediate aftermath of the genocide, Rwanda was in ruins. Those remaining in the country were primarily genocide survivors and military officials. A sense of hopelessness and chaos permeated the nation. According to Handicap International (2009), a nongovernmental organization working in Rwanda,

> The psychological suffering associated with the trauma was also accompanied by socioeconomic problems. As individuals could no longer count on the solidarity and mutual support mechanisms that were characteristic of the Rwandan community, they had to meet their needs alone, in extremely poor living conditions, their homes having mostly been destroyed and with no financial resources to meet basic needs such as feeding themselves.

Salomon Muzungu, one of BFR's founders, reflects on how this dark period motivated him to pursue a different path:

> After the genocide, we saw many genocide orphans going the wrong way, doing drugs, stealing. They were without hope. We saw those children and made a decision not to go that way. Even though we didn't have parents, we felt that we needed to search for the solution on our own. We asked ourselves, "How can we help each other?" We found our hope in each other and in God.

After the murder of family members, four boys, ages seven to twelve, banded together to form a supportive surrogate family. They first joined forces in an entrepreneurial endeavor, selling candy, gum, and cigarettes out of makeshift cardboard box-stands on the roadsides. After vending during the day, they met nightly to encourage each other, share their dreams for a better future, and strategize ways to improve their lives. In 2001, they decided to officially name themselves "Four Boys Group."

For two years, they supported and encouraged one another, sharing everything that they had. In 2004, they opened their organization to other orphans and changed their name to "Best Family Rwanda." According to Jean Claude, they chose the word "family" instead of "company" or "organization" because it better captured their subculture. He explains,

> In the genocide, we all lost family members. We were alone and no longer had parents to take care of us. We wanted to make a new family so that we could bring back those we had lost. No one in our family will see himself or herself as an orphan any longer. When you say "mom" there is a feeling, an emotion, and affection attached to that word. In Best Family Rwanda, the younger children called us "mom" and "dad." In doing so, the younger children really felt cared for, like they had new parents.

They communicated their vision for a brighter future to other orphans. At their meetings, they stressed the importance of their Christian faith, emphasizing the words in the Bible that state that God is the father to widows and orphans. They clung to their faith that God had a great plan for each of them and spent hours praying for God's help. They taught, lived, and modeled what it meant to live as Christians with good morals, values, and hope.

Where did the idea and motivation for creating a surrogate community of orphans come from? Even before the genocide, Jean Claude embraced the idea that he had the capacity to help others despite his young age and lack of monetary resources. In 1988, he was chosen to be a sponsored child by Compassion International, an organization that serves 1.3 million children in 26 countries (Wydick, Glewwe, and Rutledge 2013). Through the program, sponsors contribute US$25–US$45 a month to provide school tuition and uniforms, several meals per week, health care, and tutoring. What distinguishes Compassion projects from most government and international donor programs is that children spend at least 8 hours per week in an intensive after-school program that emphasizes their spiritual, physical, and socioemotional development.

Jean Claude attended these meetings and recalls the positive impact it had on his life,

> The meetings were so wonderful. I looked forward to them every week. They helped me to forget all the problems that I and my family were facing. I remember playing with other children. I also learned about the Bible stories and how those stories applied to my life. Compassion helped me in my spiritual life.

The Compassion program also focuses on raising children's self-esteem and aspirations. It does this by teaching children that they are valuable in God's sight and by instilling hope—that God has a better future in store for them.

Compassion connects children with sponsors through its letter writing program. When Jean Claude asked his sponsor what he did for a living, he learned that he sold puppies. Up to that point, he assumed that his sponsor was a rich American who worked in a high prestige occupation. This left an indelible mark on him: You don't need to be rich to help others. He shares,

> I learned from my sponsor Fritz that you can help others even if you are poor. You only need to have love. Fritz continued to encourage me in my spiritual life. He told me that even though Jesus was poor, he helped others and made a big impact with his life. Fritz told me that even though I was poor, I could become a highest person. All I need is to have a heart of helping, a heart of love, the capacity comes later.

Through the relational mentoring that developed between Fritz and Jean Claude, the seeds of hope, self-esteem, and aspiration were sown.

From 2001 to 2009, BFR relied exclusively on the financial resources of its own members. Things changed significantly in 2009, when they were introduced to a team of short-term missionaries from Visiting Orphans (VO), a Christian nonprofit organization based in Nashville, Tennessee. Over the next several years, VO sent short-term missions teams to meet and serve the children of BFR. A friend of a VO team member reached out to Jean Claude and expressed her desire to sponsor him so he could attend college. This unexpected gift enabled Jean Claude to complete his studies at the University of Rwanda with a degree in law.

Another strategic partnership that emerged was with a church in California. They provided financial resources and mentoring to BFR's leadership. A young married couple, who served on a short-term mission trip in 2011, also partnered with BFR to start "Kunda," a child sponsorship program based on Compassion International's model. Through Kunda, sponsors in the United States contribute $35 per month to provide health insurance, school fees, uniforms, food supplements, and other needs. Sponsors connect relationally with their children through encouraging letters, which are translated into Kinyarwandan by BFR members. With resources from Christian partners in the United States, BFR's reach has greatly expanded. Almost overnight, they grew from helping 35 children to serving nearly 120 in Kigali.

## SIX PILLARS OF BFR

BFR embraces a holistic approach to empowering children by providing material assistance in the context of a supportive, loving, familial community. Its mission is to lift children out of poverty by instilling hope and providing the necessary resources and opportunities for them to succeed. Currently, BFR operates in three impoverished villages in Kigali. BFR leaders select participants by asking village leaders to identify the neediest children in the community. Selected children are welcomed and embraced as BFR members and are given material assistance and non-material support, such as hope, mentorship, spiritual influence, and a sense of belonging to a vibrant community. Central to the organization are the following six pillars: education, health, social welfare, entertainment, civic education, and discipleship.

All of the children in the Kunda program attend their neighborhood schools. BFR pays for their school fees, uniforms, and school supplies. If children are struggling academically, BFR pays for private tutoring. Additionally, the older BFR members who are currently attending or have graduated from universities serve as mentors and role models to the younger children. According to Emmanuel, director of BFR's Kunda program,

> Education is the main way out of poverty. We must gain knowledge so we can better our lives. We make sure that our children are doing well in their schools. This is very important so that they can have a good future.

At one Saturday meeting, when the children were asked what they wanted to be, they confidently exclaimed, "I will be a doctor!" "I will be a teacher!" "I will be a lawyer." For the younger children, these occupations are not far-flung goals; their older "mothers" and "fathers" in BFR are modeling the fruit of diligence in their studies and obtaining these careers.

The second pillar that BFR embraces is health. The organization pays for each child's annual insurance premium, which covers 85% of total medical costs. However, most of the families cannot afford to pay the remaining 15%, so BFR covers out-of-pocket medical expenses. BFR also provides regular education on personal hygiene, because poor sanitation, unsafe water, and unhygienic practices are the causes of needless suffering for children in the developing (Boschi-Pinto, Velebit, and Shibuya 2008). At Saturday meetings, children are taught the importance of washing their hands, taking baths, and brushing their teeth. Another pressing issue is the lack of clean drinking water. BFR is hoping to remedy this by purchasing water purification units for each family in the program. In partnership with The Garden Christian Fellowship, BFR has also held community health clinics for the children and their families (Figure 20.1).

Social welfare is BFR's third pillar. BFR's leaders regularly visit the children's homes to assess whether there may be additional urgent needs. In the past, they've provided supplemental assistance in the form of extra food for the families, physical labor to repair homes, and household goods such as mattresses. They have also helped several families start small businesses. For example, one mother was a trained seamstress but was unable to earn a living as a tailor because she could not afford to buy a sewing machine. BFR purchased a sewing machine for her, improving her life dramatically. She now earns a steady income as her community's tailor and is able to provide for her children.

The fourth pillar is entertainment, which consists of two elements: recreation and personal talent development. Many of the children endure significant pressures and stress at home. Saturdays may be the only time in the week where they can forget those problems and play free-spiritedly. So, BFR carves out time at their meetings for the children to play games, sing, and dance. The second purpose of entertainment is to identify and nurture individual talent. According to Jean Claude,

> We, the leaders, are always observing the children to see what they are good at. When the children are playing soccer, we identify those kids who are talented and we try to encourage them. We put them on a team to complete with other organizations. This really helps with their self-esteem and confidence. When a child is gifted at singing, we encourage them to join in a choir at church. The children each have special talents given by God, and we want to help them develop those talents.

**FIGURE 20.1** Children enjoying a nutritious snack. (Photo courtesy of Sharon Kim.)

Civic Education, the fifth pillar, involves instilling patriotism, unity, and national pride. This is significant in light of the devastation that the country experienced during the genocide. Rwanda has been trying to make ethnicity a thing of the past. There are no Hutu or Tutsi in the new Rwanda; the government has wiped out the distinctions by decree. The new generation of Rwandans is taught to identify simply as "Rwandan." This new unified singular identity has helped bring healing to the country (Pottier 2002). Since BFR children are from both Hutu and Tutsi clans, this "Rwandan" identification has helped bring unity within the organization. The leaders of BFR take every opportunity to teach the children that they are one people: Rwandans.

The sixth and final pillar is discipleship. BFR seeks to develop and nurture the spiritual lives of their children. Every Saturday, BFR leaders teach Bible stories and Christian praise songs to instill the importance of trusting and obeying God. According to Kunda director Emmanuel,

> We teach the children about God. He has helped us survive the genocide and has helped us to complete our studies at Rwanda's top universities. We must put God first in our lives. He is the first priority.

## BUILDING SELF-SUFFICIENCY

BFR aims to develop productive Rwandan citizens who are able to support themselves and give back to the organization that helped them. To accomplish this, they recently started the IP. The IP team is comprised of 20 individuals who have been members of BFR for many years and have personally benefitted from the organization (Figure 20.2). Blaise, a current IP member

**FIGURE 20.2** Members of Best Family Rwanda's Intervention Program. (Photo courtesy of Sharon Kim.)

who joined in 2006, credits BFR for instilling confidence, aspirations, and values in his life. He believes that, without its influence, he would not have been able to complete his degree. Today, he works as a pharmacist and is seen as a role model by the younger members. Nearly all of the IP members have either graduated from or are currently studying at universities. The goal of the IP is to provide leadership to the organization and serve as mentors, "mothers," and "fathers" to the younger children.

IP members meet weekly to share, plan, and pray together. They also engage in special projects to advance the mission of BFR. All IP members make monthly financial contributions. Students contribute 2000 Rwandan Francs (approximately US$2.68) a month, while those with jobs give 5000 Rwandan Francs (approximately US$6.71). According to one IP leader,

> We cannot depend on those outside only. We must be self-sufficient. This is why we have restarted the contribution system. We want to become less dependent on foreign aid. Best Family Rwanda must continue and be able to support ourselves.

The money goes into the IP Fund, where it is used to help members of BFR on an "as needed" basis.

## FAITH AND FORGIVENESS

Throughout history, religion has been the source for many horrific deeds. But, it has also been the source for countless acts of compassion, forgiveness, and reconciliation. In Rwanda, the two faces of religion have been clearly evident. Scholars have documented the reality that Christian leaders aided in the genocide by giving moral support to the perpetrators' cause (Forges 1999; Longman 2001). Churches were sites of the massacres. Most of the killers were Christian; some pastors and priests participated in the slaughter. At the same time, religion in Rwanda has been the source of many powerful stories of redemption and healing.

The challenge of extending forgiveness is one that the founders of BFR know all too well. They extended this to the Hutus, many of them friends and neighbors, who had heinously murdered their parents and relatives. They found this strength in their Christian faith. "The Bible tells us that we must forgive others," notes Salomon. "God has forgiven me and he told me to forgive others." They also understand that bitterness and rage are destructive forces that will keep them in bondage. Emmanuel comments, "We had to forgive to set ourselves free. Our hearts were so heavy with bitterness and hatred toward those killers. When we forgave, we found that our hearts were free of this heaviness and hate. We need to forgive to have a good future."

Not only did they forgive the wrongdoers, the leaders of BFR also extended concrete acts of mercy and kindness to their families. For example, Claude's father, who died in prison, was one of the men who murdered Jean Claude's father and sister. Claude is one of the children in BFR's program. Ben has another powerful story. His father Benjamin and Jean Claude were close childhood friends and were in the same Compassion International program before the genocide. However, during the genocide, Benjamin's father and brothers actively engaged in the murders. Benjamin participated as well, looting goods from the homes of murdered Tutsis and selling them at the village market. Jean Claude knew that Benjamin stole items from his home but decided to forgive him and accepted Benjamin's son into BFR's program. When asked how he was able to do this, he replied, "God helped me to forgive him. I now have compassion and understanding toward Benjamin. We are now friends." Forgiveness paved the way for BFR founders to move forward with hope. Releasing bitterness and thoughts of revenge, they were able to focus on building a better future.

Over the past several decades, there has been an increasing focus on forgiveness and reconciliation in societies coming out of conflict. Previously, these concepts were the domain of philosophers and theologians but now have become integrally linked to politics, economics, and international relations. In African nations such as South Africa, Uganda, Congo, and Rwanda, apology and forgiveness have become central to societal rebuilding. The motivation to do this has largely come from religious convictions.

Shore (2009), in her analysis of the South African Truth and Reconciliation Commission (TRC), finds that Christianity played a significant role in shaping the discourse and approach that the commission took in pursuing transitional justice. Although the TRC was a political process, it also served as a national sacred space where Christian language and definitions of truth, reconciliation, and justice were incorporated. In his opening remarks, Archbishop Tutu (as cited in Shore 2009, p. 86) used overt Christian language and references,

> We are charged to unearth the truth about our dark past, to lay the ghosts of the past so they will not return to haunt us and that will thereby contribute to the healing of the traumatized and wounded people...For Christians it is a significant thing. Now the first hearing happened at Easter time, when we commemorate the victory of life over death, of light over darkness, of goodness over evil, of justice over injustice...in the glorious resurrection of our Savior Jesus Christ.

One approach to transitional justice can be summed up in secular language: perpetrators ought to be punished and victims vindicated. This approach is voiced most often by human rights activists, international lawyers, United Nations officials, and scholars. Religious conceptions differ. In addition to respect and recognition of human rights, they envision reconciliation that includes apology, forgiveness, empathetic acknowledgment of suffering, and rebuilding relationships (Philpott 2007). Reconciliation and retribution are not mutually exclusive. It is possible for the state to punish offenders while victims extend forgiveness to those who have harmed them.

## CONCLUSION

In the aftermath of the Rwandan Genocide, the founders of BFR innovatively constructed a familial community that provides personal as well as economic empowerment. Their unwavering belief in God has been a shaping force in the construction of this organization. This illustrates that religion is a powerful force in resilience, enabling the survivors to come to peace with the past and to look confidently towards the future.

This case study provides important lessons and insights for individuals and groups involved in humanitarian work in developing countries. First, there must be a movement to listen and build relationships. Rather than working from a posture of power, Westerners need to start seeing themselves as servants, relinquishing power to others. There is an impressive level of creativity, passion, and initiative among local people in the developing world. Instead of defining the agenda, Westerners need to come along side local leadership and ask, "What is your vision? Is there anything in our experiences or resources that you could use to fulfill your vision for your organization?" It is important for Westerners to encourage local and autonomous self-determination of development goals and strategies. According to Ernesto Sirolli (2012, par. 12), an economic development expert,

> We Western people are imperialist, colonialist missionaries, and there are only two ways we deal with people: We either patronize them, or we are paternalistic...you [need to] become a servant of the local passion, the servant of local people who have a dream...so what you do—you shut up. You never arrive in a community with any ideas, and you sit with the local people. We become friends, and we find out what that person wants to do.

The term "partnership" is increasingly espoused as the best relationship between members of sustainable development programs. It suggests that both parties respect one another and avoid situations in which one group dominates another. However, given the inevitable inequalities in power between Western donors and in-country partners, it is hard to put this ideal into practice. One promising approach to analyzing partnership is based on interdependence theory (Rusbult and Van Lange 2003). Donors and in-country agencies need each other in order to accomplish their shared goals. Each is an equal partner that gives and receives. One of the key factors that enable healthy partnerships is the ability and willingness to listen to one another and address tensions and conflicts in relationships. Nondefensive and active listening, coupled with the willingness to manage tensions, is the cornerstone of effective partnership (Poncelet 2001).

Second, the influence of religion must be recognized. Too often, development programs embrace a secular worldview that can privatize or problematize religion, thereby overlooking the religious sources of resilience. Religious beliefs are powerful motivators for action. The sociological expectation that modernization and globalization would lead to secularization is being proven false. Christianity is alive, well, and growing in the Global South. Instead of trivializing or marginalizing religious faith, it would be wise for development workers to acknowledge and harness the role that this plays in building lives and communities in the developing world.

Finally, short-term mission trips must be understood as part of and contributors to long-term impacts. Churches, organizations, and individuals need to view short-term mission trips as learning experiences that will be seeds for future engagement and results. Rather than seeing these as ends in themselves, individuals should see them as vision trips that can develop into long-term partnerships and ministries.

While there are limitations to generalizability of the single case approach, faith-based nonprofit organizations are valuable agents for promoting resilience in communities coming out of conflict (Rivera and Nickels 2014). In this light, the BFR case provides an example of the impact of religious faith in shaping individuals' ability to cope with trauma, reconstruct their lives and institutions, and invest their resources to empower others in their community. Further research should extend the scope of the analysis to include how faith institutions of different religions or in different locations foster resilience.

## REFERENCES

Akl, M. and E. Mullet. 2010. Forgivingness: Relationships with conceptualizations of divine forgiveness and childhood memories. *The International Journal for the Psychology of Religion* 20(1): 187–200.

Booth, D. and F. Golooba-Mutebi. 2014. Policy for agriculture and horticulture in Rwanda: A different political economy? *Development Policy Review* 32(2): 173–198.

Boschi-Pinto, C., L. Velebit, and K. Shibuya. 2008. Estimating child mortality due to diarrhea in developing countries. *Bulletin of the World Health Organization* 86(9): 710–717.

Burnet, J.E. 2008. Gender balance and the meanings of women in governance in post-genocide Rwanda. *African Affairs* 107(428): 361–386.

Daly, E. 2002. Between punitive and reconstructive justice: The Gacaca Courts in Rwanda. *International Law and Politics* 34(2): 355–396.

Dixon, R. 2014. Rwanda makes great progress 20 years after genocide. *Los Angeles Times*. http://articles.latimes.com/2014/apr/07/world/la-fg-rwanda-genocide-20140407, accessed August 5, 2015.
Forges, A. 1999. *Leave none to tell the story: Genocide in Rwanda*. New York: Human Rights Watch.
Glaser, B. 1978. *Theoretical sensitivity*. Mill Valley, CA: Sociology Press.
Handicap International. 2009. *Supporting persons living with trauma by rebuilding social and community links: An example of a community-based mental health approach after the Rwandan genocide of the Tutsis*. Lyon, France: Handicap International.
Kinzer, S. 2014. Reconciliation and development in kagame's Rwanda. *The Brown Journal of World Affairs* 20(2): 93–101.
Longman, T. 2001. Church politics and the genocide in Rwanda. *Journal of Religion in Africa* 31(2): 163–186.
Mooney, M. 2010. *Disaster, religion, and resilience*. The Immanent Frame. http://blogs.ssrc.org/tif/2010/02/24/disaster-religion-and-resilience/, accessed October 1, 2015.
Philpott, D. 2007. What religion brings to the politics of transitional justice. *Journal of International Affairs* 61(1): 93–107.
Poncelet, E.C. 2001. A kiss here and a kiss there: Conflict and collaboration in environmental partnerships. *Environmental Management* 27(1): 13–25.
Pottier, J. 2002. *Re-imagining Rwanda: Conflict, survival, and disinformation in the late twentieth century*. Cambridge: Cambridge University Press.
Rivera, J.D. and A.E. Nickels. 2014. Social capital, community resilience, and faith-based organizations in disaster recovery: A case study of Mary Queen of Vietnam Catholic Church. *Risk, Hazards and Crisis in Public Policy* 5(2): 178–211.
Rusbult, C.E. and P.A.M. Van Lange. 2003. Interdependence, interaction, and relationships. *Annual Review of Psychology* 54: 351–375.
Shore, M. 2009. *Religion and conflict resolution: Christianity and South Africa's Truth and Reconciliation Commission*. Burlington, VT: Ashgate.
Sirolli, E. 2012. Retrieved from Ted Blog. http://blog.ted.com/8-talks-on-the-importance-of-listening-and-how-to-do-a-much-better-job-of-it/, accessed August 12, 2015.
Strauss, A. and J. Corbin. 1990. *Basics of qualitative research: Grounded theory procedures and techniques*. Newbury Park, CA: Sage.
Wydick, B., P. Glewwe, and L. Rutledge. 2013. Does international child sponsorship work? A six-country study of impacts on adult life. *Journal of Political Economy* 121(2): 393–436.

# 21 Grassroots and Guerrillas
## *Radical and Insurgent Responses for Community Resilience*

*Natalie Osborne, Deanna Grant-Smith, and Edward Morgan*

## CONTENTS



**Abstract**

In this chapter, we draw from three Australasian cases to explore the strategies enacted by communities to reduce risk and respond to disasters. Each case features communities acting outside formal government processes, in what may be understood as "guerrilla governance" approaches. The first focuses on an emergent online community established in the wake of the Christchurch, New Zealand, earthquakes, the second considers the resilience-building actions of an intentional community located in Melbourne, Australia, and the third considers grassroots responses to government plans to "drought-proof" South East Queensland, Australia. Taken together, they provide the opportunity to reflect on the importance of community action in building or undermining local resilience.

## INTRODUCTION

Urban activist Jane Jacobs (1961/1993) famously noted that cities are life at its most complex and intense. This is arguably at its peak when a city is dealing with the consequences of natural disasters such as an earthquake or severe drought. While governments have a significant role to play in planning for and responding to such events, the disaster management literature suggests that communities must also play a substantive role in their own preparedness, response, and ultimate recovery (Twigg 2009; Vallance 2011a). Indeed, the social fabric of community, including social networks, support structures, and social capital, is essential for building and sustaining resilience (Hegney et al. 2008). However, what this might entail in a given context is rarely articulated.

A community may be conceptualized as a group of individuals who share a sense of interdependence. Targeting place-based communities can be an effective way to raise awareness about the hazards, risks, and vulnerabilities applicable to their shared landscape. There is also a need to consider other types of communities, including coalitions of individuals who emerge in response to shared interests, identities, and/or experiences.

We explore three examples of communities coalescing around actual and potential disasters in ways that have affected their resilience. Through these cases, we consider how community actions broadly characterized as being grassroots or even radical, insurgent, or guerrilla in nature can work to advance, or in some cases undermine, local resilience.

## COMMUNITY-DRIVEN INTERVENTIONS

Involving communities across all phases of the disaster cycle (planning, preparing, response, and recovery) can yield positive results for community resilience (Howes et al. 2013). However, while the difficulties associated with involving the community in such efforts have been recognized, it is generally accepted that taking positive action after a disaster, as an individual or as part of a community, can be cathartic and empowering, aid recovery, and contribute to resilience (Thornley, Ball, Signal, Lawson-Te Aho, and Rawson 2013; Vallance 2011a,b).

Community-driven interventions in this space may be described as "radical" or "insurgent" practices when they occur outside of formal planning and governance processes, often in response to their failures (Miraftab 2009). Those who choose to participate in radical or insurgent practices are often those marginalized or excluded from mainstream governance. More recently, scholars have used terms like "tactical urbanism" (Lydon and Garcia 2015) and "guerrilla governance" (Legacy and van den Nouwelant 2015) to describe related ideas and actions. Tactical urbanism describes the deployment of quick, cheap, small-scale, often unsanctioned interventions designed to test and demonstrate alternatives and disrupt the status quo, with a view to contributing to transformative change (Lydon and Garcia 2015). Similarly, guerrilla governance describes attempts by community groups to "open up" governance and decision-making processes (Legacy and van den Nouwelant 2015) such that they may participate more extensively in governance.

Community-driven interventions may emerge where mainstream processes around disaster risk reduction, response, and recovery are perceived to be exclusive, rigid, unresponsive, and reflective of an inherent conservatism influenced by neoliberal ideology. The cases presented in this chapter describe different types of communities who have mobilized a grassroots response to an issue that they perceived as exacerbating vulnerabilities. These cases demonstrate the possibilities of such communities working outside of, in opposition to, and/or in cooperation with governments and planning authorities with the aim of building resilience.

These cases have been the subject of earlier research by the authors and were selected as paradigmatic cases demonstrating how different types of communities come together around the threats of, or actual instances of, climate change or natural disasters. The first case considers community responses to enhance resilience in the face of postdisaster lifeline infrastructure failure through directed content analysis (Hsieh and Shannon 2005). It is informed by earlier research (see Grant-Smith 2011) and focuses on a community website celebrating the construction of personal pit latrines (Grant-Smith 2012). Through ethnographic observations conducted over five weeks and 10 semistructured interviews with community members, the second case explores how an intentional community organizes to reduce vulnerability and build capacity (Osborne 2009). The third case uses document analysis and 22 semistructured interviews with scientists and government officials in South East Queensland, Australia, regarding water governance arrangements to examine cases of community mobilization with a potentially negative impact on resilience and vulnerability (Morgan 2014).

## COMMUNITY RESPONSES TO INFRASTRUCTURE FAILURE: showusyourlongdrop.co.nz

Earthquakes can have significant impacts on the infrastructure and services that support the life of a community. Much of the postdisaster lifeline and seismic resilience research focuses on improving infrastructure resilience and asset performance (Ainuddin and Routray 2012) rather than on nurturing community resourcefulness and adaptive capacity. Indeed, impacts on and the actions of communities responding to these failures are often conceptualized as outage consequences.

The 2011 Christchurch earthquakes and aftershocks were the most expensive in New Zealand's history, causing extensive damage to sanitation networks and resulting in the dumping of raw sewage into rivers and estuaries. Approximately 50% of the city was without water for the days immediately following the earthquake; more than a third of households were without water for over a week. It was six weeks before the potentially contaminated water supply was chlorinated. It was many months before sewerage was restored to most homes (McLean, Oughton, Ellis, Wakelin, and Ruben 2012).

While damage was being assessed and rectified, many residents had to rely on alternatives to city sewage systems to manage their sanitation needs. Two distinct strategies were employed by the disaster authorities: the distribution of more than 38,000 chemical toilets for individual household use and more than 2900 portable toilets for shared use by multiple households (Noell and Meek 2012; Stevenson et al. 2011). The decision to provide chemical and portable toilets was based on the assumption that, where it was safe to do so, it would be more effective and less risky to provide some form of sanitation to people in their homes than to displace them to makeshift welfare centers (McLean, Oughton, Ellis, Wakelin, and Ruben 2012).

Swaffield (2013, p. 5) describes Christchurch becoming a "'Portaloo' city." However, because there was enormous demand for portable and chemical toilets, they were deemed "assets of importance" under legislation. Their allocation had to be coordinated by the government Civil Defence and Emergency Management authority. The equity and efficiency of their numbers, distribution, and servicing have been criticized (Potangaroa, Wilkinson, Zare, and Steinfort 2011). Many Christchurch residents resorted to constructing personal pit latrines in their backyards, colloquially referred to as "long drops." Disaster authorities released communications about how to build an emergency toilet (Poole 2012). However, there was a general feeling in the community that insufficient advice on alternative sanitation solutions was being provided (McLean, Oughton, Ellis, Wakelin, and Ruben 2012). An emergent online community sought to fill this gap.

The website www.showusyourlongdrop.co.nz was established to provide information and advice about building and maintaining a safe, temporary, outdoor long drop. The identity of the creator and curator of the website was never revealed. However, through the site narrative, it can be assumed they, and many of the contributors, were from the Christchurch area.

> This website has been set up to showcase all the creative Long Drops that are popping up around Christchurch. The earthquake disaster that occurred on 22/2/11 has been a testing time for us Cantabrians and we feel for people who have lost loved ones or property…During these tough times it is important to be with friends and family and still be able to have a good laugh. Hence the reason for this website. A bit of toilet humour is bound to put a smile on your face even if you're having a crappy day! (http://www.showusyourlongdrop.co.nz/about/)

The website provided a forum for Cantabrians to share images and stories of their experiences building, using, and maintaining long drops. The website had a largely humorous tone, including images of homemade long drops such as "the Turdis," modeled on the blue police call box of Dr Who fame. Despite this tone, it provided detailed instructions and information on a range of sanitation-related hygiene, public health, physical safety, aesthetic, and environmental issues. It also catalyzed community around these issues in a way that a purely geographical or community of interest could not. This nascent and emergent community of interest created both a local and global community of people sharing stories and strategies and expressing support and solidarity. It also provided a platform, due to its high levels of social and traditional media exposure, to assist fund raising efforts via the Red Cross appeal.

Narratives of resistance and resilience, such as those expressed on this website, can inspire processes of recovery because "urban disaster and recovery are driven and signalled by a succession of highly symbolic actions," which become rallying points (Vale and Campanella 2005, p. 16). Community initiatives like www.showusyourlongdrop.co.nz (re)affirm to contributors and demonstrate to fellow citizens that they are, and can be, resilient, ingenious, and self-reliant. Toilets (or lack thereof) may be an unlikely rallying point, but they were a tangible and practical expression of rebuilding and resilience. The website delivered practical sanitation outcomes in terms of the information it provided. It fostered camaraderie, hope, and sense of pride in the ability to adapt and be resourceful. These are important ingredients for resilience. It also provided a way to maintain and strengthen collective identity, epitomizing what is known in New Zealand lexicon as a "number 8 wire mentality." This is an expression of the personal resourcefulness and resilience that are intrinsic to their cultural identity.

Disaster management authorities may look to the example of www.showusyourlongdrop.co.nz as a guerrilla response to enhancing community resilience in three ways. First, it has the ability to fill a perceived information vacuum. Second, it is a platform for creating community connection and solidarity. Third, it is a site for promoting practical resilience and resourcefulness, which is built on an ethic of personal care and responsibility. This creates a citizen who is at once responsible for and responsive to managing the waste that they produce (Grant-Smith 2010).

## COMMUNITY CAPACITY BUILDING TO REDUCE VULNERABILITY: CENTRE FOR EDUCATION AND RESEARCH IN ENVIRONMENTAL STRATEGIES

Unlike the sudden (acute event) disaster described earlier, climate change and resource scarcity represent a kind of long, slow (chronic event) disaster. These have locally situated impacts that may be difficult to predict. Hence, some community-driven resilience activities may focus on mitigation and on shaping positive change rather than passively "coping" or reacting to disasters as they occur.

Operating since 1982, the Centre for Education and Research in Environmental Strategies (CERES) Community Environment Park, located in Melbourne, Australia, has a "localized" grassroots ethos aimed at drawing together those with a commitment to sustainable lifestyles (CERES 2008). The site on which CERES was founded was formerly a municipal garbage dump. Through local community efforts, the land has been restored to fertility and productivity, with biodiversity gains.

CERES is a not-for-profit organization that employs insurgent and guerrilla approaches to effect social and environmental change. It leverages small grants and seed-funding into self-sustaining programs and social enterprises. It guards its radical and insurgent ethos by avoiding funding structures or partners that could undermine their grassroots status or create a relationship of dependency. An important part of the CERES approach is building and leveraging community for long-term, wider cultural change. It is also a place of experimentation (discovering what works and what does not) on a small, affordable scale and identifying lessons that can be more broadly applied. Both are characteristics of tactical urbanism (Lydon and Garcia 2015) and are essential for building resilience; in that vein, CERES hosts a range of programs and activities aimed at improving equity and sustainability.

Activities hosted by the park's employees and volunteers include experimenting and demonstrating the viability of renewable energies and other innovative technologies for sustainability, urban agriculture (see Figure 21.1), providing opportunities for experiential education, and reducing car dependence via their cycling workshop. It also functions as a community hub for residents in neighboring suburbs and builds social capital, community cohesion, and shared identities by hosting festivals and events.

Diverse economies (Gibson-Graham, Cameron, and Healy 2013) contribute to disaster risk and vulnerability reduction and climate change adaptation (Twigg 2009). Through the kinds of activities listed previously, CERES facilitates "connected livelihoods" that may prove more resilient to disasters, climate change impacts, and resource scarcity by making use of local assets and networks, as well as diverse economies such as bartering, sharing, cooperatives, and social enterprises. For

**FIGURE 21.1** Urban agriculture and mosaic art at CERES Community Environment Park.

example, CERES hosts the Moreland LETS (local exchange trading system) that people can use to trade goods and services without currency.

CERES also offers training and education programs for disadvantaged and vulnerable people, improving their personal resilience by providing new opportunities. Its Seven Stars Organic Catering Enterprise grew out of a hospitality-training program, which CERES ran for Turkish and Kurdish migrant women living in the area. Many participants were quite vulnerable, due to low levels of formal education, job skills, or local connections. They gained a qualification, improved their English communication skills, and formed a social enterprise that improved economic self-sufficiency, personal resilience, and the resilience of their family and broader community (Osborne 2009). By acting as a community hub for those with a commitment to sustainability and social justice, CERES represents a leading example of how community-led organizing can reduce individual and community vulnerability. CERES remains committed to its independence and the grassroots status that facilitates radical experimentation, innovation, and the tactical demonstration of new possibilities.

## MALADAPTIVE COMMUNITY MOBILIZATION: POOwoomba

There is a longstanding assumption that the increased participation of communities in decisions that affect them will deliver positive outcomes (see Arnstein 1969). However, not all participatory activity contributes to community resilience. Some community-driven interventions may lead to maladaptive responses and fracture the community. This final example highlights the impact of a fear-driven grassroots guerrilla campaign to influence government plans to increase the security and resilience of local water supplies in the city of Toowoomba, in South East Queensland, Australia. The plans, in response to a severe drought and declining average rainfall over dam catchments, focused on supplementing the potable water supply with recycled water.

Segments of the Toowoomba community vehemently opposed this approach to drought proofing, despite the very real possibility that the water shortages being experienced in the region might be the start of a persistent change from historical conditions, either under climate change or as part of long-term natural variability (Chiew, Young, Cai, and Teng 2011). When the plan was taken to a plebiscite, it was defeated. This has been largely attributed to the effective and highly emotive grassroots "no" campaign (Hurlimann and Dolnicar 2010; Morgan and Grant-Smith 2015). This case illustrates that community actions are not necessarily "positive" and have the potential to exacerbate the vulnerability of local areas to climate change impacts and disasters.

Although the community was largely accepting of water saving measures, the prospect of recycled water was troubling for some (Fishman 2011). Some residents felt that consultation process had been inadequate and that the recycled water would be imposed upon them (Hurlimann and Dolnicar 2010). In response, a group of residents formed Citizens Against Drinking Sewage

**FIGURE 21.2** Sign on the eastern approach into Toowoomba. (Courtesy of Edward Morgan.)

(CADS) to campaign against plans for recycled water. Their campaign materials were highly emotive and divisive. Alongside slogans that evoked notions of "toilet to tap" water cycles (Hanna 2006), materials included a picture of a frightened child with the caption "I dont [*sic*] want to die Mummy!"* CADS argued that Toowoomba residents were test subjects for an unproven and potentially unsafe technology. They further asserted that the scheme would undermine their civic pride and threaten their standing in the broader community. They feared their town would be widely dubbed "POOwoomba" (Balderson 2006).

The CADS campaign diminished what was formerly broad bipartisan support for the recycled water plans across all tiers of government. Some formerly supportive elected representatives changed their position, and others chose not to vocalize their support (Morgan 2014). The CADS campaign and the controversial nature of the issue contributed to the polarization of the community and undermined the ability of stakeholders to "engage in constructive dialogue…the debate which the decision was based on was limited and divisive" (Hampton 2009, p. 229). This was further exacerbated by the decision to take the plan to a plebiscite, which reduced complex issues to a simple "yes" or "no" question and constructed a divide between those who were "for" or "against" the water recycling plan.

The mobilization against recycled water was potentially maladaptive and may have increased exposure to future, likely worsening, drought events. Yet, despite opposition to water recycling, many residents voluntarily undertook a number of personal measures to reduce their water consumption. These included widespread adoption of water-saving devices and installation of household water tanks to meet the 200 L/person/day water restrictions, which were enforceable through fines and sanctions (Figure 21.2). The personal approaches were reinforced by statewide government initiatives, including community education programs about water use, fiscal incentives and rebates, and the introduction of transparent water billing systems and enforceable restrictions (England 2009). As a result, Toowoomba's water usage dropped significantly. This demonstrates that, despite the controversy, the community worked to change their water footprint in a way that may have reduced their vulnerability to drought events, at least in the short-term. This also indicates that the rejection of the water recycling proposal was directly related to its scatological nature, rather than objections to behavior change or government regulation of water demand more generally (Grant-Smith 2011).

* For more examples, see Morgan 2014.

## THE POTENTIAL OF GRASSROOTS AND GUERRILLA RESPONSES FOR BUILDING COMMUNITY RESILIENCE

"Community" is widely understood to be a contested term that resists oversimplified or decontextualized definitions, particularly in the context of disaster risk reduction and resilience (Howes et al. 2013). These cases demonstrate that community is embedded in specific contexts and places. It can be built around any group of individuals who share a sense of connection, interdependence, and/or mutual interests.

Descriptions of communities within the disaster management and climate change literature have typically depicted them as geographical communities or communities of place (e.g., towns, regions, or neighborhoods), which are formed by proximity through shared spaces (Cutter et al. 2008), although they may share little else. In the age of globalization, this conceptualization of community has been critiqued as too narrow. Yet, the trend toward (re)localization is emphasizing the local geographical community in planning and policy responses. A return to this scale and form of community may be particularly influential, because many of the impacts of disasters, such as floods and cyclones, are experienced in local places and contexts. In the context of climate change, local geographies may present additional hazards or exacerbate risks and vulnerabilities such as through sea-level rise.

Targeting geographical communities can be effective for raising awareness about the hazards and risks applicable to the shared landscape and environs (Cutter et al. 2008; United Kingdom Cabinet Office [UKCO] 2010). An example of this is planning for and responding to the risks of bushfires. Local communities can be involved in a range of community-driven and government-sponsored activities, which can positively impact resilience. However, it is important that intragroup difference and the social, as well as spatial, construction of vulnerabilities are recognized when planning for and with geographical communities (Twigg 2009).

All the case communities included geographical elements, but geography alone did not create them. Other kinds, or elements, of communities, including coalitions of individuals who emerge in response to shared interests, identities, commitments, values, and/or experiences, must also be considered (Stewart 2011). Communities of interests are formed as a result of shared values, activities, land, or interests (UKCO 2010). The "fabric" of these communities may be civil society organizations, social networks (both online and offline), club membership, or attendance at particular events. Communities of interest are not necessarily distinct from geographical communities. Residents in an ecovillage, for example, may be both a geographical community who share a neighborhood and a community of interest, as they have chosen to live there because of a shared commitment to living more sustainably. As CERES demonstrates, communities of interest may be able to mobilize particular resources to respond to disasters, including expertise and other forms of capital, and can be critical for reducing vulnerability.

Communities of interest may have their genesis as "emergent" communities or communities of circumstance (Maguire and Cartwright 2008; UKCO 2010). These are often catalyzed in the wake of disasters and other urgent issues, as individuals seek a way to mobilize a response. What distinguishes emergent communities from other communities of interest is that they may form without building on any preexisting relationships, networks, or shared identity (Maguire and Cartwright 2008). Rather, those relationships, networks, and identities are catalyzed by a disaster or other disruptive event. For instance, where a particular disaster affects some and not others, a new sense of community based on shared experience may emerge among those affected. This may be strengthened by a sense of being "marked" by it or through a feeling of being alienated from those who were unaffected (Convery et al. 2008). What these communities often share and what may motivate their emergence are a shared experience of a threat, whether in the form of a natural disaster, such as in Christchurch, or of an externally imposed policy change, as in Toowoomba. These communities emerged or mobilized in response to perceived and actual vulnerabilities and a desire to make themselves and each other more resilient, self-sufficient, and capable of coping.

It is overly simplistic to suggest that a given community is "vulnerable" or "resilient" or that the formation of specific communities will positively impact vulnerability or resilience. While it is important, it is not a panacea for vulnerability, as communities are composed of diverse individuals and contradictory practices. The case of Toowoomba shows that communities can simultaneously form and mobilize in ways that can both exacerbate and mitigate their vulnerability to hazards and risks.

Focusing on community-driven and insurgent practices as inherently transformative or transgressive in the pursuit of resilience is likewise limiting. Although that capacity exists, as evidenced by both CERES and showusyourlongdrop.co.nz, Toowoomba reminds us that practices like guerrilla governance may be used to resist changes, as well as to pursue or embrace them. The practice of engaging communities for disaster risk reduction and climate change adaptation must come with a recognition of the inherent contradictions and complexities of "community" both as a concept and as a collective. Greater consideration of their geographical, interest, and emergent elements must be taken into account. Planners must seek to work with them in ways that do not perpetuate what is ultimately an artificial divide between decision makers and the community. Further, it is important to encourage the innovation and experimentation that grassroots, insurgent, and guerrilla approaches may offer without assuming that all community-based responses will contribute positively to resilience. Resilience requires complementary but multipronged and multifaceted approaches driven by different actors, so that where some initiatives fail, others may succeed.

Despite these cautions, the examples of communities constituted by geographical, interest, and emergent elements explored here highlight the potential power and efficacy of grassroots responses to disasters. Showusyourlongdrop.co.nz demonstrates how new networks and communities may form in the aftermath of a disaster; they may be quicker and more innovative than governments in addressing particular problems. This emergent community was ephemeral. In contrast, CERES demonstrates the potential of grassroots approaches embedded within geographical communities and communities of interest to work for resilience over a longer timeframe. Although there is considerable value for disaster managers and planners to collaborate with communities, it may be important that they remain independent and genuinely grassroots. This may protect the innovation, creativity, and authenticity that are derived from their insurgent nature.

## REFERENCES


Ainuddin, A. and J.K. Routray. 2012. Community resilience framework for an earthquake prone area in Baluchistan. *International Journal of Disaster Risk Reduction* 2: 25–36.

Arnstein, S. 1969. A ladder of citizen participation. *Journal of the American Institute of Planners* 35(4): 216–224.

Balderson, S. 2006. Anti-recycling campaigners voice their defiance. *The Chronicle*, May 29. www.thechronicle.come.au/news/apn-anti-recycling-campaigners-voice-thei/3880/, accessed October 26, 2015.

Centre for Education and Research in Environmental Strategies. 2008. *CERES annual report 2007/2008*. CERES: Brunswick East.

Chiew, F.H.S., W.J. Young, W. Cai, and J. Teng. 2011. Current drought and future hydroclimate projections in southeast Australia and implications for water resources management. *Stochastic Environmental Research and Risk Assessment* 25(4): 601–612.

Convery, I., M. Mort, J. Baxter, C. Bailey. 2008. *Animal disease and human trauma: Emotional geographies of disaster*. Hampshire: Palgrave Macmillan.

Cutter, S., L. Barnes, M. Berry, C. Burton, E. Evans, E. Tate, and J. Webb. 2008. A place-based model for understanding community resilience to natural disasters. *Global Environmental Change* 18: 598–606.

England, P. 2009. Managing urban water in Australia: The planned and the unplanned. *Management of Environmental Quality* 20(5): 592–608.

Fishman, C. 2011. *The big thirst: The secret life and turbulent future of water*. New York: Free Press.

Gibson-Graham, J.K., J. Cameron, and S. Healy. 2013. *Take back the economy: An ethical guide for transforming our communities*. Minneapolis, MN: University of Minnesota Press.

Grant-Smith, D. 2012. The potential contribution of scatological art to post-disaster resilience and community building. Presentation: Creative Communities 3 Conference, September 26–28, Gold Coast.

_____. 2011. *Regulating the unspeakable: A policy story of boaters, floaters and voters*. PhD thesis. Brisbane, Australia: Griffith University.

_____. 2010. Constructing the shitting citizen: The promise of scatological art as environmental and social activism. *Reconstruction: Studies in Contemporary Culture*, 10(3): 1–11.

Hampton, G. 2009. Narrative policy analysis and the integration of public involvement in decision making. *Policy Sciences* 42(3): 227–242.

Hanna, C. 2006. Fears will wash away with time. *Queensland Times* (Ipswich edition), August 1. http://www.qt.com.au/news/apn-fears-will-wash-away-with/82097/, accessed November 20, 2015.

Hegney, D., H. Ross, P. Baker, C. Rogers-Clark, C. King, E. Buikstra, A. Watson-Luke, K. McLachlan, and L. Stallard. 2008. *Building resilience in rural communities: Toolkit*. Toowoomba, Queensland: University of Queensland and University of Southern Queensland. http://learningforsustainability.net/pubs/Building_Resilience_in_Rural_Communities_Toolkit.pdf, accessed October 26, 2015.

Howes, M., D. Grant-Smith, K. Reis, K. Bosomworth, P. Tangney, M. Heazle, D. McEvoy, and P. Burton. 2013. *Rethinking disaster risk management and climate change adaptation*. Gold Coast: National Climate Change Adaptation Research Facility, Griffith University. https://www.nccarf.edu.au/sites/default/files/attached_files_publications/Howes_2013_Rethinking_disaster_risk_management.pdf, accessed October 26, 2015.

Hsieh, H.F. and S.E. Shannon. 2005. Three approaches to qualitative content analysis. *Qualitative Health Research* 15(9): 1277–1288.

Hurlimann, A. and S. Dolnicar. 2010. When public opposition defeats alternative water projects: The case of Toowoomba, Australia. *Water Research* 44(1): 287–297.

Jacobs, J. (1961/1993). *The life and death of great American cities*. New York: Modern Library.

Legacy, C. and R. van den Nouwelant. 2015. Negotiating strategic planning's transitional spaces: The case of 'guerrilla governance' in infrastructure planning. *Environment and Planning A* 47(1): 209–226.

Lydon, M. and A. Garcia. 2015. *Tactical urbanism: Short-term action for long-term change*. Washington, DC: Island Press.

Maguire, B. and S. Cartwright. 2008. *Assessing a community's capacity to manage change: A resilience approach to social assessment*. Canberra: Bureau of Rural Sciences. http://data.daff.gov.au/brs/brsShop/data/dewha_resilience_sa_report_final_4.pdf, accessed October 26, 2015.

McLean, I., D. Oughton, S. Ellis, B. Wakelin, and C. Ruben. 2012. *Review of the Civil Defence Emergency Management response to the 22 February Christchurch Earthquake*. Report prepared for Civil Defence and Emergency Management, New Zealand Government. http://civildefence.govt.nz/assets/Uploads/publications/Review-CDEM-Response-22-February-Christchurch-Earthquake.pdf, accessed October 26, 2015.

Miraftab, F. 2009. Insurgent planning: Situating radical planning in the global south. *Planning Theory* 8(1): 32–50.

Morgan, E.A. 2014. Science and sustainability: The use of science and the science-policy interface in sustainable water resource management. PhD thesis. Brisbane, Australia: Griffith University.

Morgan, E.A. and D. Grant-Smith. 2015. Tales of science and defiance: The case for co-learning and collaboration in bridging the science/emotion divide. *Journal of Environmental Planning & Management* 58(10): 1770–1788.

Noell, B. and R. Meek. 2012. A day in the life of an earthquake sewer recovery operation Hurunui District Council Strategy and Policy Committee. http://www.pdp.co.nz/documents/2012NoellMeek1.pdf, accessed October 26, 2015.

Osborne, N. 2009. Acting locally: A community-based approach to resiliency. Honours dissertation. Brisbane, Australia: Griffith University.

Poole, M. 2012. Public information management in Christchurch following the February 2011 earthquakes: Lessons learned. *Australian Journal of Emergency Management* 27(4): 7–14.

Potangaroa, R., S. Wilkinson, M. Zare, and P. Steinfort. 2011. The management of portable toilets in the eastern suburbs of Christchurch after the February 22, 2011 Earthquake. *Australasian Journal of Disaster and Trauma Studies* 2011–2012: 35–48.

Stevenson, J.R., H. Kachali, Z. Whitman, E. Seville, J. Vargo, and T. Wilson. 2011. Preliminary observations of the impacts of the 22 February Christchurch Earthquake on organisations and the economy: A report from the field. *New Zealand Society for Earthquake Engineering Bulletin* 44(2): 65–76.

Stewart, J. 2011. *The dilemmas of engagement: The role of consultation in governance*. Acton: Australian National University E-Press.

Swaffield, S. 2013. Place, culture and landscape after the Christchurch Earthquake. In *Space, Place, Culture*, ed. H. Sykes, 1–27. Albert Park, Victoria: Future Leaders. http://www.futureleaders.com.au/book_chapters/pdf/Space-Place-Culture/Simon-Swaffield.pdf, accessed October 26, 2015.

Thornley, L., J. Ball, L. Signal, K. Lawson-Te Aho, and E. Rawson. 2013. *Building community resilience: Learning from the Canterbury earthquakes*. Final Report to Health Research Council and Medical Research Foundation. New Zealand. http://www.healthychristchurch.org.nz/media/101584/buildingcommunityresilience_march2013.pdf, accessed October 26, 2015.

Twigg, J. 2009. *Characteristics of a disaster-resilient community*. London: Aon Benfield UCL Hazard Research Centre. http://community.eldis.org/.59e907ee/Characteristics2EDITION.pdf, accessed October 26, 2015.

United Kingdom Cabinet Office (UKCO). 2010. *Draft strategic national framework on community resilience*. London: Cabinet Office.

Vale, L.J. and T.J. Campanella. 2005. Introduction: The cities rise again. In *The resilient city: How modern cities recover from disaster*, eds. L.J. Vale and T.J. Campanella, 3–26. Oxford: Oxford University Press.

Vallance, S. 2011a. Early disaster recovery: A guide for communities. *Australasian Journal of Disaster and Trauma Studies* 2011–2012: 19–25.

_____. 2011b. Communities and resilience: Burning or building bridges. *Lincoln Planning Review* 3(1): 4–8.

# 22 "Prepper" as Resilient Citizen
## *What Preppers Can Teach Us about Surviving Disasters*

*Chad Huddleston*

## CONTENTS



**Abstract**

"Prepping" is a social movement of individuals and small groups that are attempting to build resiliency at microlevels within their communities. They aim to learn how to effectively survive potential disasters and long-term change within their locale. Preppers choose to prepare for potential disaster through self-education, training, and the gathering of necessary materials to meet their own individual/familial needs. Keenly aware of community vulnerabilities, they also avidly support organizational attempts at building resilience. By building small, linked cells of microresiliency, communities are able to construct a stronger web that acts to support the larger community when disaster strikes. This allows prepared individuals to become responders instead of victims. This study introduces preppers and gives a brief history of the movement, followed by specific ethnographic examples to illustrate their efforts at resiliency construction.

## INTRODUCTION

In the *World Disasters Report* by the International Federation of Red Cross and Red Crescent Societies (2014), an emphasis is placed on the importance of local cultural understandings of disaster, risk, and resiliency in order to comprehend how populations prepare for, manage, and respond to adverse events. Similarly, this chapter is enhanced through a case study, which presents an ethnographic profile of "Zombie Squad" (ZS), a group that fits into a more general category of disaster preparation enthusiast called "preppers." While there is an ongoing discussion of the meaning of resilience and its place in preparing for disasters, the average community member around the world is more concerned with engaging in practices that will help them to survive the event.

Preppers are focused on learning and spreading such practices. This research clearly shows that they are also capable of contributing to the construction of resilient systems. The Resilience

Alliance's (2010) website defines resilience as (1) the amount of disturbance a system can absorb and still remain within the same state or domain of attraction; (2) the degree to which the system is capable of self-organization, and; (3) the degree to which the system can build and increase the capacity for learning and adaptation. As will be shown, preppers excel at increasing learning and adaptation, while self-organizing in order to support established systems in order to withstand disturbances.

Because of the particular history in which these kinds of practices have been negatively framed in the United States, it is necessary to situate the movement in its cultural context (Johnston and Noakes 2005). As discussed here, preppers are often associated with survivalists, who practice similar behaviors but have different motivations. While survivalists have been linked to criminal behavior and extremist perspectives, preppers have tried to escape that stereotype by defining a new frame that focuses on individuals enacting the same behaviors but with inclusive, community-supported goals that engage the general public. This is in direct opposition to the survivalist frame, which emphasizes that skills and resources should be focused exclusively within their specific groups. Because of such differences, understanding what preppers are and what prompts their behavior is essential to gaining insight into how they construct micro-resilient networks that support well-established systems of disaster response in their communities and why we should nurture these.

## METHODS

This ongoing research was conducted primarily from 2009 from 2012 in the Midwestern United States with the original ZS chapter (001). Because ZS is a public group, entrée was through their open monthly meetings. After initial discussion with their leadership board, I started "complete participant observation" (Spradley 1980). This type of participant observation focuses on becoming a member of the group; I attended meetings, participated in charity events, and had hundreds of hours of conversations with preppers at bars, while camping, at the shooting range, at charity events, and at disaster preparation seminars. This participation-heavy method facilitates asking questions, taking observational notes, and having detailed conversations while in the field, permitting the researcher to learn the group-specific "rules" quickly (DeWalt and DeWalt 2011). Members would often seek me out to add some information to previously asked questions. They reciprocated my overtly participatory role in the group with participation in the research.

I recorded semistructured interviews with group leadership, chosen for their roles on the organization's board. Selection was based on the "snowball" method, where participants suggest the next round of people to contact (O'Reilly 2012), resulting in phone and e-mail interviews with members from other chapters around the country and in Canada. Because members are volunteers, not everyone participates at the same rate. The snowball method assisted in reaching individuals who had ties to the group but did not regularly attend all events. To widen my scope of understanding, I engaged with members on the online forum. These conversations were focused on the topic in each particular thread rather than directed questions within the research. Additionally, I conducted semistructured interviews with representatives from community organizations that had relationships with ZS.

As with any participant-based, qualitative research, reliability can be a concern. To achieve accuracy and understanding, direct experiential participation that uses mixed methods as a means to test the data is essential (DeWalt and DeWalt 2011). I have participated in and observed ZS's annual events over several calendar years, giving me a chance to test my observations and understanding of their "rules" and relationships. Supplementing my "complete participation" with semistructured interviews provides another method to test reliability.

## DIFFERENTIATING PREPPERS FROM SURVIVALISTS

Unfortunately for preppers, there is a weighty discourse in American society framing some of the behaviors in which they engage as fringe activity and perspectives. This is particularly true of those labeled as "survivalists" in the 1970–1990s. Philip Lamy (1996) has broadly defined "survivalists" as a wide spectrum of groups focusing on disaster preparedness. They range from those who are prepared for difficult times to white supremacists, antigovernment groups, and apocalyptic cults. Militias are a common addition to this list (Berlet 2004; Lamy 1992; Weeber and Rodeheaver 2003). These survivalists are often depicted as shaved-headed youths, marching about with swastikas, American flags, or signs preaching against homosexuals, abortion, or any number of ethnic groups (Lamy 1996; Mitchell 2002). They are also depicted with weapons, carrying out paramilitary training scenarios, or preaching that the "End is coming" (Lamy 1992, p. 422).

Because of these portrayals, survivalists are often equated with the "radical right" (Berry 1999; Lamy 1996; Mitchell 2002). While this is true for some, such as the Hutaree Militia (Temple-Raston 2010) or the Militia of Montana (Caron 2011), it is not true of all. It is the extreme type of survivalist groups that are used to construct frames presented by media to the public due to their actions and their perceived threat. This contributes to the construction of media-influenced memory in American culture.

These groups often follow some form of religious or secular millennial myth that helps them to interpret and explain their social experience, allowing them to contextualize that experience in any way they choose (Hill, Hickman, and McLendon 2001; Lamy 1992; Tapia 2003). Most commonly, those that claim to be survivalists focus on ideologies that lead them to prepare for adverse conditions. They focus on social/political/economic collapse or change that will bring about a dystopian situation, where they will need to defend themselves and their families or communities from those that they perceive as a threat.

The goal of prepping, alternatively, is to learn how to effectively survive disasters and adapt to long-term change within a local area. According to preppers I interviewed, the most important adverse events to anticipate were those most likely to occur—house fires, strong storms, flooding, tornados, and earthquakes. However, participants report that the preparations and skills necessary to weather these events are the same as those used to respond to large-scale events (e.g., social unrest). The need for food, water, and safety are paramount regardless.

This explanation is important because there is a common misperception of preppers by those familiar with the term. The primary sources of misconception come from television shows on the National Geographic (NatGeo) channel. *Doomsday Preppers*, the most well known, has made the public more aware of prepping. However, the show is biased toward one extreme within prepping—those that can afford the time and money to gather exorbitant amounts of material and gear and have extraordinary views on the events that would lead to using it.

The preppers participating in this research were not able to construct such arsenals. They consider the show as a bit of a spectacle, purposely showing fringe elements of the movement in order to make it NatGeo's most watched series over the past three years (North 2012). However, the show creates a lasting discourse that frames stereotypes of preppers in American society, the kinds of events that influence them, and how much time, money, and effort they are willing to expend in ways that can be problematic in the future (discussed below). The *Doomsday Preppers* website supports this notion of preppers as "Other," painting participants on the show as irrational agents, prepping for the coming apocalypse (Meet the Experts 2012). Thus, anyone claiming to be a prepper is often framed as resembling the show's participants and emulating their extreme behaviors. My contention is that there is a distinct difference between such fringe elements of the past and the average prepper of today. Furthermore, these differences are what allow for the construction of microresiliencies within communities that can bolster established systems.

## Zombie Squad

Preppers are different from survivalists. To illustrate this, I will introduce one well-established prepping organization—ZS. Founded by a group of five friends in 2003, in St. Louis, Missouri, ZS has grown into a grassroots, nonprofit (501c3). It is an all-volunteer disaster preparedness and awareness organization. Their tagline is "ZS is the nation's premier non-stationary cadaver suppression task force" (ZS 2009). This message emphasizes that, if you are prepared for a zombie apocalypse, then you are prepared for anything.

The organization has a standard corporate structure that is headed by an "international board" that oversees the ZS brand, deals with media, maintains the extensive online forum, and manages the larger charity functions. Fifty-one "chapters" in the United States and ZS's only international chapter in Southern Ontario, Canada, support the international board. Chapters, consisting of at least three active members, are required to host public, monthly meetings (often held in local bars or restaurants), as well as seminars and charity drives to bring disaster preparedness education to their communities. They often conduct these events while dressed in black tactical ("tacticool") gear and preaching against the dangers of zombies. It should be noted that members do not consider zombies or a zombie apocalypse to be a realistic threat. Rather, these are representational of emerging threats for which it is possible to prepare (Curtis 2012; McIntosh and Leverette 2008).

Because ZS is not strict on membership being a prerequisite to participating in the group, there is no accurate count of the "card-carrying" members. As of October 2015, its online forum had nearly 52,000 active participants. This suggests that the organization has wide online appeal. However, that appeal is tempered by the homogeneity of group chapters. While a detailed discussion is beyond the scope of this paper, it is important to note that preppers in this research tended to be primarily male (about 80%). Females tend to be partnered with males (15%), although about 5% are single. Participants are middle class (income over US$30,000) and almost entirely ethnically "white."

Despite this homogeneity, the organization's message is inclusive and public. While there are some latent political overtones to ZS's ideals, such as supporting the rights of gun owners (which tends toward the political right), their ideas on inclusivity and their opposition to stereotypical survivalist ideologies lean toward the political left. Political or religious talk is not allowed at meetings, gatherings, or on online boards. The organization feels these topics only lead to divisiveness. ZS is attempting to build a community of common knowledge without the ideology that is so important in survivalist circles. This was a conscious decision on the part of ZS founders. One member posted the following statement to explain why these policies are important to organizational continuation:

> ZS is where rabid republicans can sit down and talk trigger tuning jobs on AR [a type of rifle] variants with devout democrats; where successful businessmen, doctors and lawyers can sit down and talk about backpacks and hydration pouches with struggling students and minimum wagers...and it's because of the things we don't talk about when we sit down to talk that this is so. (ZS 2011)

Despite its name, the members of ZS are rational, well-informed individuals who are simply concerned with being prepared for adverse possibilities. The name "Zombie Squad" was intentional. As one founder of the group stated in an interview, "No one would show up if we called ourselves the St. Louis Tornado group. Zombies are cool and it gets people interested."

Members pay to join the organization and volunteer for activities. They report joining for the knowledge and the social aspects. They want to connect with others who are interested in learning and talking about survival strategies, gear, and end-of-the-world scenarios in a serious manner. Being a member becomes a part of their identity. They project this by wearing logoed clothes, patches, and gear. It also becomes the lens through which they view the world: they try to see how each context or item in their environment might be useful in different situations.

Embracing this identity has made ZS members a respected group in the local disaster preparedness community; it altered the local framing of preppers in the eye of the media, local citizens, and organizations. Further, ZS gives members a public outlet for their experience, knowledge, and willingness to assist the community. While members may never have to respond to a disaster situation, they still act as nodes of preparedness around the community. Thus, they function the same as any department within an organization's disaster preparedness plan.

### Commonalities

Aspects of survivalism and prepping overlap where the focus is on building knowledge about how to adapt to and survive adverse events. This reflects ZS's mission and mostly consists of learning how to procure and treat water and food and how to maintain safety in any given situation. Other skills that are emphasized include first-aid, communications (especially short-wave radio), and firearms training. For ZS, these skills are often taught through the assembly of a "bug-out bag." This is a backpack or duffle with the gear that individuals need if they are forced to leave their residence. The bag is prepared for immediate need (3–5 days), with the idea that other types of assistance will be provided within a matter of days by governmental or nongovernmental agencies.

The contents of the bag depend on the individual and his/her level of skill. ZS members often noted that the more skill you have, the lighter your bag. If you know of potential clean water sources or have a way to filter it, for instance, then you don't need to constantly carry five pounds of water. Thus, survivalists and preppers share a desire for training and skill building. The key to understanding the difference between the two groups isn't the behavior; it is the impetus behind the behaviors.

### Tactics and Sharing

The rationale behind learning, practicing, and disseminating skills and strategies differentiates survivalist and preppers. Also, with whom they share those skills and strategies differ vastly. ZS, at one end of the spectrum, wants every person in their communities to be prepared at a minimum bug-out bag level. The fact that ZS does this without overt calls to political, religious, or exclusionary ideologies differentiates it from survivalist groups. Survivalist groups generally want to keep these skills within their ideological communities to the exclusion of others. They may have notions of using those skills/strategies against the rest of society in order to fulfill ideas of revolution or apocalypse (Lamy 1996; Mitchell 2002). Survivalist groups often envision using the potential chaos created by an adverse event to generate a new society based on their ideologies (Berlet 2004; Hill, Hickman, and McLendon 2001). In opposition to this, preppers, like ZS, want to contribute to current forms of society, as well as recognized disaster response systems, by making it more resilient.

### Why These Differences Matter

If preppers are equated with the stereotypical survivalist, then potential relationships between preppers and other individuals, organizations, and agencies within their communities may be hindered. As discussed here, ZS has been successful in showing that its members are something new in the disaster preparedness community. In so doing, ZS has been able to construct a loose web of micro-resilient areas that could act as nodes for information, resources, safety, and communications, supporting a larger effort by response organizations and agencies.

## BUILDING RESILIENCY

The United States has a wide-ranging system of disaster and emergency preparedness and assistance-based agencies. The Federal Emergency Management Agency (FEMA) acts as the primary organizing agency for other federal, state, and local disaster management agencies and first responders. Additionally, international organizations, like the American Red Cross, have local chapters across the country, supplementing the government network. FEMA's Citizen Corp (2009) found that 61% of 4461 households surveyed would rely on these agencies given a local disaster. Even among those who reported they were "prepared" for local disaster, less than 30% had knowledge of their community evacuation routes and only 34% knew how to get information on local hazards (2009). The survey showed low levels of participation in preparedness activities and general knowledge on what to do, what to have available, or how to get help.

From the perspective of the prepper community, this is problematic, as the agencies (local, regional, or federal) cannot respond to disaster quickly. Thus, preppers plan for self-sufficiency until help arrives or in the case that it never does. In conversations and interviews, research participants repeatedly cited Hurricane Katrina, referring to the fact that help never arrived for some. Members of ZS have repeatedly reminded me that they fully support response agencies and recognize that these services are important. While they may have detailed, well-considered plans, they are just as vulnerable as the rest of society. Thus, they may be limited in their ability to respond. This is why members prep.

Members spoke heatedly, noting that if the rate of prepping were higher, the average person might be able to avoid some of the problems seen with Katrina. They do admit that prepping does not necessarily keep one from being vulnerable. In any disaster, you may lose your gear, food, and shelter and be unable to avoid some depravation. However, ZS argues that once you have certain skills, they are always with you. Basic survival knowledge and skill is what makes members resilient.

In this regard, prepping is a process, not an outcome. When asked if you could ever consider yourself prepared, members of ZS had strong responses.

*GB*: "I don't think so!...it's almost like a sport, always improving your game. But, you're never gonna say, 'done.' You continually get a little better, a little better, a little better."

*BC*: "Oh no, it's definitely a spectrum of preparedness…Preparedness, it's a journey not a destination. [*laughs*] Because in the end, even the really prepared guy is not necessarily prepared for everything, there's a lot of stuff he's not prepared for…there's no guarantees."

The process allows for vulnerabilities but attempts to reduce them by finding creative ways to adapt. ZS members often talk about being responsive to a changing world, especially in times of crisis, when services and resources may be unreliable or unavailable. This also means, at least on the small scale, that conceptions of resiliency encompass all services and resources needed by the individual or small group. Thus, preppers are adaptation-oriented in terms of constructing resiliency because that is what is necessary at the microlevel.

Members of ZS are not just constructing resiliency. They are influencing others to do so as well. ZS realized it could not achieve its goal of public education independently, but few organizations wanted to work with the group based on their name alone. Even fewer organizations wanted to work with, or be associated with, a group of young, tattooed, and pierced people dressed in black, military-style clothes. Still, building partnerships not only furthers ZS's goal of spreading the ideals of prepping, it also exemplifies its notion that resilient systems are redundant ones. Members have a saying to demonstrate this: "Two is one, one is none." The idea is that everything will fail, so maintaining redundancies is essential.

Members of ZS tend to think of these redundant systems in terms of gear and skills they can gain. However, as an organization, ZS has attempted to develop their adaptive capacity (Carpenter, Walker, Anderies, and Abel 2001) and adaptability (Walker, Abel, Anderies, and Ryan 2009) by building networks with other organizations in the area. ZS was able to forge relationships with three sectors within the community that have proved to be vital in gaining legitimacy for the organization: local community centers and organizations, law enforcement, and the nonprofit sector.

The first step was gaining legitimacy with the local chapter of the American Red Cross by hosting successful blood donation campaigns at local community centers and union halls. At these venues, the group was able to mix its membership with community partners not only to raise the number of blood donors but also to raise community awareness of the group. This gave ZS instant access to community organization structures to which it might not otherwise have contact. The American Red Cross publicly acknowledged the hard work and dedication ZS put into their blood drives by presenting them with official letters of thanks and coproducing fliers and banners to advertise future events.

ZS continued to plan regular charity events such as movie nights, canned food drives, and donation-based events at those same locations and local bars, leading to thousands of dollars going to local and international organizations. For example, in interviews, the international board reported that its dedicated networking allowed them to raise more than $13,000 in a matter of weeks for the Japan disaster in 2011. ZS received letters of thanks and recognition from local nonprofits and larger ones such as the American Cancer Society, Direct Relief International, and Save the Children for sponsoring fund-raising events. This legitimization helps to frame the group as a serious organization whose membership is focused on disaster preparation and helping communities affected by adverse events.

The ties to local and regional law enforcement developed in a similar way. Members of ZS, some of who are former military or have worked for or with police organizations, volunteer to act as "criminals" and "victims" for trainings. Additionally, about 48% of members of ZS who participated in this research are also members of Citizen Emergency Response Teams (CERTs). These small neighborhood teams are part of FEMA's plan to localize emergency response (www.fema.gov 2015). Being a part of these teams also builds ties with local law enforcement and with first responders.

For example, after training with regional, interdepartmental SWAT (Special Weapons and Tactics) teams covering 11 counties in Illinois, where ZS members had played the role of "terrorists," several officers voiced concern over the level of tactical skills and firearm knowledge held by the members. In an interview with the regional commander of the training, he related that "3 or 4" of his officers were not comfortable with the idea that ZS members were training with, and thus observing, "law enforcement strategies, armaments and training dynamics." Yet, when questioned, the reason for this was the connection between this kind of knowledge and how it has been used in the past by antigovernment survivalists. It is this kind of framing that can destroy community relationships that ZS has worked so hard to build.

Aware of these misgivings, ZS has continued to build legitimacy and foster relationships with each of these organizations independently through its work, knowledge, and the experience of the members. While this has not resulted in any of these organizations formally including ZS in their plans, it has altered the response landscape for emergencies and disasters in the localized St. Louis metro area (which covers the city of St. Louis, Missouri, and the adjacent counties in Illinois). In fact, the relationships that the home chapter of ZS has built in this area over the past ten years directly relate to the types of volunteer services it is able to supply to the community during or after an event: search and rescue, triage, and first aid (CERT and American Red Cross), distribution of resources and services (Red Cross and local law enforcement in the St. Louis metro area), supplemental security, and communications (CERT and local law enforcement in the St. Louis metro area). This example is specific to the St. Louis chapter of ZS; however, interviews with other chapters in the United States point to much the same relationships in other chapter's areas.

Furthermore, in interviews supplemented with conversations at charity events and trainings with representatives from the American Red Cross, local and regional law enforcement, and CERT instructors in the St. Louis metro area, there is respondent consensus that, when ZS members show up, they are there to work and are willing and interested in learning new skills. The organizations know members tend to have some knowledge and experience in training for disaster situations. They also know that ZS members often have some of their own supplies and will not be reliant on response systems in the short-term.

## CONCLUSION

The concept of resiliency needs to have some metrics, such as infrastructure, economy, ecology, and community systems, in order for policy makers and organizations to determine how a community might respond to an adverse event (Cutter, Burton, and Emrich 2010). However, because they are difficult to account for within these larger scales, individuals and small groups within communities are not likely to be counted in such metrics, even if they hold significant resources in terms of preparedness and knowledge (Cutter, Burton, and Emrich 2010). In addition, preppers and others may not hold to those same metrics when assessing their preparedness and ability to respond to events.

My observations and conversations have shown that preppers spend a great deal of time researching and contributing to the communal, organizational, and agency-based knowledge about how best to prepare, adapt, and survive various events. This communal sourcing of knowledge allows people from all over the political, social, and economic spectrums to share information with like-minded others. So, while the group may be localized, the expertise they gain and share may originate from a much wider area. Technical experts from various fields and regions contribute to that pool of knowledge. This corresponds to the definition of resiliency, presented earlier, in terms of building capacity and knowledge in order to construct resilient systems.

How these knowledge and experience are then applied to behaviors and networking will vary. Not all groups prepare in the same way, have the same resources, or are likely to be confronted by or be able to manage the same threats. Because these are individuals, small groups, or loosely organized larger groups, their adaptability is fluid. While preppers would never be able to respond to a large-scale disaster en masse, that is not their aim. Their goal is to be able to apply their knowledge and skills during an event, so that they can avoid needing assistance from large-scale organizations or be able to lend support to those in need. This type of self-organization (part 2 of the Resilience Alliance's definition of resiliency, given previously) is also important should the established plans fail due to the scale of the disaster. The hope, according to conversations with research participants, is that preppers could act as nodes of assistance, resources, and security until the response organizations could recover.

Admittedly, this is an untested web of relationships. Though ZS members have volunteered after disasters (e.g., Katrina, local tornadoes, and floods), there has yet to be a need for large-scale, prolonged response from any of the ZS chapters. As with any organization's disaster preparation, the true test occurs when the plan is implemented for the first time. You can only be so ready. But, this is where the power of ZS's goals and membership shines. ZS members continue to develop best practices, share information, and adapt, as any resilient system must. Moreover, as they build individual competency and legitimacy with multiscalar organizations, their microresilience bolsters the larger local systems, regardless of whether they are included in those systems.

The lessons learned from the example of ZS are twofold. First, communities can always be more prepared. It is possible to move communities toward preparedness by mobilizing the public to collectively plan and engage in skill building as per their resources. Plans can be created with little to no resources and still save lives. Being adaptive to emerging conditions is the key to preparedness. Second, being adaptive is more possible in a context of collaboration and consensus building. It is most beneficially adaptive when communities, government, and nongovernmental organizations work together on plans and how best to utilize resources, including each other.

This is the kind of resiliency-construction leaders and policy makers need to nurture. ZS's saying "two is one, one is none" exemplifies this idea through the creation of supportive systems. While they are not a duplicate system by any means, the unique set of skills preppers are able to provide does offer a small-scale redundant system that may help some communities withstand a disaster to which they may have otherwise succumbed.

## REFERENCES

Berlet, C. 2004. Militias in the frame. *Contemporary Sociology* 33(5): 514–521.

Berry, B. 1999. *Social rage*. London: Routledge.

Caron, C. 2011. Montana manhunt for David Burgert, survivalist militia leader. Retrieved from: http://abcnews.go.com/US/montana-manhunt-david-burgert-survivalist-militia-leader/story?id=13841307&page=2, accessed May 28, 2015.

Carpenter, S., B. Walker, J. Anderies, and N. Abel. 2001. From metaphor to measurement: Resilience of what to what? *Ecosystems* 4(8): 765–781.

Curtis, C.P. 2012. *Postapocalyptic fiction and the social contract*. Lanham, MD: Lexington.

Cutter, S.L., C.G. Burton, and C.T. Emrich. 2010. Disaster resilience indicators for benchmarking baseline conditions. *Journal of Homeland Security and Emergency Management* 7(1): 1–22.

DeWalt, K. and B. DeWalt. 2011. *Participant observation*. Lanham, MD: Altamira.

Federal Emergency Management Agency. 2015. Retrieved from: http://www.fema.gov/community-emergency-response-teams, accessed February 19, 2015.

Hill, H., J. Hickman, and J. McLendon. 2001. Cults and sects and doomsday groups, oh my: Media treatment of religion on the eve of the millennium. *Review of Religious Research* 43(1): 24–38.

International Federation of Red Cross and Red Crescent Societies. 2014. *World disasters report 2014: Focus on culture and risk*. Retrieved from: http://www.ifrc.org/world-disasters-report-2014, accessed June 9, 2015.

Johnston, H. and J.A. Noakes. 2005. *Frames of protest*. Lanham, MD: Rowman and Littlefield.

Lamy, P. 1992. Millennialism in the mass media: The case of "Solider of Fortune" magazine. *Journal for the Scientific Study of Religion* 31(4): 408–424.

Lamy, P. 1996. *Millennium rage*. New York: Plenum Press.

McIntosh, S. and M. Leverette. 2008. *Zombie culture*. Lanham, MD: Scarecrow.

Meet the Experts. 2012. Retrieved from: http://channel.nationalgeographic.com/doomsday-preppers/articles/meet-the-experts/, accessed October 9, 2015.

Mitchell, Jr. R. 2002. *Dancing at Armageddon*. Chicago: University of Chicago Press.

North, J. 2012. "Doomsday Preppers" casting director aims to be prepared, too. *Asheville Daily Planet*. Retrieved from: http://www.ashevilledailyplanet.com/news/2771-doomsday-preppers-casting-director-aims-to-be-prepared-too, accessed May 28, 2015.

O'Reilly, K. 2012. *Ethnographic methods*. London: Routledge.

Resilience Alliance. 2010. Assessing and managing resilience in social-ecological systems: A practitioner's workbook, Version 2.0. Retrieved from: http://www.resalliance.org/3871.php, accessed October 9, 2015.

Spradley, J. 1980. *Participant observation*. New York: Holt, Rinehart and Winston.

Tapia, A. 2003. Technomillennialism: A subcultural response to the technological threat of Y2K. *Science, Technology, & Human Values* 28(4): 483–512.

Temple-Raston, D. 2010. How the FBI got inside the Hutaree militia. Retrieved from: http://www.npr.org/templates/story/story.php?storyId=125856761, accessed June 15, 2015.

Walker, B., N. Abel, J.M. Anderies, and P. Ryan. 2009. Resilience, adaptability, and transformability in the Goulburn-Broken Catchment Australia. *Ecology and Society* 14(1): 12.

Weeber, S. and D. Rodeheaver. 2003. Militias at the millennium: A test of Smelser's theory of collective behavior. *The Sociological Quarterly* 44(2): 181–204.

Zombie Squad (ZS). 2009. What is Zombie Squad? St. Louis: Zombie Squad. Retrieved from: http://zombiehunters.org/downloads/index.php#flyers, accessed January 10, 2010.

Zombie Squad (ZS). 2011. Zombie Squad forum rules: Read me! Retrieved from: http://zombiehunters.org/forum/viewtopic.php?f=44&t=19895, accessed January 21, 2012.

# 23 All the Years Combine
## *The Expansion and Contraction of Time and Memory in Disaster Response*

*A.J. Faas*

### CONTENTS



**Abstract**

Disaster response is a process that entails neutralizing a biophysical hazard while mitigating effects sustained by humans, animals, and their property and environment. These are sites in which histories of relationships among communities, institutions, and in environments are thrown into relief, where parties to disaster response draw on memories in acts of narrative construction in discourse with the past. This paper explores how these memories are produced, negotiated, and translated in multiple contexts by contrasting two bundles of stories drawn from studies of disaster-induced resettlements in highland Ecuador and wildfires in the northwestern United States. In Ecuador, I identify ways in which practice informed memory; among wildfire responders, I find memories informing practice. They draw on existing cultural repertoires and recollections that are simultaneously compressed under the weight of time, retelling, and shared cultural meanings that reduce difference and idiosyncrasy in individual experience. This study also points to the ways in which the spatiotemporal expansions and contractions of memory affect practice in neutralizing hazards, mitigating impacts, and resettlement and recovery.

### INTRODUCTION

Catastrophic events often register as cultural traumas, threatening a palpable loss of identity on top of the frequently staggering material losses. Inevitably, following cataclysmic events, stories of the experience emerge and circulate among survivors and others. While remembrances may serve many functions, the shared recollections and retellings of common experiences, places, and times are often sources of healing for disaster survivors. Retelling and recollection may be means to recover identity and a sense of both personal and shared cultural wholeness (Eyerman 2004;

Hawdon and Ryan 2008; Komac 2009). Memories are also social reconstructions wrought by present concerns (Halbwachs 1992; Trouillot 1995), reaffirming, as Ricoeur (2004) says, that the recursive process of memory (re)construction makes the distinction between recall and imagination an often elusive pursuit.

I have found that invocations of memory are common among the people I have studied in post-disaster resettlement in the Andean highlands of Ecuador and in wildfire response in the American northwest. In this paper, I consider their significance for the interpretation of human behavior in disaster response and recovery. I have been concerned primarily with investigating the ways in which memories inform practice and, perhaps, the ways in which practice informs memory. Here, I contrast two stories to point to the ways in which the parties to disaster response engage in what Ogden (2011, p. 25) calls "remembering as critical practice."

In my analysis, remembering, as critical practice, takes shape in several ways. First, as Ogden (2011, p. 26) points out, these rememberings are not deconstructing critiques. Rather, they are acts of construction of narratives in discourse with both the past and the present. Second, memories of disaster frequently undergo a sort of compression or noise reduction, largely brought on through social retelling and forgetting over time, such that nuance and variation in individual experience are often blended into collective versions. In this way, tragedies can be sources of cohesion and solidarity for a community and a means of recovery from cultural trauma (Hawdon and Ryan 2008; Moulton 2015). Third, in the moments in which a disaster is unfolding, people scan their mental catalogues and cultural repertoires for cues to inform action.

## METHODOLOGY

This chapter is based on data collected as part of two separate studies of networks of social relationships in disaster contexts. Data for the Ecuadorian case were collected as part of an ethnographic study of two disaster-induced resettlements and multiple displaced communities around Mt. Tungurahua in the central Andean cordillera. Data for this chapter come from focus groups I conducted in 2009, although the ethnographic context is based upon 10 months of fieldwork in 2009 and another 6 months of fieldwork in 2011. During this time, I conducted dozens of ethnographic interviews and administered approximately 230 semistructured interviews, which contribute to my contextualization of the focus group case.

Data from the American Pacific Northwest are drawn from my participation in the Fire Chasers' Improving Community Response to Wildfire project, a larger study of wildfire response network in Idaho, Montana, Oregon, and Washington. Data for this chapter are drawn from 25 key informant interviews with experienced wildfire responders in the study region. These interviews were conducted by myself and two colleagues (Branda Nowell and Toddi Steelman), with members of federal and state Incident Management Teams (IMTs),* US Department of Agriculture Forest Service fire staff, county fire chiefs, county sheriffs, and county government from September 2012 through March 2013.

Analysis of both bodies of data followed the same procedure. I collected passages of interviews and observations where people spoke of the memories and past experience and examined them for themes. I inductively coded passages of text according to salient themes and recursively revisited passages to correct and confirm my coding as new themes emerged (Krippendorf 2012). I revised my coding continuously until no new themes were detectable.

* IMTs provide a paramilitary management infrastructure for the logistical coordination of state, local, and federal emergency responders and government and nongovernmental agencies. IMTs are primarily for wildfire response but may be deployed in response to other hazards. Type I and Type II wildfire incidents are of the largest and most complex, requiring national resources in response. Type I IMTs are state or federally certified and have the highest levels of training and experience. Type II teams are also state or federally certified and their training and experience are second only to Type I teams.

## THE COMPRESSION OF MEMORY AFTER A VOLCANIC ERUPTION

In March 2009, my colleagues and I hosted a series of focus groups in the Penipe Nuevo resettlement in the Andean highlands of Ecuador. Roughly six months prior, the 287 houses in this small, periurban township had been granted to 1500 agro-pastoralists displaced from their villages by the eruptions of Mt. Tungurahua in 1999 and 2006. This tripled the predisaster size of the town (Faas 2015). The first focus group discussed several important events and processes that had occurred since the catastrophe. Families had been separated during evacuations, and separations often lasted months or years. Most resettlers now lacked access to land, productive resources, or employment. The group noted that a host of other all-too-common postdisaster and resettlement hardships had also taken place.

In the second group, an unexpected quarrel broke out after our first several questions. In response to the query, "How did you first become aware that the volcano was erupting?" Rafael Ocaña,* a soft-spoken, portly farmer who was pushing 70, began to tell the story of hearing sirens as soon as he felt tremors from the eruptions. He indicated that the time was roughly 9 am on October 15, 1999. He had barely uttered these words when eight men from the other side of the room protested, rudely shouting that the tremors were felt first several minutes prior to 9 am, and the sirens did not wail for another 20 minutes. Sr. Ocaña politely reiterated that these were the facts as he recalled them, that he and his family had spent no small amount of time recalling them, and that the local bus service arrived near his home within 20 minutes of hearing the alarms. Again, the chorus of angry voices rose from the other end of the room, yelling that Ocaña was in gross error and that the buses did not arrive for more than an hour.

As my study progressed, I came to see the dynamics of the focus group quarrel as pertaining to local processes through which practice informed memory. While Sr. Ocaña was from the village of Pungal de Puela, on the southern flank of the volcano and nearer the parish's main road, the other men in the room were from Manzano, a smaller village on the southwest flank of the volcano, on an auxiliary extension of the main road. What later became clear was that memories of these experiences were central to ongoing political conflict and competition between villages, and most especially in the resettlements, for access to state, nongovernmental, and private resources since the disasters. Neighboring villages had long competed for access these scarce resources as part of the clientalist political system that characterizes Ecuador's rural periphery (Faas in press), but competition was more heated and frequent in the wake of the eruptions and displacement.

In 2008 and 2009, a few years after the last great eruptions, displaced villagers often engaged in a "politics of deservingness," contesting distinctions between those deemed deserving and undeserving of aid in the form of housing, relief goods, and program inclusion by contrasting their suffering with that of others. Having just started fieldwork with the focus groups, I did not anticipate the relative importance of the times and spaces of the initial disaster events and evacuation processes in marking these domains of suffering and, hence, deservingness. When households from one village displaced by the eruptions were perceived to be deprived of a form of aid, a typical rejoinder was "everyone from [some other village] receives houses and aid and they never suffered the way we did!"

It is not uncommon for memories to undergo a smoothing process, minimizing variation and indeterminacy to provide a sort of stabilization that may aid in healing processes (Moulton 2015). Things imagined, remembered, and experienced can become "time stories" that form schematics for organizing thoughts and practice (Fincher, Barnett, Graham, and Hurlimann 2014, p. 203). Disaster memories in Penipe solidified around definite times, spaces, and events among, and sometimes in contrast to, certain groups.

To a limited extent, the different locations of villages along the flanks of Mt. Tungurahua can explain some degree of variation in what Komac (2009) called "geographical memory" or memories

* All names of individuals and wildfire incidents are pseudonyms.

whose vantage points are affected by spatial relationships with a given phenomenon. However, I know from numerous ethnographic interviews with members of each village that most were not at their homes or village centers when the eruptions occurred. Many were scattered in their fields or among their animals in the hills around the volcano. Others were in neighboring villages. Yet, within each village, strikingly consistent renditions of the time stories of the events, alarms, and the arrival of evacuation assistance emerged.

The spatiotemporal details of memory in these villages compressed under the weight of perpetual retelling. They became political instruments frequently deployed in the competition between villagers from different villages for scarce resources in resettlement and recovery. Disaster memories were invoked in contexts of competition over the flows of outside aid as well as local resources. For example, in a parish council meeting in August 2011, nearly three years after resettlement, a local delegate stood up to accuse members of the council from neighboring villages of corruption, claiming that people who did not truly suffer from the volcano received houses in the resettlement while other deserving families went without. Another woman later stood up at the same meeting, claiming that some villages get selected for aid projects because they appear more organized, not because they are particularly deserving as a result of their suffering.

In her ethnography of the impacts of the 2004 tsunami in Sri Lanka, Gamburd (2013) found that accusations of corruption were common where local leaders are active agents in the distribution of aid. Like those noted by Gamburd, the accusations I recorded were rarely, if ever, substantiated. However, they did have the impact of imposing a sort of moral economy over aid administration processes by forcing leaders to be exceedingly transparent in their dealings to avoid any accusation of impropriety.

Back in the Penipe Nuevo resettlement, two women from Manzano, emboldened by the politics of deservingness that is so animated in local affairs, gained notoriety for spying on other resettlers and reporting them to the corresponding agencies for failing to fulfill occupancy requirements. In truth, many residents, including the reconnoitering women themselves, frequently abandoned the resettlements for days on end to tend to their fields and animals on the slopes of the volcano. Yet, the passionately held view, bolstered by retelling of disaster suffering, was that these women and their neighbors were simply more deserving of these resources than the others. This resulted in several of those accused being threatened with eviction and heightened acrimony between neighbors from different villages in the resettlements.

## WILDFIRE AND THE EXPANSES OF MEMORY

While practice informs memory in postdisaster resettlements in Ecuador, I encountered the inverse when I began studying wildfire response in the American Northwest. I noted the ways in which memory informs practice for decision making and help seeking. When communities experience a wildfire and complex responder networks (local, state, federal) mobilize, both responders and those affected are focused on the present and emerging conditions, but thoughts also fan out into the past. People scan their memories for experiences that help make sense of what is currently happening. They recall past fires and interactions with various personnel and agencies involved in response. They remember how those interactions shaped and affected their livelihoods and culture. One IMT Incident Commander, with 30 years of fire management experience, notes,

> Communities have amazing memories. I mean, oh my gosh, you come into some of these communities and there was a bad fire 20 years ago—for instance, if you go fight fire in Augusta, Montana, you will hear about the Canyon Creek fire in 1988. It is fresh in their memories and there's a lot of other places like that with a lot of other fires.

I joined the Fire Chasers Project at North Carolina State University in 2012. We launched a large-scale study of interorganizational networks in wildfire response. We began by conducting dozens of interviews with national (Type I and Type II) IMT personnel and others in wildfire service. We wanted to map the contours of the ways in which wildfire team leaders identified, prioritized, and managed relational risks (the interpersonal, cultural, and political aspects of fire management) in the social life of wildfire incident response. One of the more salient issues that stood out during these interviews was that IMT and other wildfire personnel were often quite attuned to the ways in which memories shape perceptions, relations, and action for themselves and the individuals, groups, and organizations with whom they communicate and coordinate in an incident. In what follows, I identify some of the themes that emerged in their chronicles of wildfire response.

First, some IMT personnel speak of entering communities where bitter memories of past incidents and IMTs linger; they discuss how they have to actively work to build and repair relationships with local agencies and communities who felt they had been unfairly treated by outside agencies in the past (see also Carroll, Cohn, Seesholtz, and Higgins 2005; Carroll, Higgins, Cohn, and Burchfield 2006). One local fire chief, with experience working on IMTs for dozens of Type I fires, recalls a story:

> We had a fire in…"07" I think it was—called the Pole Summit Fire in Montana, that burned over the continental divide and we ended up catching it on the Indian Reservation. They had had a fire there several years before called the Eagle Ridge fire, which ended up with…very poor relationships, not just between the [Native American Group] and the Forest Service, but even between different forests on the Forest Service.…So going into the Pole Summit fire, that was…an absolute priority to not have a similar experience as had occurred on the Eagle Ridge fire.
>
> The catalyst to bring them all together to communicate again was the Pole Summit Fire. So prior to that they struggled to even find common ground…to work to fix the communication and it ended up being the fire that became the catalyst. And it ended up very well, very positive in fact.

On the other hand, the absence of memory and a lack of wildfire culture can be a source of tension. Several IMT personnel told us that fear and uncertainty run deep and wide in communities without previous experience with wildfire. One Fire Management Officer, who also served as an Incident Commander for the past seven years, spoke of returning to Colorado for a fire three years after having been there for the Terrapin Fire. He noted that no one except for the sheriff remembered him or how they had worked effectively together in the past to avoid disaster.

> So the first press conference I'm thinking these people are scared. I mean, they were fearful that the fire was coming right in to the edge of town. It was going to take out all the neighborhoods. So my first press conference, the first thing I said was my team's goal is to alleviate the effects on this community as quickly and as effectively as we can…We're not going away until it's taken care of. People said, "Okay. It was good. I'm glad you said that." And next thing, you've got to work to kind of build up some credibility that you understand their issues, that you understand their fears, all that stuff. And I think if you can figure out how to do that, you're going to get up to speed in terms of community support quicker.

In some places, memories extend to bygone times when livelihoods and culture were tied to local resources to which the US Forest Service now restricts access. Although changes in Asian export demands and the globalization of lumber markets in the late 1980s and 1990s contributed significantly to the decline in logging (Daniels 2005), many continue to point reductions in timber harvesting in Pacific Northwest forests as the result of the US Fish and Wildlife Service listing the northern spotted owl as "threatened" in 1990 under the 1973 Endangered Species Act. These reductions were enforced by the US Forest Service. Thus, when Forest Service personnel and IMTs, many of whom also work for the Forest Service in their day jobs, enter a community during a wildfire, memories of the roles their agencies have played in people's lives are still very central. One IMT Operations

Chief with 24 years of experience on the US Forest Service fire staff tells a story that reflects popular memory of the decline in logging and attendant animosity toward the agency.

> As you well know, the Forest Service used to cut a lot of timber and was typically well inserted into small communities throughout the West as a result. Now, right, wrong, or indifferent, and because of the discovery of the Spotted Owl and the lack of numbers of Spotted Owl...and the requirement for us to protect the habitat for the Spotted Owl, obviously, we pretty much stopped cutting timber. And that goes everywhere from the corner of Oregon all the way down there to the southeast corner of New Mexico.
>
> So, as a result, we had a lot of small communities whose livelihood depended on the logging industry. Their economies basically fell apart...So there was a lot of animosity against the Forest Service because all they knew is that the Forest Service stopped cutting timber...all they remember is that the Forest Service was responsible for their lack of the livelihood that they knew for generations. Because, in a lot of those small towns, it was the grandfathers, the fathers, and the sons—they were all loggers, and they were proud of what they did.

This rendition is an exaggeration of the historical influence of the role of the Forest Service in the decline of logging. However, it is illustrates the ways in which tensions over resource extraction and conservation stand out as salient features in land and wildfire management in the American West (Faas, Jones, Whiteford, Tobin, and Murphy 2014). These tensions occasionally flare up and make national news, as with the armed confrontation of Bureau of Land Management personnel on the Bundy Ranch in Nevada in 2014.

People's attachments to their past are often tied to senses of place that are intimately bound to the landscape (Frake 1996). Landscapes themselves often "reflect a buildup of memory, history, and experience that is as compositional to landscapes as are layers of rock" (Ogden 2011, p. 28). Sawmills, now abandoned and dilapidated, are key memorial fixtures in the landscape. In these places, the perception of the Forest Service and other outside federal agencies as responsible for loss of livelihood can loom large. One seasoned Operations Chief explained,

> And so what I've seen...is that we go into some of these small communities that used to be timber-based—and you can still see the mills in the towns, so that the mills are closed and everything is falling apart. And because of that animosity against the Forest Service, there is not a good relationship between the private citizen and the Forest Service. And those are the communities where we have a really hard time.

Perceptions and practice in the social environment of incident response are borne of multiple jurisdictional, functional, cultural, and social differences in disaster response networks. Breakdowns in one part of response networks cascade into other areas, with potentially devastating effects (Nowell and Steelman 2015). When the fire is over, the flames vanish, and the smoke is cleared, the social life of the incident lingers in people's recollections. These memories endure and change through retelling and reconstruction and will become features of the social lives of future incidents. An Incident Commander with 23 years of experience in fire service notes,

> Let me tell you something, it's very critical that I learned a long time ago. Wildfires have one thing in common, they are all going to go out, whether you put them out, whether the weather puts them out, and burns itself out...they are all going to go out. What an IMT gets remembered for is how we conduct to the business of the fire.

An IMT Public Information Officer with 28 years of experience in wildfire management in the northwest states,

> The fire goes out and it's over and people don't you know they remember the smoke and flames especially if they lost their homes. But what they're gonna remember more is how did you deal with me

> when I lost my home. How quickly was I evacuated, how good was the information that you gave me, how much did I feel that you cared. All of those things are the feeling that are left a long time after... you to squirt water on the fire and put it out.

## DISCUSSION

Human relationships with the past may be no more definite and no less precarious than our relationships with the future. In Penipe, practice informed memory, whereas among disaster responders and IMTs, memories informed practice. While it would be unwise to generalize too broadly from these cases, it is important to note that these patterns should not be seen as mutually exclusive. Rather, I encountered moments of practice informing memory at a particular time in the Ecuadorian resettlements and recollections of memory informing practice in wildfire response in the American northwest. In both instances, people's thoughts radiate outward and expand the spatiotemporal scale of emerging response contexts. They draw on existing cultural repertoires and recollections that are simultaneously compressed under the weight of time, retelling, and shared cultural meanings that have reduced difference and idiosyncrasy.

The contraction of time and memory postdisaster can become political, as shared recollections can foster solidarity around who gets what, when, and how (after Lasswell 1936). Likewise, in an ongoing crisis, memories may be anchored to the politics of resource management, extraction, and conservation; they affect interaction, communication, and relationships rooted in human–environmental entanglements. These memories occupy the interstices between individual experience and the shared interpretive and behavioral repertoires we refer to as culture. One interesting dynamic can be found in the ways people anticipate working with other agencies in wildfire response networks (Faas, Velez, Nowell, and Steelman in press). The interpretive frames constructed from shared experience and retellings have fostered preferences for working with local and familiar leaders and agencies during the response. This is often to the exclusion of federal and other external agencies. However, effective coordination requires working across jurisdictional and other insider/outsider divisions. While there is some evidence that people are able to reframe these cognitive preferences in practice during actual wildfires and cooperate across preexisting divisions, there is a great deal of room for improvement in these relationships that could be better dealt with prior to emergency operations (see Lessons Learned below).

It is well established that processes of disaster planning, preparation, mitigation, response, and recovery are fundamentally relational processes. In many ways, actors in disaster response networks are engaging in relationships with relationships (after Dombrowski 2014). Community members, local responders, and IMTs are engaging not only in relational interactions with each other but also with relationships between publics and local, state, and federal agencies, past IMTs, people and resources, and, significantly, people and their memories. For IMTs and emergency managers, these memories become objects of study and intervention (Foucault 1990), part of cognitive and relational fields that inform action.

## LESSONS LEARNED

In studying wildfire response, my colleagues and I were constantly impressed with the degree of attention paid by members of outside IMTs to local cultures and locals' memories of and experiences with past wildfire incidents and the ways in which these phenomena affect disaster response practices. Local sensitivity emerged as a very salient issue in the majority of our conversations with IMT personnel. And yet, there is reason to point to relational risks that can persist in spite of, perhaps even because of, this awareness. One is the risk of committing the error I made in focus groups in the postdisaster resettlements in Ecuador—a failure to appreciate the alternatively subtle and stark differences in the perceptions, memories, and practices of key stakeholders. All too often, scholars, policy makers, and practitioners imagine local culture as static, unchanging, or holistic, which blinds us to the variegated, shifting, and contingent compositions of culture(s) in a given locale (Faas and Barrios 2015; Hoffman 2014). A priori characterizations of local cultures limit our ability to get to know and build relationships with real people and increase the likelihood of problems in communication and coordination. Operational priorities (i.e., neutralizing hazards and securing populations and values at risk) are also likely to place certain limits on the capacity of outside agencies to work with all parties immediately.

The divisions of social interaction and perception described throughout this chapter often result in the (re)production of sociotechnical systems of disaster response and recovery operations where scientific instruments, expert knowledge, and organizational practices are in discord with the social, cultural, and biophysical contexts in which they are applied (Faas and Barrios 2015). While no one strategy for overcoming enduring divisions is feasible or even desirable, there are at least three broad approaches worth suggesting. The first would be to work through local actors who can serve as social bridges to facilitate coordinated action across preexisting divisions (Faas, Velez, Nowell, and Steelman in press). Bridging actors connect otherwise disconnected groups and individuals, facilitating the flow of information and resources in emergency and recovery contexts. This has been documented as vital to successful incident response (Steelman, Nowell, Bayoumi, and McCaffrey 2014) and recovery (Faas, Jones, Whiteford, Tobin, and Murphy 2014; Faas, Jones, Tobin, Whiteford, and Murphy 2015; Halvorson and Hamilton 2007).

The second recommendation would be to identify ways to build and maintain relationships between groups and organizations involved in disaster response and recovery outside of disaster context. This could help foster the development of familiarity, trust, and shared knowledge. Simple meetings and retreats involving community members in hazard-prone communities and members of organizations involved in planning, prevention, response, and recovery could aid in the establishment of relationships outside emergency context that could facilitate more effective communication and coordination in emergency and recovery contexts. Preseason relationship-building activities could help reduce insider/outsider tensions that arise during response operations by helping attune external actors to local concerns and capacities in response. It can also familiarize locals with the response capabilities and priorities of outside actors.

Finally, bringing communities and agencies together can and often does entail going beyond simple meetings to conducting tabletop exercises and other response drills and planning activities, including recovery. These contexts allow people and agencies to share tools such as maps, archives, reports, symbols, and instruments that can serve as boundary objects (Star and Griesemer 1989). Such objects may originate in seemingly distinct social or epistemological domains but may serve to facilitate communication and translation of knowledge in ways that span these boundaries.

## ACKNOWLEDGMENTS

Key informant interviews with wildland fire personnel were drawn from a larger dataset collected by the Firechasers Research Program at North Carolina State University (Branda Nowell and Toddi Steelman, principle investigators), with funding provided by the National Science Foundation (8-1-2 4-01), the Joint Fire Science Program, and the US Forest Service Northern Research Station. Research for the Ecuadorian case study was funded in part by the National Science Foundation (0751264/0751265, Collaborative Research—Social Networks in Chronic Disasters: Exposure, Evacuation, and Resettlement), a National Science Foundation Dissertation Improvement Grant (1123962), and the Public Entity Risk Institute's (PERI) Dissertation Fellowship in Hazards, Risk, and Disasters. All views expressed in this article are those of the author.

## REFERENCES

Carroll, M.S., P.J. Cohn, D.N. Seesholtz, and L.L. Higgins. 2005. Fire as a galvanizing and fragmenting influence on communities: The case of the Rodeo–Chediski Fire. *Society & Natural Resources: An International Journal* 18(4): 301–320.

Carroll, M.S., L.L. Higgins, P.J. Cohn, and J. Burchfield. 2006. Community wildfire events as a source of social conflict. *Rural Sociology* 71(2): 261–280.

Daniels, J.M. 2005. *The rise and fall of the Pacific Northwest log export market*. Portland, OR: United States Department of Agriculture, Forest Service, Pacific Northwest Research Station, General Technical Report PNW-GTR-624.

Dombrowski, K. 2014. A novel formalization of peer influence incorporating both self-directed and alter-directed sentiment and disposition. Paper delivered at the 34th Annual International Sunbelt Social Network Conference, St. Pete Beach, FL, February 18–24.

Eyerman, R. 2004. Cultural trauma: Slavery and the formation of African American identity. In *Cultural trauma and collective identity*, ed. J.C. Alexander, 60–111. Berkeley: University of California Press.

Faas, A.J. in press. Reciprocity and vernacular statecraft: Changing practices of Andean cooperation in post-disaster highland Ecuador. *Journal of Latin American and Caribbean Anthropology*.

_____. 2015. Disaster resettlement organizations, NGOs, and the culture of cooperative labor in the Ecuadorian Andes. In *Disaster's Impact on Livelihoods and Cultural Survival: Losses, Opportunities, and Mitigation*, ed. M. Companion, 51–62. Boca Raton, FL: CRC Press.

Faas, A.J. and R. Barrios. 2015. Applied anthropology of risk, hazards, and disasters. *Human Organization* 74(4): 287–296.

Faas, A.J., E.C. Jones, G.A. Tobin, L.M. Whiteford, and A.D. Murphy. 2015. Critical aspects of social networks in a resettlement setting. *Development in Practice* 25(2): 221–233.

Faas, A.J., E.C. Jones, L.M. Whiteford, G.A. Tobin, and A.D. Murphy. 2014. Gendered access to formal and informal resources in post disaster development in the Ecuadorian Andes. *Mountain Research and Development* 34(3): 223–234.

Faas, A.J., A. Velez, B. Nowell, and T. Steelman. In press. Patterns of preference and practice: Bridging actors in wildfire response networks in the American Northwest. *Disasters* 41(3).

Fincher, R., J. Barnett, S. Graham, and A. Hurlimann. 2014. Time stories: Making sense of futures in anticipation of sea-level rise. *Geoforum* 56: 201–210.

Foucault, M. 1990. *The history of sexuality, volume 1: An introduction*. New York: Vintage Books.

Frake, C. 1996. Pleasant places, past times and sheltered identity in rural East Anglia. In *Senses of place*, eds. S. Feld and K.H. Basso, 229–258. Santa Fe: School of American Research Press.

Gamburd, M. 2013. *The golden wave: Culture and politics after Sri Lanka's tsunami disaster*. Bloomington, IN: University of Indiana Press.

Halbwachs, M. 1992. *On collective memory*. Chicago: University of Chicago Press.

Halvorson, S.J. and J.P. Hamilton. 2007. Vulnerability and the erosion of seismic culture in mountainous central Asia. *Mountain Research and Development* 27(4): 322–330.

Hawdon, J. and J. Ryan. 2008. From individual to community: The "framing" of 4–16 and the display of social solidarity. *Traumatology* 14(1): 43–51.

Hoffman, S. 2014. Discussant remarks for the panel "(Re)Constructing Culture: Critical Reflections on the Concept of Culture in Disaster Research" at the 113th Annual Meeting of The American Anthropological Association, Washington, DC, December 7–11.

Krippendorf, K. 2012. *Content analysis: An introduction to its methodology, Third Ed.* Los Angeles: Sage.

Lasswell, H.D. 1936. *Politics: Who gets what, when, and how*. New York: McGraw-Hill.

Komac, B. 2009. Social memory and geographical memory of natural disaster. *Geografski zbornik/Acta Geographica Slovenica* 49(1): 199–226.

Moulton, S.M. 2015. How to remember: The interplay of memory and identity formation in post-disaster communities. *Human Organization* 74(4): 319–328.

Nowell, B. and T.A. Steelman. 2015. Communication under fire: The role of embeddedness in the emergence and efficacy of disaster response communication networks. *Journal of Public Administration Research and Theory* 25(3): 929–952.

Ogden, L.A. 2011. *Swamplife: People, gators, and mangroves entangled in the Everglades*. Minneapolis, MN: University of Minnesota Press.

Ricoeur, P. 2004. *Memory, history, forgetting*. Chicago: University of Chicago Press.

Star, S. and J. Griesemer. 1989. Institutional ecology, "translations" and boundary objects: Amateurs and professionals in Berkeley's Museum of Vertebrate Zoology, 1907–39. *Social Studies of Science* 19(3): 387–420.

Steelman, T.A., B. Nowell, D. Bayoumi, and S. McCaffrey. 2014. Understanding information exchange during disaster response: Methodological insights from infocentric analysis. *Administration & Society* 46(6): 707–743.

Trouillot, M. 1995. *Silencing the past: Power and the production of history*. Boston: Beacon Press.

# Index

## D



## E



## F

## L



## M



## N



## O



## P



## Q



## R

## U



## V



## W



## Y



## Z